TEEN TITANS ACADEMY

VOL. 1: X MARKS THE SPOT

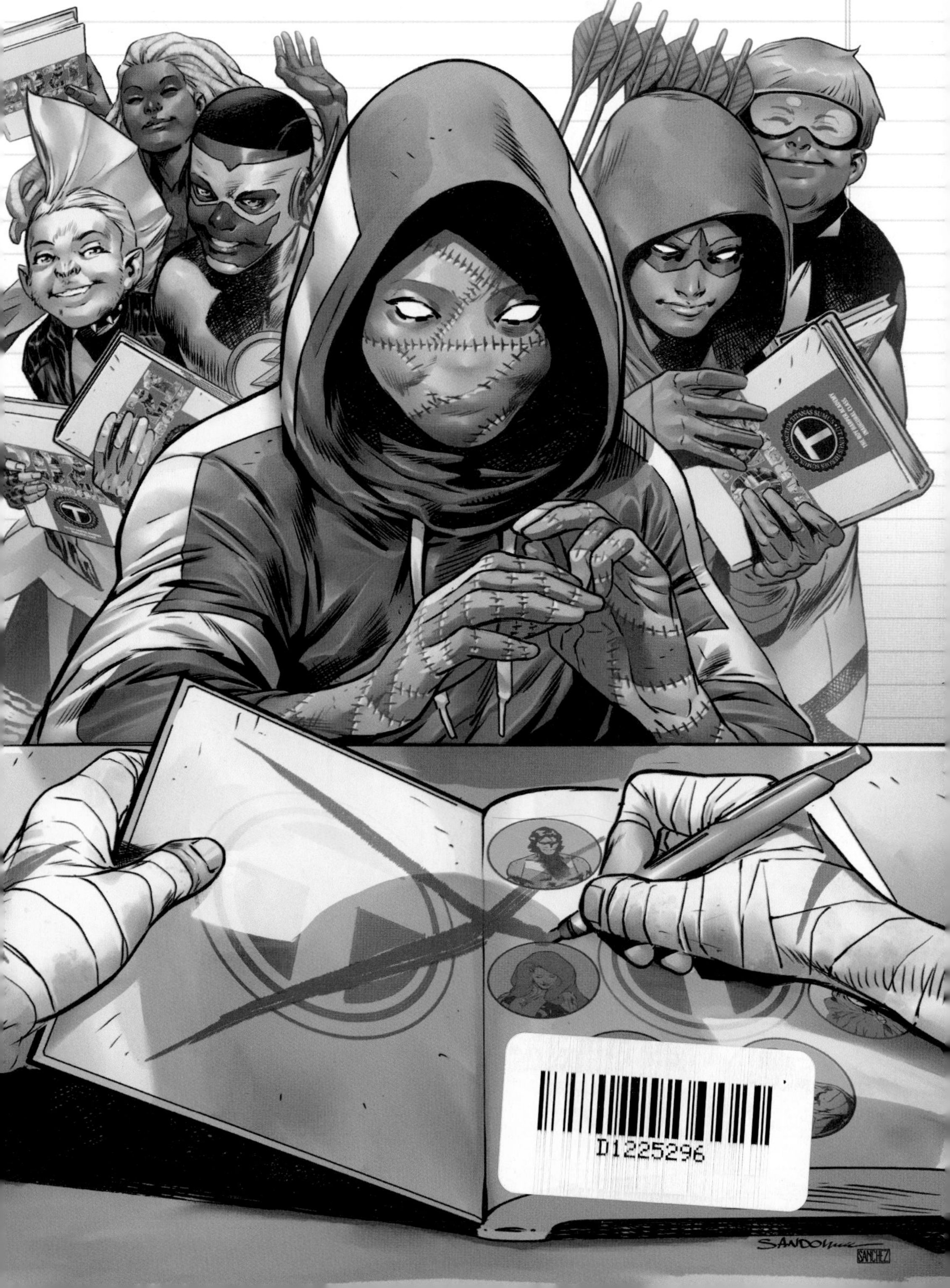

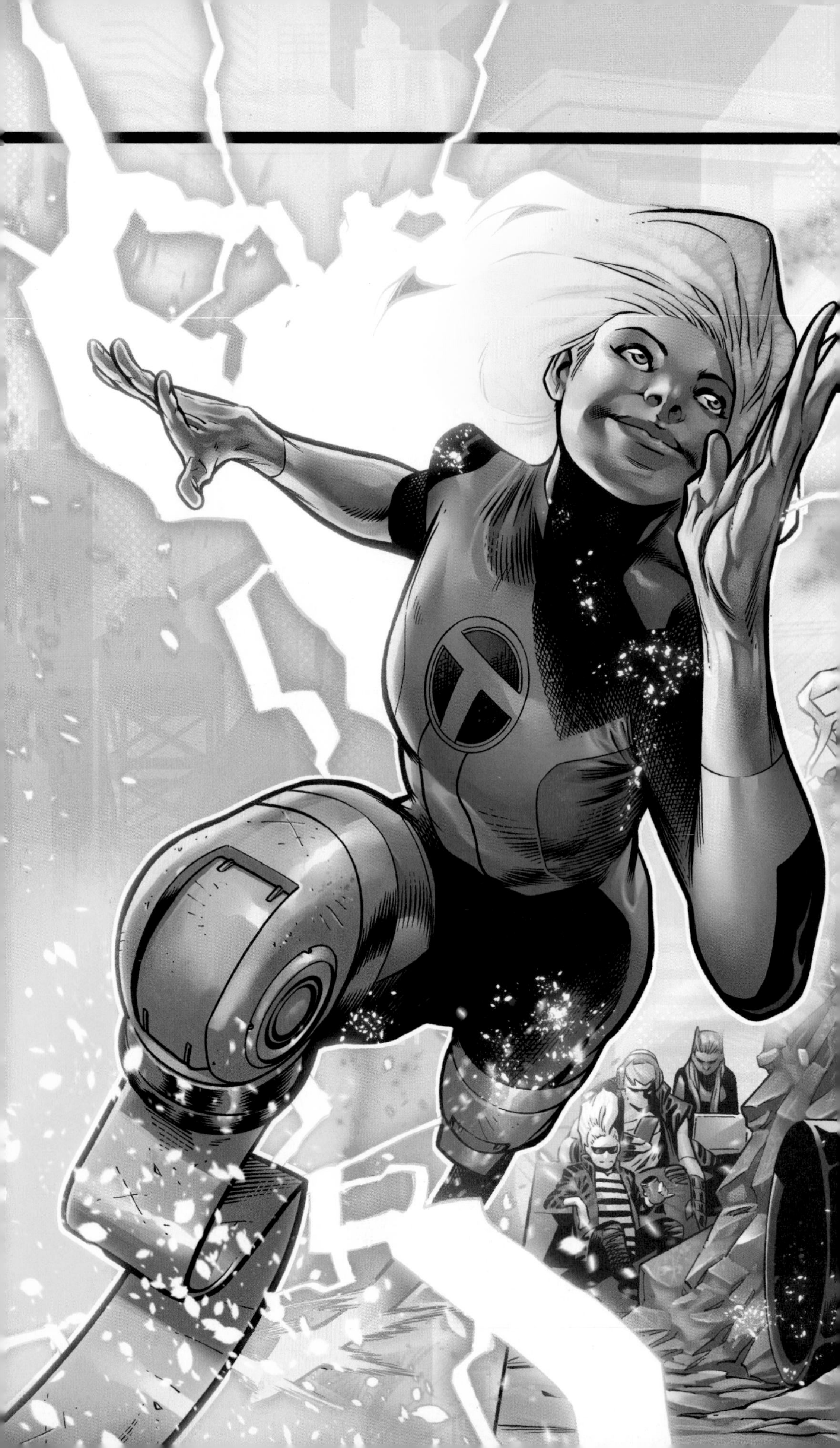

TEEN TITANS ACADEMY

VOL. 1: X MARKS THE SPOT

TIM SHERIDAN
ROBBIE THOMPSON
writers

RAFA SANDOVAL
JORDI TARRAGONA
STEVE LIEBER
EDUARDO PANSICA
JULIO FERREIRA
MAX RAYNOR
BERNARD CHANG
MARCO SANTUCCI
DARKO LAFUENTE
artists

ALEJANDRO SÁNCHEZ
DAVE STEWART
ALEX SINCLAIR
MARCELO MAIOLO
MICHAEL ATIYEH
MIQUEL MUERTO
colorists

ROB LEIGH
WES ABBOTT
letterers

RAFA SANDOVAL and
ALEJANDRO SÁNCHEZ
collection cover artists

SUPERBOY created
by JERRY SIEGEL
By special arrangement
with the Jerry Siegel family

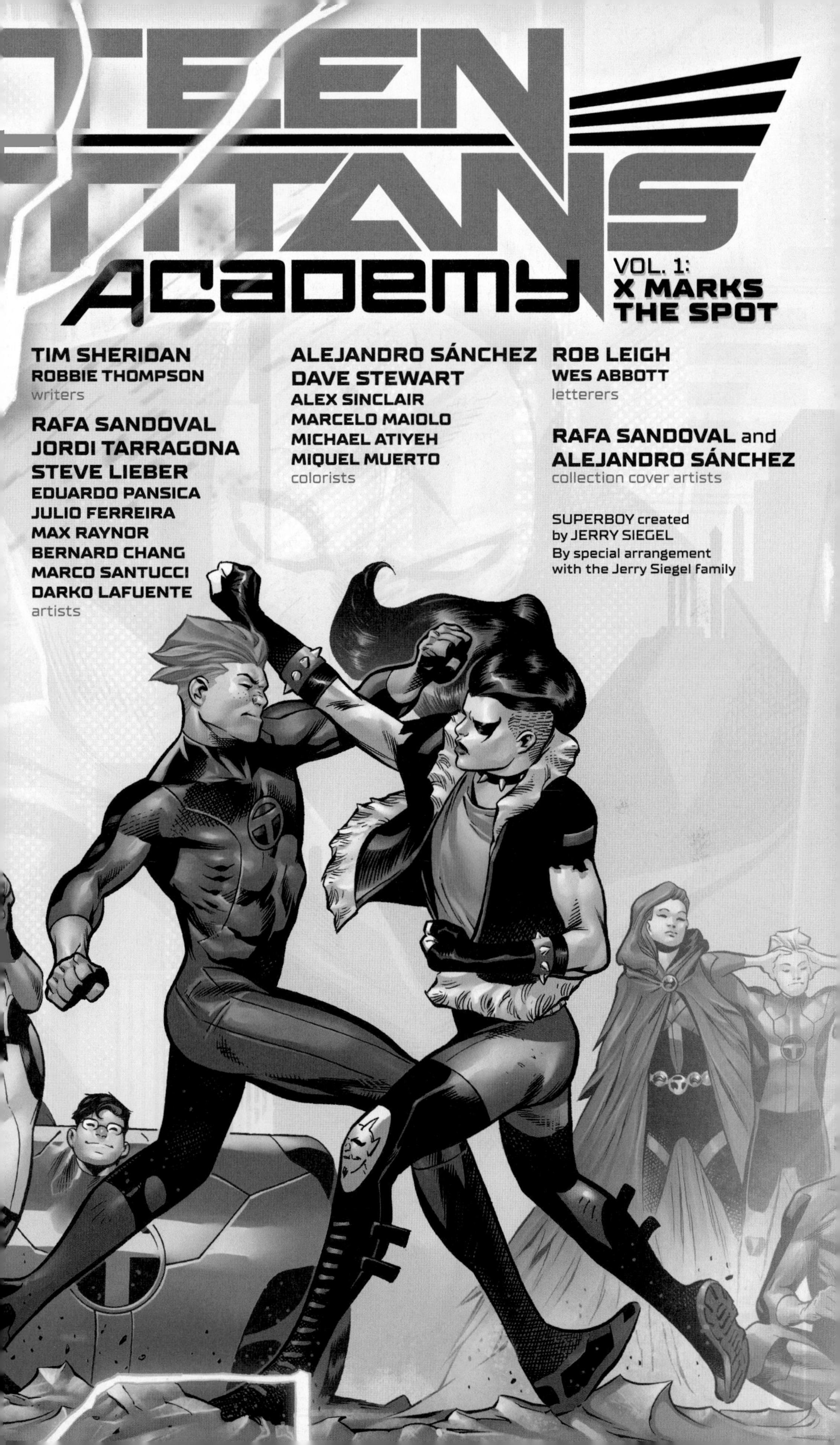

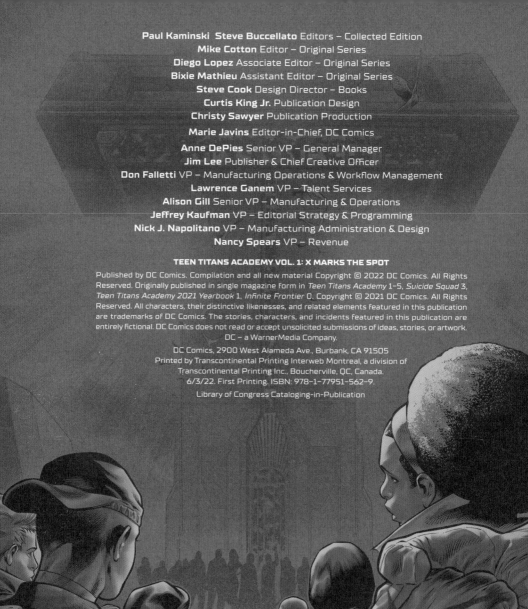

Paul Kaminski Steve Buccellato Editors – Collected Edition
Mike Cotton Editor – Original Series
Diego Lopez Associate Editor – Original Series
Bixie Mathieu Assistant Editor – Original Series
Steve Cook Design Director – Books
Curtis King Jr. Publication Design
Christy Sawyer Publication Production

Marie Javins Editor-in-Chief, DC Comics

Anne DePies Senior VP – General Manager
Jim Lee Publisher & Chief Creative Officer
Don Falletti VP – Manufacturing Operations & Workflow Management
Lawrence Ganem VP – Talent Services
Alison Gill Senior VP – Manufacturing & Operations
Jeffrey Kaufman VP – Editorial Strategy & Programming
Nick J. Napolitano VP – Manufacturing Administration & Design
Nancy Spears VP – Revenue

TEEN TITANS ACADEMY VOL. 1: X MARKS THE SPOT

DC Comics, 2900 West Alameda Ave., Burbank, CA 91505
Printed by Transcontinental Printing Interweb Montreal, a division of
Transcontinental Printing Inc., Boucherville, QC, Canada.
6/3/22. First Printing. ISBN: 978-1-77951-562-9.
Library of Congress Cataloging-in-Publication

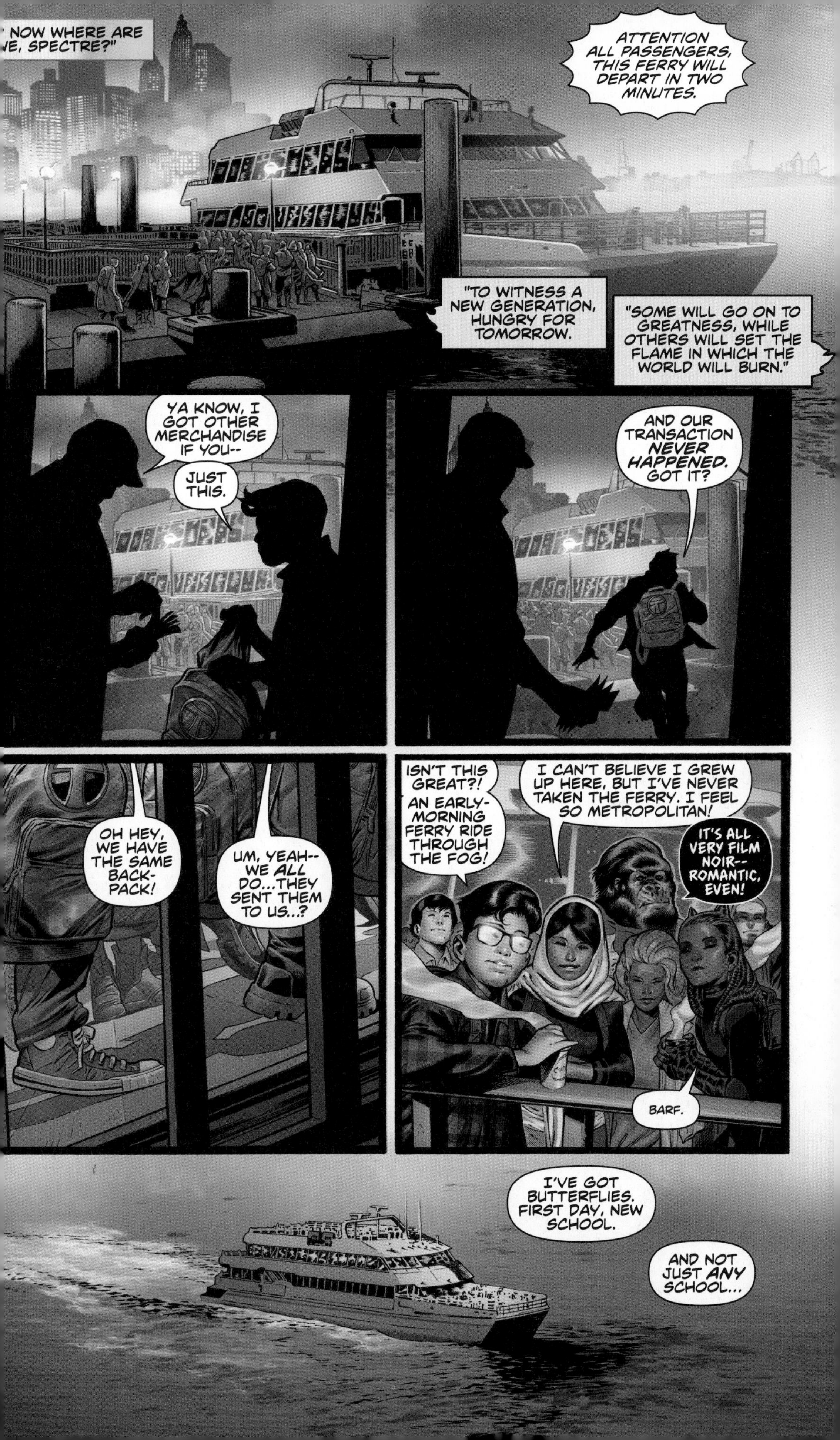
"NOW WHERE ARE WE, SPECTRE?"
ATTENTION ALL PASSENGERS, THIS FERRY WILL DEPART IN TWO MINUTES.
"TO WITNESS A NEW GENERATION, HUNGRY FOR TOMORROW.
"SOME WILL GO ON TO GREATNESS, WHILE OTHERS WILL SET THE FLAME IN WHICH THE WORLD WILL BURN."
YA KNOW, I GOT OTHER MERCHANDISE IF YOU--
JUST THIS.
AND OUR TRANSACTION NEVER HAPPENED. GOT IT?
OH HEY, WE HAVE THE SAME BACK-PACK!
UM, YEAH-- WE ALL DO...THEY SENT THEM TO US..?
ISN'T THIS GREAT?! AN EARLY-MORNING FERRY RIDE THROUGH THE FOG!
I CAN'T BELIEVE I GREW UP HERE, BUT I'VE NEVER TAKEN THE FERRY. I FEEL SO METROPOLITAN!
IT'S ALL VERY FILM NOIR-- ROMANTIC, EVEN!
BARF.
I'VE GOT BUTTERFLIES. FIRST DAY, NEW SCHOOL.
AND NOT JUST ANY SCHOOL...

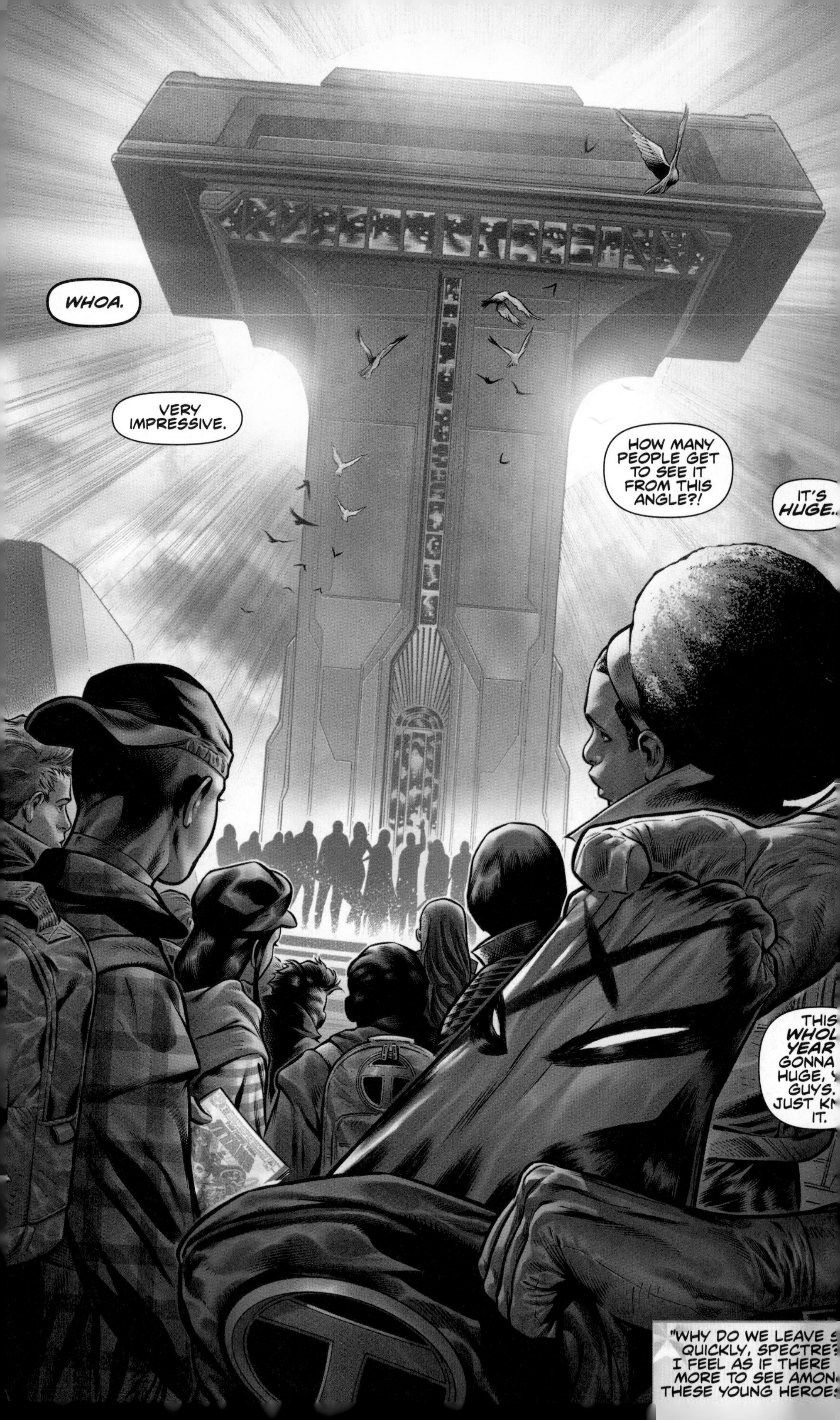
WHOA.
VERY IMPRESSIVE.
HOW MANY PEOPLE GET TO SEE IT FROM THIS ANGLE?!
IT'S HUGE..
THIS WHOL YEAR GONNA HUGE, GUYS. JUST KN IT.
"WHY DO WE LEAVE QUICKLY, SPECTRE? I FEEL AS IF THERE MORE TO SEE AMON THESE YOUNG HEROE

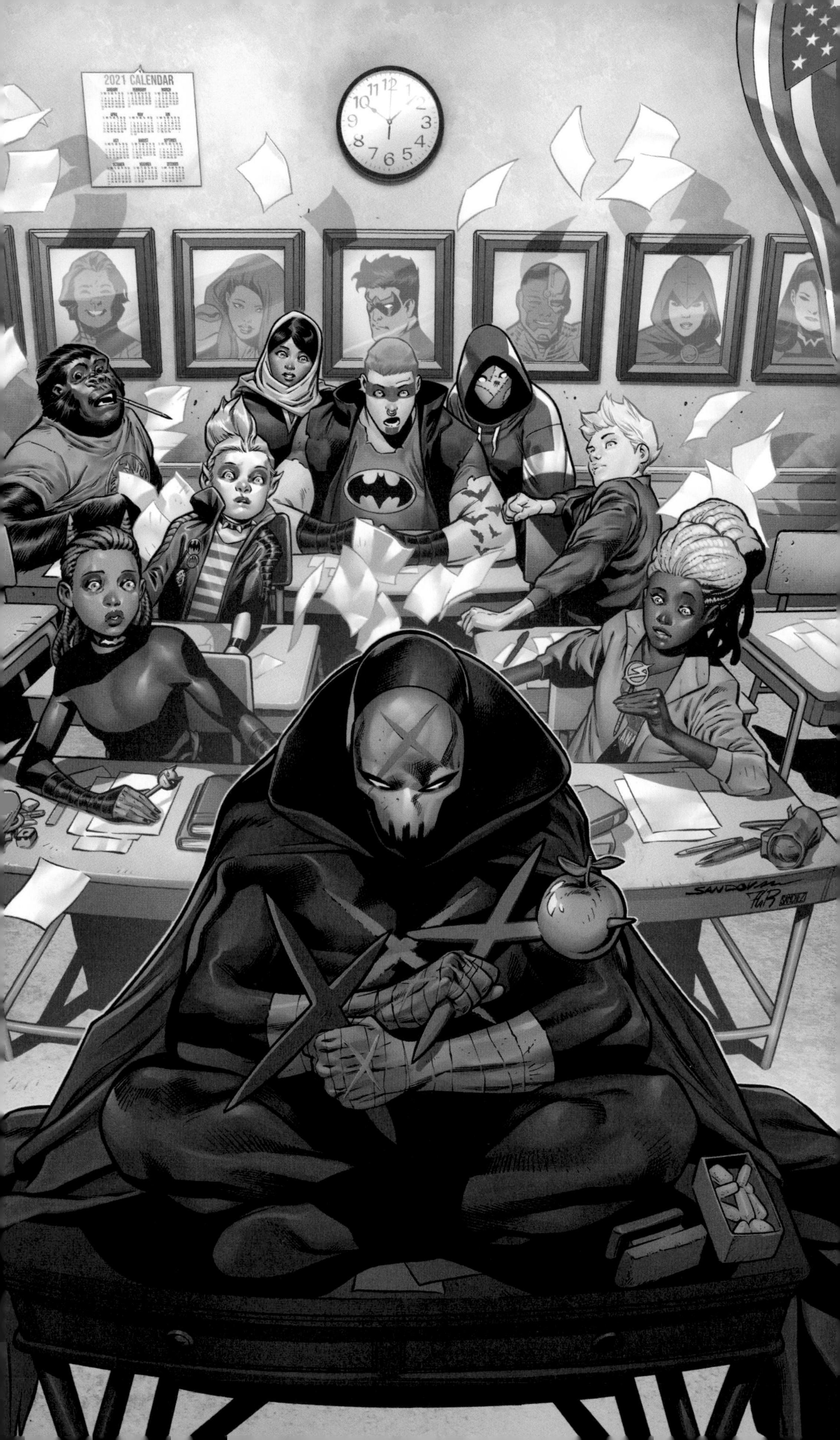
2021 CALENDAR

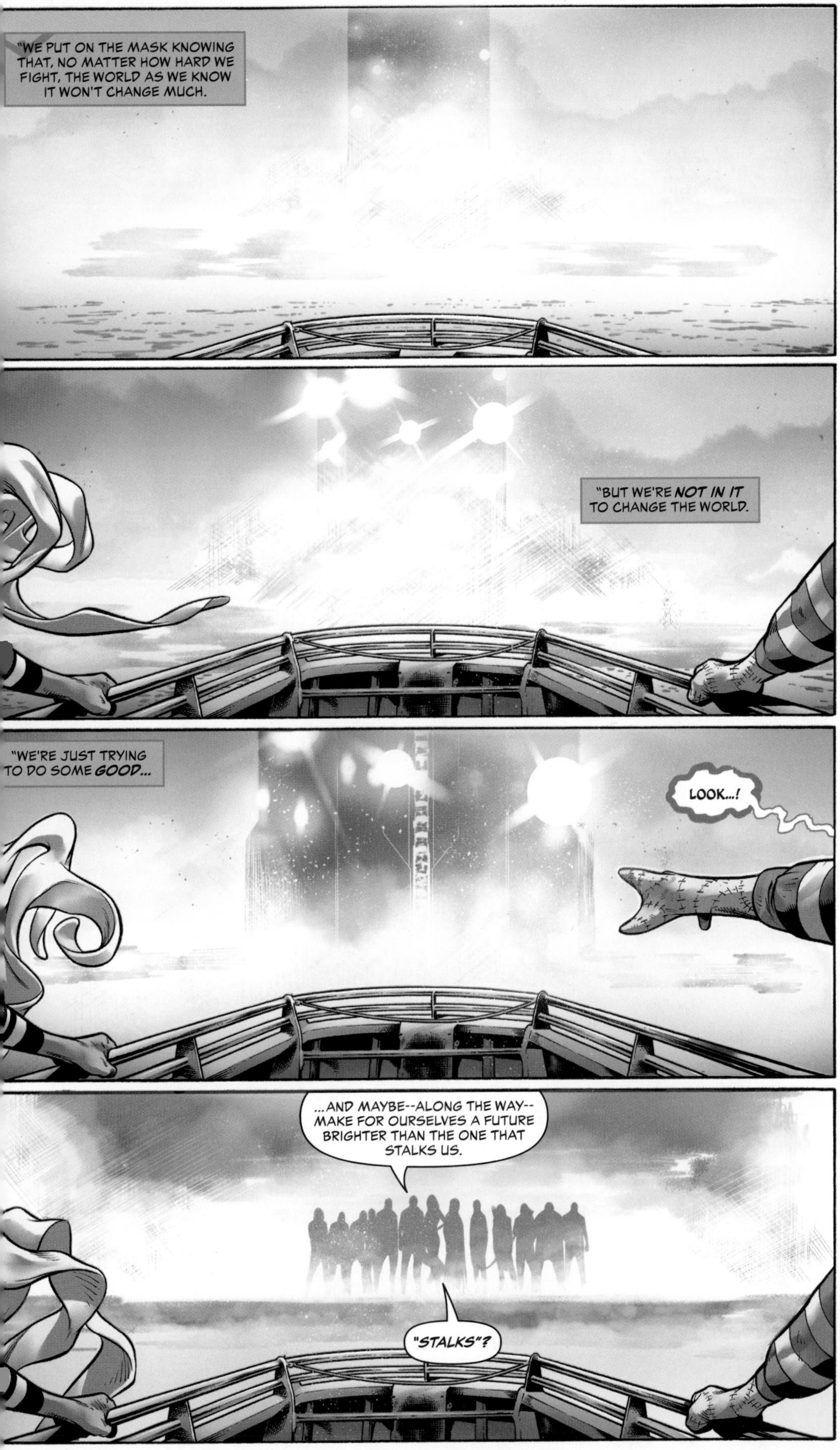
"WE PUT ON THE MASK KNOWING THAT, NO MATTER HOW HARD WE FIGHT, THE WORLD AS WE KNOW IT WON'T CHANGE MUCH.
"BUT WE'RE NOT IN IT TO CHANGE THE WORLD.
"WE'RE JUST TRYING TO DO SOME GOOD...
LOOK...!
...AND MAYBE--ALONG THE WAY--MAKE FOR OURSELVES A FUTURE BRIGHTER THAN THE ONE THAT STALKS US.
"STALKS"?

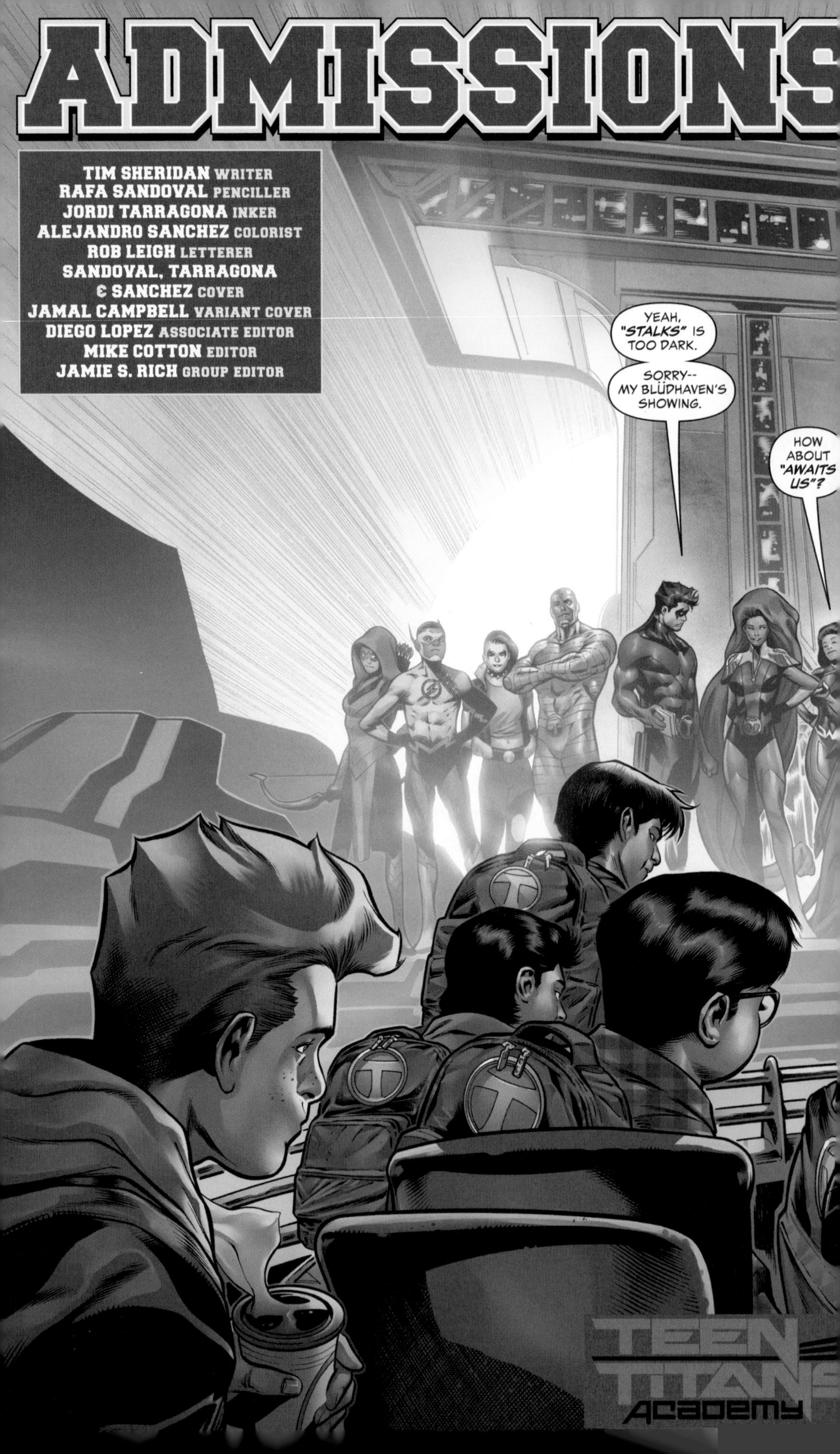
ADMISSIONS
TIM SHERIDAN WRITER
RAFA SANDOVAL PENCILLER
JORDI TARRAGONA INKER
ALEJANDRO SANCHEZ COLORIST
ROB LEIGH LETTERER
SANDOVAL, TARRAGONA
& SANCHEZ COVER
JAMAL CAMPBELL VARIANT COVER
DIEGO LOPEZ ASSOCIATE EDITOR
MIKE COTTON EDITOR
JAMIE S. RICH GROUP EDITOR
YEAH, "STALKS" IS TOO DARK.
SORRY-- MY BLÜDHAVEN'S SHOWING.
HOW ABOUT "AWAITS US"?
TEEN TITANS ACADEMY

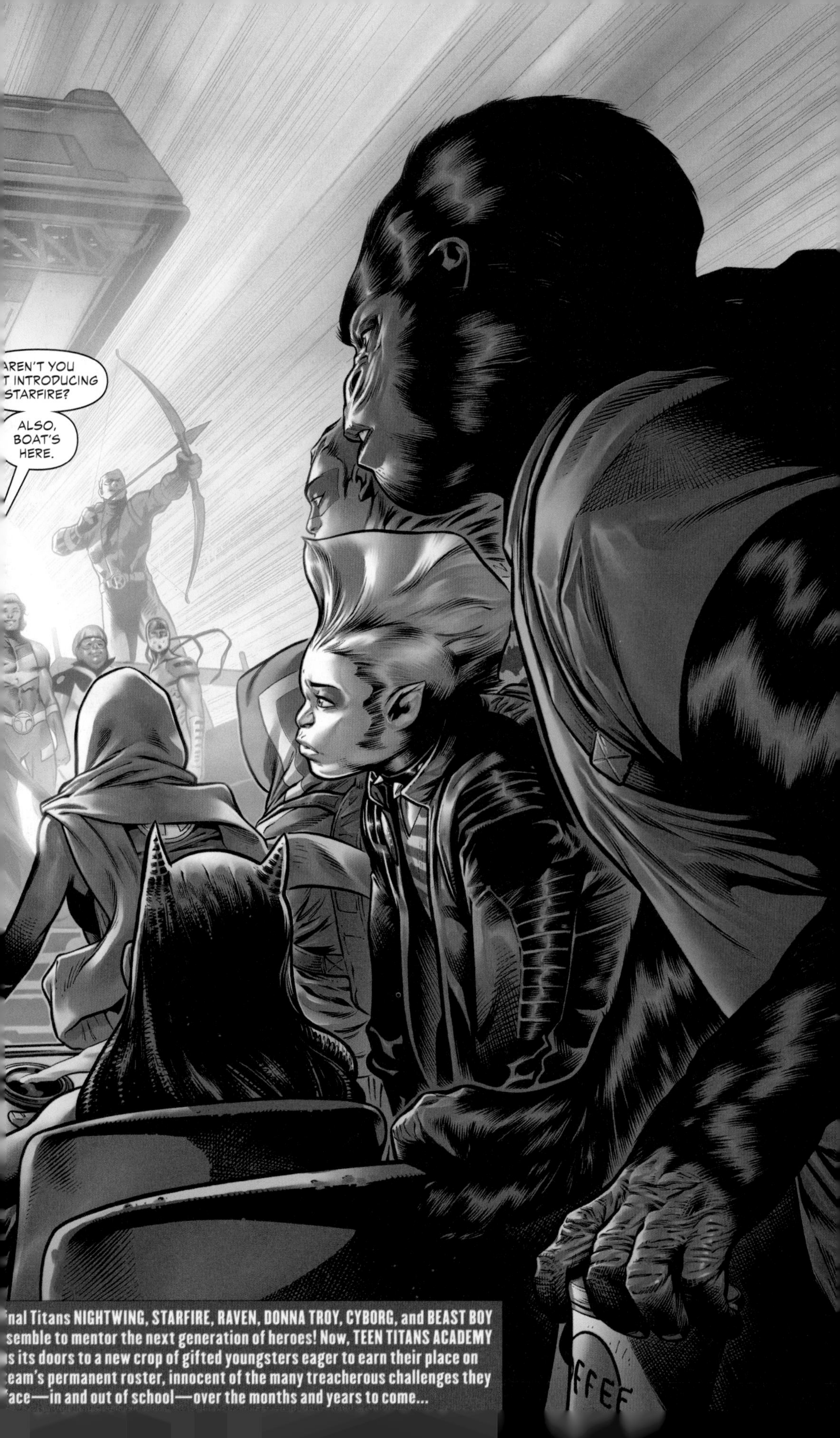
AREN'T YOU
T INTRODUCING
STARFIRE?
ALSO, BOAT'S HERE.
nal Titans NIGHTWING, STARFIRE, RAVEN, DONNA TROY, CYBORG, and BEAST BOY
semble to mentor the next generation of heroes! Now, TEEN TITANS ACADEMY
s its doors to a new crop of gifted youngsters eager to earn their place on
eam's permanent roster, innocent of the many treacherous challenges they
ace—in and out of school—over the months and years to come...

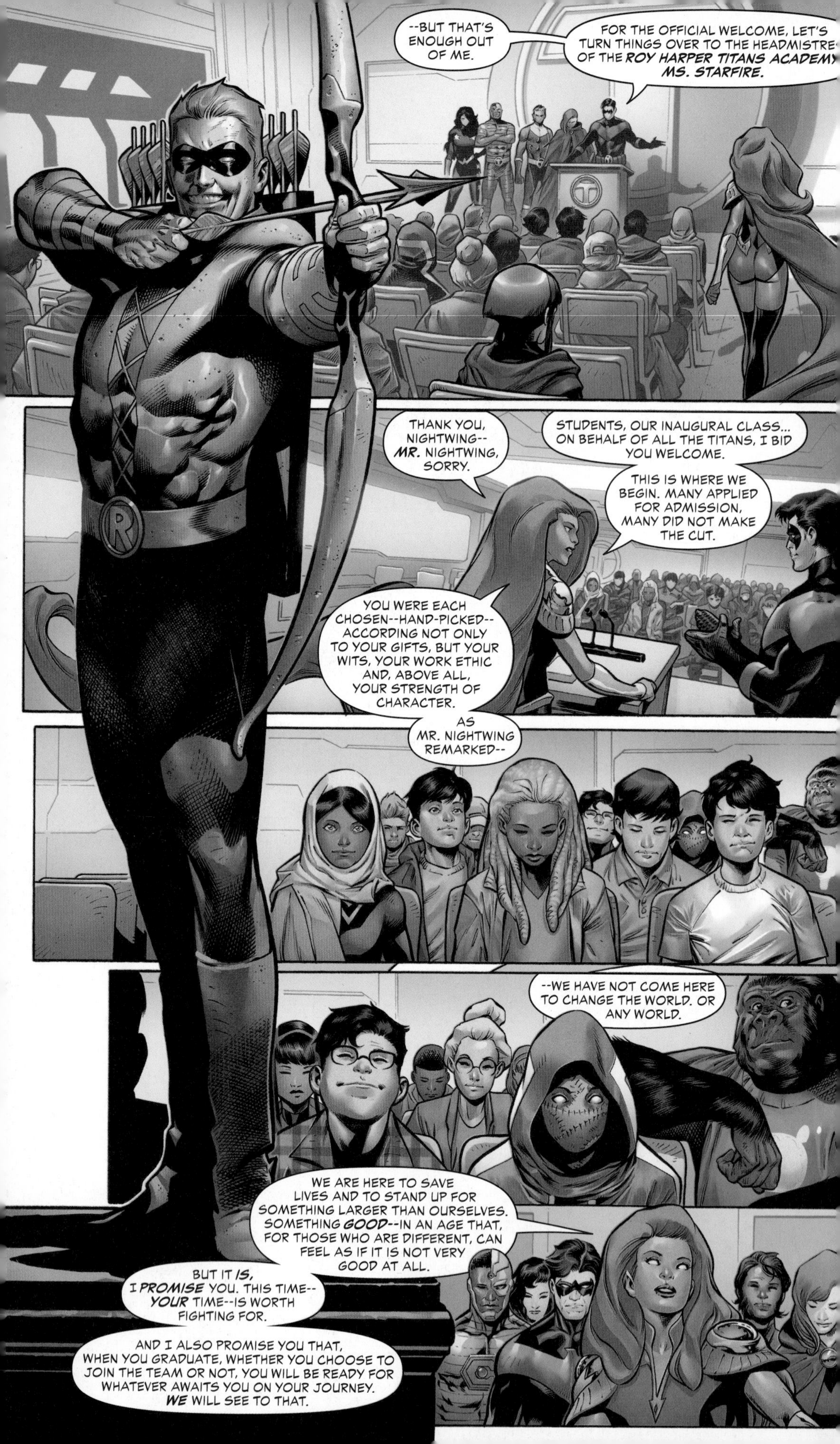
--BUT THAT'S ENOUGH OUT OF ME.
FOR THE OFFICIAL WELCOME, LET'S TURN THINGS OVER TO THE HEADMISTRESS OF THE ROY HARPER TITANS ACADEMY, MS. STARFIRE.
THANK YOU, NIGHTWING-- MR. NIGHTWING, SORRY.
STUDENTS, OUR INAUGURAL CLASS... ON BEHALF OF ALL THE TITANS, I BID YOU WELCOME.
THIS IS WHERE WE BEGIN. MANY APPLIED FOR ADMISSION, MANY DID NOT MAKE THE CUT.
YOU WERE EACH CHOSEN--HAND-PICKED--ACCORDING NOT ONLY TO YOUR GIFTS, BUT YOUR WITS, YOUR WORK ETHIC AND, ABOVE ALL, YOUR STRENGTH OF CHARACTER.
AS MR. NIGHTWING REMARKED--
--WE HAVE NOT COME HERE TO CHANGE THE WORLD. OR ANY WORLD.
WE ARE HERE TO SAVE LIVES AND TO STAND UP FOR SOMETHING LARGER THAN OURSELVES. SOMETHING GOOD--IN AN AGE THAT, FOR THOSE WHO ARE DIFFERENT, CAN FEEL AS IF IT IS NOT VERY GOOD AT ALL.
BUT IT IS, I PROMISE YOU. THIS TIME--YOUR TIME--IS WORTH FIGHTING FOR.
AND I ALSO PROMISE YOU THAT, WHEN YOU GRADUATE, WHETHER YOU CHOOSE TO JOIN THE TEAM OR NOT, YOU WILL BE READY FOR WHATEVER AWAITS YOU ON YOUR JOURNEY. WE WILL SEE TO THAT.

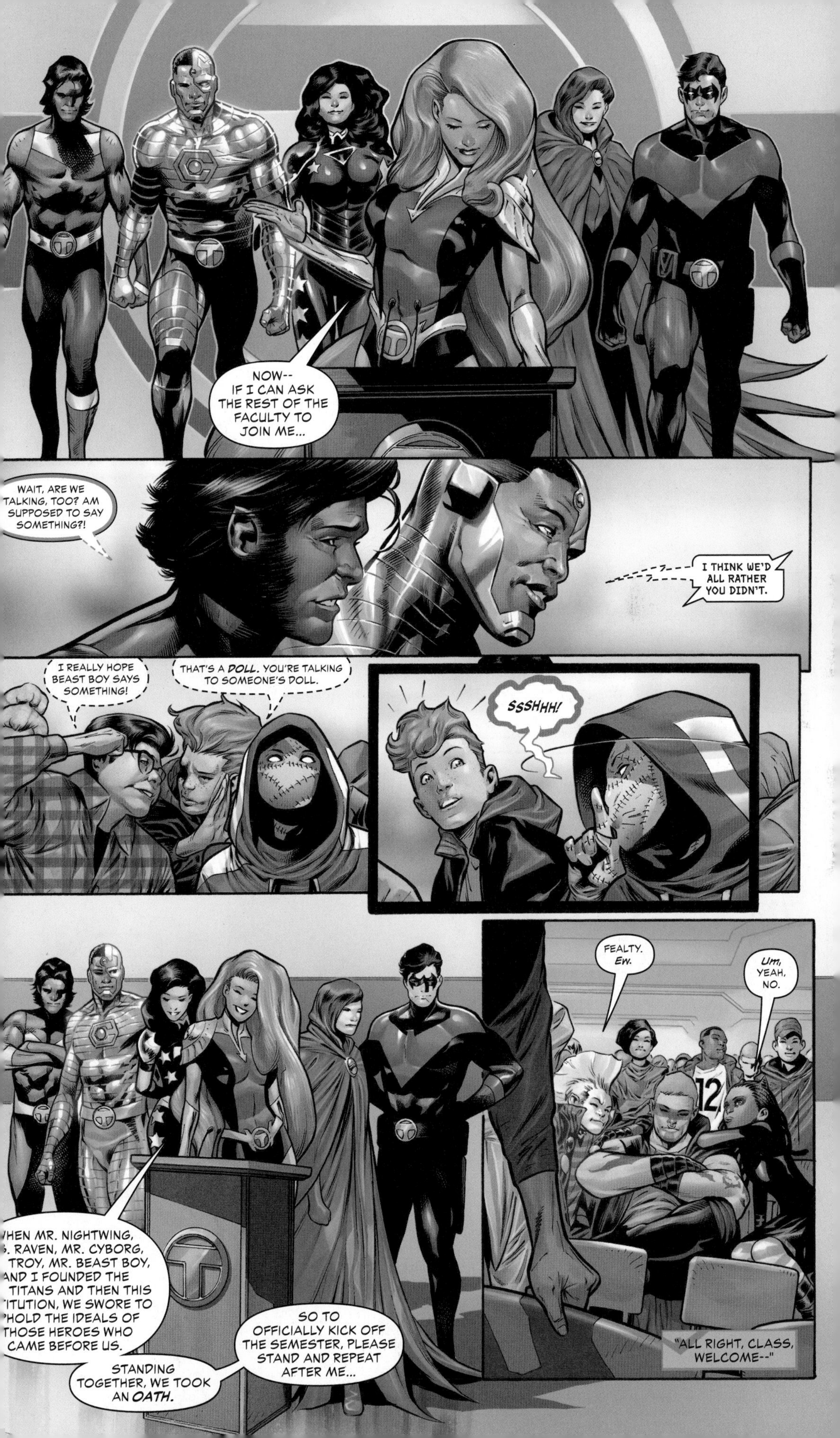
NOW-- IF I CAN ASK THE REST OF THE FACULTY TO JOIN ME...
WAIT, ARE WE TALKING, TOO? AM SUPPOSED TO SAY SOMETHING?!
I THINK WE'D ALL RATHER YOU DIDN'T.
I REALLY HOPE BEAST BOY SAYS SOMETHING!
THAT'S A DOLL. YOU'RE TALKING TO SOMEONE'S DOLL.
SSSHHH!
"ALL RIGHT, CLASS, WELCOME--"
FEALTY. Ew.
Um, YEAH, NO.
WHEN MR. NIGHTWING, S. RAVEN, MR. CYBORG, TROY, MR. BEAST BOY, AND I FOUNDED THE TITANS AND THEN THIS TITUTION, WE SWORE TO PHOLD THE IDEALS OF THOSE HEROES WHO CAME BEFORE US.
STANDING TOGETHER, WE TOOK AN OATH.
SO TO OFFICIALLY KICK OFF THE SEMESTER, PLEASE STAND AND REPEAT AFTER ME...

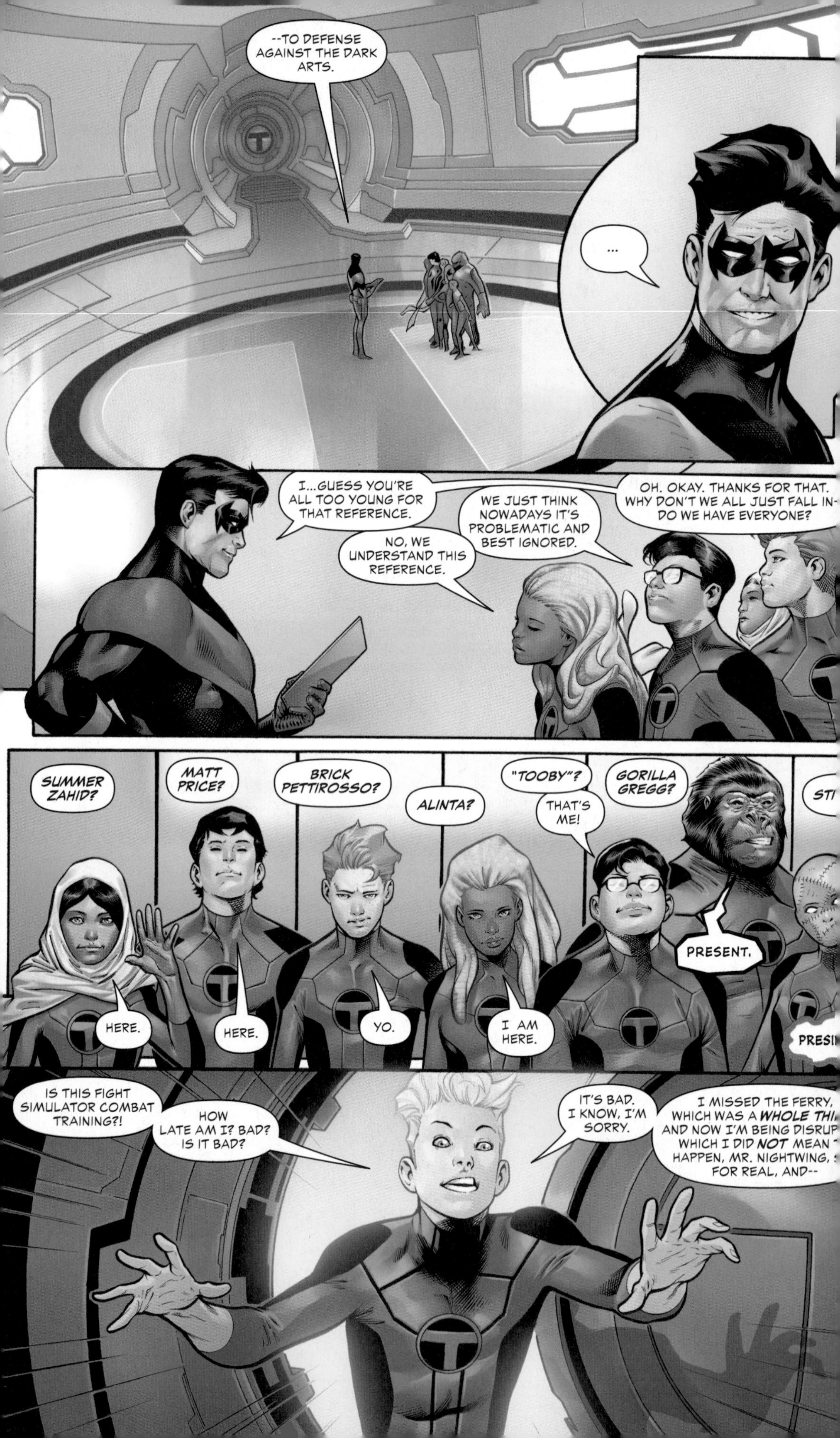
--TO DEFENSE AGAINST THE DARK ARTS.
...
I...GUESS YOU'RE ALL TOO YOUNG FOR THAT REFERENCE.
NO, WE UNDERSTAND THIS REFERENCE.
WE JUST THINK NOWADAYS IT'S PROBLEMATIC AND BEST IGNORED.
OH. OKAY. THANKS FOR THAT. WHY DON'T WE ALL JUST FALL IN- DO WE HAVE EVERYONE?
SUMMER ZAHID?
HERE.
MATT PRICE?
HERE.
BRICK PETTIROSSO?
YO.
ALINTA?
I AM HERE.
"TOOBY"?
THAT'S ME!
GORILLA GREGG?
PRESENT.
STI
PRESI
IS THIS FIGHT SIMULATOR COMBAT TRAINING?!
HOW LATE AM I? BAD? IS IT BAD?
IT'S BAD. I KNOW, I'M SORRY.
I MISSED THE FERRY, WHICH WAS A WHOLE THI AND NOW I'M BEING DISRUP WHICH I DID NOT MEAN HAPPEN, MR. NIGHTWING, FOR REAL, AND--

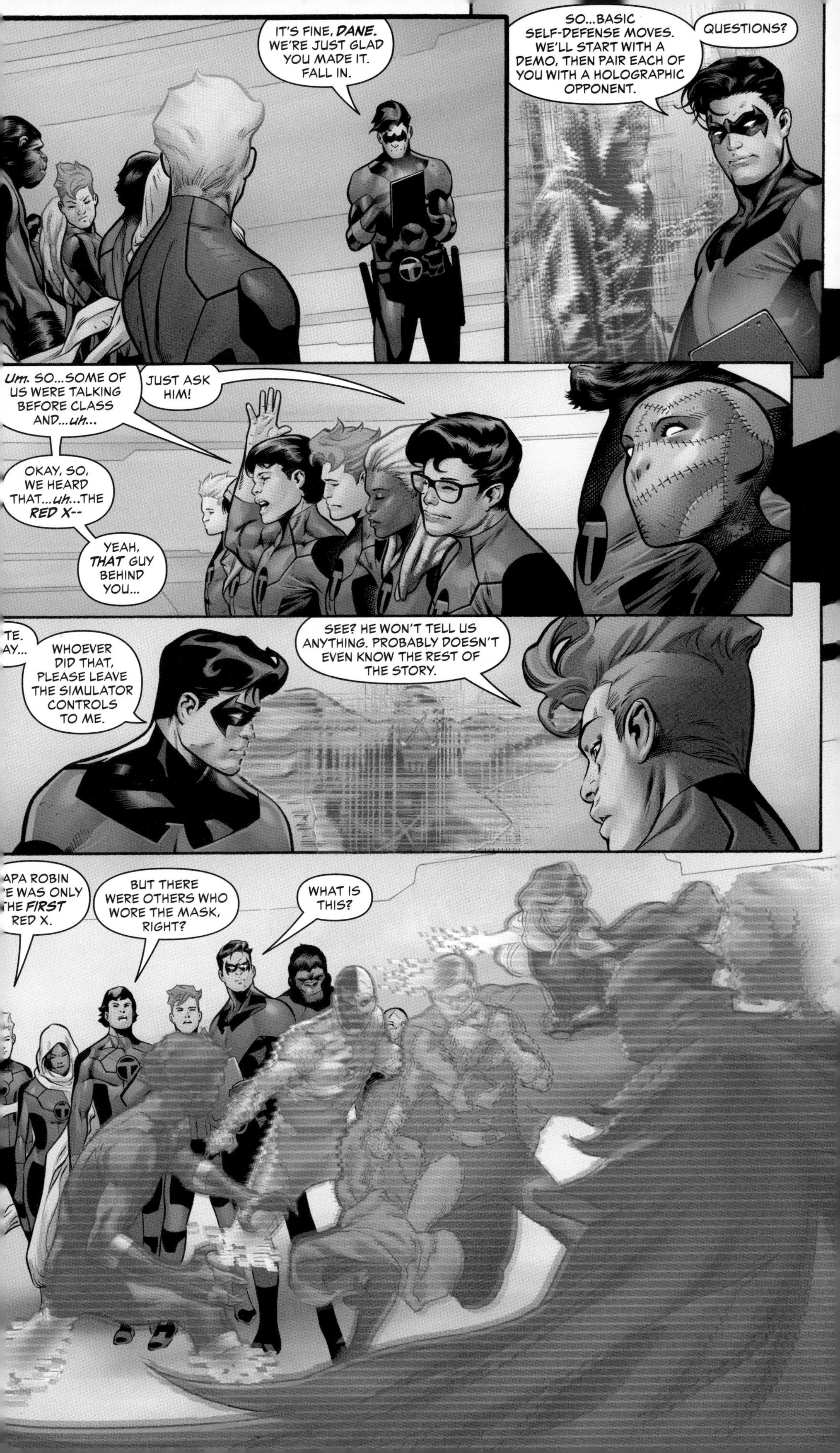
IT'S FINE, DANE. WE'RE JUST GLAD YOU MADE IT. FALL IN.
SO...BASIC SELF-DEFENSE MOVES. WE'LL START WITH A DEMO, THEN PAIR EACH OF YOU WITH A HOLOGRAPHIC OPPONENT.
QUESTIONS?
Um. SO...SOME OF US WERE TALKING BEFORE CLASS AND...uh...
JUST ASK HIM!
OKAY, SO, WE HEARD THAT...uh...THE RED X--
YEAH, THAT GUY BEHIND YOU...
TE. AY...
WHOEVER DID THAT, PLEASE LEAVE THE SIMULATOR CONTROLS TO ME.
SEE? HE WON'T TELL US ANYTHING. PROBABLY DOESN'T EVEN KNOW THE REST OF THE STORY.
APA ROBIN E WAS ONLY HE FIRST RED X.
BUT THERE WERE OTHERS WHO WORE THE MASK, RIGHT?
WHAT IS THIS?

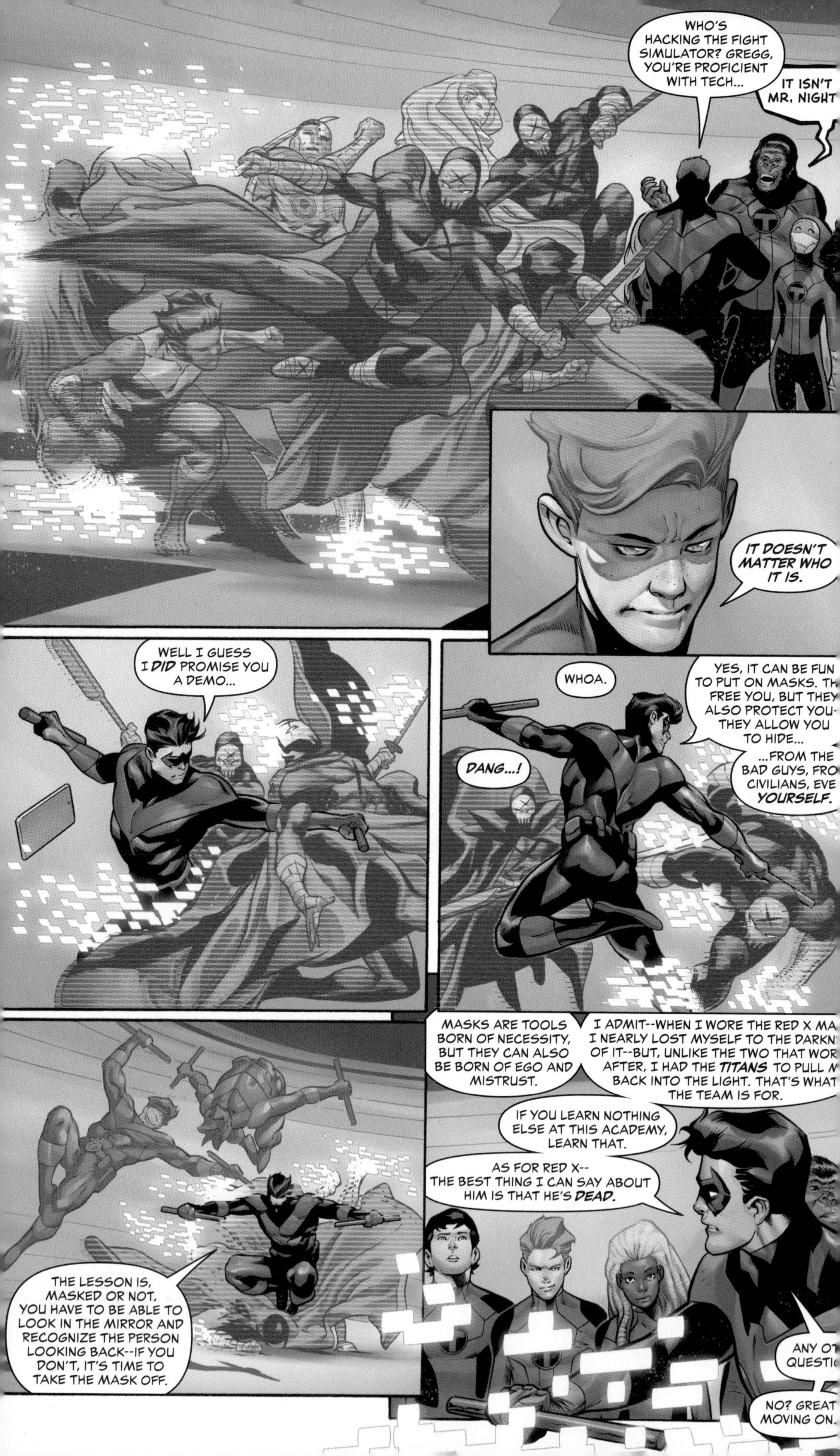
WHO'S HACKING THE FIGHT SIMULATOR? GREGG, YOU'RE PROFICIENT WITH TECH...
IT ISN'T MR. NIGHT
IT DOESN'T MATTER WHO IT IS.
WELL I GUESS I DID PROMISE YOU A DEMO...
WHOA.
DANG...!
YES, IT CAN BE FUN TO PUT ON MASKS. TH FREE YOU, BUT THEY ALSO PROTECT YOU- THEY ALLOW YOU TO HIDE...
...FROM THE BAD GUYS, FRO CIVILIANS, EVE YOURSELF.
THE LESSON IS, MASKED OR NOT, YOU HAVE TO BE ABLE TO LOOK IN THE MIRROR AND RECOGNIZE THE PERSON LOOKING BACK--IF YOU DON'T, IT'S TIME TO TAKE THE MASK OFF.
MASKS ARE TOOLS BORN OF NECESSITY, BUT THEY CAN ALSO BE BORN OF EGO AND MISTRUST.
I ADMIT--WHEN I WORE THE RED X MA I NEARLY LOST MYSELF TO THE DARKN OF IT--BUT, UNLIKE THE TWO THAT WOR AFTER, I HAD THE TITANS TO PULL M BACK INTO THE LIGHT. THAT'S WHAT THE TEAM IS FOR.
IF YOU LEARN NOTHING ELSE AT THIS ACADEMY, LEARN THAT.
AS FOR RED X-- THE BEST THING I CAN SAY ABOUT HIM IS THAT HE'S DEAD.
ANY OT QUESTI
NO? GREAT MOVING ON.

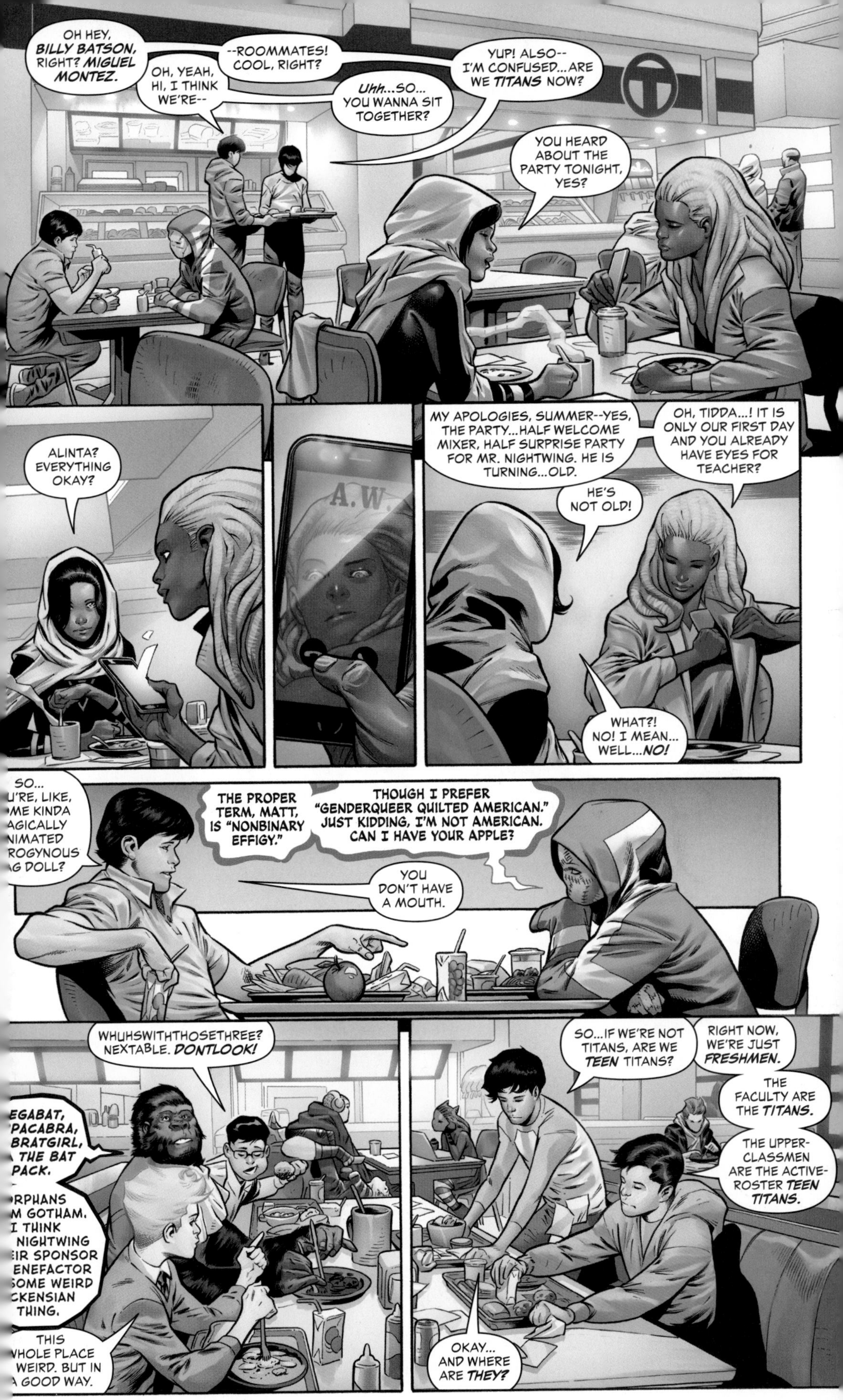

OH HEY, BILLY BATSON, RIGHT? MIGUEL MONTEZ.
OH, YEAH, HI, I THINK WE'RE--
--ROOMMATES! COOL, RIGHT?
Uhh...SO... YOU WANNA SIT TOGETHER?
YUP! ALSO-- I'M CONFUSED...ARE WE TITANS NOW?
YOU HEARD ABOUT THE PARTY TONIGHT, YES?
ALINTA? EVERYTHING OKAY?
A.W.
MY APOLOGIES, SUMMER--YES, THE PARTY...HALF WELCOME MIXER, HALF SURPRISE PARTY FOR MR. NIGHTWING. HE IS TURNING...OLD.
HE'S NOT OLD!
OH, TIDDA...! IT IS ONLY OUR FIRST DAY AND YOU ALREADY HAVE EYES FOR TEACHER?
WHAT?! NO! I MEAN... WELL...NO!
SO... U'RE, LIKE, ME KINDA AGICALLY NIMATED ROGYNOUS G DOLL?
THE PROPER TERM, MATT, IS "NONBINARY EFFIGY."
THOUGH I PREFER "GENDERQUEER QUILTED AMERICAN." JUST KIDDING, I'M NOT AMERICAN. CAN I HAVE YOUR APPLE?
YOU DON'T HAVE A MOUTH.
WHUHSWITHTHOSETHREE? NEXTABLE. DONTLOOK!
EGABAT, PACABRA, BRATGIRL, THE BAT PACK.
RPHANS M GOTHAM. I THINK NIGHTWING EIR SPONSOR ENEFACTOR SOME WEIRD CKENSIAN THING.
THIS WHOLE PLACE WEIRD. BUT IN A GOOD WAY.
SO...IF WE'RE NOT TITANS, ARE WE TEEN TITANS?
RIGHT NOW, WE'RE JUST FRESHMEN.
THE FACULTY ARE THE TITANS.
THE UPPER-CLASSMEN ARE THE ACTIVE-ROSTER TEEN TITANS.
OKAY... AND WHERE ARE THEY?

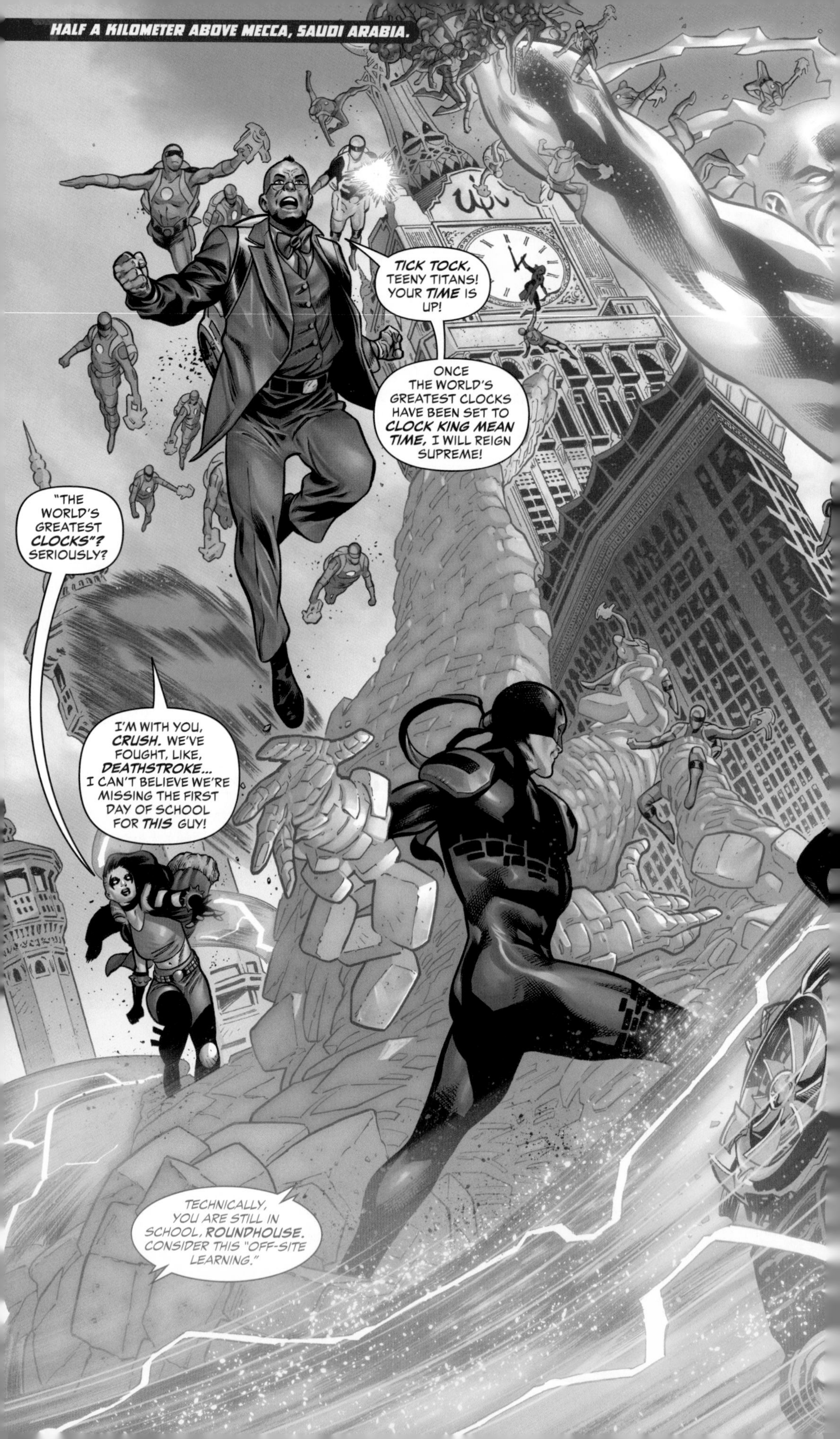
HALF A KILOMETER ABOVE MECCA, SAUDI ARABIA.
TICK TOCK, TEENY TITANS! YOUR TIME IS UP!
ONCE THE WORLD'S GREATEST CLOCKS HAVE BEEN SET TO CLOCK KING MEAN TIME, I WILL REIGN SUPREME!
"THE WORLD'S GREATEST CLOCKS"? SERIOUSLY?
I'M WITH YOU, CRUSH. WE'VE FOUGHT, LIKE, DEATHSTROKE... I CAN'T BELIEVE WE'RE MISSING THE FIRST DAY OF SCHOOL FOR THIS GUY!
TECHNICALLY, YOU ARE STILL IN SCHOOL, ROUNDHOUSE. CONSIDER THIS "OFF-SITE LEARNING."

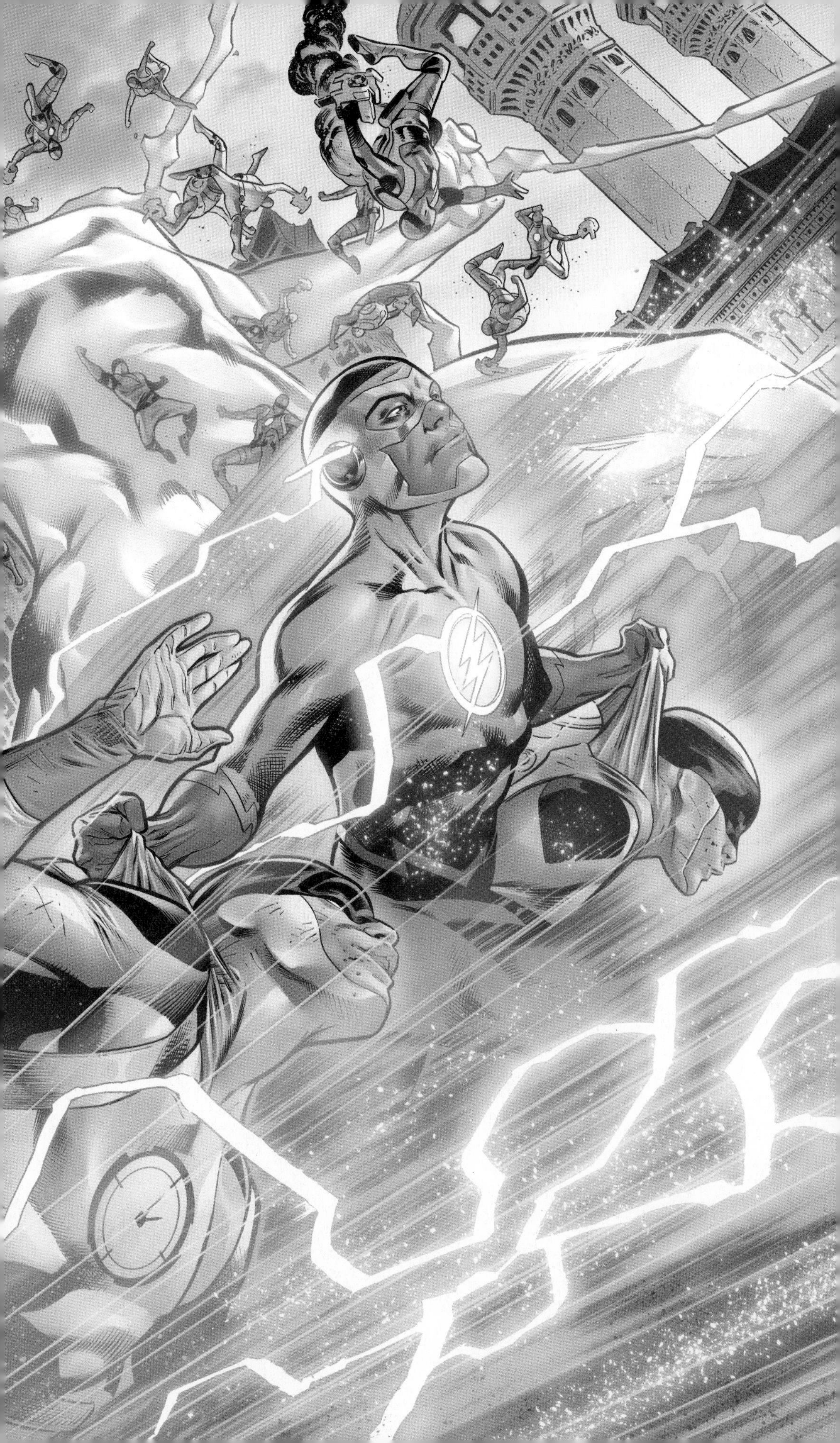

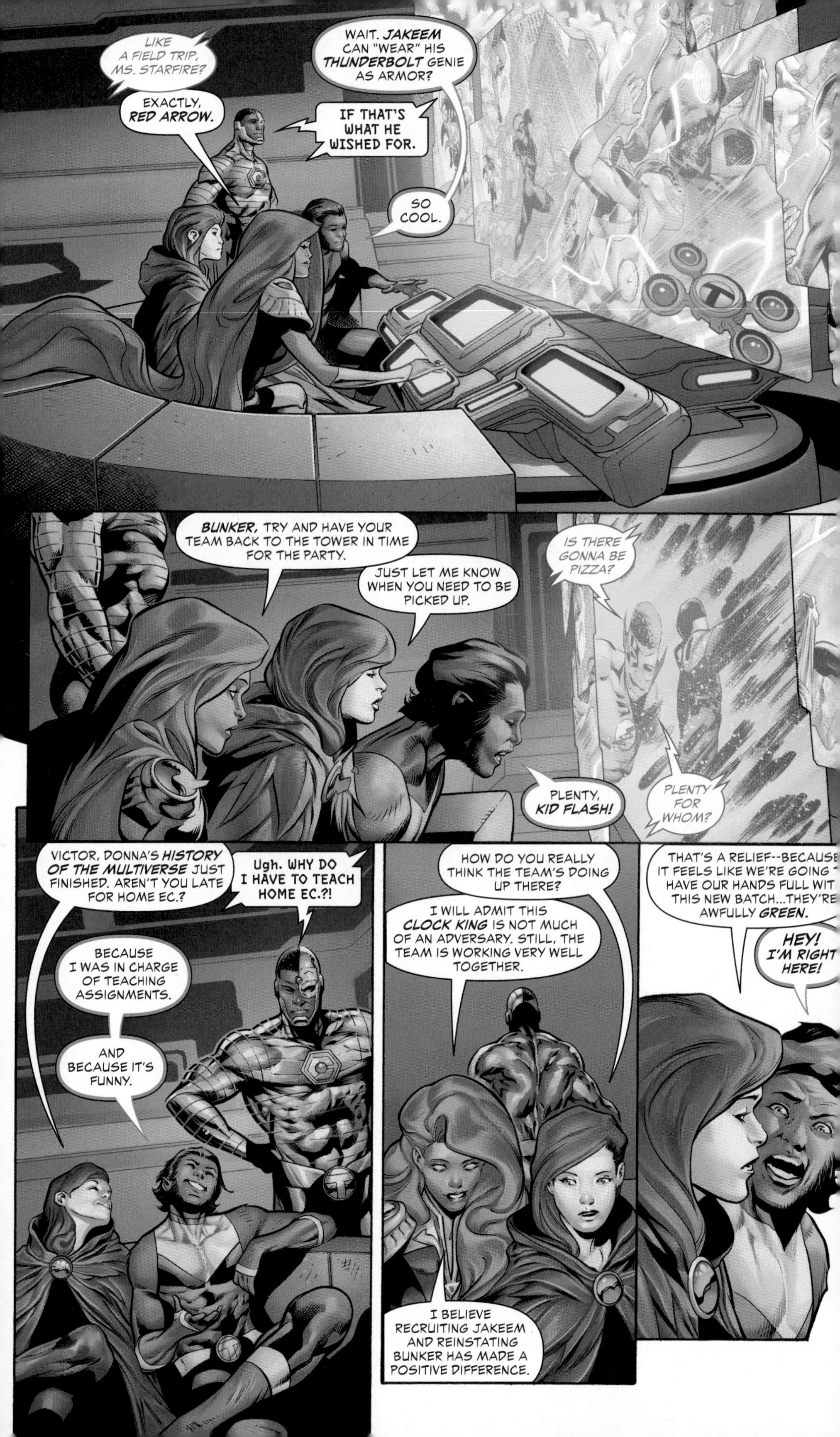

LIKE A FIELD TRIP, MS. STARFIRE?
EXACTLY, RED ARROW.
WAIT. JAKEEM CAN "WEAR" HIS THUNDERBOLT GENIE AS ARMOR?
IF THAT'S WHAT HE WISHED FOR.
SO COOL.
BUNKER, TRY AND HAVE YOUR TEAM BACK TO THE TOWER IN TIME FOR THE PARTY.
JUST LET ME KNOW WHEN YOU NEED TO BE PICKED UP.
IS THERE GONNA BE PIZZA?
PLENTY, KID FLASH!
PLENTY FOR WHOM?
VICTOR, DONNA'S HISTORY OF THE MULTIVERSE JUST FINISHED. AREN'T YOU LATE FOR HOME EC.?
Ugh. WHY DO I HAVE TO TEACH HOME EC.?!
BECAUSE I WAS IN CHARGE OF TEACHING ASSIGNMENTS.
AND BECAUSE IT'S FUNNY.
HOW DO YOU REALLY THINK THE TEAM'S DOING UP THERE?
I WILL ADMIT THIS CLOCK KING IS NOT MUCH OF AN ADVERSARY. STILL, THE TEAM IS WORKING VERY WELL TOGETHER.
I BELIEVE RECRUITING JAKEEM AND REINSTATING BUNKER HAS MADE A POSITIVE DIFFERENCE.
HEY! I'M RIGHT HERE!

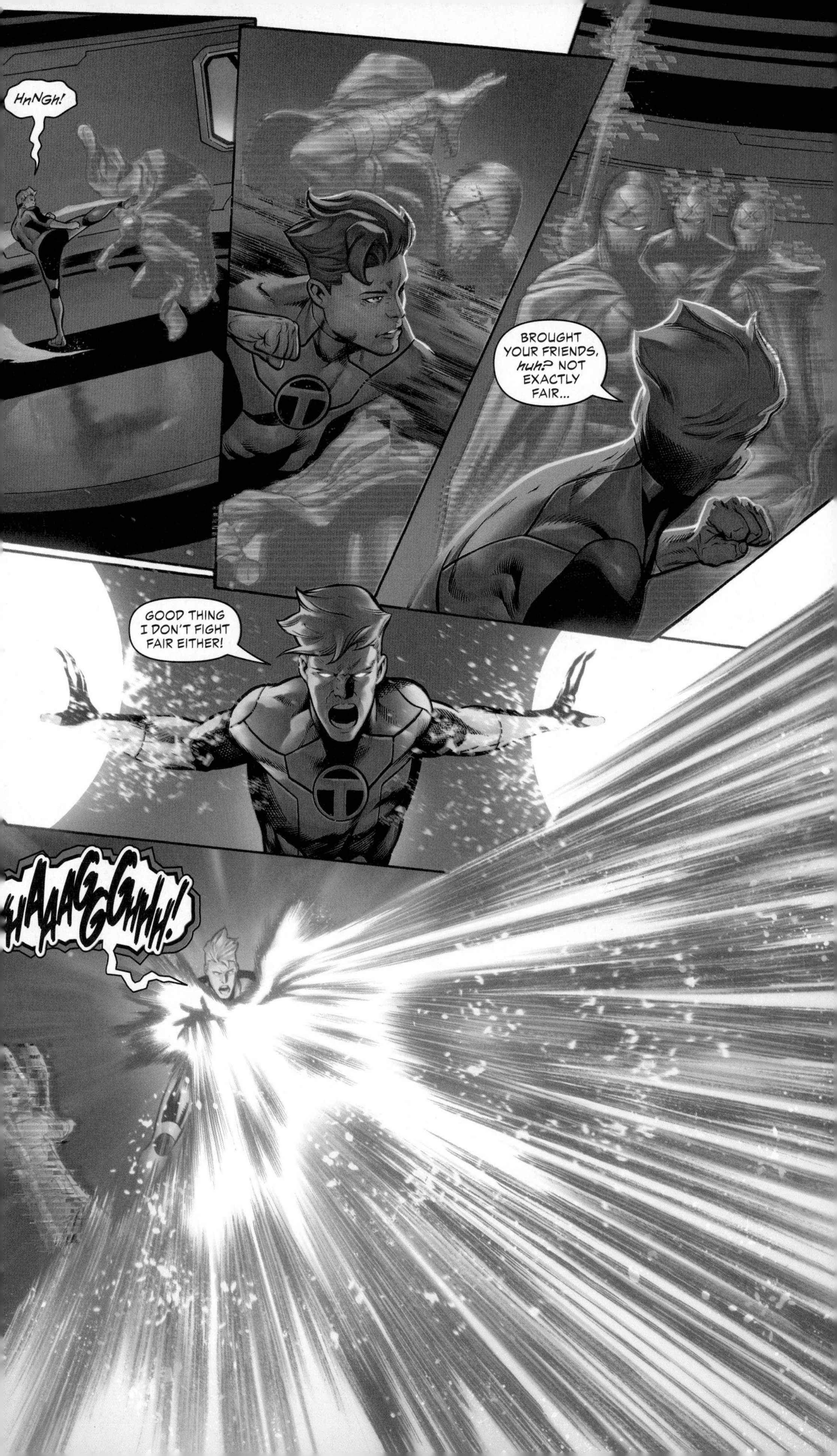
HnNGh!
BROUGHT YOUR FRIENDS, huh? NOT EXACTLY FAIR...
GOOD THING I DON'T FIGHT FAIR EITHER!
HAAAGGHHH!

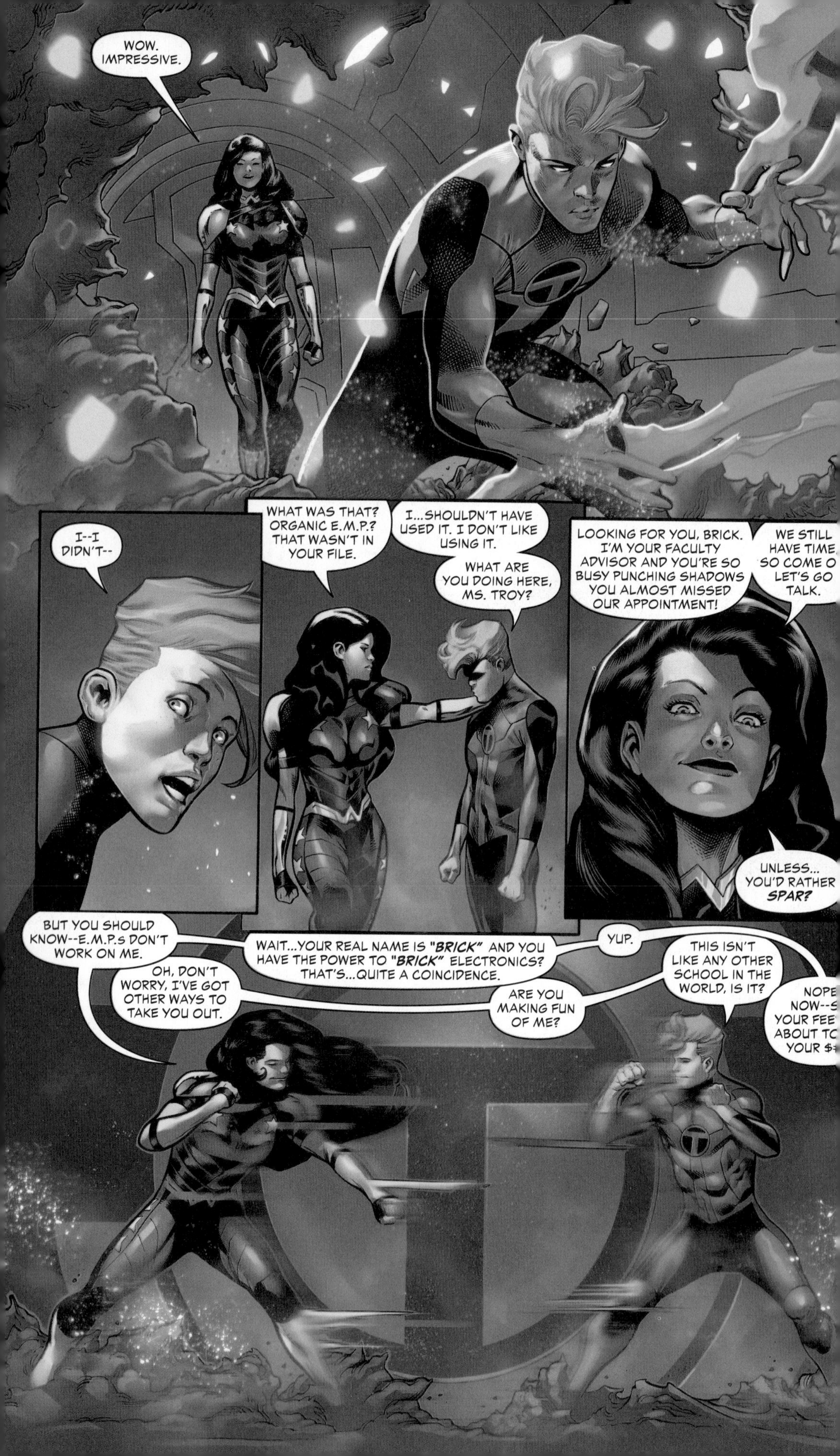

WOW. IMPRESSIVE.
I--I DIDN'T--
WHAT WAS THAT? ORGANIC E.M.P.? THAT WASN'T IN YOUR FILE.
I...SHOULDN'T HAVE USED IT. I DON'T LIKE USING IT.
WHAT ARE YOU DOING HERE, MS. TROY?
LOOKING FOR YOU, BRICK. I'M YOUR FACULTY ADVISOR AND YOU'RE SO BUSY PUNCHING SHADOWS YOU ALMOST MISSED OUR APPOINTMENT!
WE STILL HAVE TIME, SO COME O LET'S GO TALK.
UNLESS... YOU'D RATHER SPAR?
BUT YOU SHOULD KNOW--E.M.P.s DON'T WORK ON ME.
OH, DON'T WORRY, I'VE GOT OTHER WAYS TO TAKE YOU OUT.
WAIT...YOUR REAL NAME IS "BRICK" AND YOU HAVE THE POWER TO "BRICK" ELECTRONICS? THAT'S...QUITE A COINCIDENCE.
ARE YOU MAKING FUN OF ME?
YUP.
THIS ISN'T LIKE ANY OTHER SCHOOL IN THE WORLD, IS IT?
NOPE NOW--S YOUR FEE ABOUT TO YOUR $

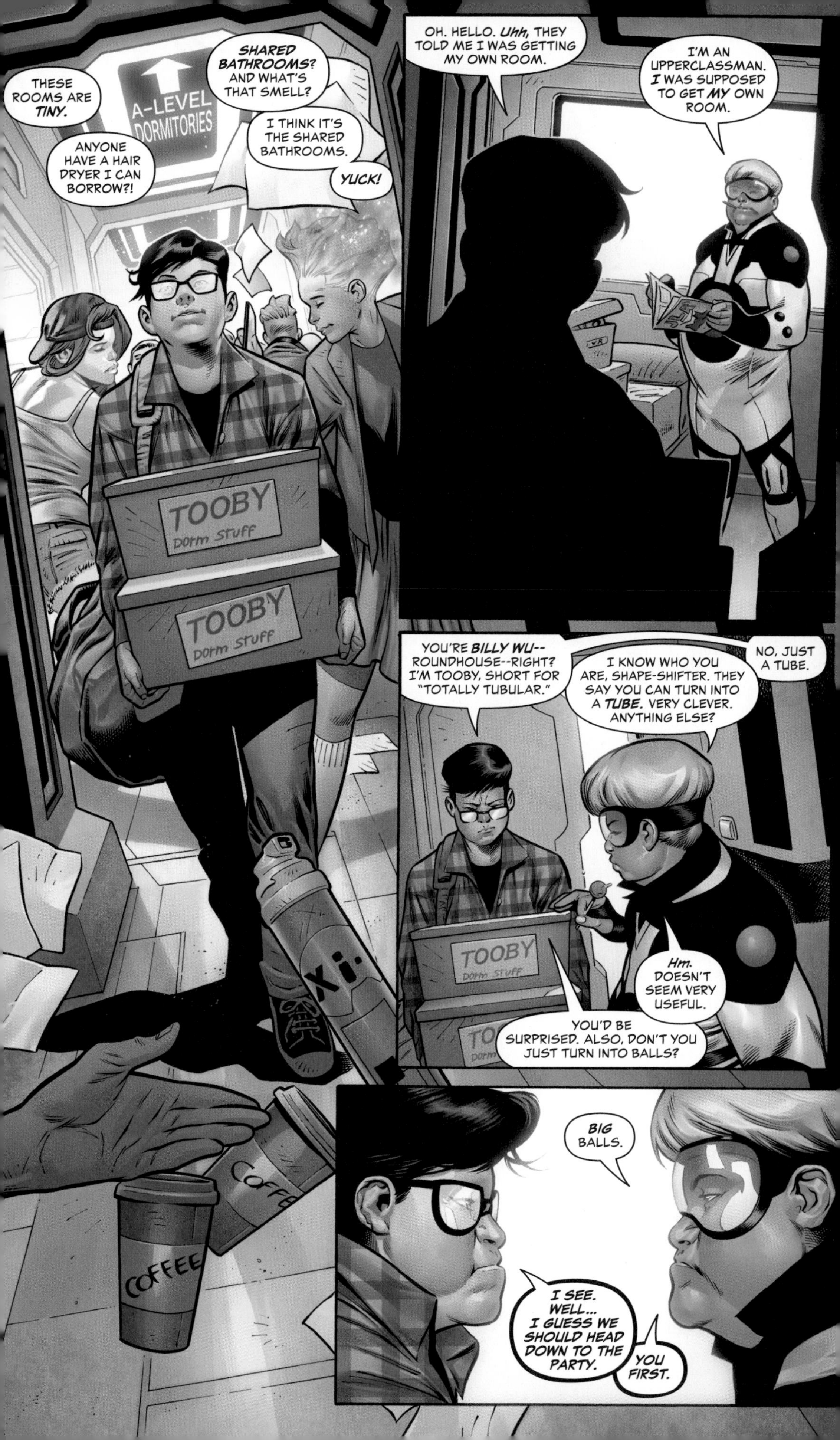
THESE ROOMS ARE TINY.
A-LEVEL DORMITORIES
ANYONE HAVE A HAIR DRYER I CAN BORROW?!
SHARED BATHROOMS? AND WHAT'S THAT SMELL?
I THINK IT'S THE SHARED BATHROOMS.
YUCK!
TOOBY Dorm Stuff
TOOBY Dorm Stuff
Xi
COFFEE
OH. HELLO. Uhh, THEY TOLD ME I WAS GETTING MY OWN ROOM.
I'M AN UPPERCLASSMAN. I WAS SUPPOSED TO GET MY OWN ROOM.
YOU'RE BILLY WU--ROUNDHOUSE--RIGHT? I'M TOOBY, SHORT FOR "TOTALLY TUBULAR."
I KNOW WHO YOU ARE, SHAPE-SHIFTER. THEY SAY YOU CAN TURN INTO A TUBE. VERY CLEVER. ANYTHING ELSE?
NO, JUST A TUBE.
TOOBY Dorm Stuff
Hm. DOESN'T SEEM VERY USEFUL.
YOU'D BE SURPRISED. ALSO, DON'T YOU JUST TURN INTO BALLS?
BIG BALLS.
I SEE. WELL... I GUESS WE SHOULD HEAD DOWN TO THE PARTY.
YOU FIRST.

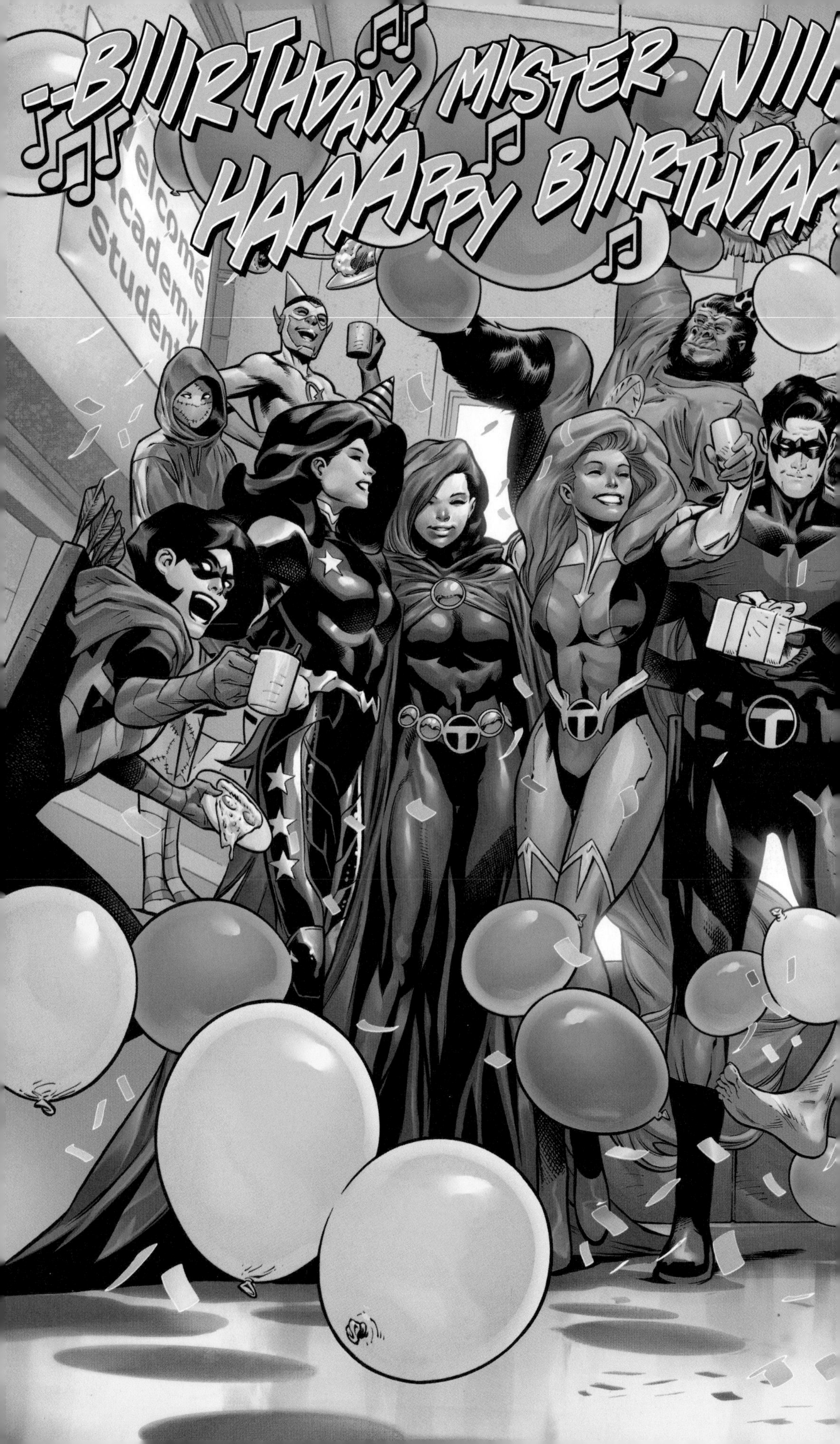

--BIIIRTHDAY, MISTER NIII
HAAAAPPY BIIIRTHDA
Welcome Academy Students

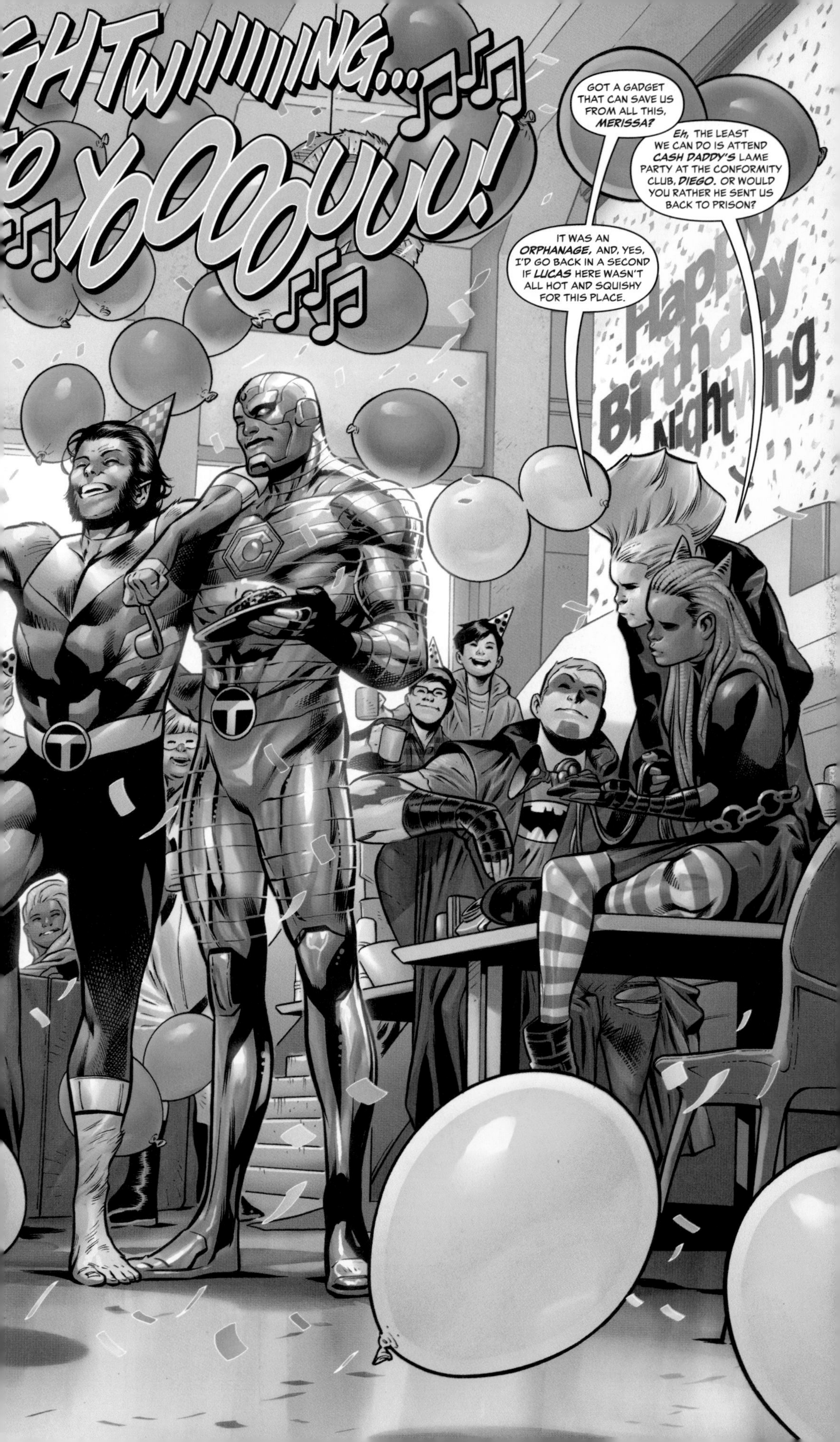

GHTWIIIIIIING... TO YOOOOUUU!
GOT A GADGET THAT CAN SAVE US FROM ALL THIS, MERISSA?
Eh, THE LEAST WE CAN DO IS ATTEND CASH DADDY'S LAME PARTY AT THE CONFORMITY CLUB, DIEGO. OR WOULD YOU RATHER HE SENT US BACK TO PRISON?
IT WAS AN ORPHANAGE, AND, YES, I'D GO BACK IN A SECOND IF LUCAS HERE WASN'T ALL HOT AND SQUISHY FOR THIS PLACE.
Happy Birthday Nightwing

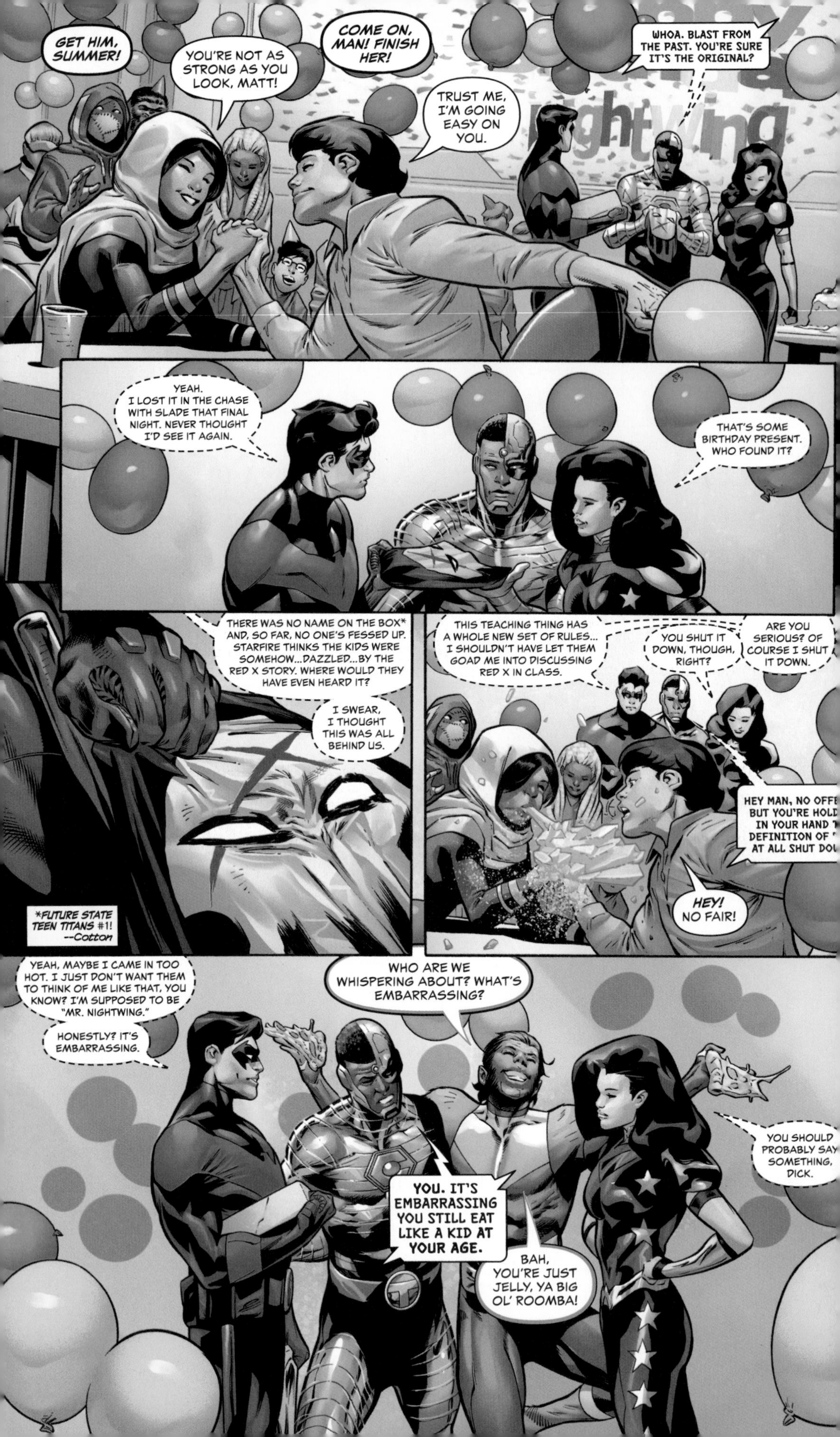
GET HIM, SUMMER!
YOU'RE NOT AS STRONG AS YOU LOOK, MATT!
COME ON, MAN! FINISH HER!
TRUST ME, I'M GOING EASY ON YOU.
WHOA. BLAST FROM THE PAST. YOU'RE SURE IT'S THE ORIGINAL?
YEAH. I LOST IT IN THE CHASE WITH SLADE THAT FINAL NIGHT. NEVER THOUGHT I'D SEE IT AGAIN.
THAT'S SOME BIRTHDAY PRESENT. WHO FOUND IT?
THERE WAS NO NAME ON THE BOX* AND, SO FAR, NO ONE'S FESSED UP. STARFIRE THINKS THE KIDS WERE SOMEHOW...DAZZLED...BY THE RED X STORY. WHERE WOULD THEY HAVE EVEN HEARD IT?
I SWEAR, I THOUGHT THIS WAS ALL BEHIND US.
*FUTURE STATE TEEN TITANS #1! --Cotton
THIS TEACHING THING HAS A WHOLE NEW SET OF RULES... I SHOULDN'T HAVE LET THEM GOAD ME INTO DISCUSSING RED X IN CLASS.
YOU SHUT IT DOWN, THOUGH, RIGHT?
ARE YOU SERIOUS? OF COURSE I SHUT IT DOWN.
HEY! NO FAIR!
YEAH, MAYBE I CAME IN TOO HOT. I JUST DON'T WANT THEM TO THINK OF ME LIKE THAT, YOU KNOW? I'M SUPPOSED TO BE "MR. NIGHTWING."
HONESTLY? IT'S EMBARRASSING.
WHO ARE WE WHISPERING ABOUT? WHAT'S EMBARRASSING?
YOU SHOULD PROBABLY SAY SOMETHING, DICK.
YOU. IT'S EMBARRASSING YOU STILL EAT LIKE A KID AT YOUR AGE.
BAH, YOU'RE JUST JELLY, YA BIG OL' ROOMBA!

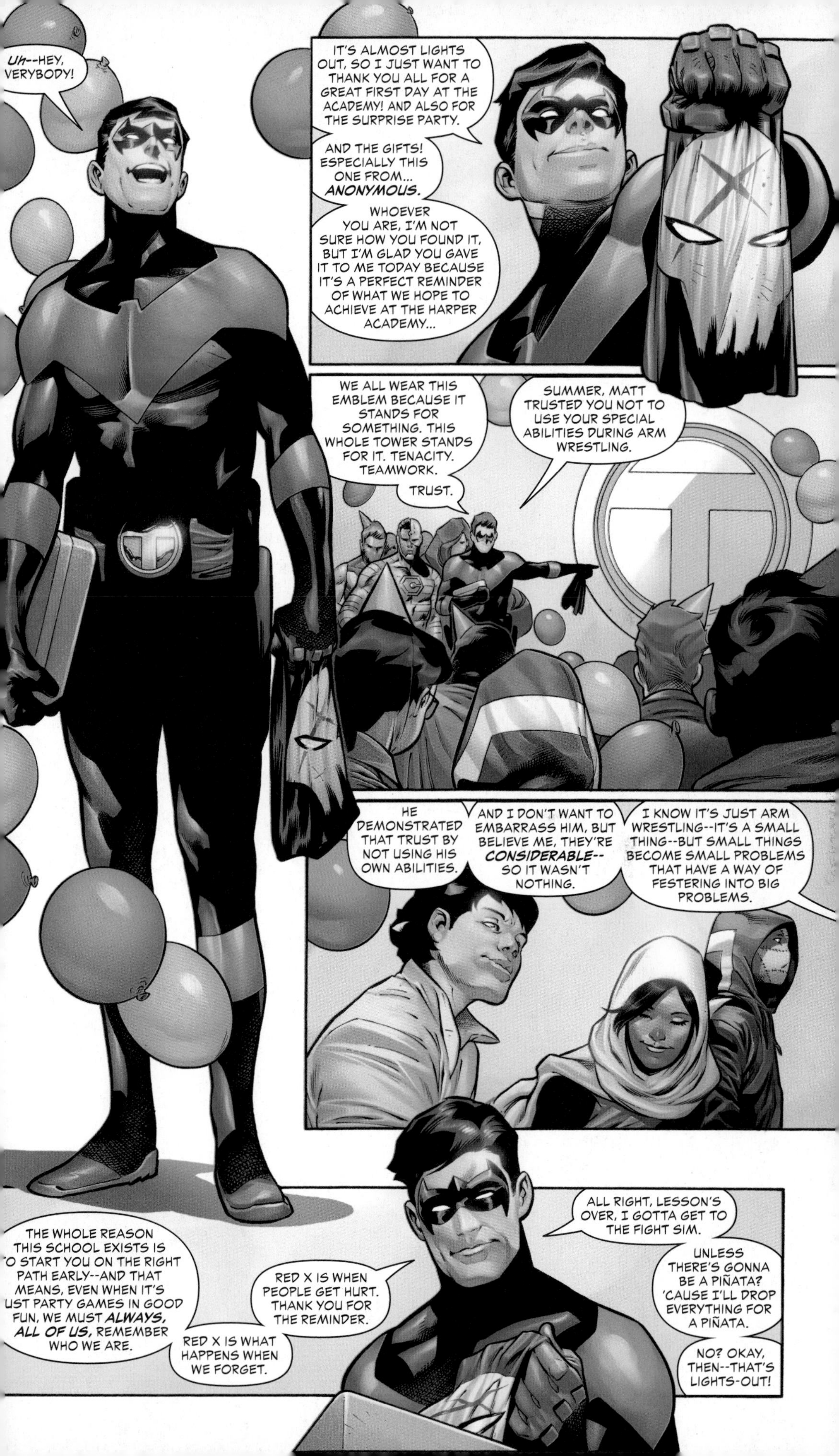
Uh--HEY, VERYBODY!
IT'S ALMOST LIGHTS OUT, SO I JUST WANT TO THANK YOU ALL FOR A GREAT FIRST DAY AT THE ACADEMY! AND ALSO FOR THE SURPRISE PARTY.
AND THE GIFTS! ESPECIALLY THIS ONE FROM... ANONYMOUS.
WHOEVER YOU ARE, I'M NOT SURE HOW YOU FOUND IT, BUT I'M GLAD YOU GAVE IT TO ME TODAY BECAUSE IT'S A PERFECT REMINDER OF WHAT WE HOPE TO ACHIEVE AT THE HARPER ACADEMY...
WE ALL WEAR THIS EMBLEM BECAUSE IT STANDS FOR SOMETHING. THIS WHOLE TOWER STANDS FOR IT. TENACITY. TEAMWORK.
TRUST.
SUMMER, MATT TRUSTED YOU NOT TO USE YOUR SPECIAL ABILITIES DURING ARM WRESTLING.
HE DEMONSTRATED THAT TRUST BY NOT USING HIS OWN ABILITIES.
AND I DON'T WANT TO EMBARRASS HIM, BUT BELIEVE ME, THEY'RE CONSIDERABLE-- SO IT WASN'T NOTHING.
I KNOW IT'S JUST ARM WRESTLING--IT'S A SMALL THING--BUT SMALL THINGS BECOME SMALL PROBLEMS THAT HAVE A WAY OF FESTERING INTO BIG PROBLEMS.
THE WHOLE REASON THIS SCHOOL EXISTS IS TO START YOU ON THE RIGHT PATH EARLY--AND THAT MEANS, EVEN WHEN IT'S JUST PARTY GAMES IN GOOD FUN, WE MUST ALWAYS, ALL OF US, REMEMBER WHO WE ARE.
RED X IS WHAT HAPPENS WHEN WE FORGET.
RED X IS WHEN PEOPLE GET HURT. THANK YOU FOR THE REMINDER.
ALL RIGHT, LESSON'S OVER, I GOTTA GET TO THE FIGHT SIM.
UNLESS THERE'S GONNA BE A PIÑATA? 'CAUSE I'LL DROP EVERYTHING FOR A PIÑATA.
NO? OKAY, THEN--THAT'S LIGHTS-OUT!

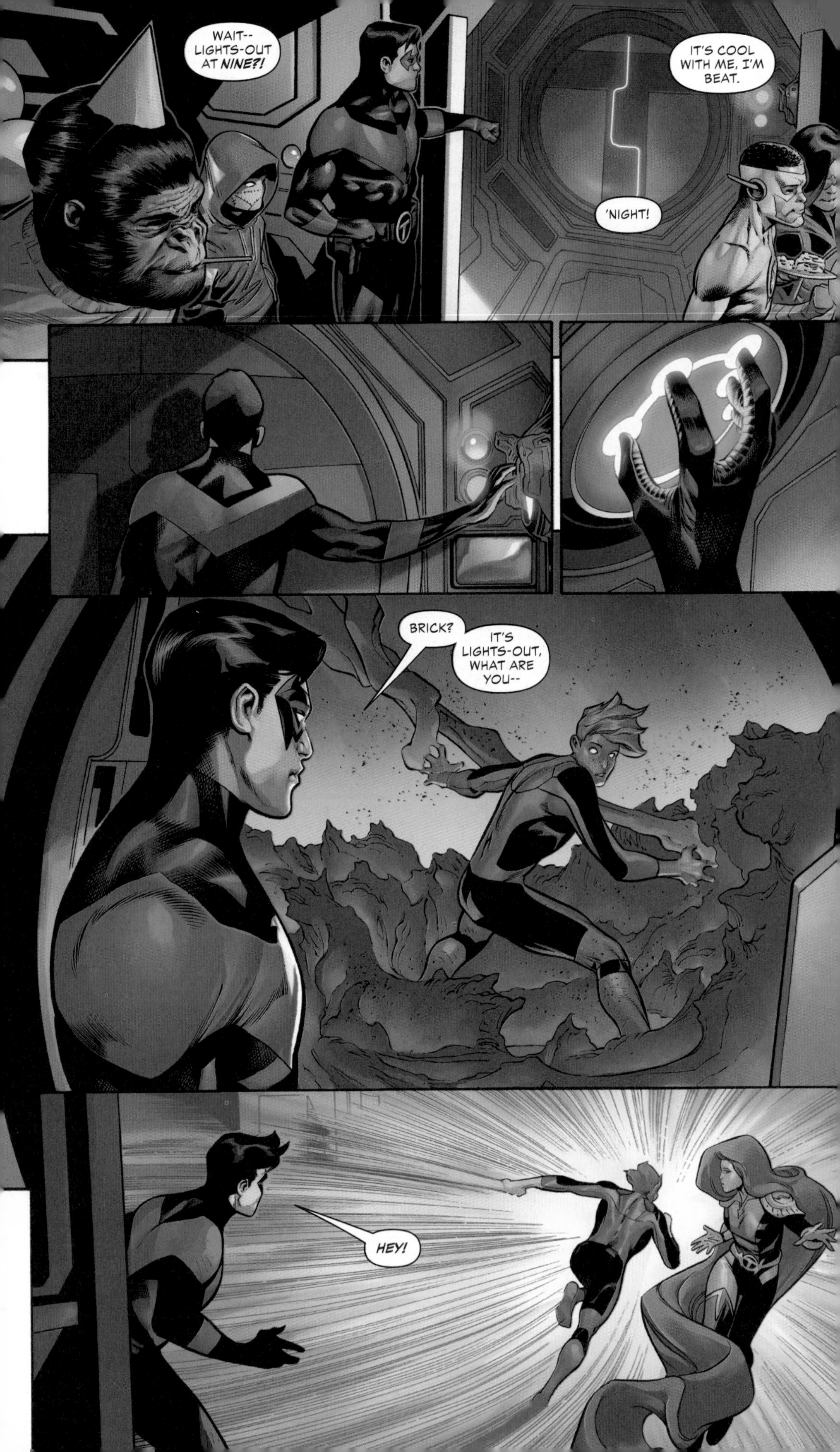
WAIT-- LIGHTS-OUT AT NINE?!
IT'S COOL WITH ME, I'M BEAT.
'NIGHT!
BRICK?
IT'S LIGHTS-OUT, WHAT ARE YOU--
HEY!

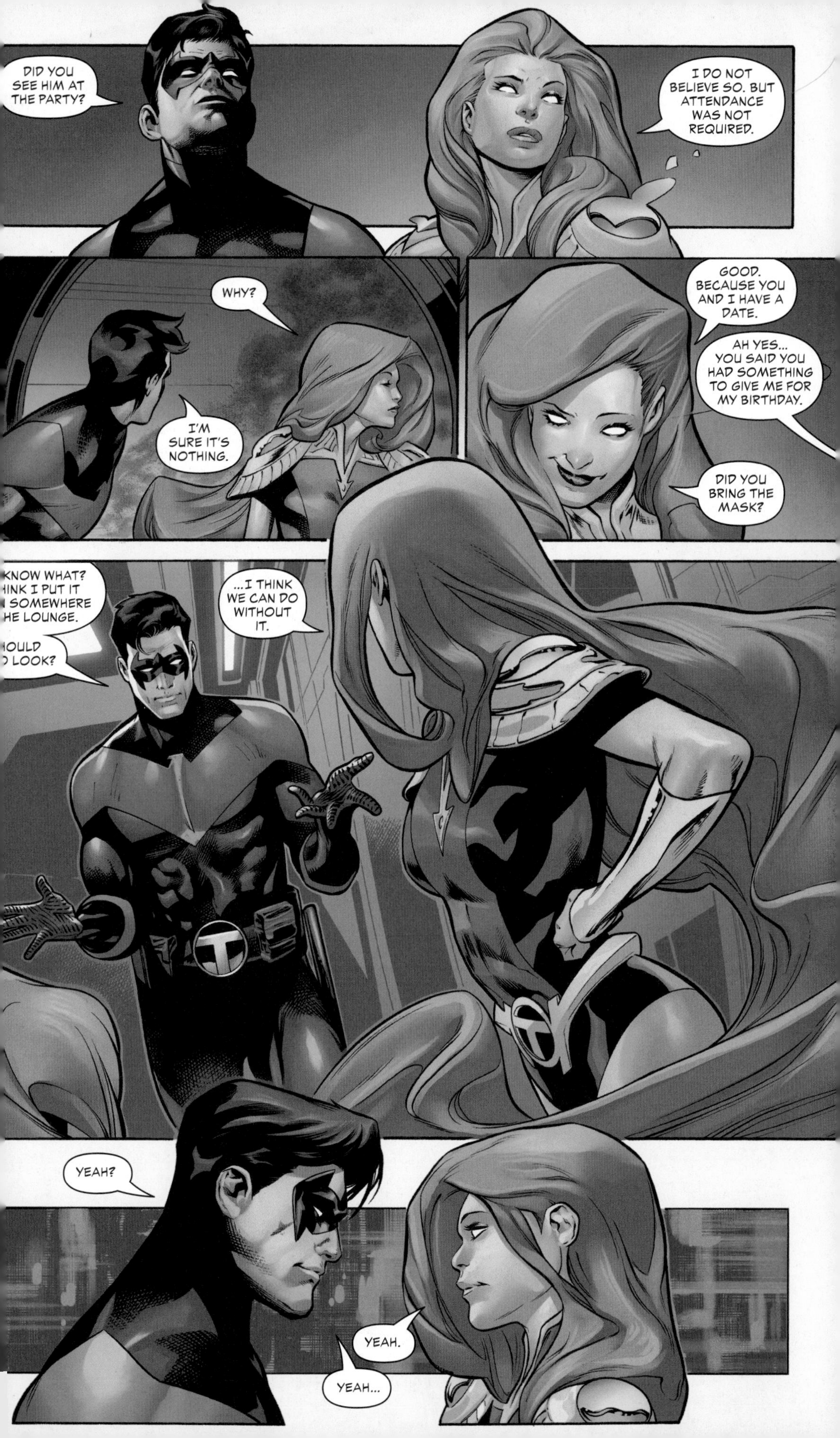
DID YOU SEE HIM AT THE PARTY?
I DO NOT BELIEVE SO. BUT ATTENDANCE WAS NOT REQUIRED.
WHY?
I'M SURE IT'S NOTHING.
GOOD. BECAUSE YOU AND I HAVE A DATE.
AH YES... YOU SAID YOU HAD SOMETHING TO GIVE ME FOR MY BIRTHDAY.
DID YOU BRING THE MASK?
KNOW WHAT? HINK I PUT IT SOMEWHERE HE LOUNGE.
HOULD LOOK?
...I THINK WE CAN DO WITHOUT IT.
YEAH?
YEAH.
YEAH...

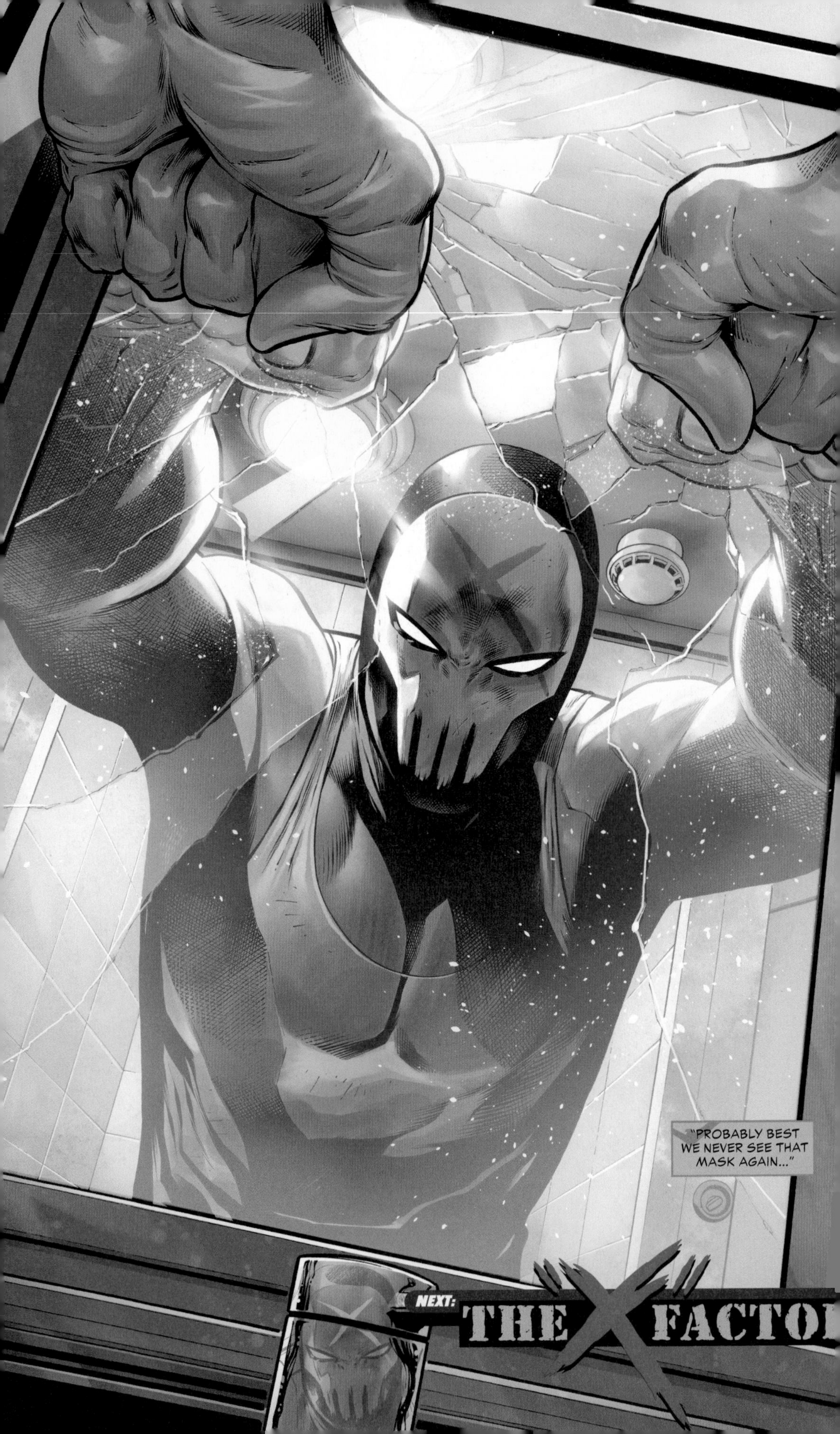
"PROBABLY BEST WE NEVER SEE THAT MASK AGAIN..."
NEXT: THE X FACTOR

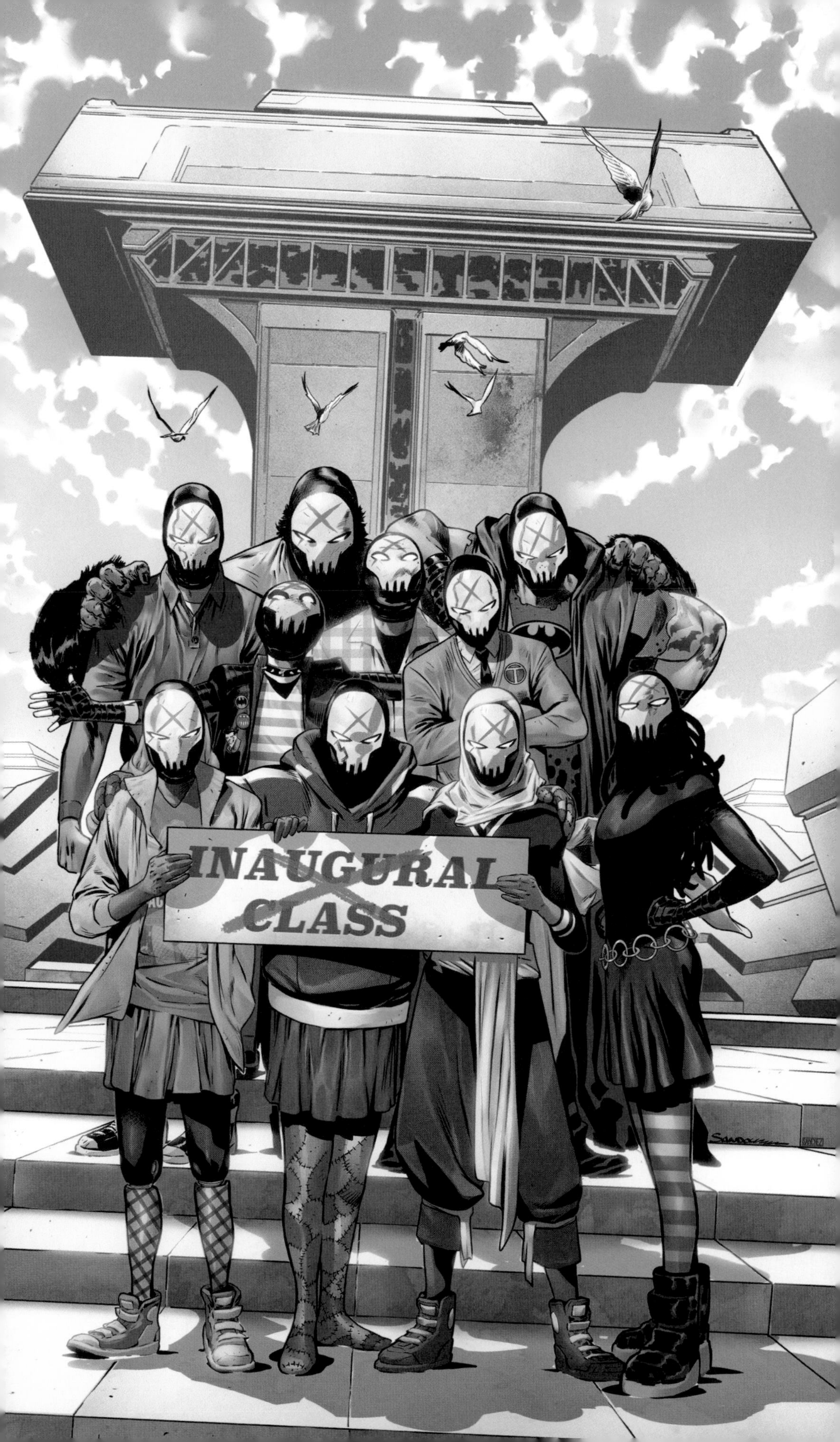
INAUGURAL
CLASS

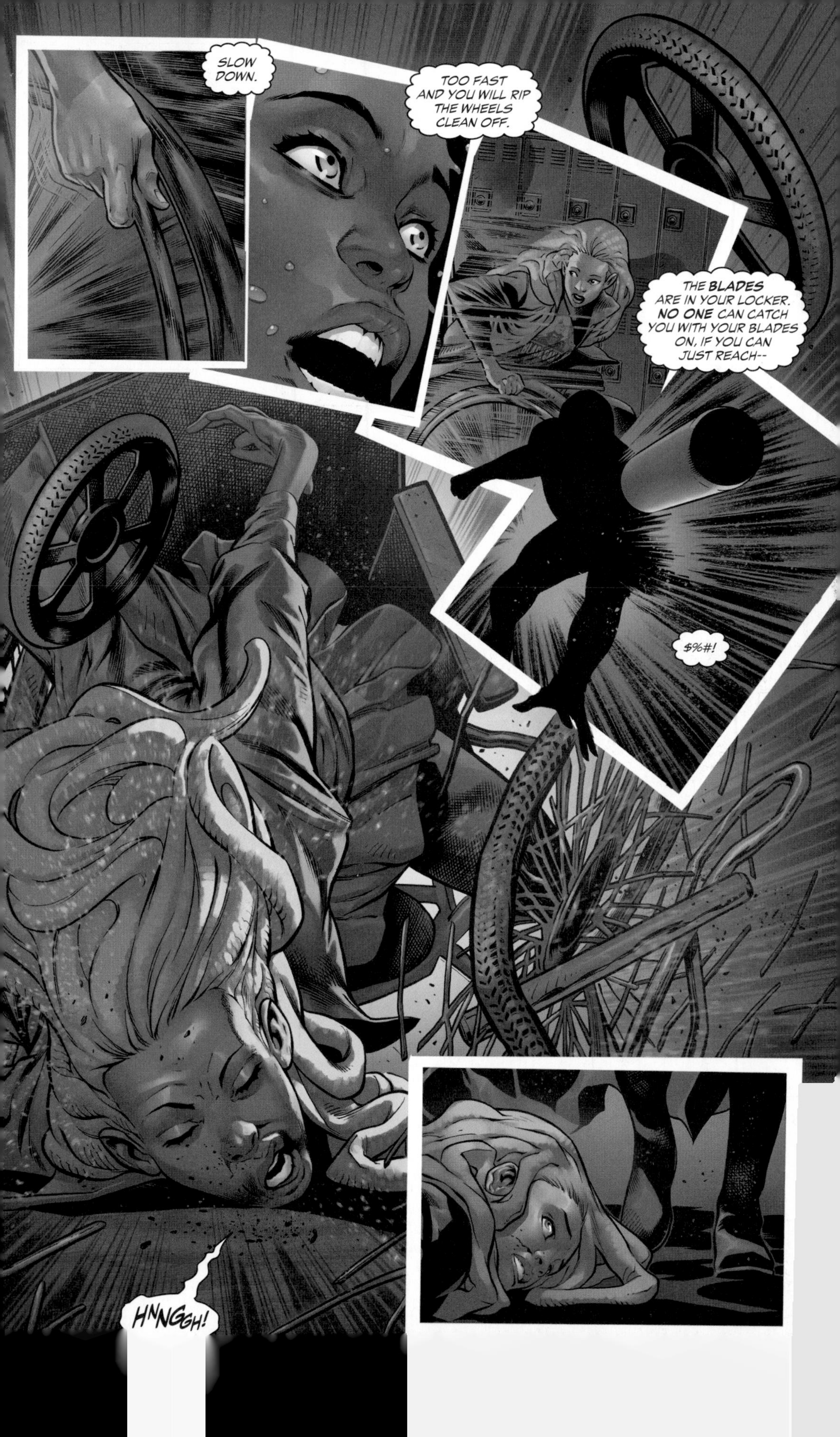
SLOW DOWN.
TOO FAST AND YOU WILL RIP THE WHEELS CLEAN OFF.
THE BLADES ARE IN YOUR LOCKER. NO ONE CAN CATCH YOU WITH YOUR BLADES ON, IF YOU CAN JUST REACH--
$%#!
HNNGGH!

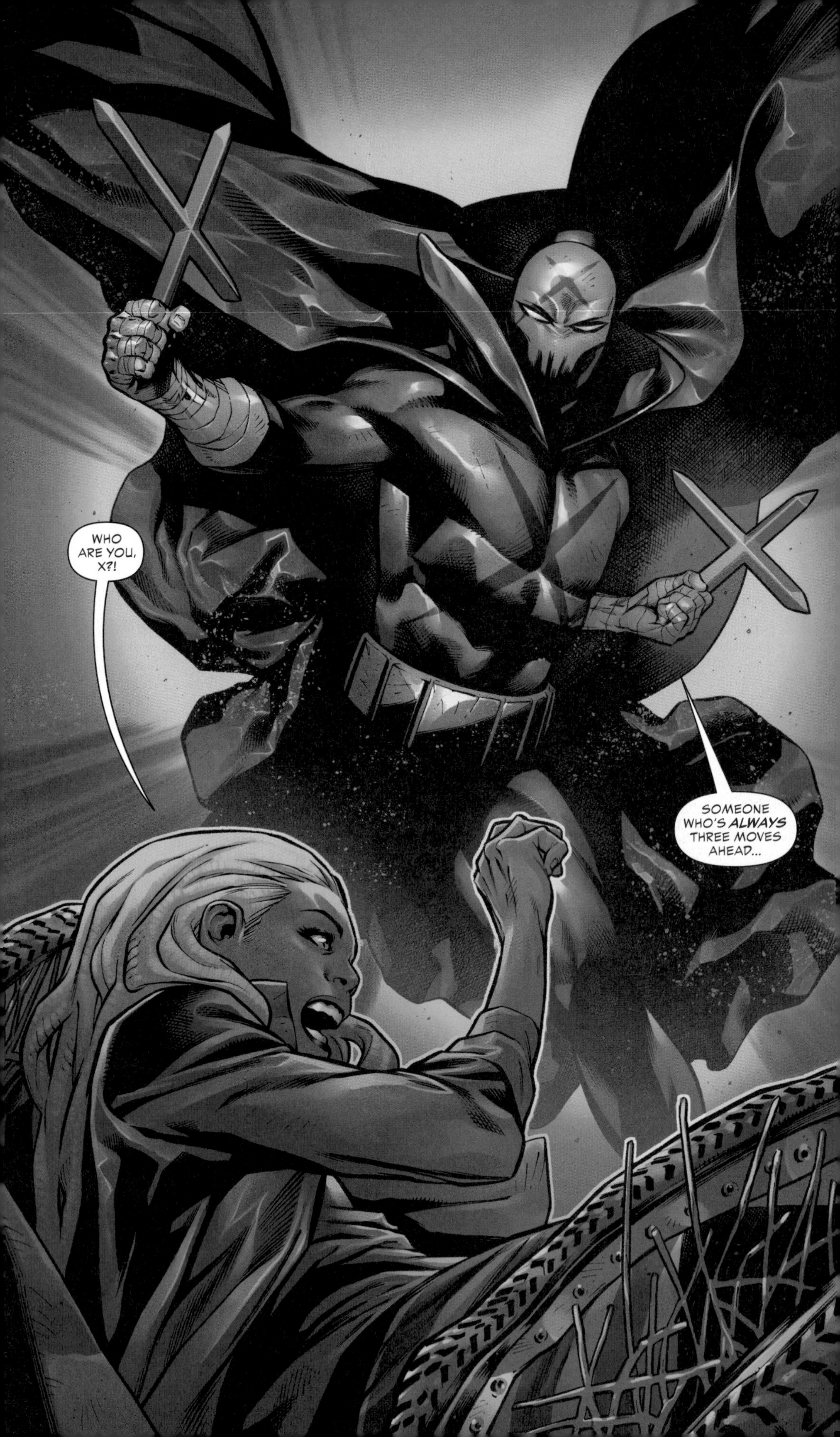
WHO ARE YOU, X?!
SOMEONE WHO'S *ALWAYS* THREE MOVES AHEAD...

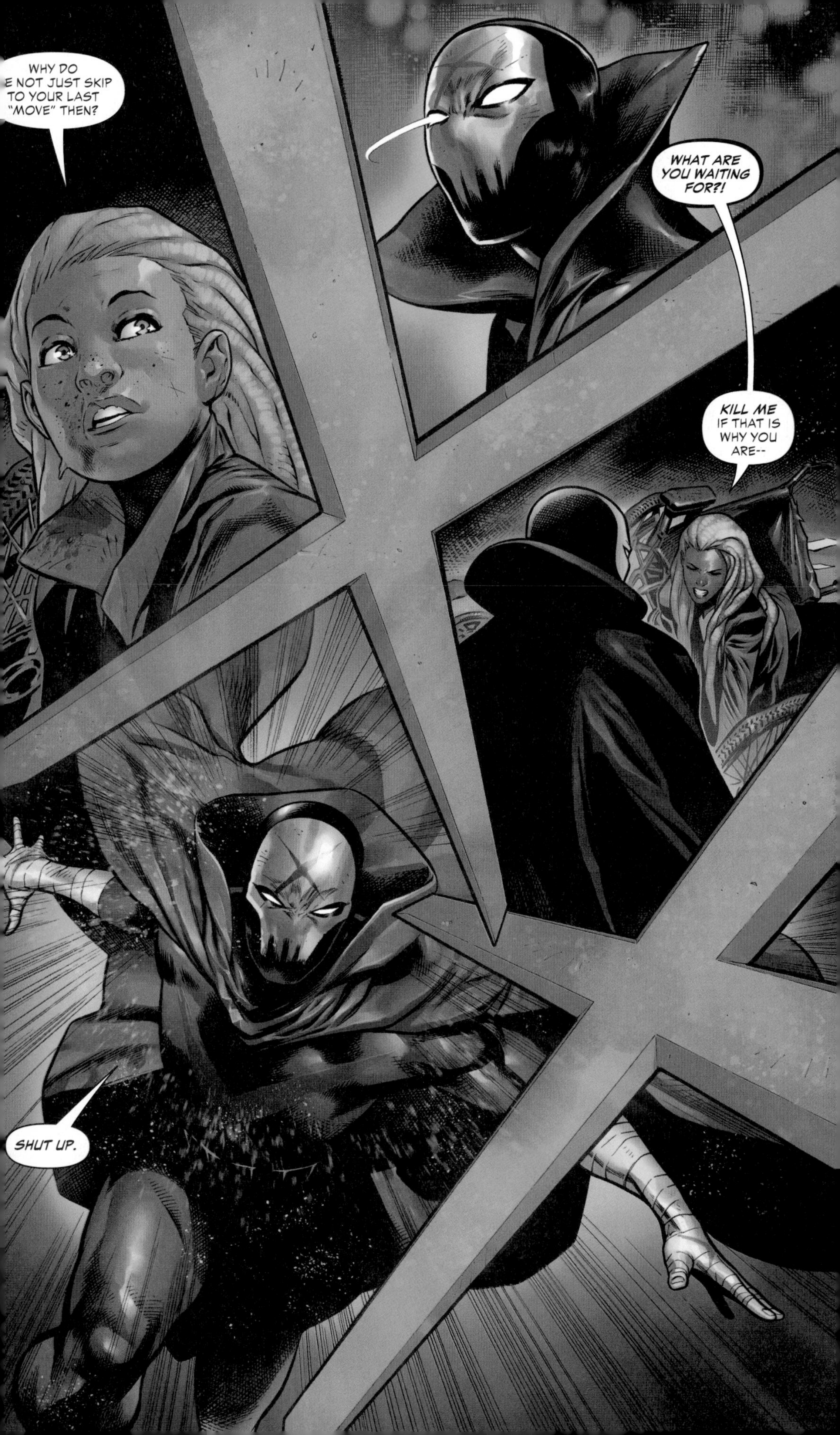
WHY DO
E NOT JUST SKIP TO YOUR LAST "MOVE" THEN?
WHAT ARE YOU WAITING FOR?!
KILL ME IF THAT IS WHY YOU ARE--
SHUT UP.

THE X FACTOR

TIM SHERIDAN
writer
RAFA SANDOVAL
penciller
JORDI TARRAGONA
inker
ALEJANDRO SANCHEZ
colorist
ROB LEIGH
letterer
SANDOVAL & SANCHEZ
cover
PHILIP TAN &
ELMER SANTOS
variant cover
DIEGO LOPEZ
associate editor
MIKE COTTON
editor
JAMIE S. RICH
group editor

Original Titans NIGHTWING, STARFIRE, RAVEN, DONNA TROY, CYBORG, and BEAST BOY reassemble to mentor the next generation of heroes! Now, TEEN TITANS ACADEMY opens its doors to a new crop of gifted youngsters eager to earn their place on the team's permanent roster, innocent of the many treacherous challenges they will face—in and out of school—over the months and years to come...

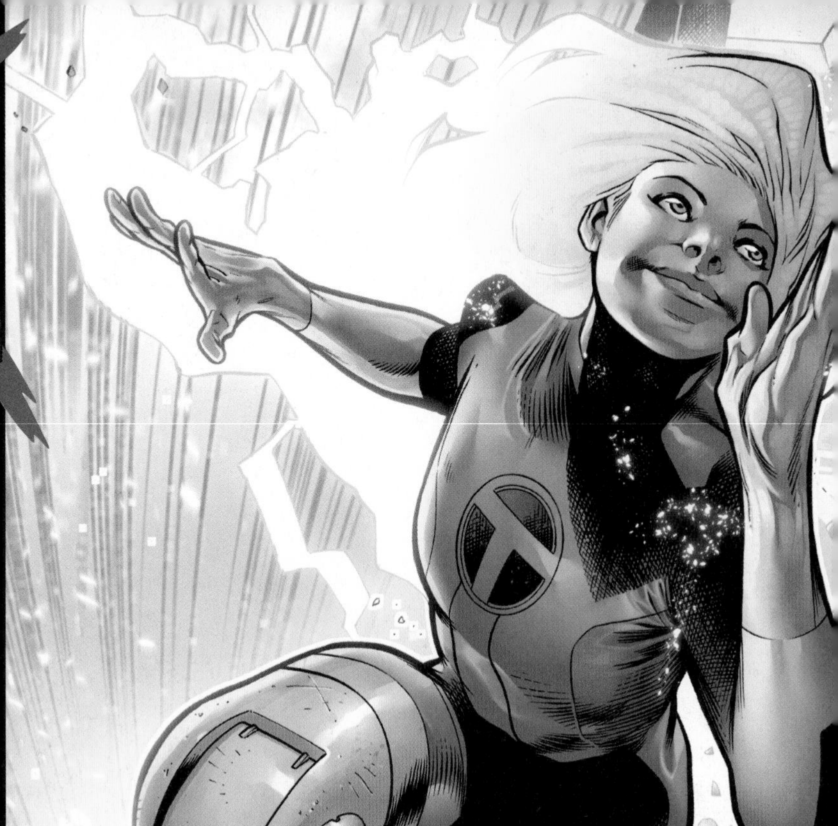

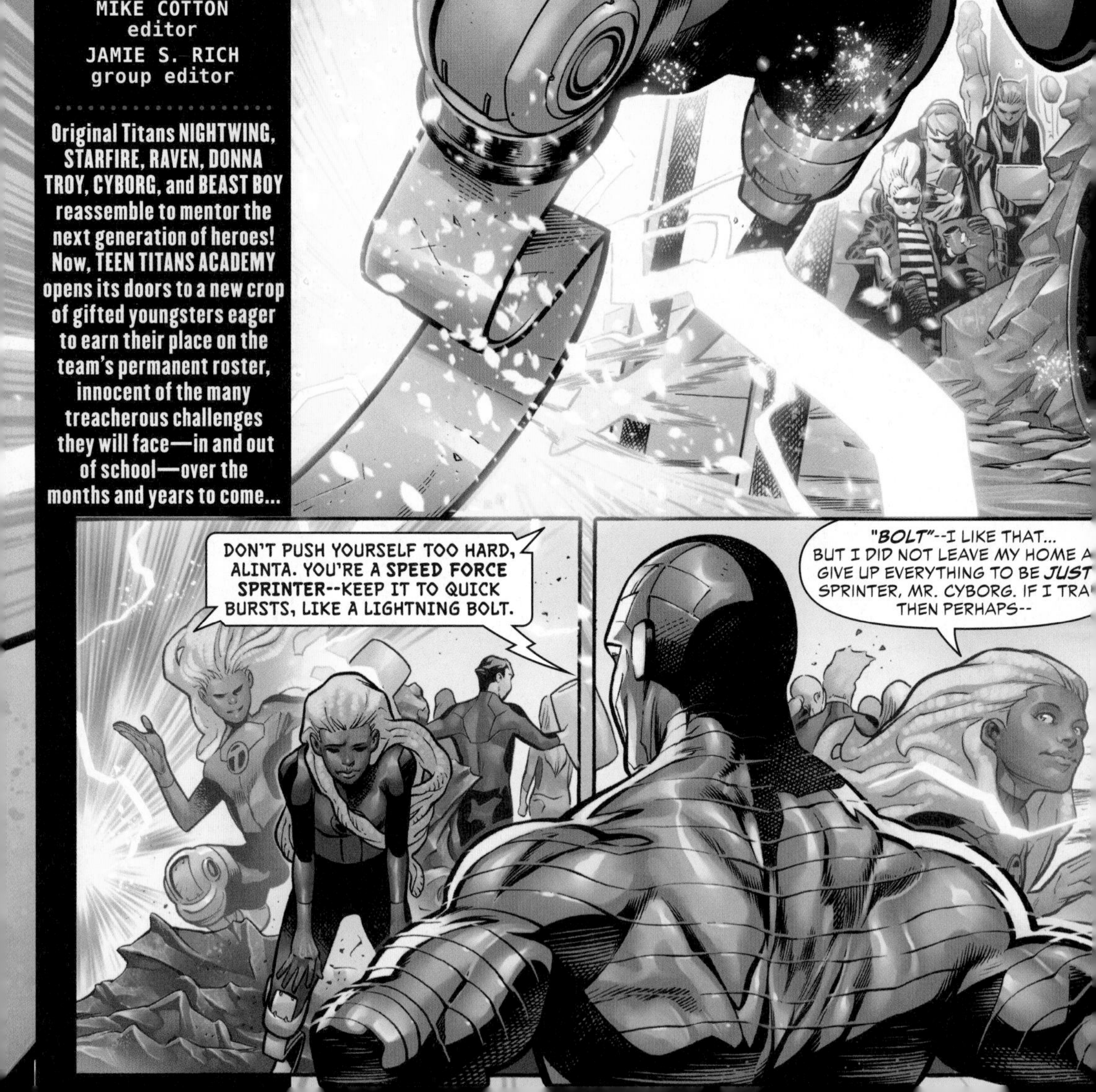
DON'T PUSH YOURSELF TOO HARD, ALINTA. YOU'RE A **SPEED FORCE SPRINTER**--KEEP IT TO QUICK BURSTS, LIKE A LIGHTNING BOLT.
"***BOLT***"--I LIKE THAT... BUT I DID NOT LEAVE MY HOME A GIVE UP EVERYTHING TO BE ***JUST*** SPRINTER, MR. CYBORG. IF I TRA THEN PERHAPS--

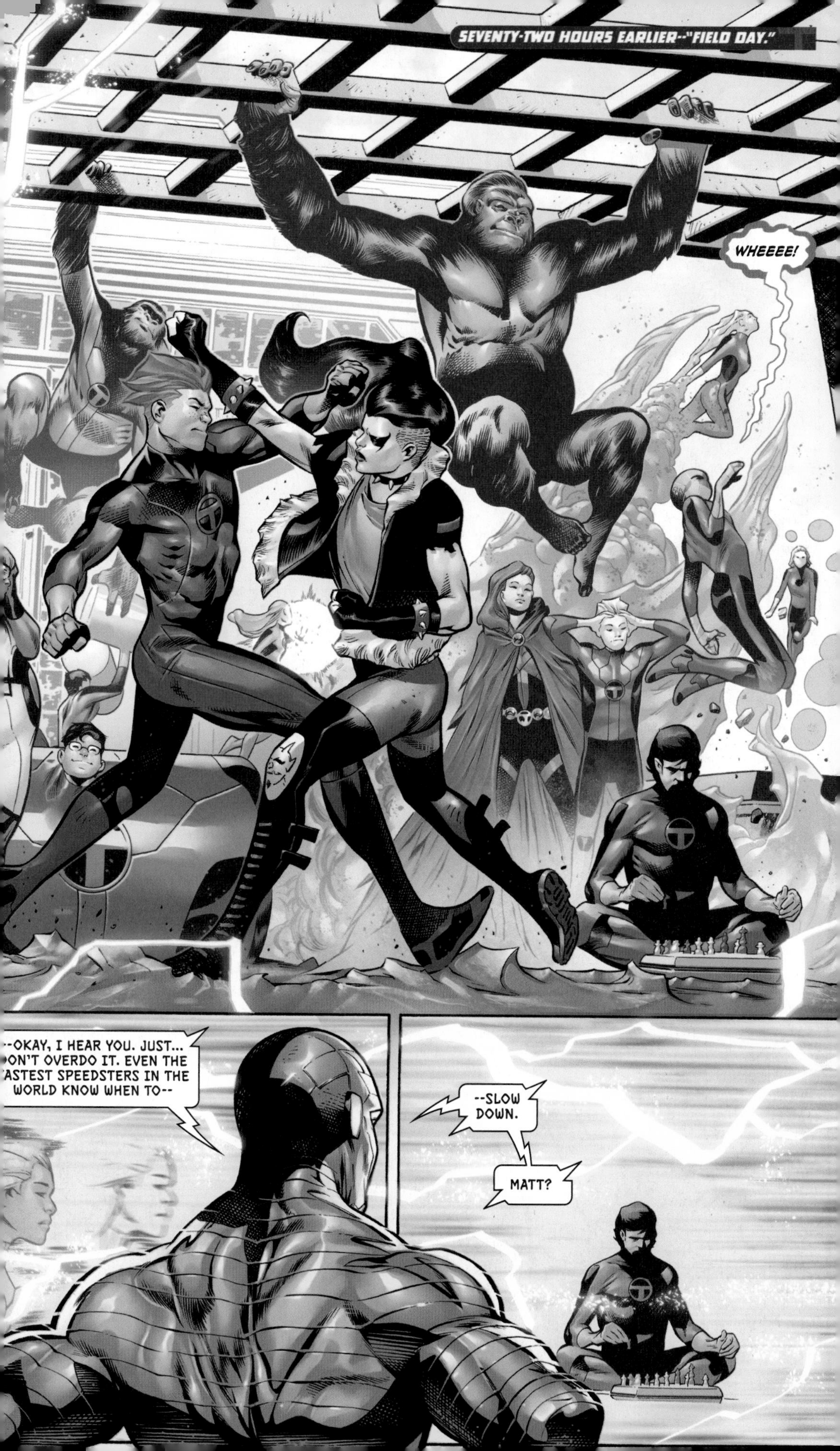
SEVENTY-TWO HOURS EARLIER--"FIELD DAY."
WHEEEE!
--OKAY, I HEAR YOU. JUST... DON'T OVERDO IT. EVEN THE FASTEST SPEEDSTERS IN THE WORLD KNOW WHEN TO--
--SLOW DOWN.
MATT?

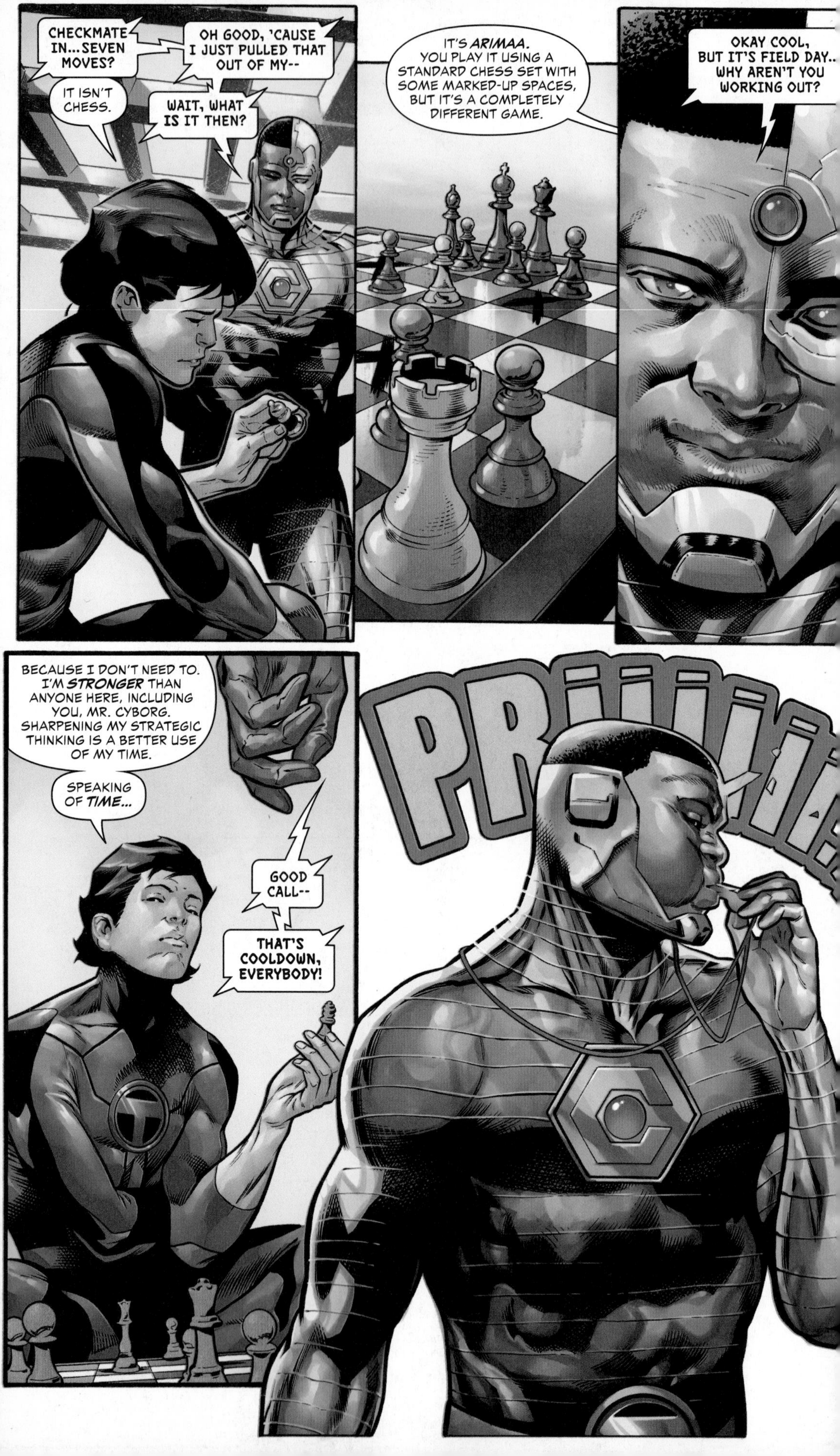
CHECKMATE IN...SEVEN MOVES?
OH GOOD, 'CAUSE I JUST PULLED THAT OUT OF MY--
IT ISN'T CHESS.
WAIT, WHAT IS IT THEN?
IT'S ARIMAA. YOU PLAY IT USING A STANDARD CHESS SET WITH SOME MARKED-UP SPACES, BUT IT'S A COMPLETELY DIFFERENT GAME.
OKAY COOL, BUT IT'S FIELD DAY.. WHY AREN'T YOU WORKING OUT?
BECAUSE I DON'T NEED TO. I'M STRONGER THAN ANYONE HERE, INCLUDING YOU, MR. CYBORG. SHARPENING MY STRATEGIC THINKING IS A BETTER USE OF MY TIME.
SPEAKING OF TIME...
GOOD CALL--
THAT'S COOLDOWN, EVERYBODY!

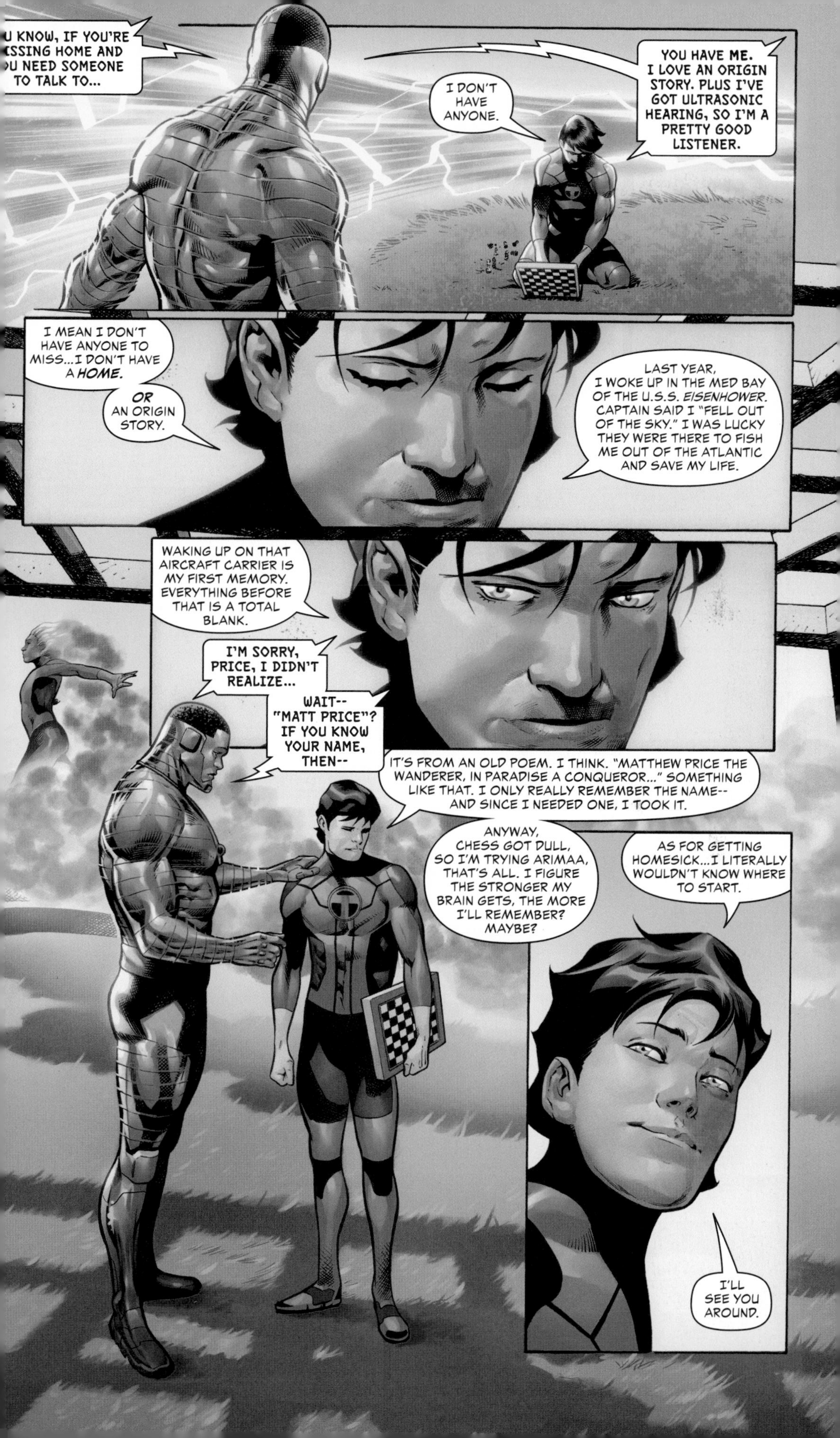

U KNOW, IF YOU'RE
ISSING HOME AND
U NEED SOMEONE
TO TALK TO...
I DON'T HAVE ANYONE.
YOU HAVE ME. I LOVE AN ORIGIN STORY. PLUS I'VE GOT ULTRASONIC HEARING, SO I'M A PRETTY GOOD LISTENER.
I MEAN I DON'T HAVE ANYONE TO MISS...I DON'T HAVE A HOME.
OR AN ORIGIN STORY.
LAST YEAR, I WOKE UP IN THE MED BAY OF THE U.S.S. EISENHOWER. CAPTAIN SAID I "FELL OUT OF THE SKY." I WAS LUCKY THEY WERE THERE TO FISH ME OUT OF THE ATLANTIC AND SAVE MY LIFE.
WAKING UP ON THAT AIRCRAFT CARRIER IS MY FIRST MEMORY. EVERYTHING BEFORE THAT IS A TOTAL BLANK.
I'M SORRY, PRICE, I DIDN'T REALIZE...
WAIT-- "MATT PRICE"? IF YOU KNOW YOUR NAME, THEN--
IT'S FROM AN OLD POEM. I THINK. "MATTHEW PRICE THE WANDERER, IN PARADISE A CONQUEROR..." SOMETHING LIKE THAT. I ONLY REALLY REMEMBER THE NAME-- AND SINCE I NEEDED ONE, I TOOK IT.
ANYWAY, CHESS GOT DULL, SO I'M TRYING ARIMAA, THAT'S ALL. I FIGURE THE STRONGER MY BRAIN GETS, THE MORE I'LL REMEMBER? MAYBE?
AS FOR GETTING HOMESICK...I LITERALLY WOULDN'T KNOW WHERE TO START.
I'LL SEE YOU AROUND.

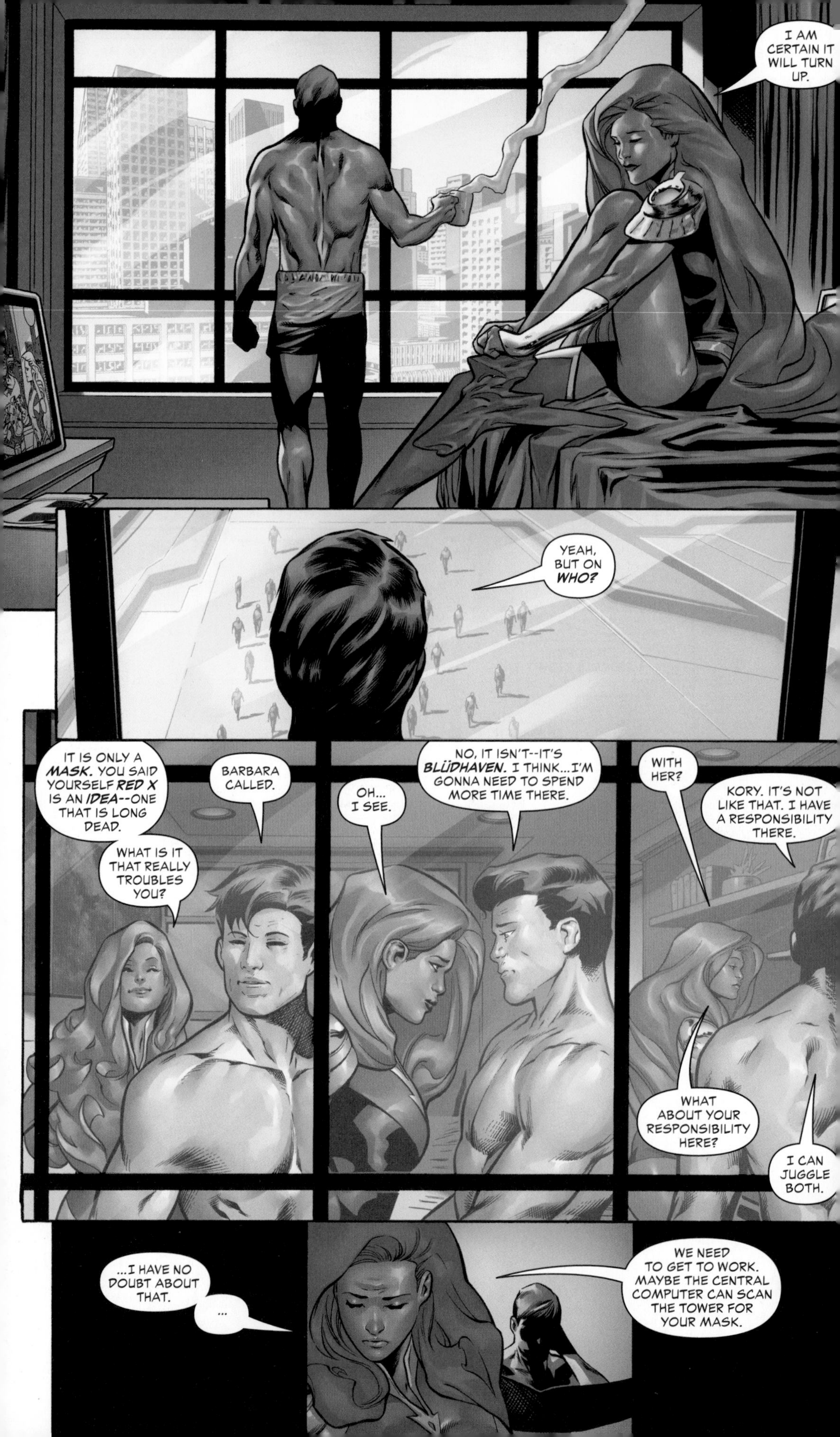
I AM CERTAIN IT WILL TURN UP.
YEAH, BUT ON WHO?
BARBARA CALLED.
IT IS ONLY A MASK. YOU SAID YOURSELF RED X IS AN IDEA--ONE THAT IS LONG DEAD.
WHAT IS IT THAT REALLY TROUBLES YOU?
NO, IT ISN'T--IT'S BLÜDHAVEN. I THINK...I'M GONNA NEED TO SPEND MORE TIME THERE.
OH... I SEE.
WITH HER?
KORY. IT'S NOT LIKE THAT. I HAVE A RESPONSIBILITY THERE.
WHAT ABOUT YOUR RESPONSIBILITY HERE?
I CAN JUGGLE BOTH.
...I HAVE NO DOUBT ABOUT THAT.
...
WE NEED TO GET TO WORK. MAYBE THE CENTRAL COMPUTER CAN SCAN THE TOWER FOR YOUR MASK.

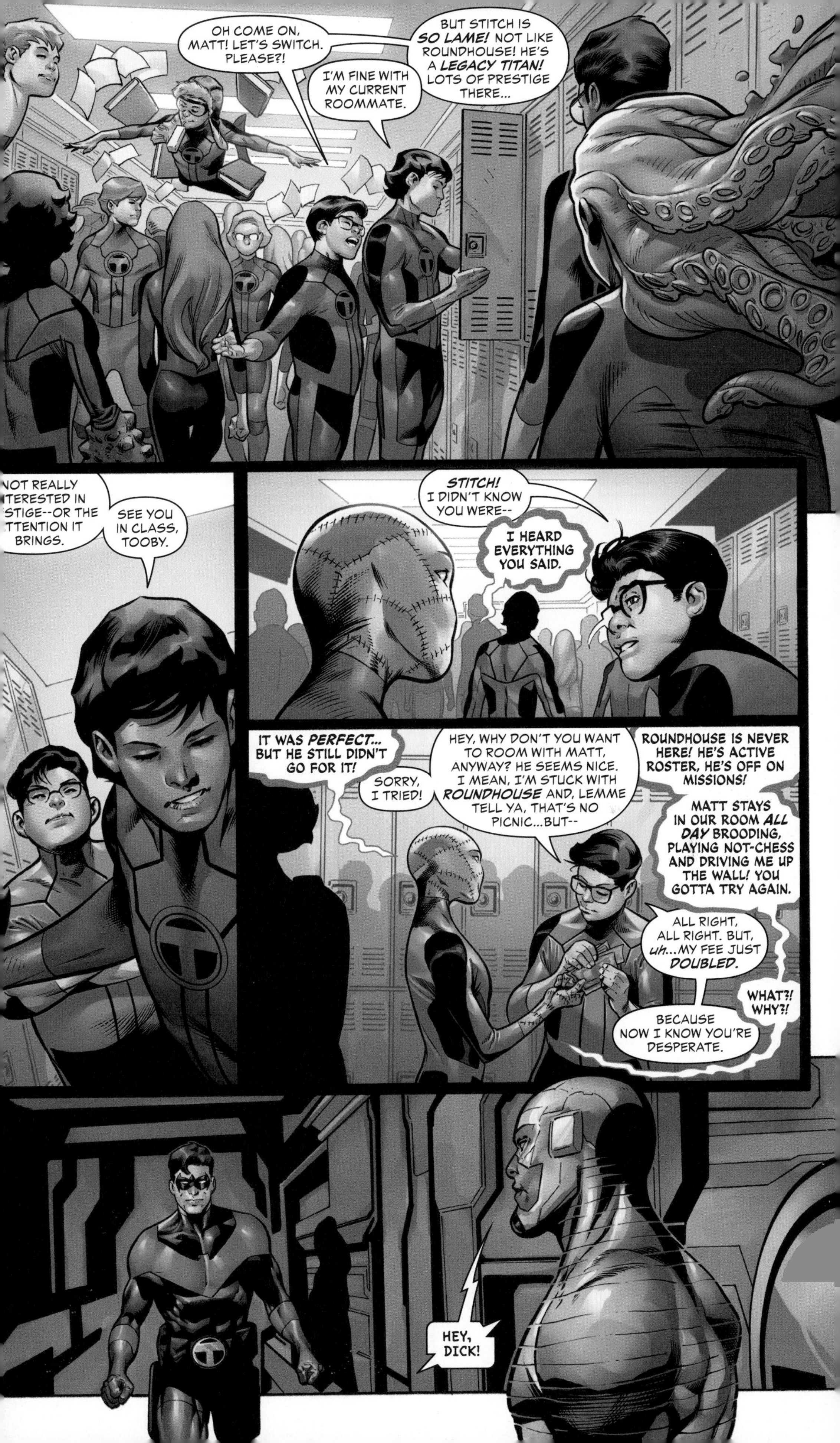
OH COME ON, MATT! LET'S SWITCH. PLEASE?!
I'M FINE WITH MY CURRENT ROOMMATE.
BUT STITCH IS SO LAME! NOT LIKE ROUNDHOUSE! HE'S A LEGACY TITAN! LOTS OF PRESTIGE THERE...
NOT REALLY TERESTED IN STIGE--OR THE TTENTION IT BRINGS.
SEE YOU IN CLASS, TOOBY.
STITCH! I DIDN'T KNOW YOU WERE--
I HEARD EVERYTHING YOU SAID.
IT WAS PERFECT... BUT HE STILL DIDN'T GO FOR IT!
SORRY, I TRIED!
HEY, WHY DON'T YOU WANT TO ROOM WITH MATT, ANYWAY? HE SEEMS NICE. I MEAN, I'M STUCK WITH ROUNDHOUSE AND, LEMME TELL YA, THAT'S NO PICNIC...BUT--
ROUNDHOUSE IS NEVER HERE! HE'S ACTIVE ROSTER, HE'S OFF ON MISSIONS!
MATT STAYS IN OUR ROOM ALL DAY BROODING, PLAYING NOT-CHESS AND DRIVING ME UP THE WALL! YOU GOTTA TRY AGAIN.
ALL RIGHT, ALL RIGHT. BUT, uh...MY FEE JUST DOUBLED.
WHAT?! WHY?!
BECAUSE NOW I KNOW YOU'RE DESPERATE.
HEY, DICK!

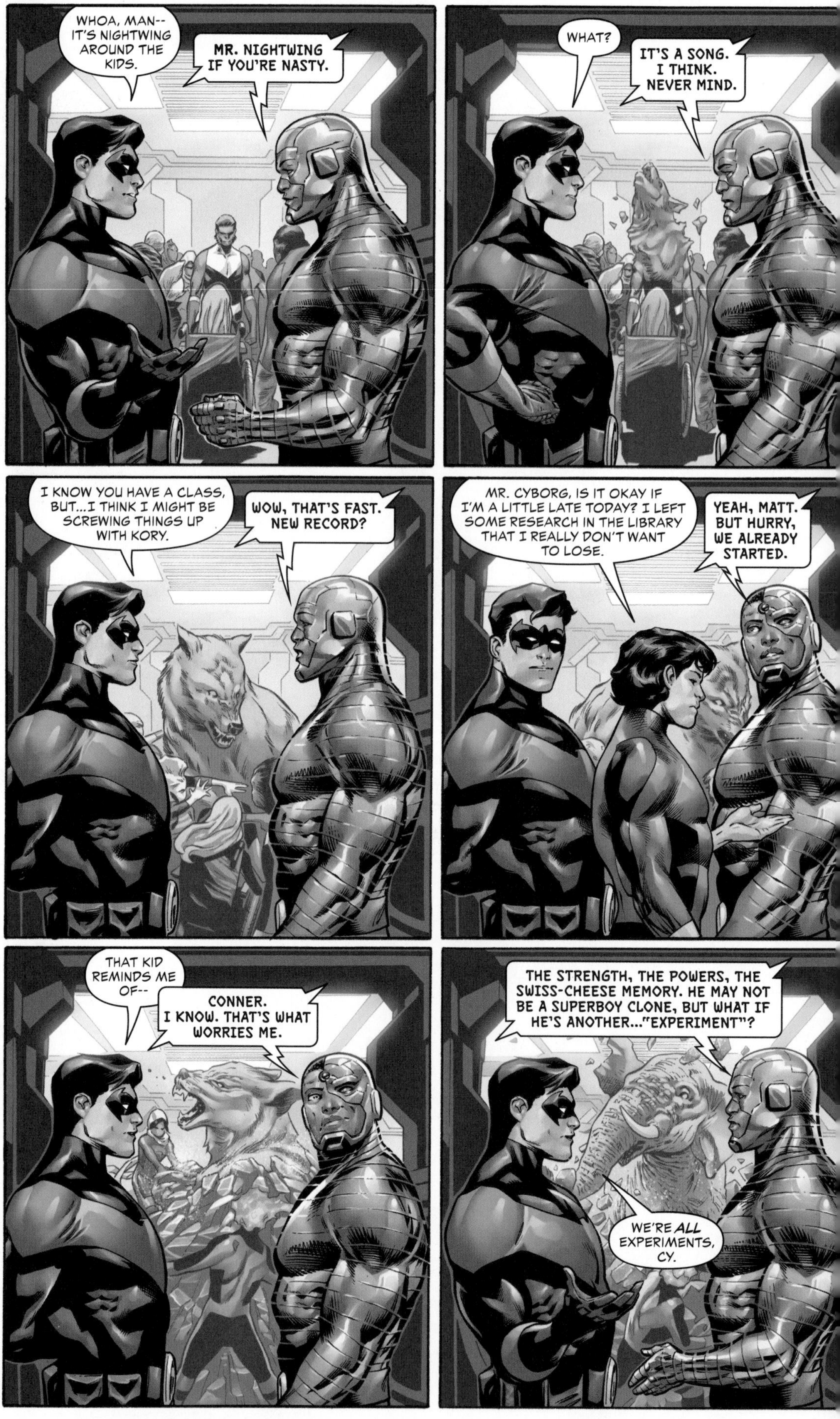
WHOA, MAN-- IT'S NIGHTWING AROUND THE KIDS.
MR. NIGHTWING IF YOU'RE NASTY.
WHAT?
IT'S A SONG. I THINK. NEVER MIND.
I KNOW YOU HAVE A CLASS, BUT...I THINK I MIGHT BE SCREWING THINGS UP WITH KORY.
WOW, THAT'S FAST. NEW RECORD?
MR. CYBORG, IS IT OKAY IF I'M A LITTLE LATE TODAY? I LEFT SOME RESEARCH IN THE LIBRARY THAT I REALLY DON'T WANT TO LOSE.
YEAH, MATT. BUT HURRY, WE ALREADY STARTED.
THAT KID REMINDS ME OF--
CONNER. I KNOW. THAT'S WHAT WORRIES ME.
THE STRENGTH, THE POWERS, THE SWISS-CHEESE MEMORY. HE MAY NOT BE A SUPERBOY CLONE, BUT WHAT IF HE'S ANOTHER..."EXPERIMENT"?
WE'RE *ALL* EXPERIMENTS, CY.

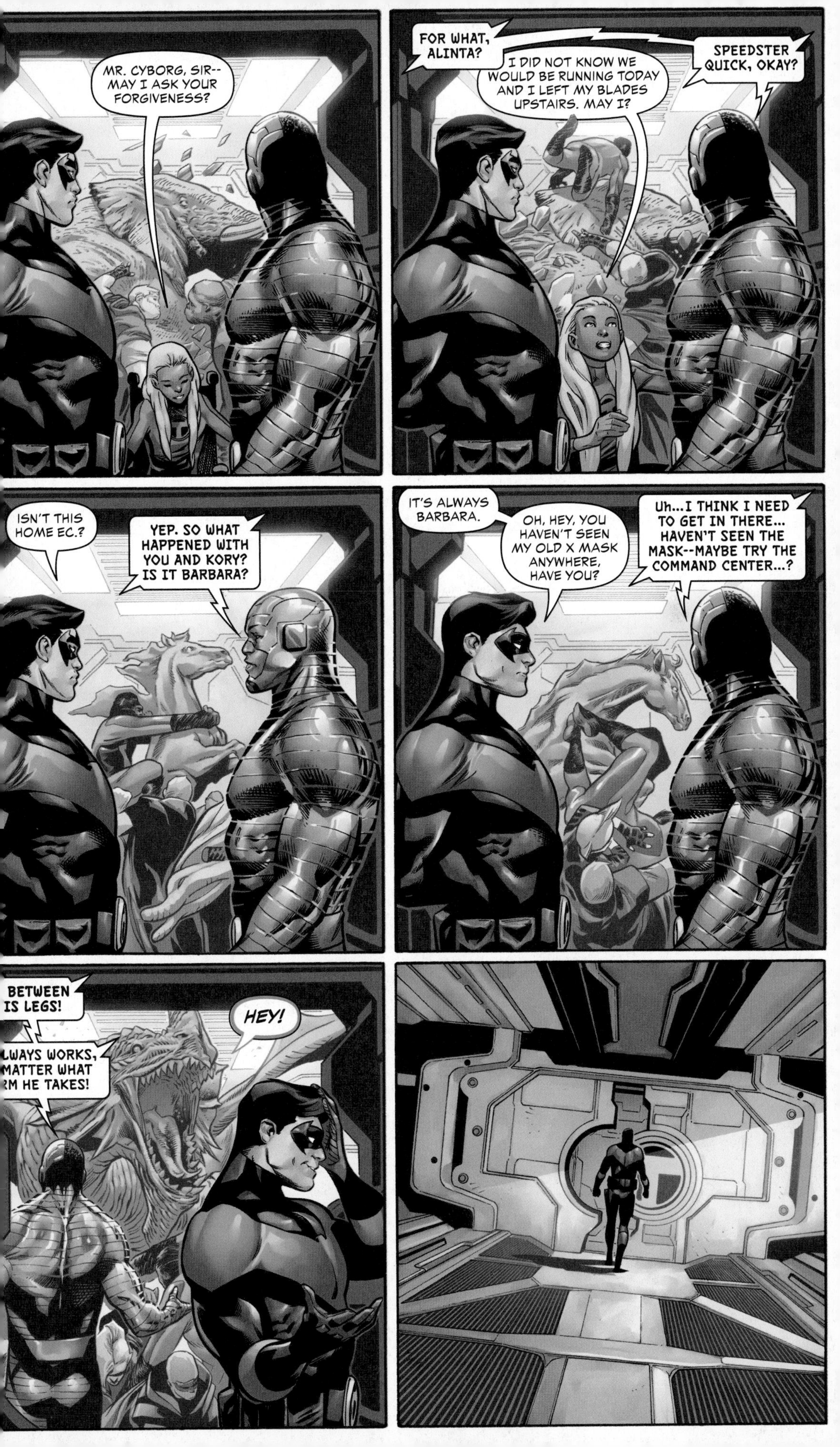
MR. CYBORG, SIR--
MAY I ASK YOUR
FORGIVENESS?
FOR WHAT,
ALINTA?
I DID NOT KNOW WE
WOULD BE RUNNING TODAY
AND I LEFT MY BLADES
UPSTAIRS. MAY I?
SPEEDSTER
QUICK, OKAY?
ISN'T THIS
HOME EC.?
YEP. SO WHAT
HAPPENED WITH
YOU AND KORY?
IS IT BARBARA?
IT'S ALWAYS
BARBARA.
OH, HEY, YOU
HAVEN'T SEEN
MY OLD X MASK
ANYWHERE,
HAVE YOU?
Uh...I THINK I NEED
TO GET IN THERE...
HAVEN'T SEEN THE
MASK--MAYBE TRY THE
COMMAND CENTER...?
BETWEEN
IS LEGS!
LWAYS WORKS,
MATTER WHAT
RM HE TAKES!
HEY!

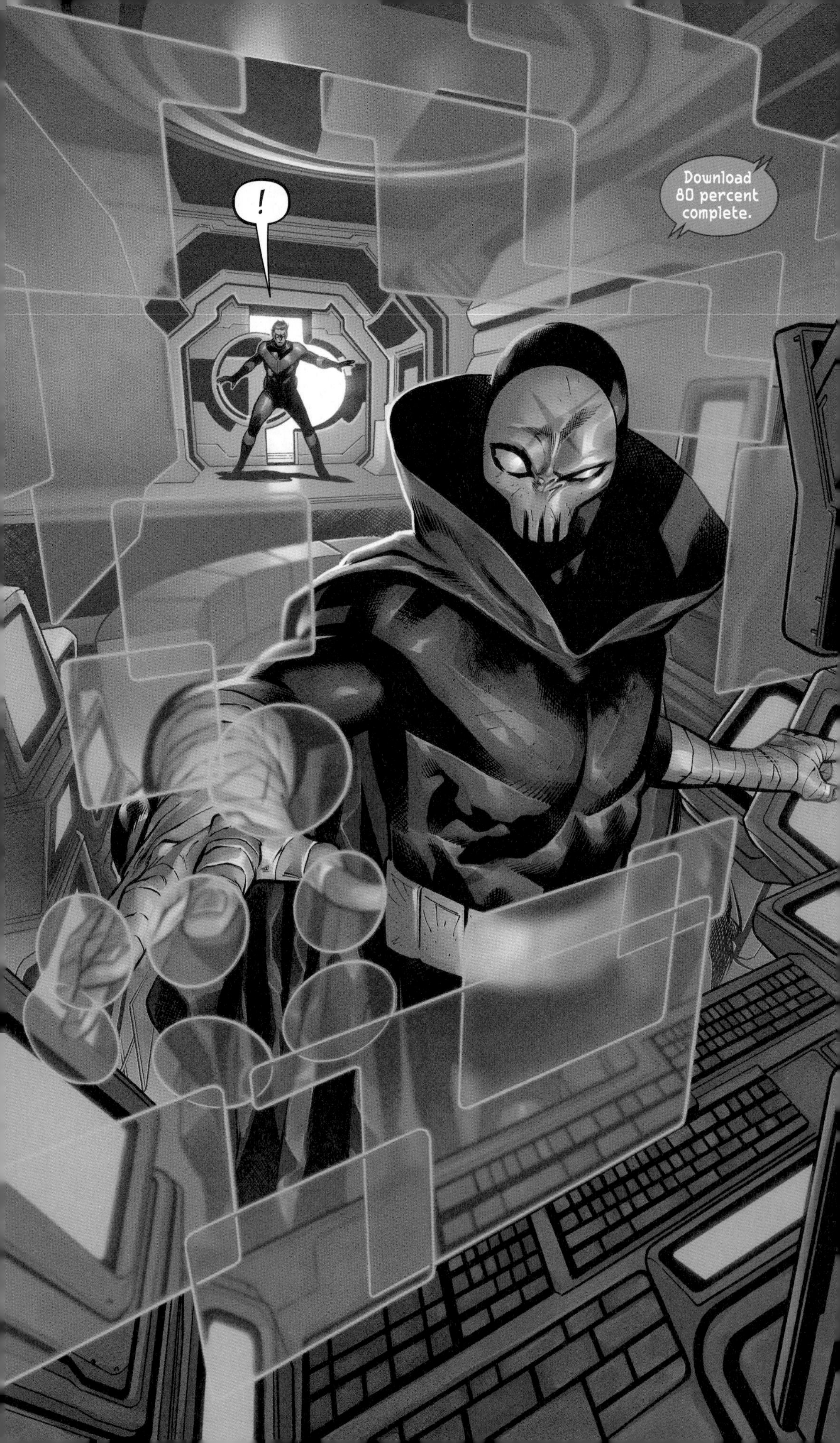
!
Download 80 percent complete.

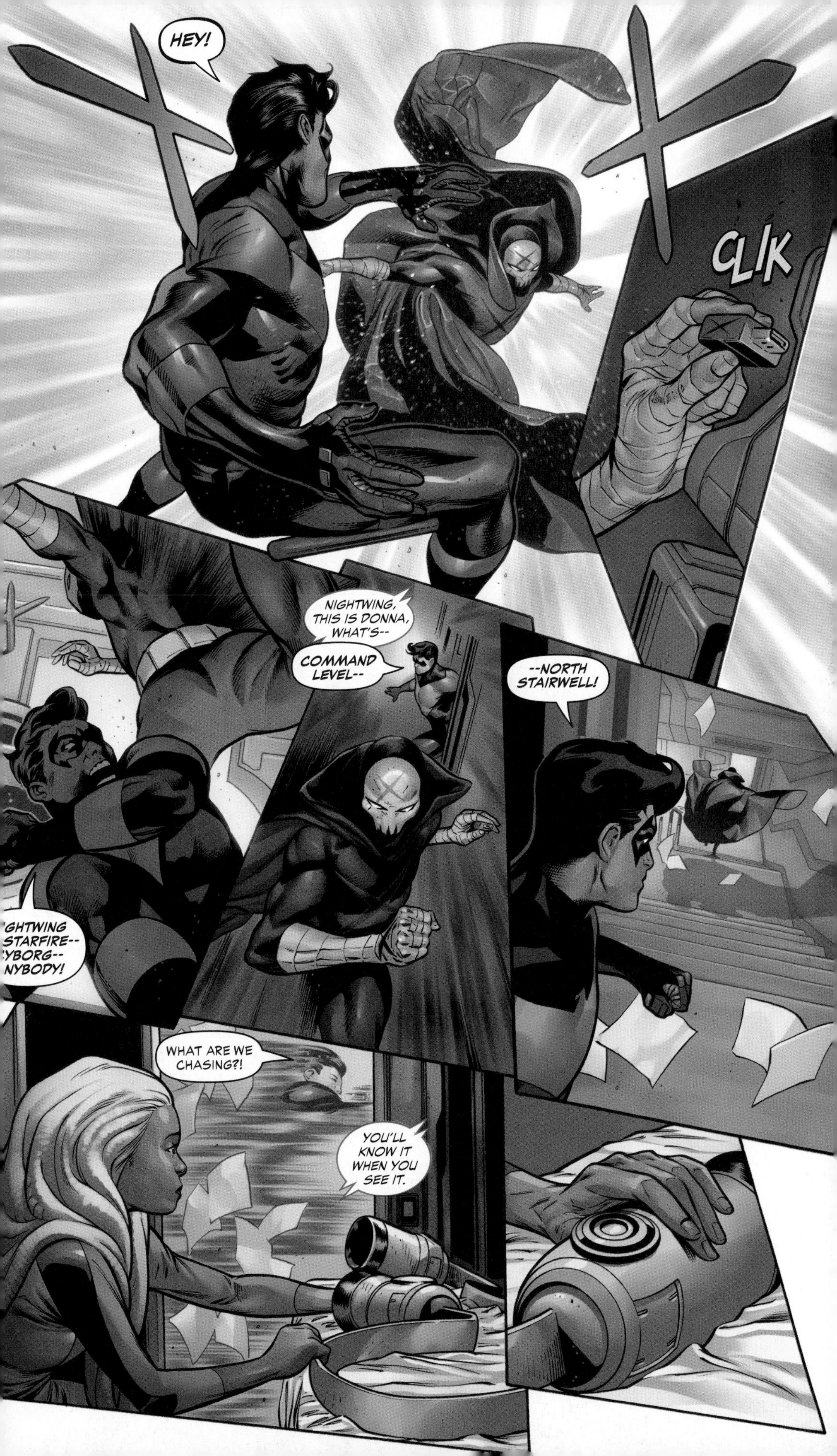
HEY!
CLIK
NIGHTWING, THIS IS DONNA, WHAT'S--
COMMAND LEVEL--
--NORTH STAIRWELL!
GHTWING STARFIRE-- YBORG-- NYBODY!
WHAT ARE WE CHASING?!
YOU'LL KNOW IT WHEN YOU SEE IT.

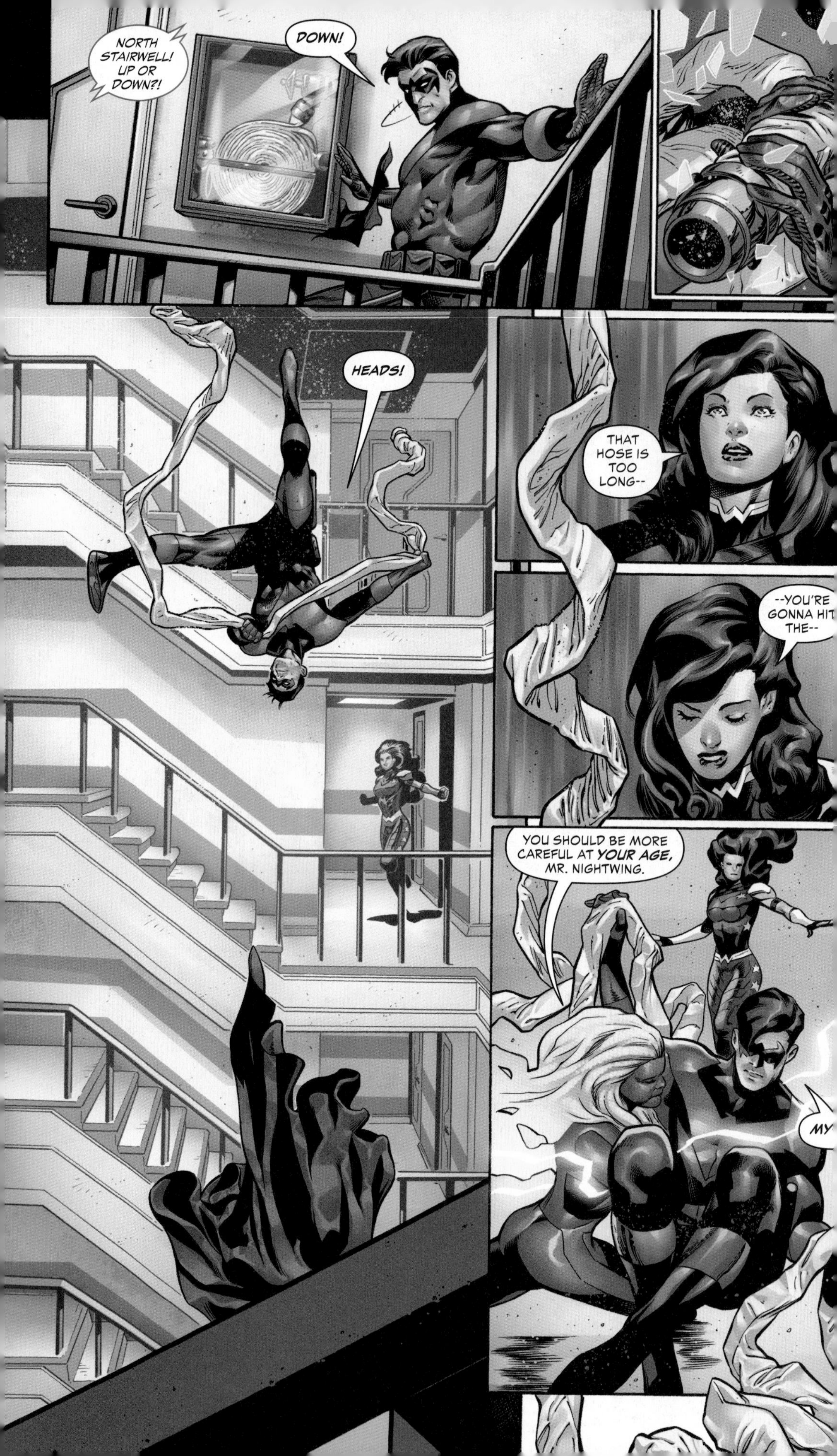
NORTH STAIRWELL! UP OR DOWN?!
DOWN!
HEADS!
THAT HOSE IS TOO LONG--
--YOU'RE GONNA HIT THE--
YOU SHOULD BE MORE CAREFUL AT YOUR AGE, MR. NIGHTWING.
MY

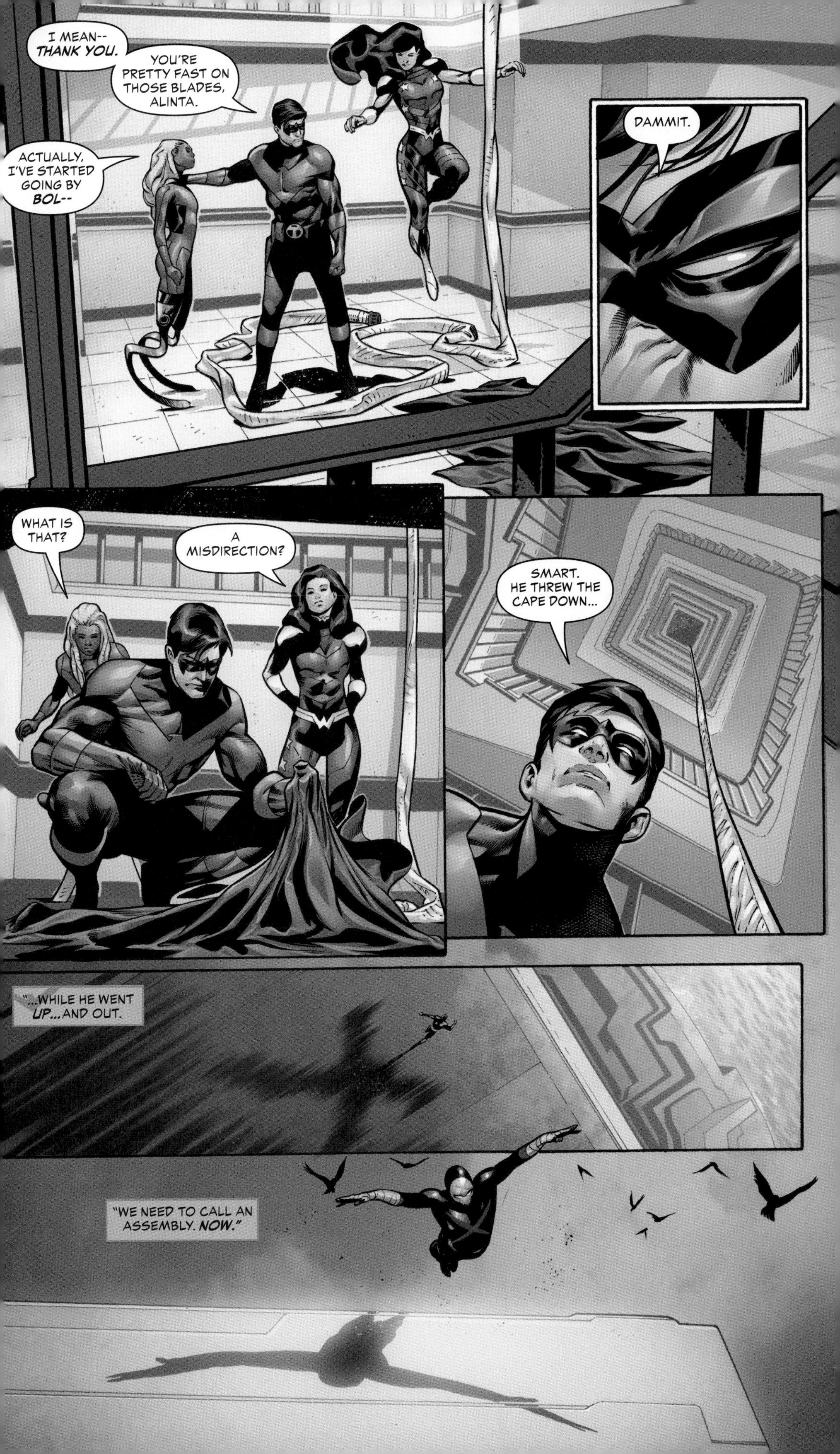
I MEAN-- THANK YOU.
YOU'RE PRETTY FAST ON THOSE BLADES, ALINTA.
ACTUALLY, I'VE STARTED GOING BY BOL--
DAMMIT.
WHAT IS THAT?
A MISDIRECTION?
SMART. HE THREW THE CAPE DOWN...
"...WHILE HE WENT UP...AND OUT.
"WE NEED TO CALL AN ASSEMBLY. NOW."

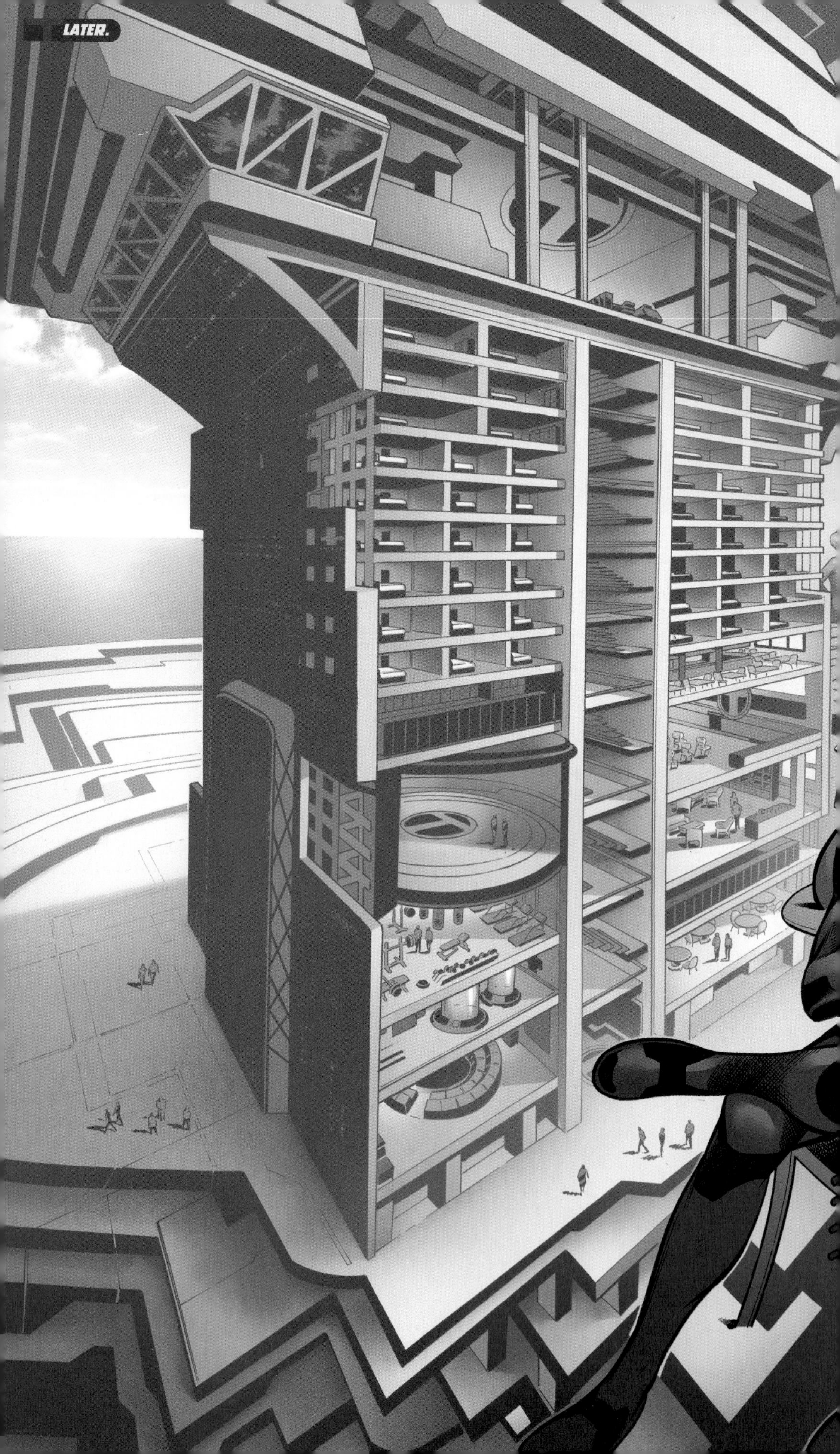
LATER.

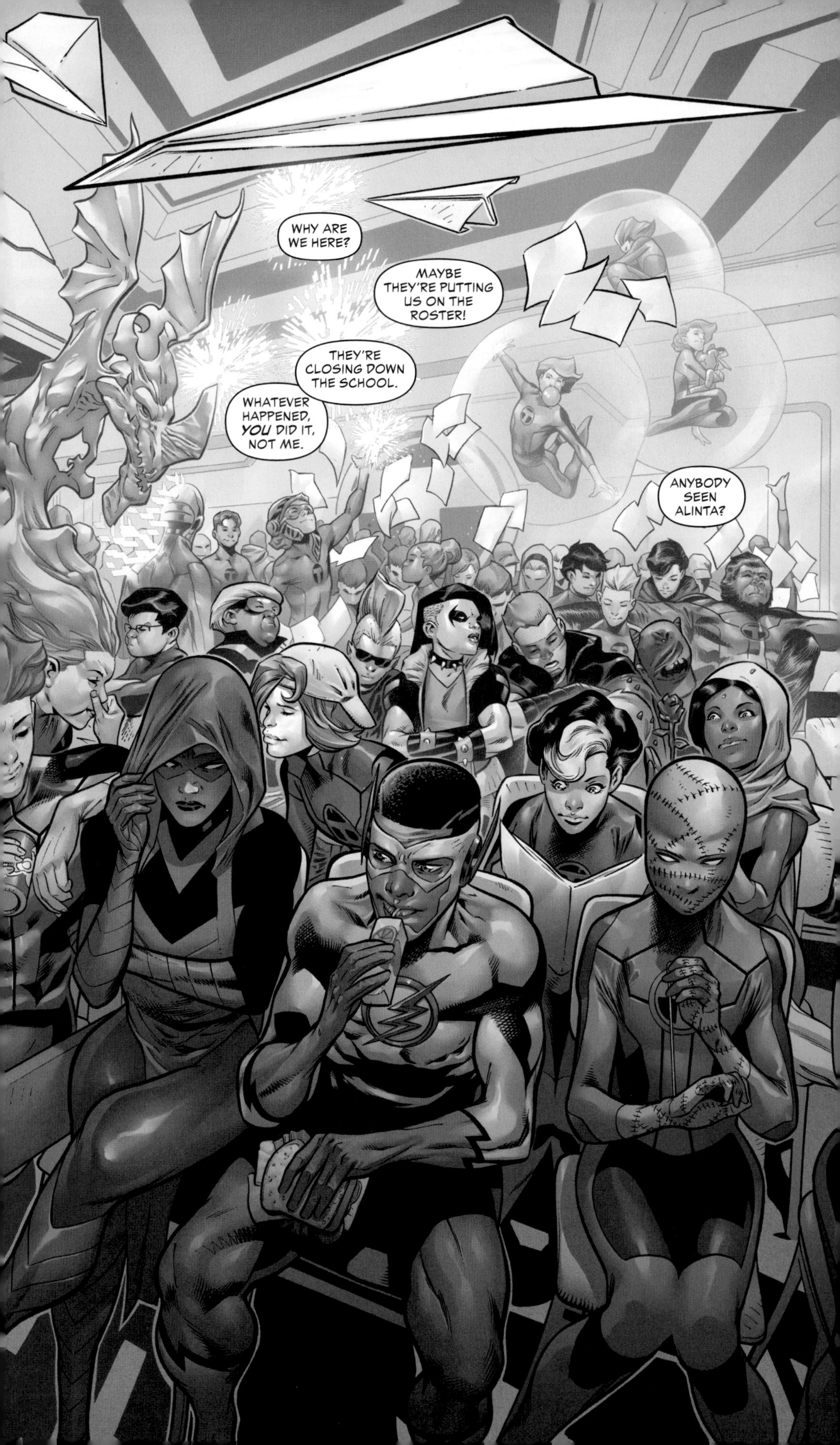
WHY ARE WE HERE?
MAYBE THEY'RE PUTTING US ON THE ROSTER!
THEY'RE CLOSING DOWN THE SCHOOL.
WHATEVER HAPPENED, *YOU* DID IT, NOT ME.
ANYBODY SEEN ALINTA?

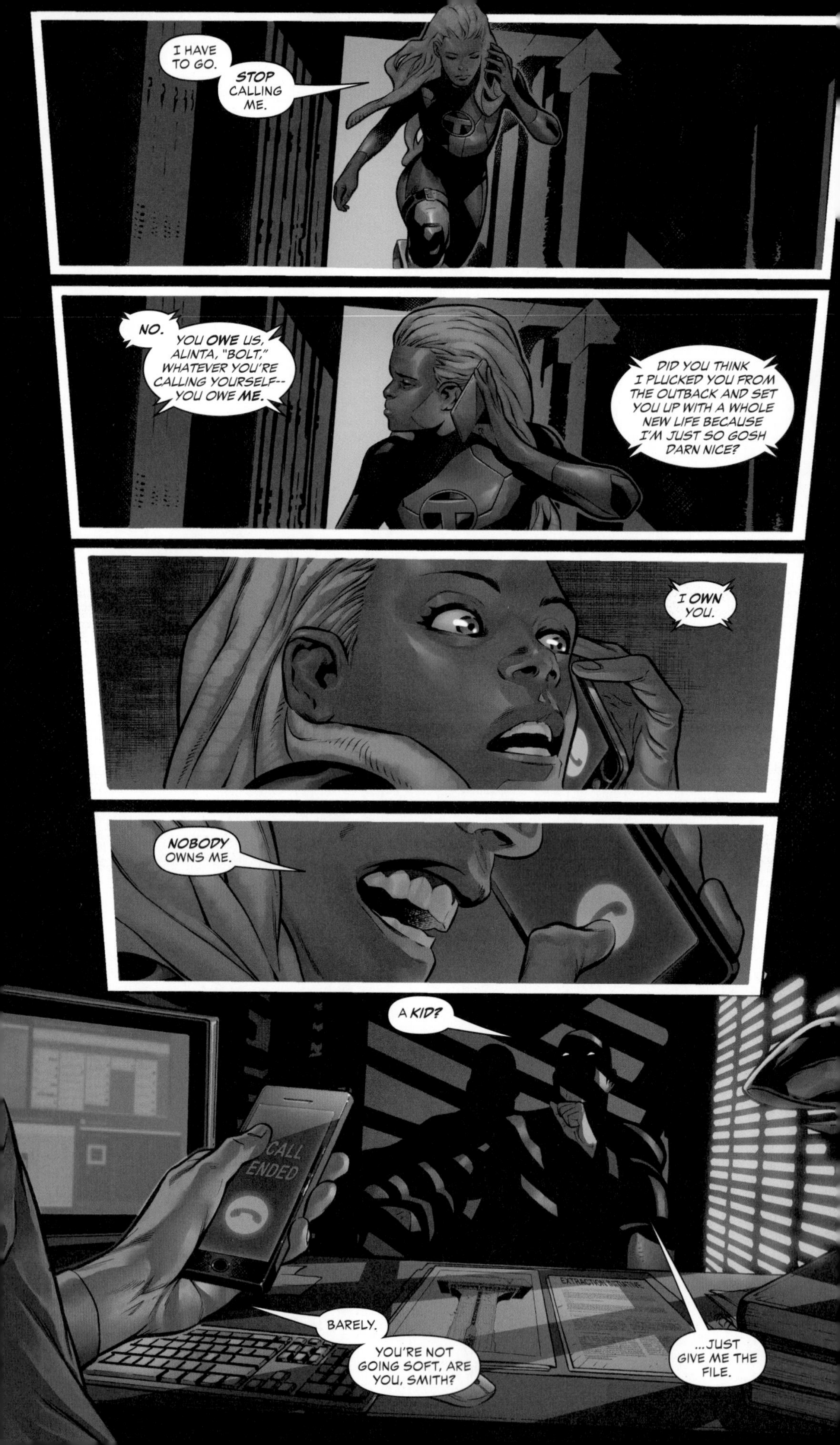
I HAVE TO GO.
STOP CALLING ME.
NO.
YOU OWE US, ALINTA, "BOLT," WHATEVER YOU'RE CALLING YOURSELF-- YOU OWE ME.
DID YOU THINK I PLUCKED YOU FROM THE OUTBACK AND SET YOU UP WITH A WHOLE NEW LIFE BECAUSE I'M JUST SO GOSH DARN NICE?
I OWN YOU.
NOBODY OWNS ME.
A KID?
CALL ENDED
BARELY.
YOU'RE NOT GOING SOFT, ARE YOU, SMITH?
...JUST GIVE ME THE FILE.

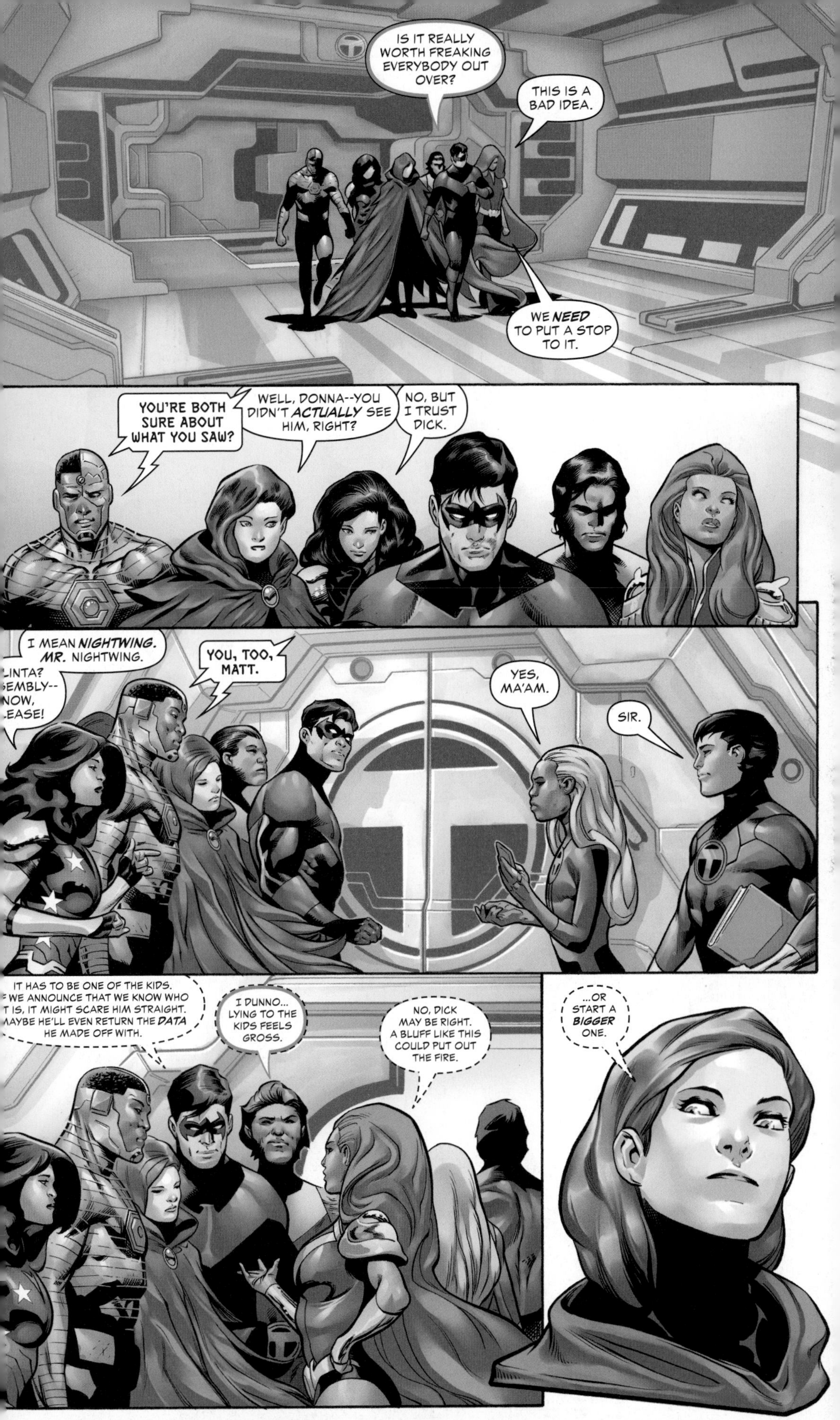
IS IT REALLY WORTH FREAKING EVERYBODY OUT OVER?
THIS IS A BAD IDEA.
WE NEED TO PUT A STOP TO IT.
YOU'RE BOTH SURE ABOUT WHAT YOU SAW?
WELL, DONNA--YOU DIDN'T ACTUALLY SEE HIM, RIGHT?
NO, BUT I TRUST DICK.
I MEAN NIGHTWING. MR. NIGHTWING.
YOU, TOO, MATT.
YES, MA'AM.
SIR.
IT HAS TO BE ONE OF THE KIDS.
I DUNNO... LYING TO THE KIDS FEELS GROSS.
NO, DICK MAY BE RIGHT. A BLUFF LIKE THIS COULD PUT OUT THE FIRE.
...OR START A BIGGER ONE.

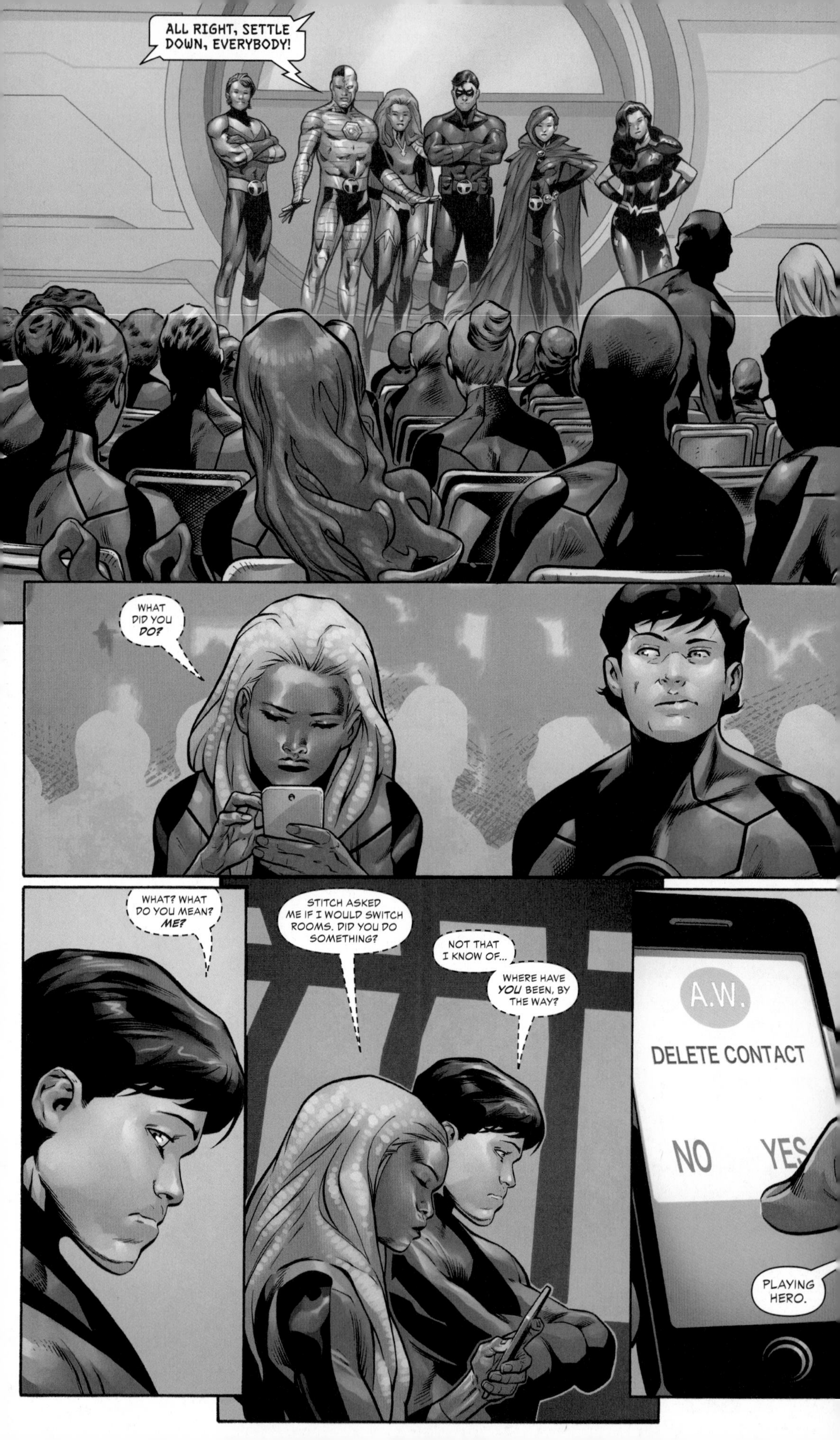
ALL RIGHT, SETTLE DOWN, EVERYBODY!
WHAT DID YOU *DO?*
WHAT? WHAT DO YOU MEAN? ***ME?***
STITCH ASKED ME IF I WOULD SWITCH ROOMS. DID YOU DO SOMETHING?
NOT THAT I KNOW OF...
WHERE HAVE *YOU* BEEN, BY THE WAY?
A.W.
DELETE CONTACT
NO
YES
PLAYING HERO.

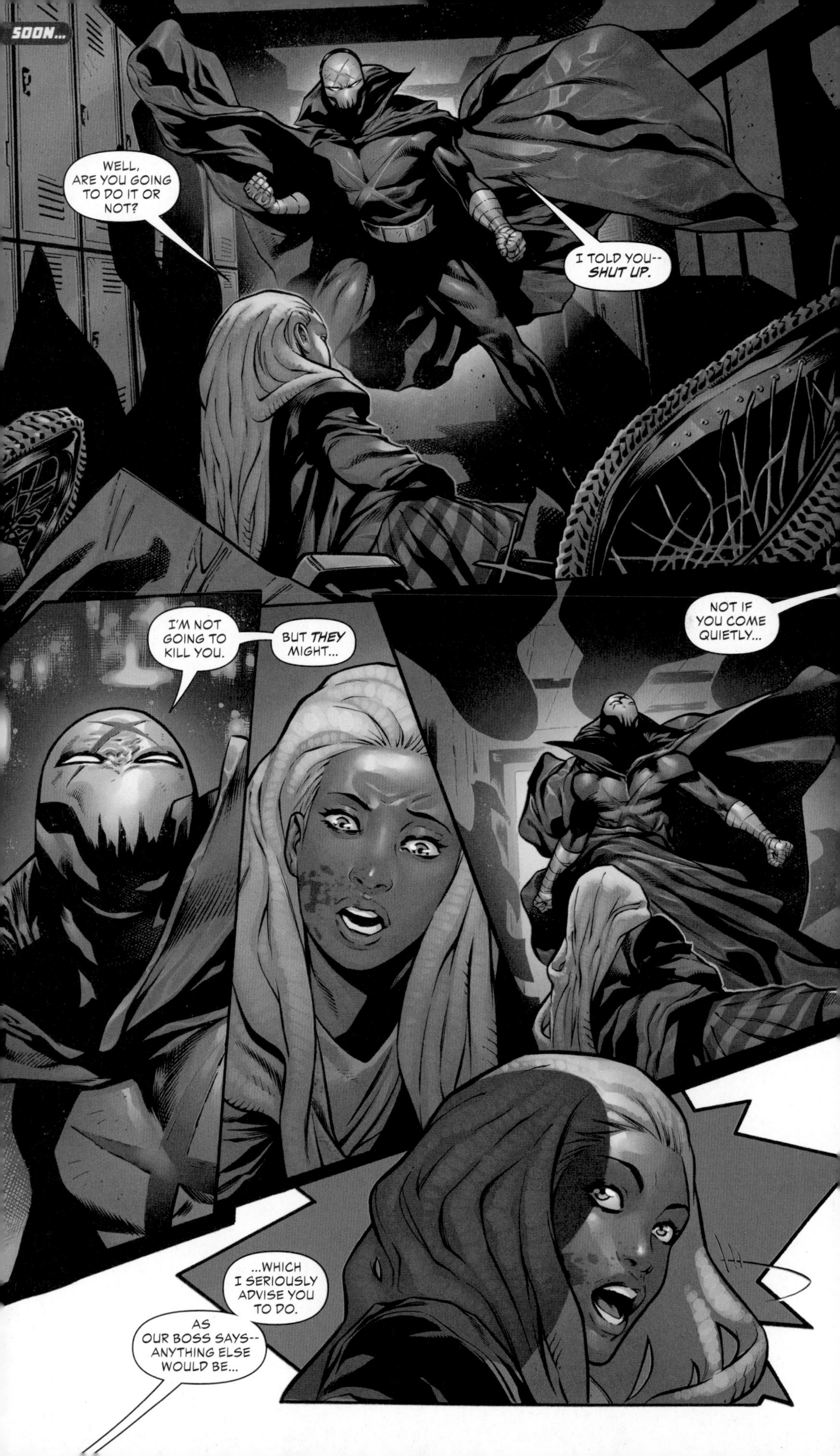
SOON...
WELL, ARE YOU GOING TO DO IT OR NOT?
I TOLD YOU-- SHUT UP.
I'M NOT GOING TO KILL YOU.
BUT THEY MIGHT...
NOT IF YOU COME QUIETLY...
...WHICH I SERIOUSLY ADVISE YOU TO DO.
AS OUR BOSS SAYS-- ANYTHING ELSE WOULD BE...

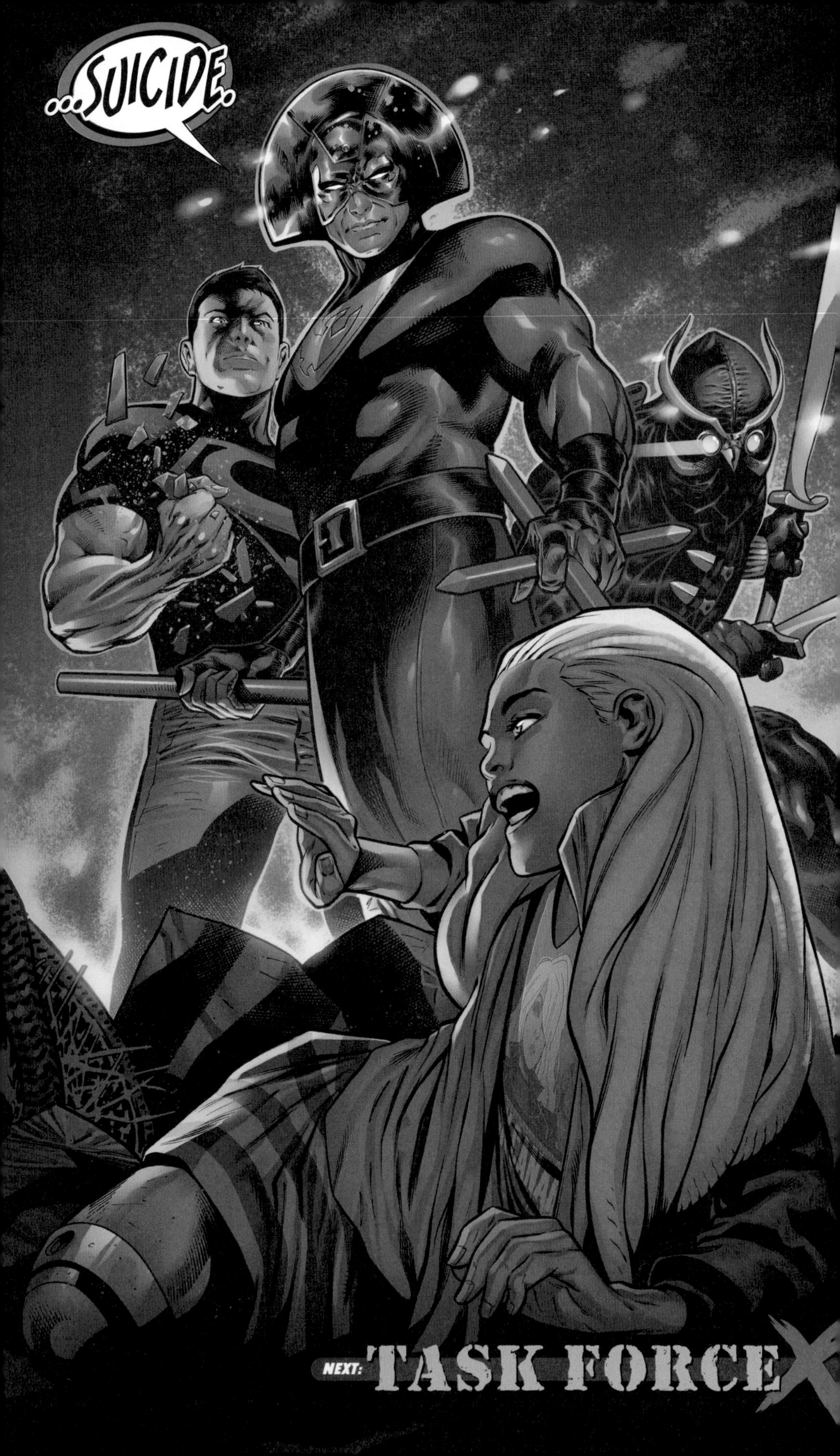
...SUICIDE.
NEXT: TASK FORCE X

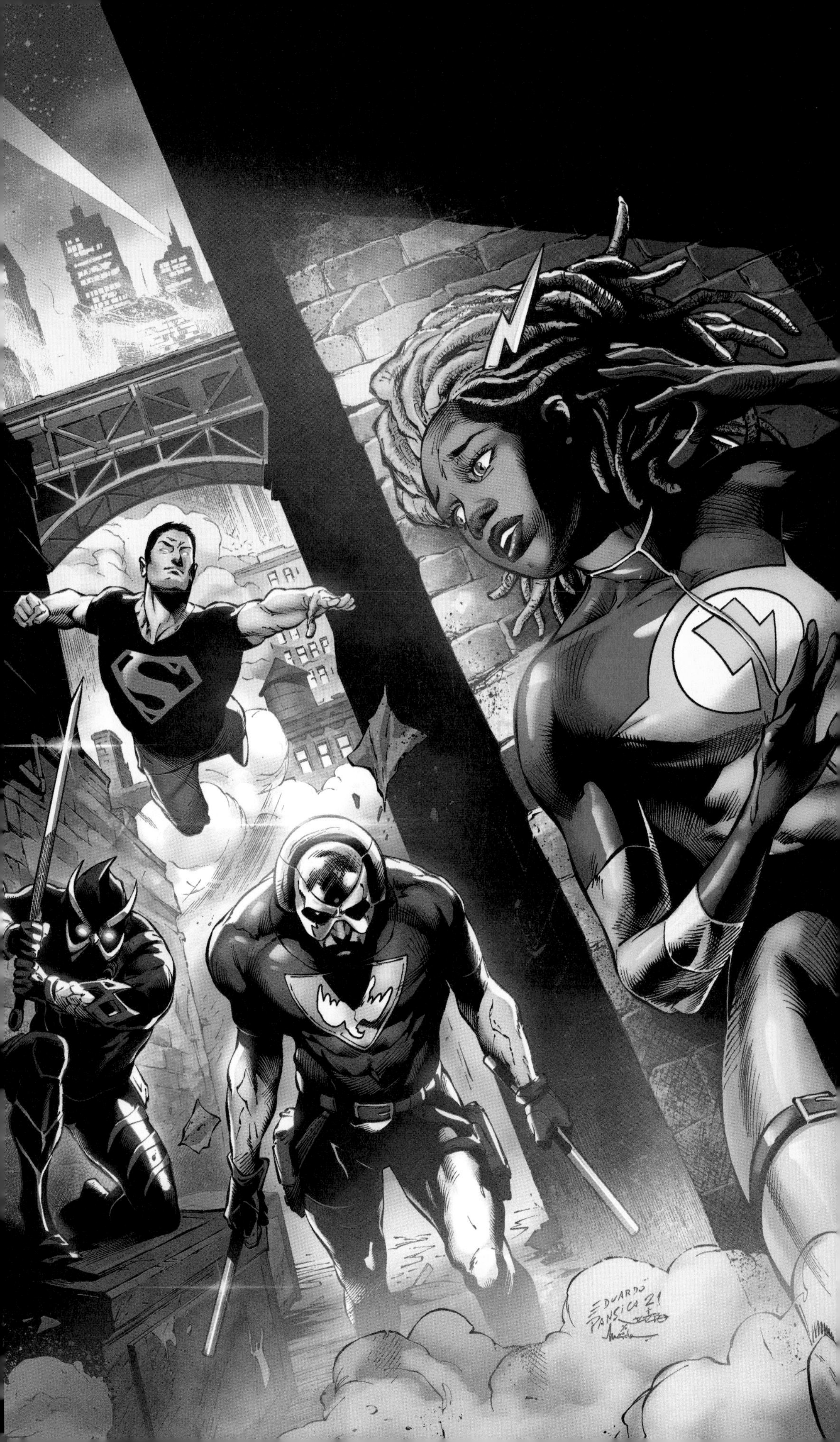
EDUARDO PANSICA 21

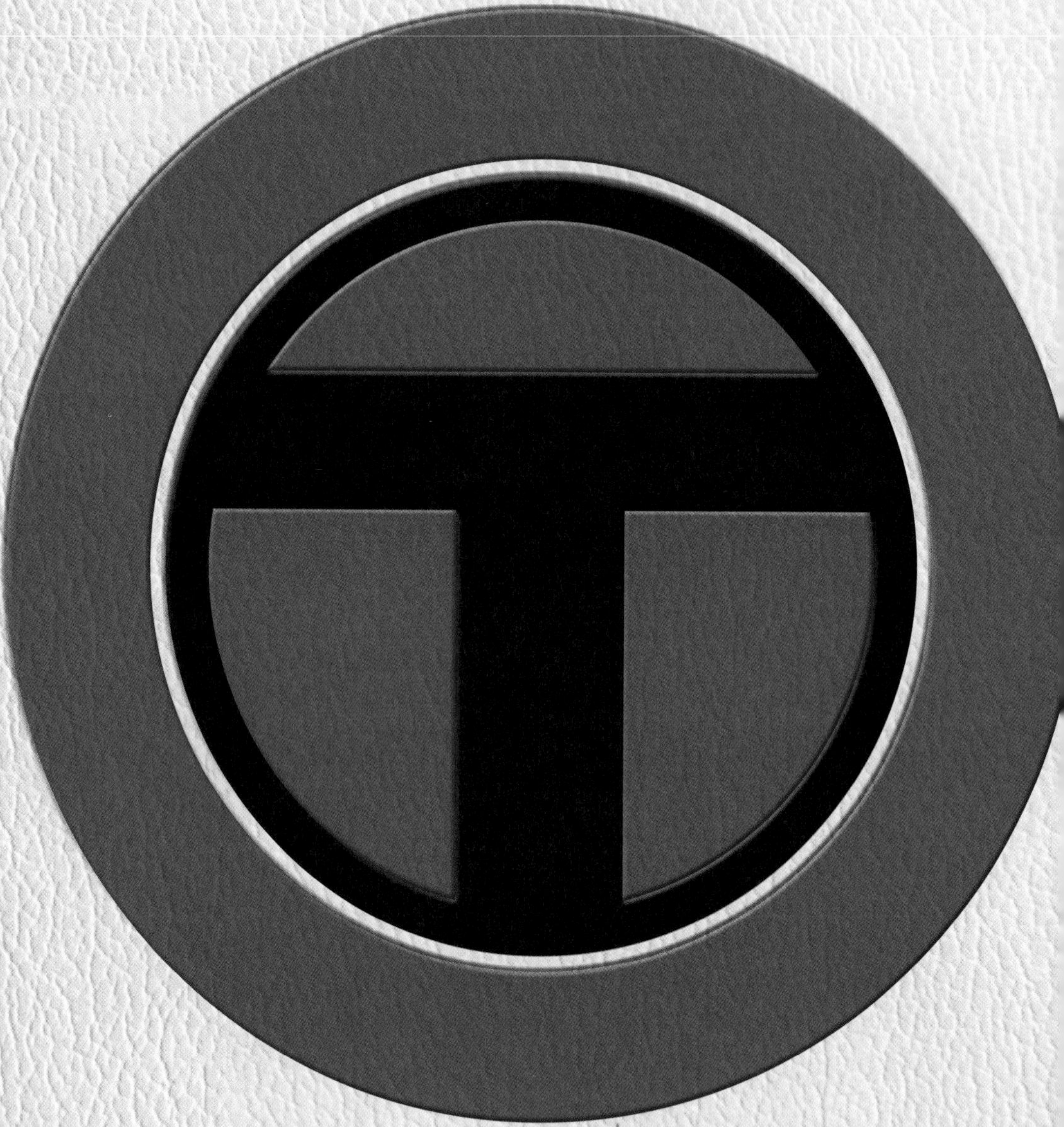

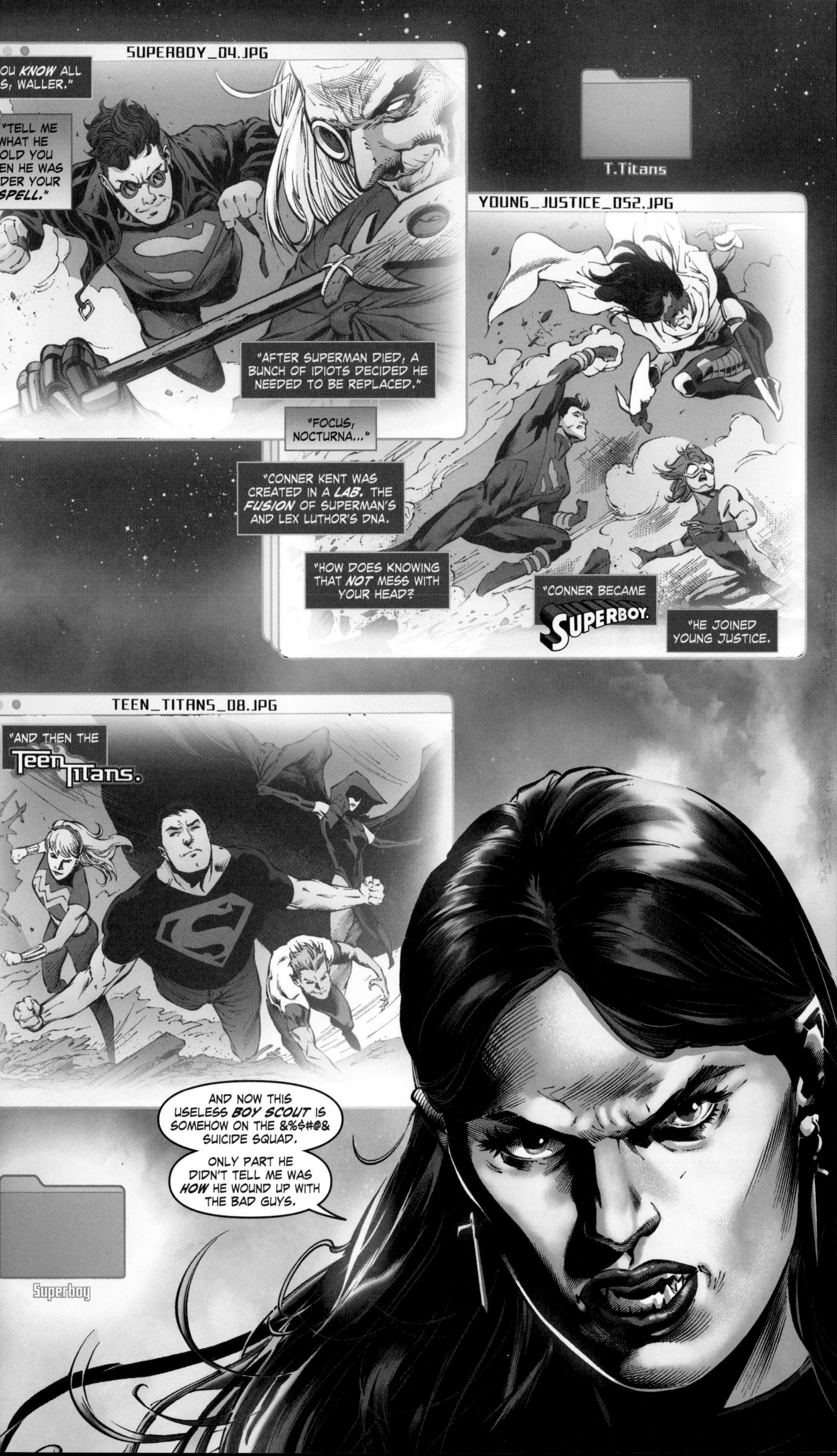
SUPERBOY_04.JPG
OU KNOW ALL
S, WALLER."
"TELL ME
WHAT HE
OLD YOU
EN HE WAS
DER YOUR
SPELL."
T.Titans
YOUNG_JUSTICE_052.JPG
"AFTER SUPERMAN DIED, A BUNCH OF IDIOTS DECIDED HE NEEDED TO BE REPLACED."
"FOCUS, NOCTURNA..."
"CONNER KENT WAS CREATED IN A LAB. THE FUSION OF SUPERMAN'S AND LEX LUTHOR'S DNA.
"HOW DOES KNOWING THAT NOT MESS WITH YOUR HEAD?
"CONNER BECAME SUPERBOY.
"HE JOINED YOUNG JUSTICE.
TEEN_TITANS_08.JPG
"AND THEN THE TEEN TITANS.
AND NOW THIS USELESS BOY SCOUT IS SOMEHOW ON THE &%$#@& SUICIDE SQUAD.
ONLY PART HE DIDN'T TELL ME WAS HOW HE WOUND UP WITH THE BAD GUYS.
Superboy

THAT'S CLASSIFIED.
BOTTOM-LINE IT FOR ME, NOCTURNA.
YOU USED YOUR GLAMOUR ON HIM, GOT HIM TALKING...
DC COMICS PROUDLY PRESENTS
SUICIDE SQUAD IN
NEED FOR SPEED
PART 1

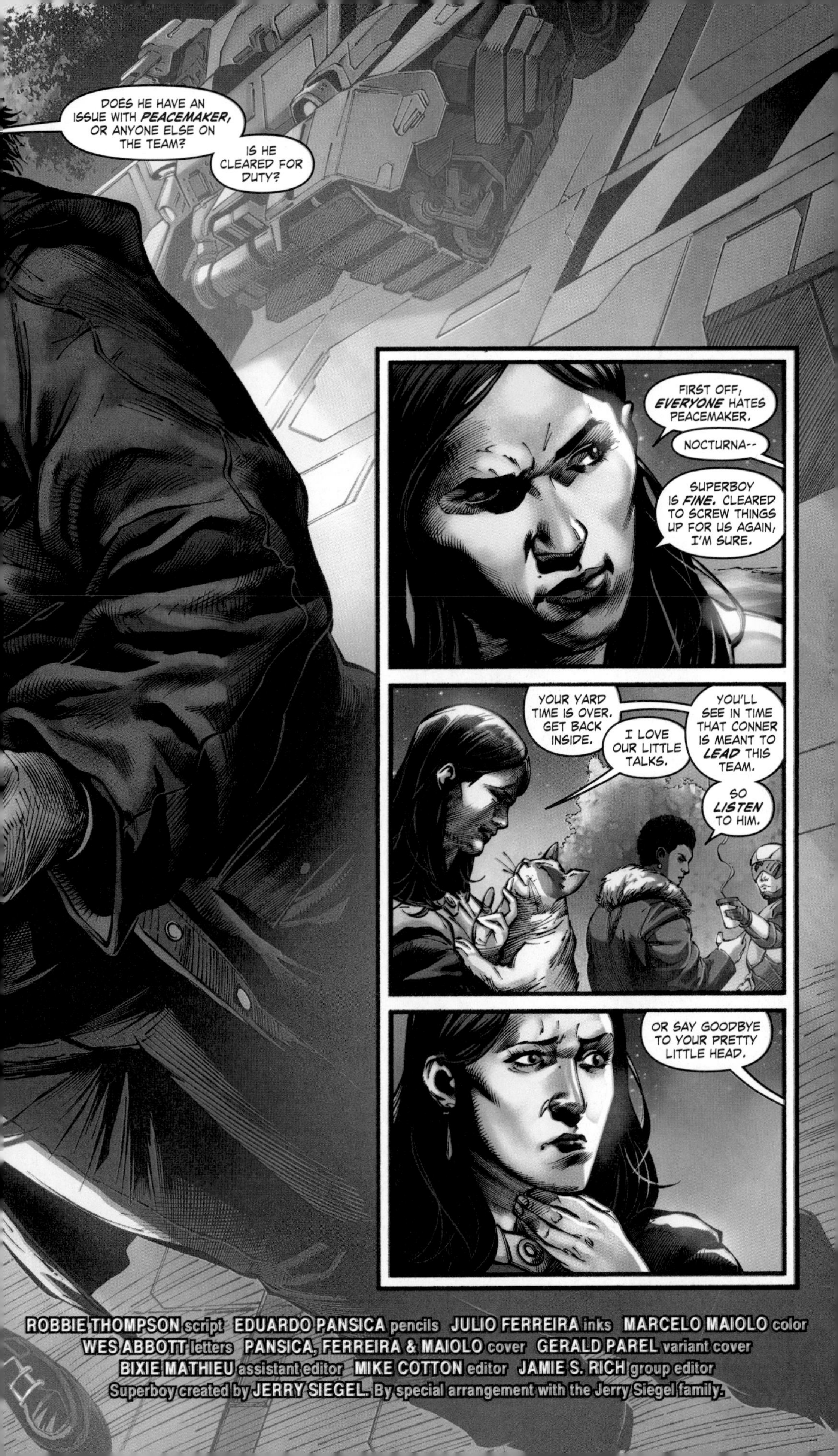

DOES HE HAVE AN ISSUE WITH PEACEMAKER, OR ANYONE ELSE ON THE TEAM?
IS HE CLEARED FOR DUTY?
FIRST OFF, EVERYONE HATES PEACEMAKER.
NOCTURNA--
SUPERBOY IS FINE. CLEARED TO SCREW THINGS UP FOR US AGAIN, I'M SURE.
YOUR YARD TIME IS OVER. GET BACK INSIDE.
I LOVE OUR LITTLE TALKS.
YOU'LL SEE IN TIME THAT CONNER IS MEANT TO LEAD THIS TEAM.
SO LISTEN TO HIM.
OR SAY GOODBYE TO YOUR PRETTY LITTLE HEAD.

ROBBIE THOMPSON script EDUARDO PANSICA pencils JULIO FERREIRA inks MARCELO MAIOLO color
WES ABBOTT letters PANSICA, FERREIRA & MAIOLO cover GERALD PAREL variant cover
BIXIE MATHIEU assistant editor MIKE COTTON editor JAMIE S. RICH group editor
Superboy created by JERRY SIEGEL. By special arrangement with the Jerry Siegel family.

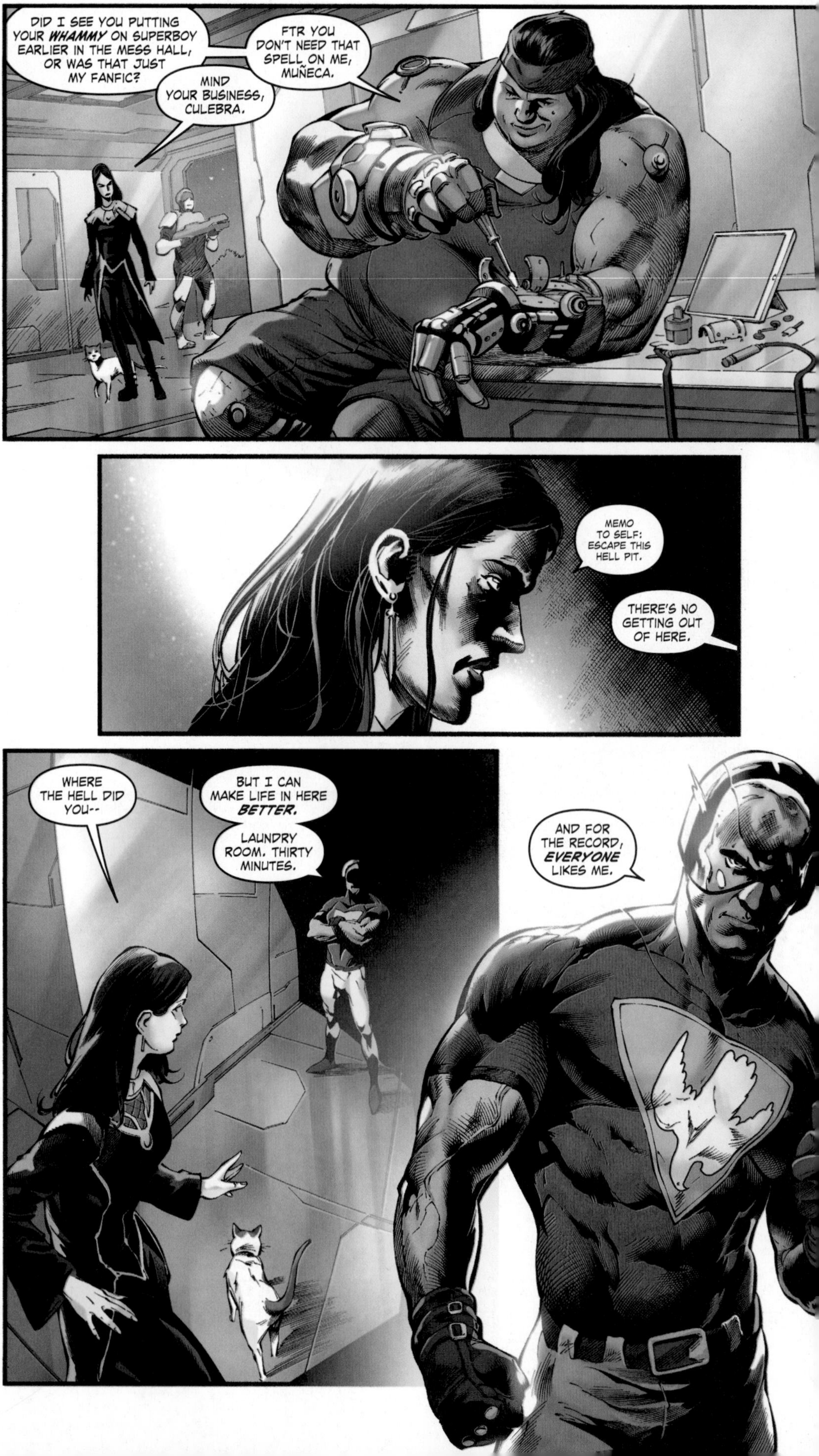
DID I SEE YOU PUTTING YOUR *WHAMMY* ON SUPERBOY EARLIER IN THE MESS HALL, OR WAS THAT JUST MY FANFIC?
FTR YOU DON'T NEED THAT SPELL ON ME, MUÑECA.
MIND YOUR BUSINESS, CULEBRA.
MEMO TO SELF: ESCAPE THIS HELL PIT.
THERE'S NO GETTING OUT OF HERE.
WHERE THE HELL DID YOU--
BUT I CAN MAKE LIFE IN HERE *BETTER.*
LAUNDRY ROOM. THIRTY MINUTES.
AND FOR THE RECORD, *EVERYONE* LIKES ME.

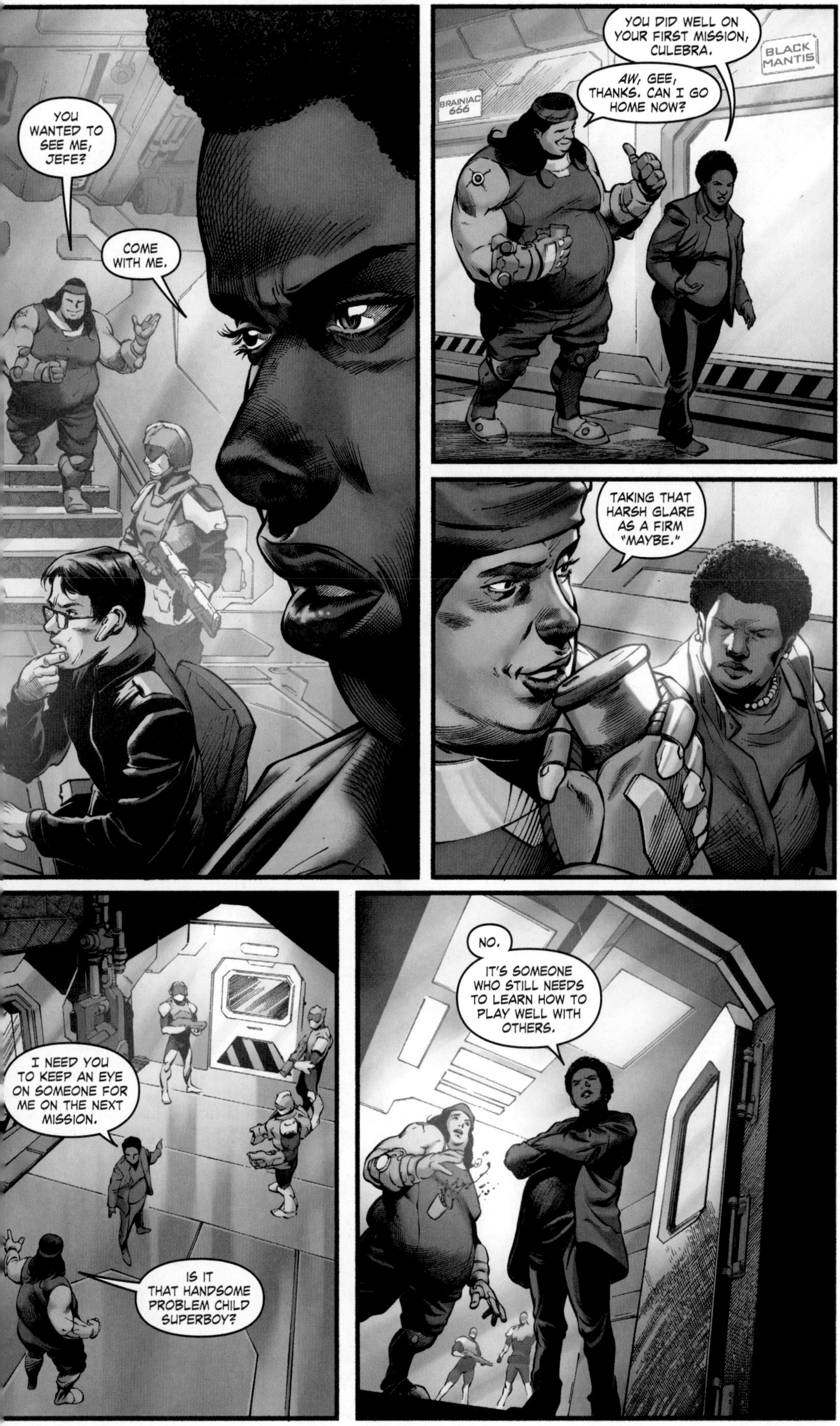
YOU WANTED TO SEE ME, JEFE?
COME WITH ME.
YOU DID WELL ON YOUR FIRST MISSION, CULEBRA.
BLACK MANTIS
BRAINIAC 666
AW, GEE, THANKS. CAN I GO HOME NOW?
TAKING THAT HARSH GLARE AS A FIRM "MAYBE."
I NEED YOU TO KEEP AN EYE ON SOMEONE FOR ME ON THE NEXT MISSION.
IS IT THAT HANDSOME PROBLEM CHILD SUPERBOY?
NO.
IT'S SOMEONE WHO STILL NEEDS TO LEARN HOW TO PLAY WELL WITH OTHERS.

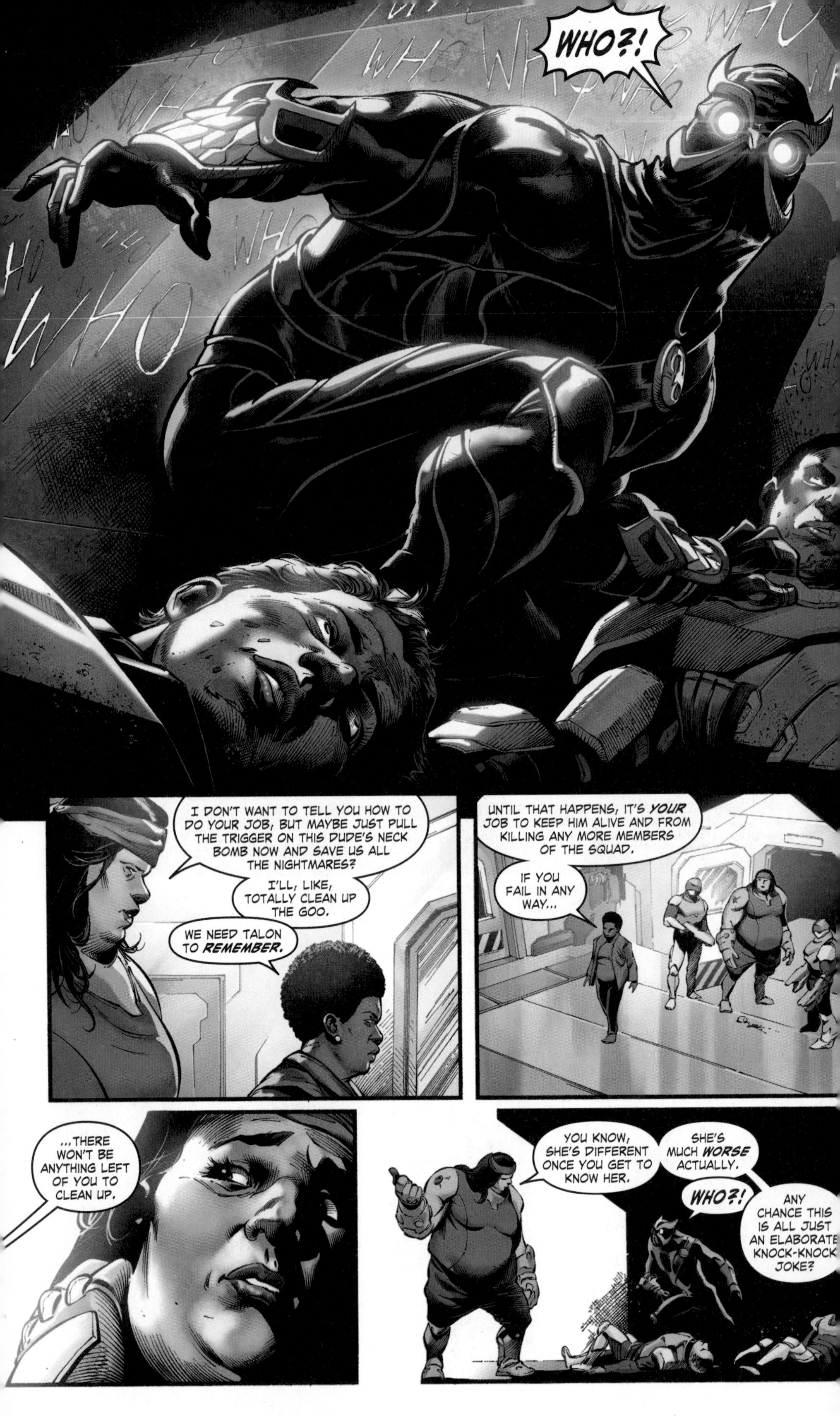
WHO?!
I DON'T WANT TO TELL YOU HOW TO DO YOUR JOB, BUT MAYBE JUST PULL THE TRIGGER ON THIS DUDE'S NECK BOMB NOW AND SAVE US ALL THE NIGHTMARES?
I'LL, LIKE, TOTALLY CLEAN UP THE GOO.
WE NEED TALON TO **REMEMBER.**
UNTIL THAT HAPPENS, IT'S ***YOUR*** JOB TO KEEP HIM ALIVE AND FROM KILLING ANY MORE MEMBERS OF THE SQUAD.
IF YOU FAIL IN ANY WAY...
...THERE WON'T BE ANYTHING LEFT OF YOU TO CLEAN UP.
YOU KNOW, SHE'S DIFFERENT ONCE YOU GET TO KNOW HER.
SHE'S MUCH ***WORSE*** ACTUALLY.
WHO?!
ANY CHANCE THIS IS ALL JUST AN ELABORATE KNOCK-KNOCK JOKE?

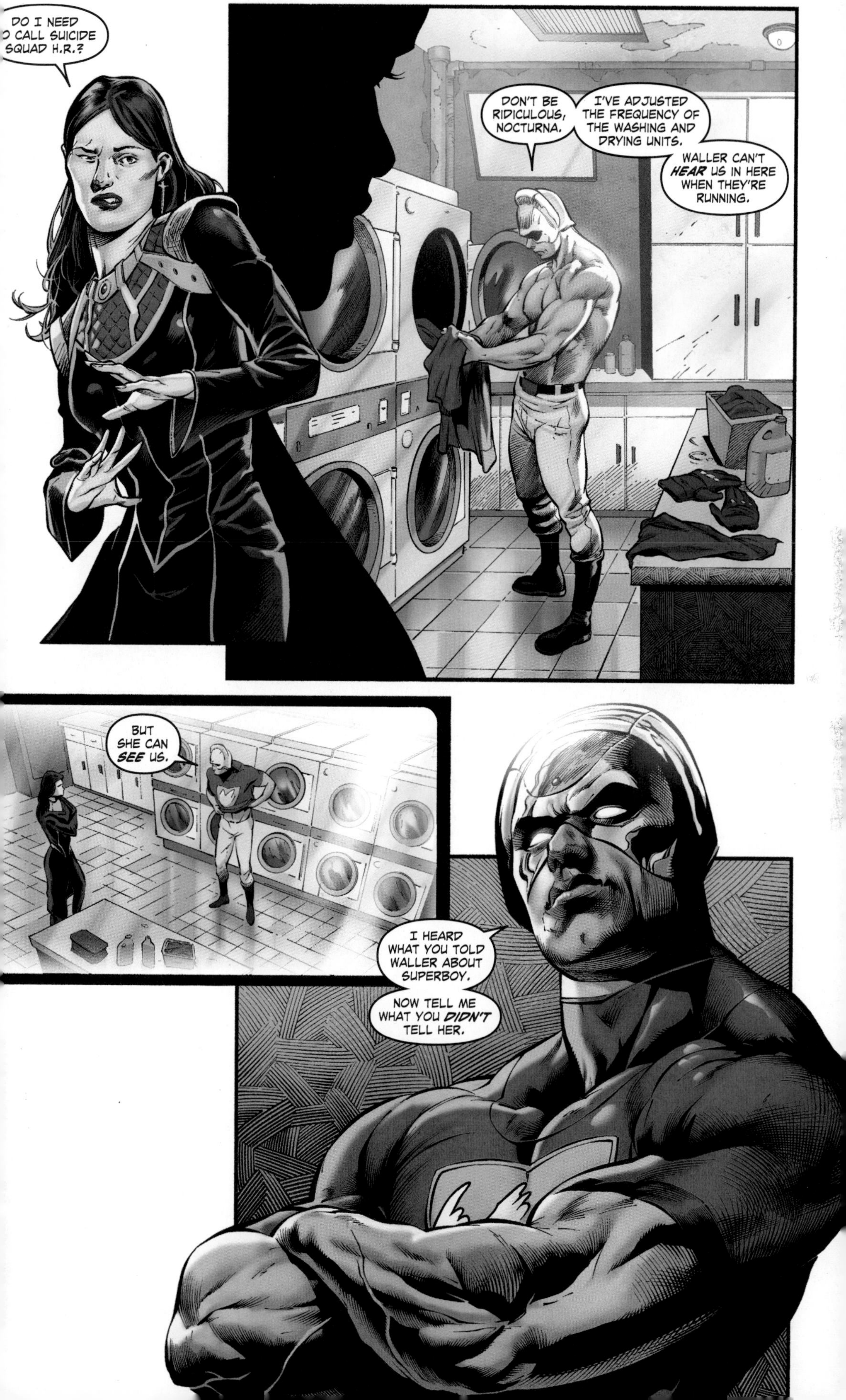
DO I NEED TO CALL SUICIDE SQUAD H.R.?
DON'T BE RIDICULOUS, NOCTURNA.
I'VE ADJUSTED THE FREQUENCY OF THE WASHING AND DRYING UNITS.
WALLER CAN'T *HEAR* US IN HERE WHEN THEY'RE RUNNING.
BUT SHE CAN *SEE* US.
I HEARD WHAT YOU TOLD WALLER ABOUT SUPERBOY.
NOW TELL ME WHAT YOU *DIDN'T* TELL HER.

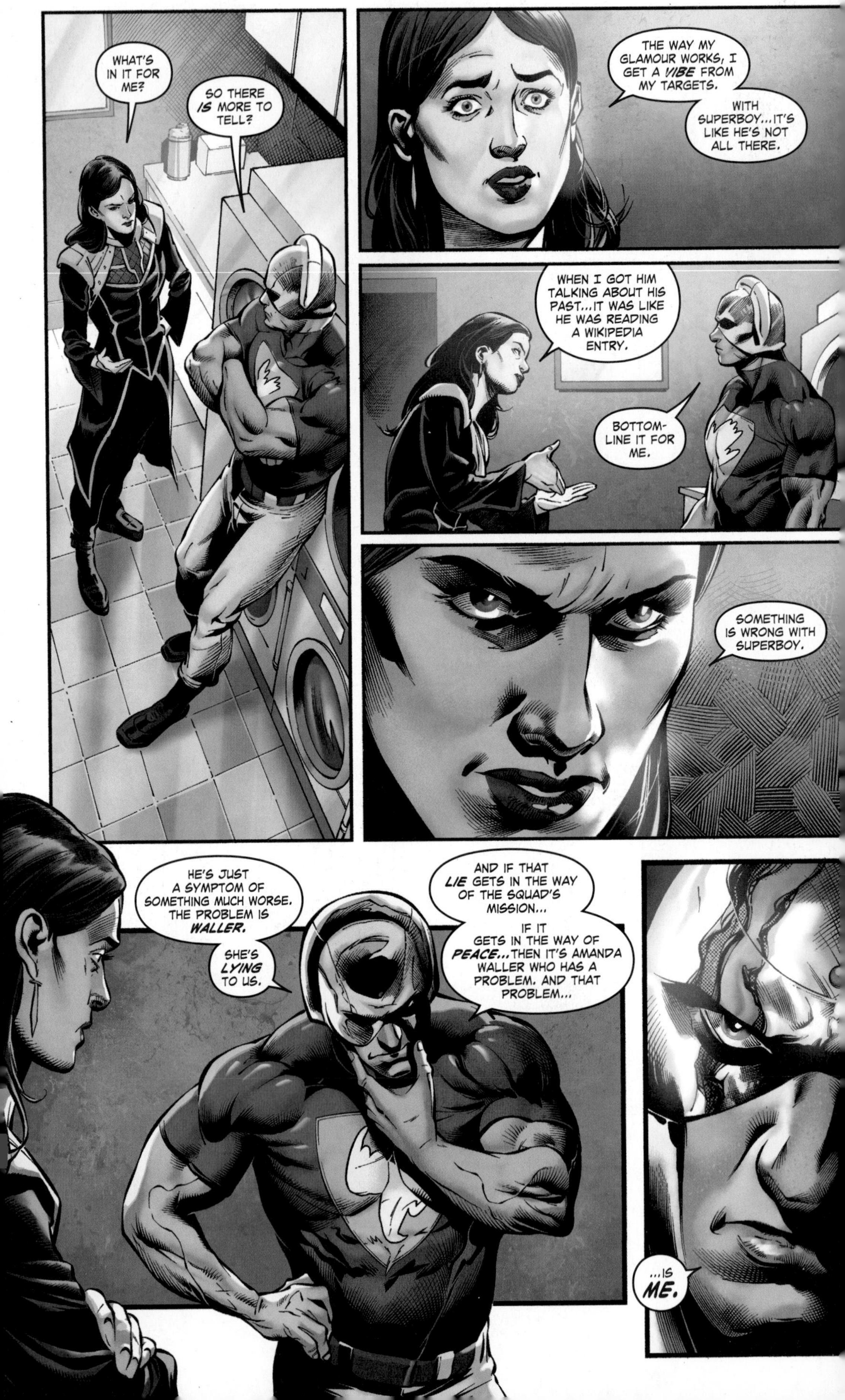
WHAT'S IN IT FOR ME?
SO THERE IS MORE TO TELL?
THE WAY MY GLAMOUR WORKS, I GET A VIBE FROM MY TARGETS.
WITH SUPERBOY...IT'S LIKE HE'S NOT ALL THERE.
WHEN I GOT HIM TALKING ABOUT HIS PAST...IT WAS LIKE HE WAS READING A WIKIPEDIA ENTRY.
BOTTOM-LINE IT FOR ME.
SOMETHING IS WRONG WITH SUPERBOY.
HE'S JUST A SYMPTOM OF SOMETHING MUCH WORSE. THE PROBLEM IS WALLER.
SHE'S LYING TO US.
AND IF THAT LIE GETS IN THE WAY OF THE SQUAD'S MISSION...
IF IT GETS IN THE WAY OF PEACE...THEN IT'S AMANDA WALLER WHO HAS A PROBLEM. AND THAT PROBLEM...
...IS ME.

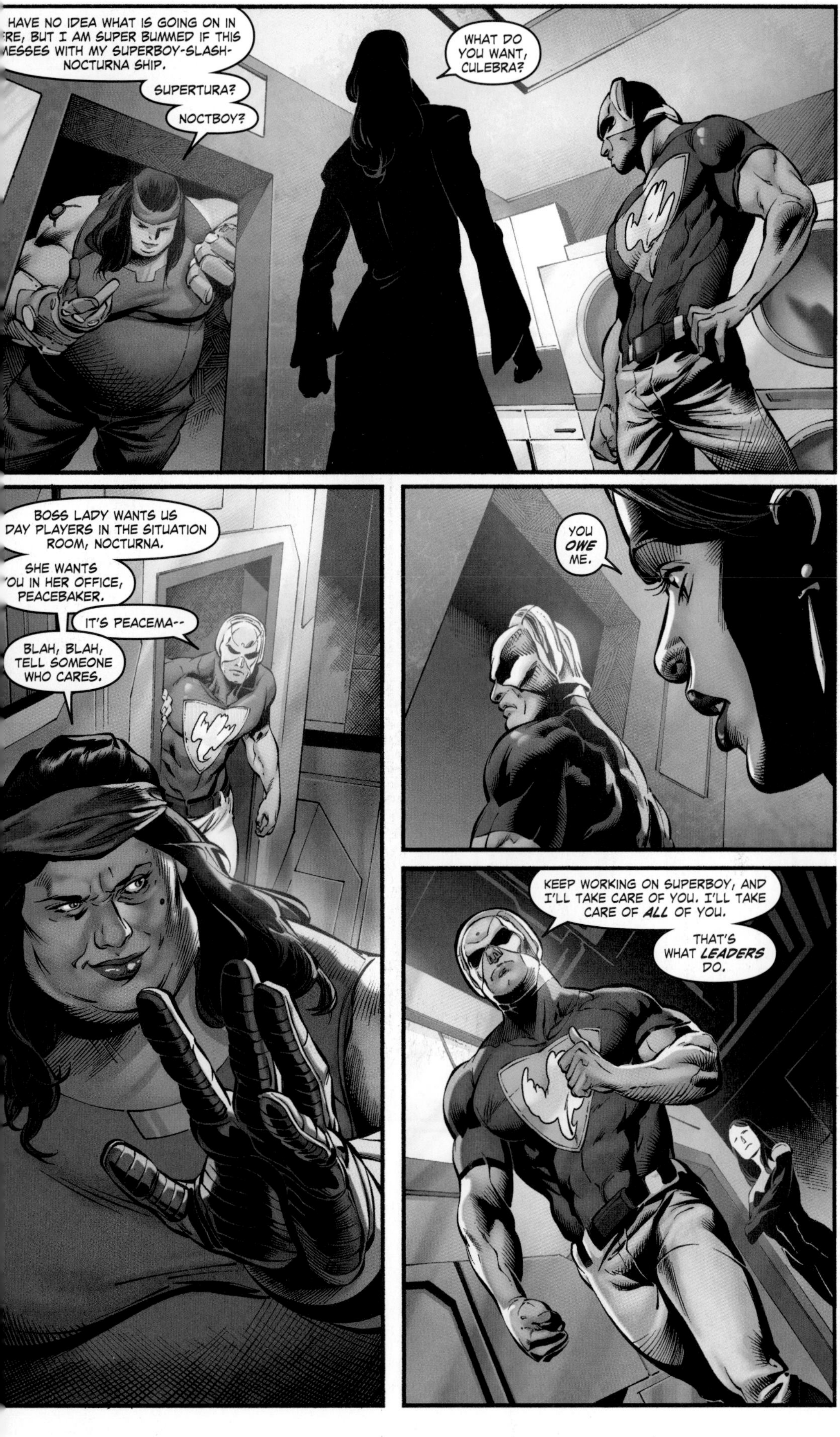
HAVE NO IDEA WHAT IS GOING ON IN
ERE, BUT I AM SUPER BUMMED IF THIS
MESSES WITH MY SUPERBOY-SLASH-
NOCTURNA SHIP.
SUPERTURA?
NOCTBOY?
WHAT DO YOU WANT, CULEBRA?
BOSS LADY WANTS US DAY PLAYERS IN THE SITUATION ROOM, NOCTURNA.
SHE WANTS OU IN HER OFFICE, PEACEBAKER.
IT'S PEACEMA--
BLAH, BLAH, TELL SOMEONE WHO CARES.
YOU *OWE* ME.
KEEP WORKING ON SUPERBOY, AND I'LL TAKE CARE OF YOU. I'LL TAKE CARE OF *ALL* OF YOU.
THAT'S WHAT *LEADERS* DO.

A KID?

YOU'RE NOT GOING SOFT ARE YOU, SMITH?

...JUST GIVE ME THE FILE.

MAKE IT *FAST*.

WHAT MAKES HER MORE SPECIAL THAN THE OTHER KIDS ON TITANS' ISLAND?

SHE'S ONE OF THE FASTEST *METAHUMANS* ON THE PLANET.

FAST ENOUGH TO ESCAPE YOU?

...

LET'S ASSEMBLE THE TEAM.

PERFECT. WHO ARE YOU ASSIGNING TO MY MISSION?

THERE IS NO *YOUR* MISSION, PEACEMAKER. THERE IS ONLY *MY* MISSION.

YOU'RE RUNNING POINT FO TODAY. NOTHING MORE.

"TARGET IS A SPEED FORCE WANNABE CALLING HERSELF *BOLT*."

HE HAS BURSTS [OF] SPEED. CAN'T CONTINUOUSLY [USE] THE FLASH.

[WE]'RE GOING TO [U]SE THAT TO [OU]R ADVANTAGE. [T]RIGGER HER [FIGH]T-OR-FLIGHT, [E]MPHASIS ON FLIGHT.

"SHE CURRENTLY [I]S BUNKED UP WITH THE TEEN TITANS.

"SHE AND I MADE A DEAL. TONIGHT WE HOLD HER TO THAT DEAL."

"WE PULLED HER OUT OF AUSTRALIA.

"AND TONIGHT SHE JOINS THE TEAM. OR DIES."

THAT WAS SO AWESOME. LET'S WATCH IT AGAIN.

WE HAVE CURFEW, BRICK.

AND EVEN OUR HOMEWORK HAS HOMEWORK.

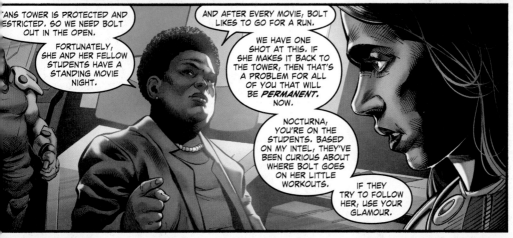

[TIT]ANS TOWER IS PROTECTED AND [R]ESTRICTED. SO WE NEED BOLT OUT IN THE OPEN.

FORTUNATELY, SHE AND HER FELLOW STUDENTS HAVE A STANDING MOVIE NIGHT.

AND AFTER EVERY MOVIE, BOLT LIKES TO GO FOR A RUN.

WE HAVE ONE SHOT AT THIS. IF SHE MAKES IT BACK TO THE TOWER, THEN THAT'S A PROBLEM FOR ALL OF YOU THAT WILL BE PERMANENT. NOW.

NOCTURNA, YOU'RE ON THE STUDENTS. BASED ON MY INTEL, THEY'VE BEEN CURIOUS ABOUT WHERE BOLT GOES ON HER LITTLE WORKOUTS.

IF THEY TRY TO FOLLOW HER, USE YOUR GLAMOUR.

OKAY, I'M GONNA GO FOR MY RUN.

BUT WHAT ABOUT--

I'LL BE BACK BEFORE YOU GUYS EVEN MAKE IT HALFWAY TO THE TOWER.

WHERE DO YOU THINK SHE GOES? MAYBE WE SHOULD FOLLOW HER?

HOW?

I DUNNO. WE'LL FIGURE IT OUT. THINK OF IT AS HOMEWORK.

AWESOME. MORE HOMEWORK.

WHAT A WONDERFUL TIME I'M NOT HAVING.

ACTUALLY, WE SHOULD HEAD BACK. C'MON, GUYS.

JEEZ, MAKE UP YOUR MIND ALREADY.

OR HAVE SOMEONE ELSE MAKE IT UP FOR YOU.

OKAY, WALLER, DUMB JUSTICE ARE HEADED HOME. YOU'RE UP--

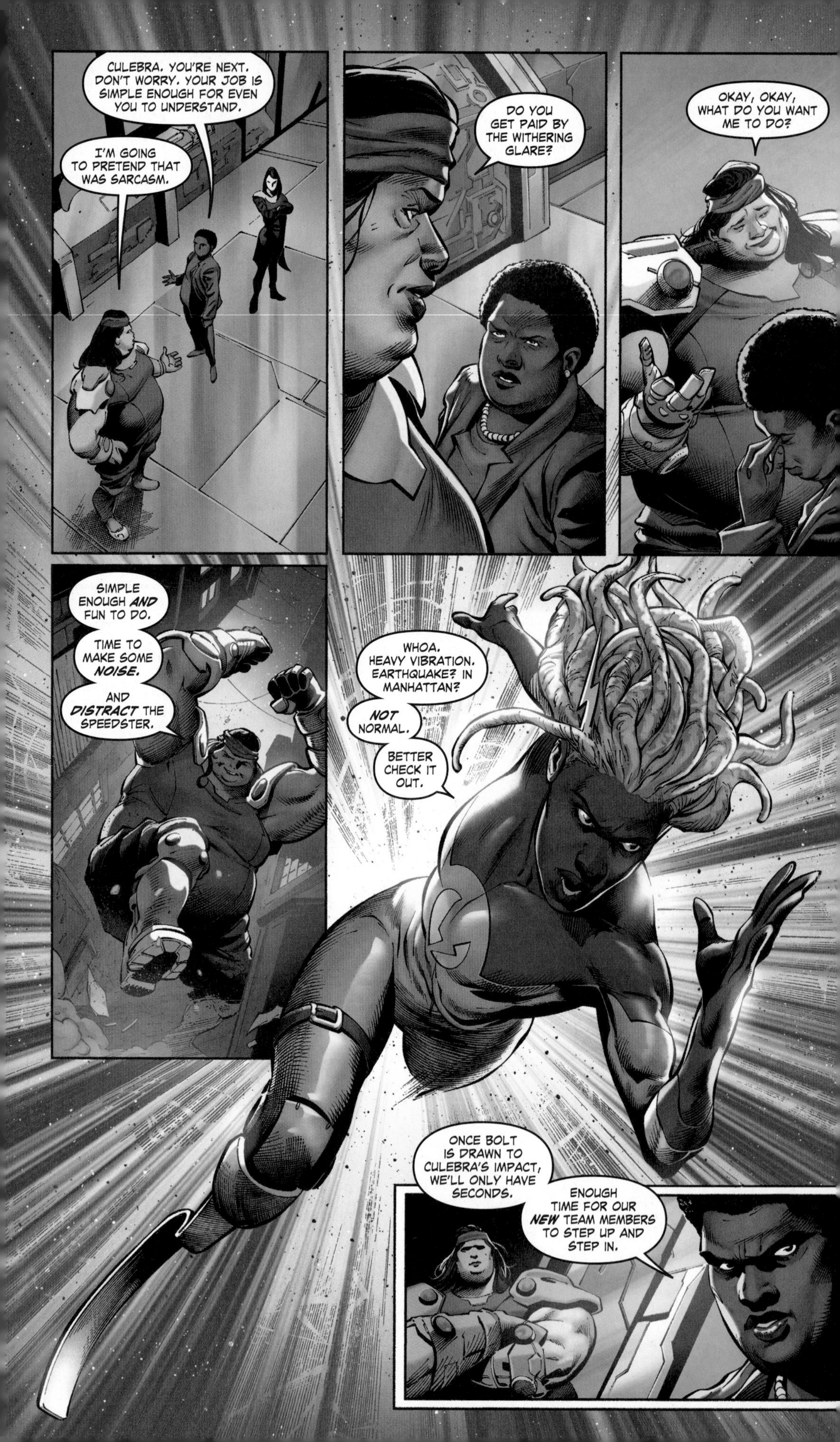
CULEBRA. YOU'RE NEXT. DON'T WORRY. YOUR JOB IS SIMPLE ENOUGH FOR EVEN YOU TO UNDERSTAND.
I'M GOING TO PRETEND THAT WAS SARCASM.
DO YOU GET PAID BY THE WITHERING GLARE?
OKAY, OKAY, WHAT DO YOU WANT ME TO DO?
SIMPLE ENOUGH AND FUN TO DO.
TIME TO MAKE SOME NOISE.
AND DISTRACT THE SPEEDSTER.
WHOA. HEAVY VIBRATION. EARTHQUAKE? IN MANHATTAN?
NOT NORMAL.
BETTER CHECK IT OUT.
ONCE BOLT IS DRAWN TO CULEBRA'S IMPACT, WE'LL ONLY HAVE SECONDS.
ENOUGH TIME FOR OUR NEW TEAM MEMBERS TO STEP UP AND STEP IN.

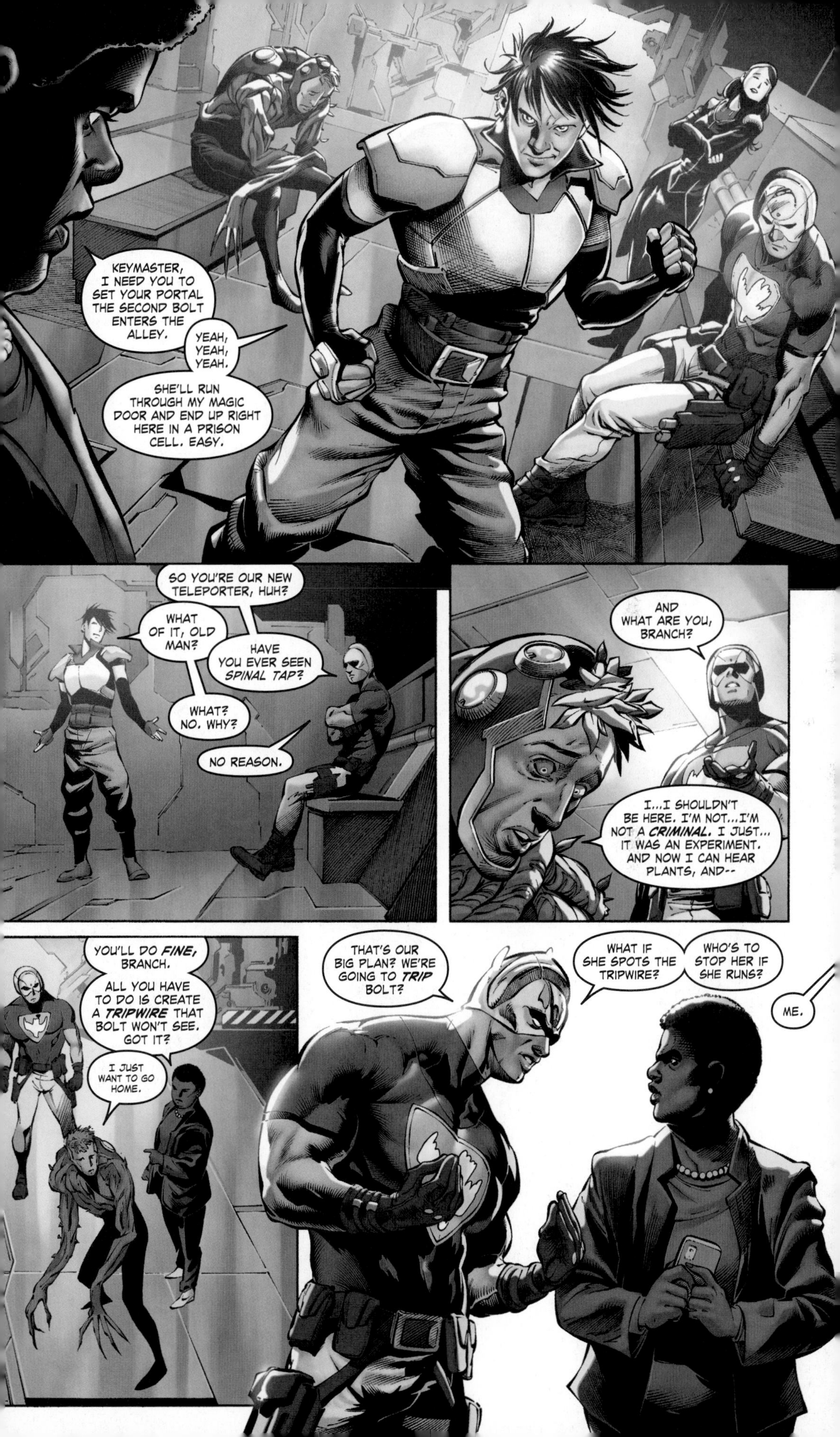
KEYMASTER, I NEED YOU TO SET YOUR PORTAL THE SECOND BOLT ENTERS THE ALLEY.
YEAH, YEAH, YEAH.
SHE'LL RUN THROUGH MY MAGIC DOOR AND END UP RIGHT HERE IN A PRISON CELL. EASY.
SO YOU'RE OUR NEW TELEPORTER, HUH?
WHAT OF IT, OLD MAN?
HAVE YOU EVER SEEN *SPINAL TAP*?
WHAT? NO. WHY?
NO REASON.
AND WHAT ARE YOU, BRANCH?
I...I SHOULDN'T BE HERE. I'M NOT...I'M NOT A ***CRIMINAL.*** I JUST... IT WAS AN EXPERIMENT. AND NOW I CAN HEAR PLANTS, AND--
YOU'LL DO ***FINE,*** BRANCH.
ALL YOU HAVE TO DO IS CREATE A ***TRIPWIRE*** THAT BOLT WON'T SEE. GOT IT?
I JUST WANT TO GO HOME.
THAT'S OUR BIG PLAN? WE'RE GOING TO ***TRIP*** BOLT?
WHAT IF SHE SPOTS THE TRIPWIRE?
WHO'S TO STOP HER IF SHE RUNS?
ME.

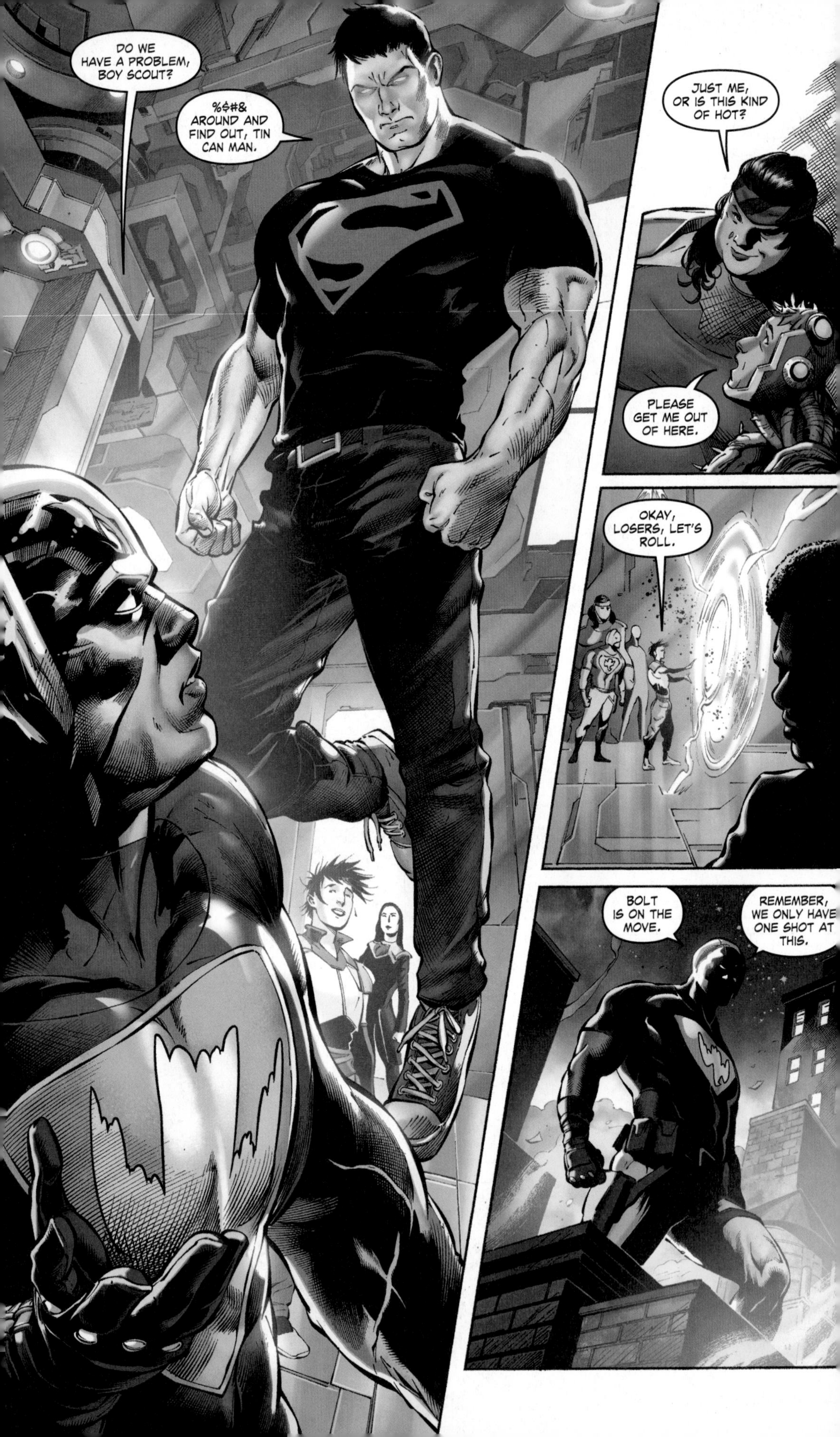
DO WE HAVE A PROBLEM, BOY SCOUT?
%$#& AROUND AND FIND OUT, TIN CAN MAN.
JUST ME, OR IS THIS KIND OF HOT?
PLEASE GET ME OUT OF HERE.
OKAY, LOSERS, LET'S ROLL.
BOLT IS ON THE MOVE.
REMEMBER, WE ONLY HAVE ONE SHOT AT THIS.

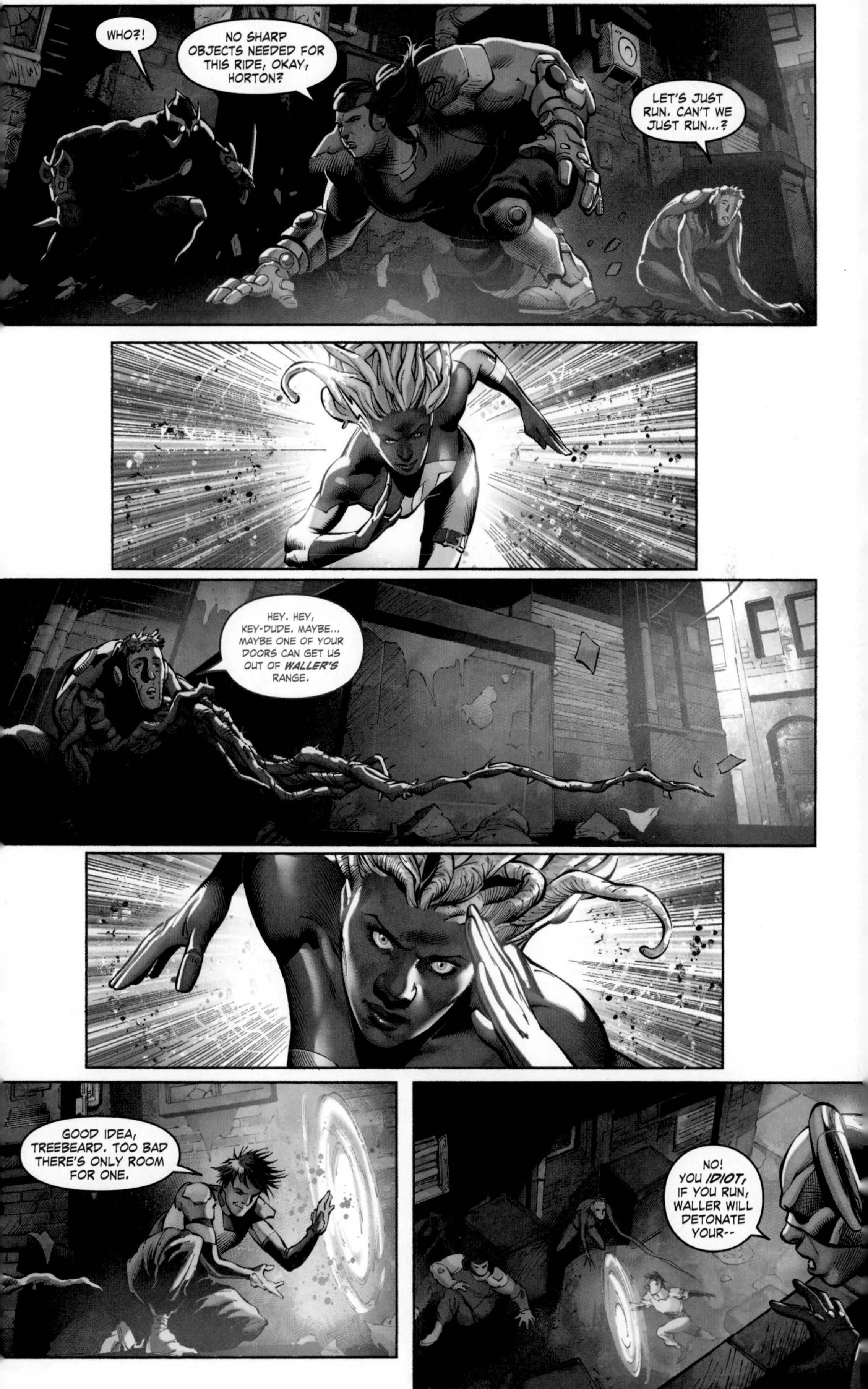
WHO?!
NO SHARP OBJECTS NEEDED FOR THIS RIDE, OKAY, HORTON?
LET'S JUST RUN. CAN'T WE JUST RUN...?
HEY. HEY, KEY-DUDE. MAYBE... MAYBE ONE OF YOUR DOORS CAN GET US OUT OF WALLER'S RANGE.
GOOD IDEA, TREEBEARD. TOO BAD THERE'S ONLY ROOM FOR ONE.
NO! YOU IDIOT, IF YOU RUN, WALLER WILL DETONATE YOUR--

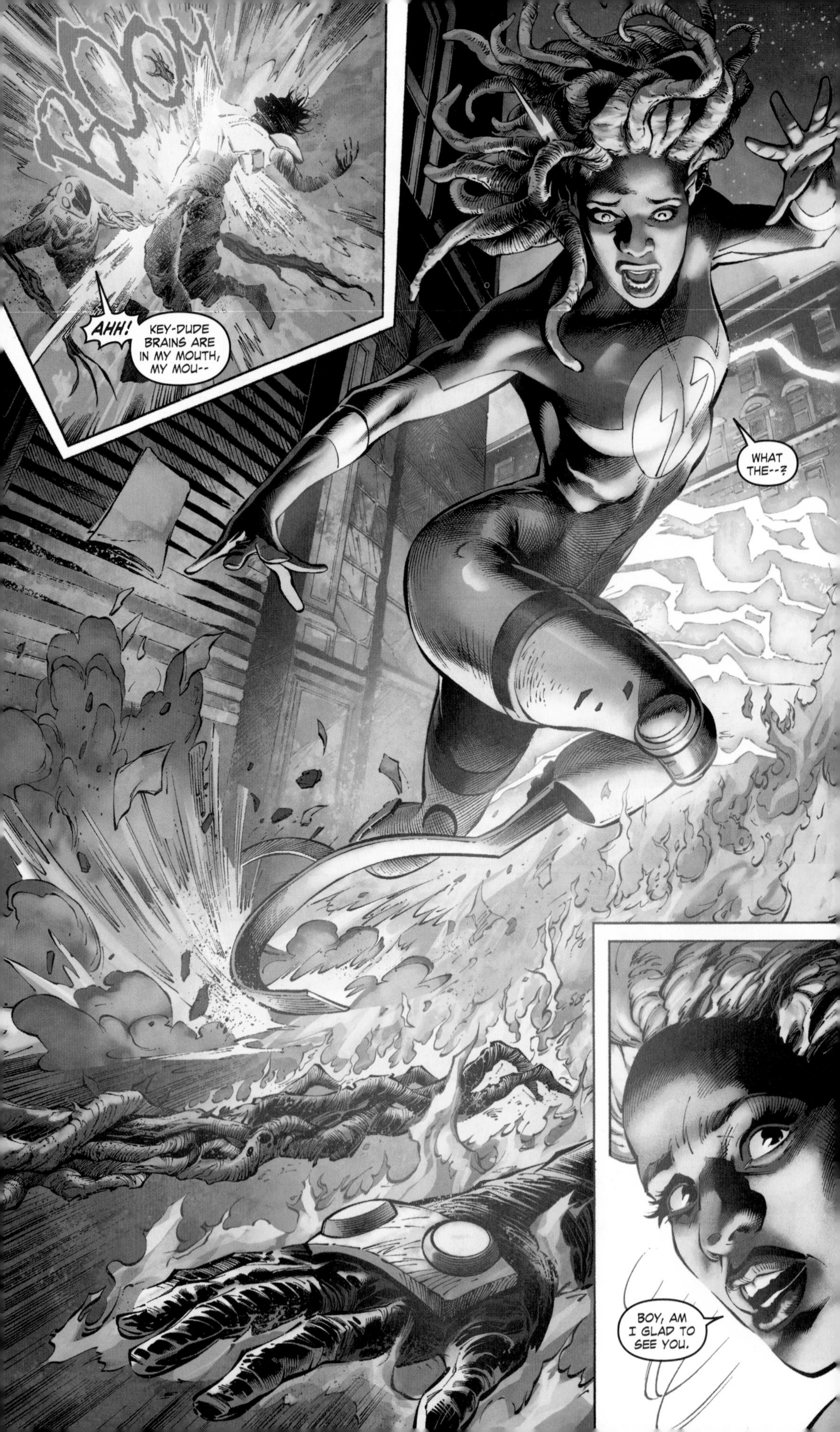
BOOM
AHH!
KEY-DUDE BRAINS ARE IN MY MOUTH, MY MOU--
WHAT THE--?
BOY, AM I GLAD TO SEE YOU.

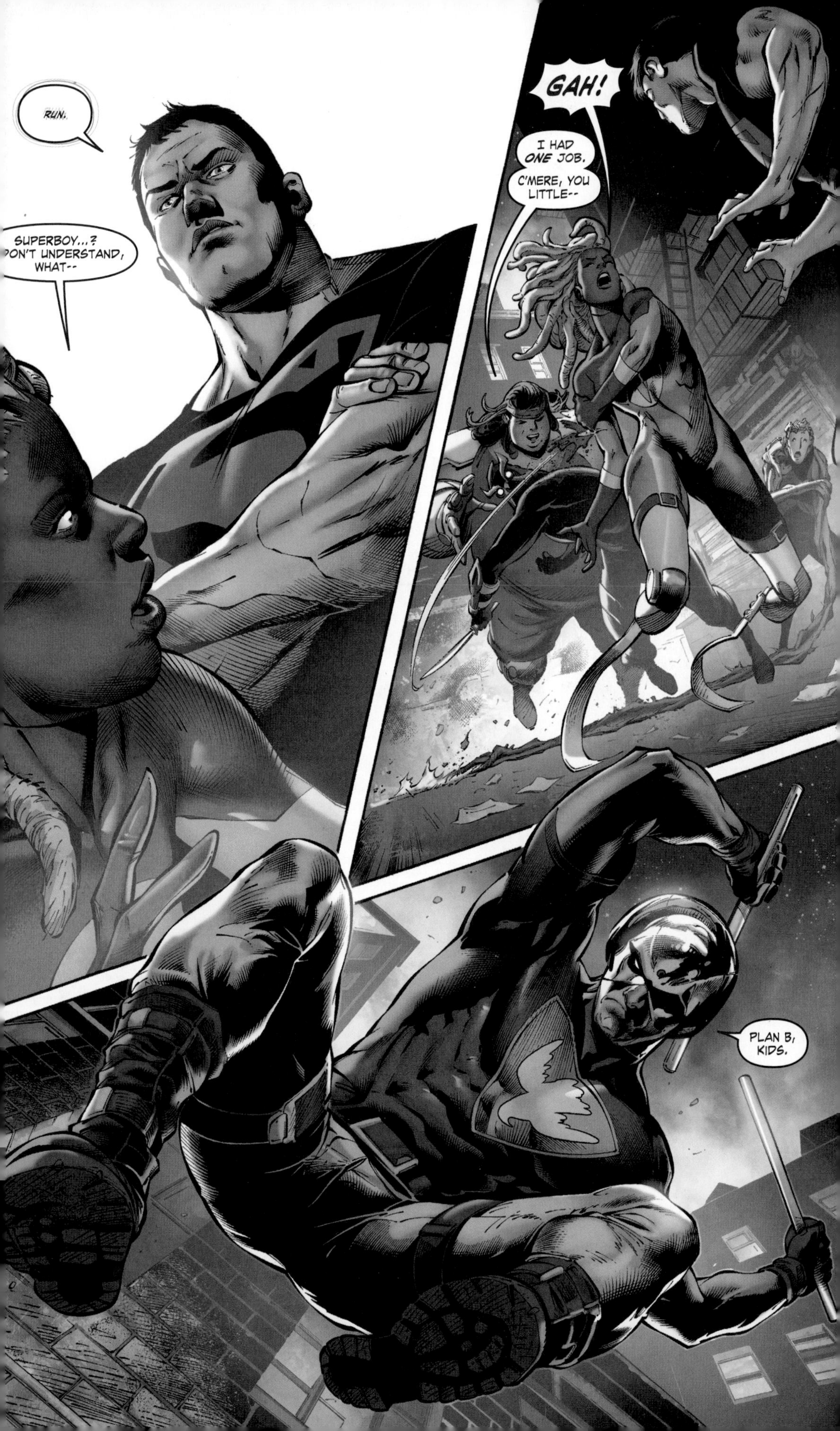
RUN.
SUPERBOY...? DON'T UNDERSTAND, WHAT--
GAH!
I HAD ONE JOB.
C'MERE, YOU LITTLE--
PLAN B, KIDS.

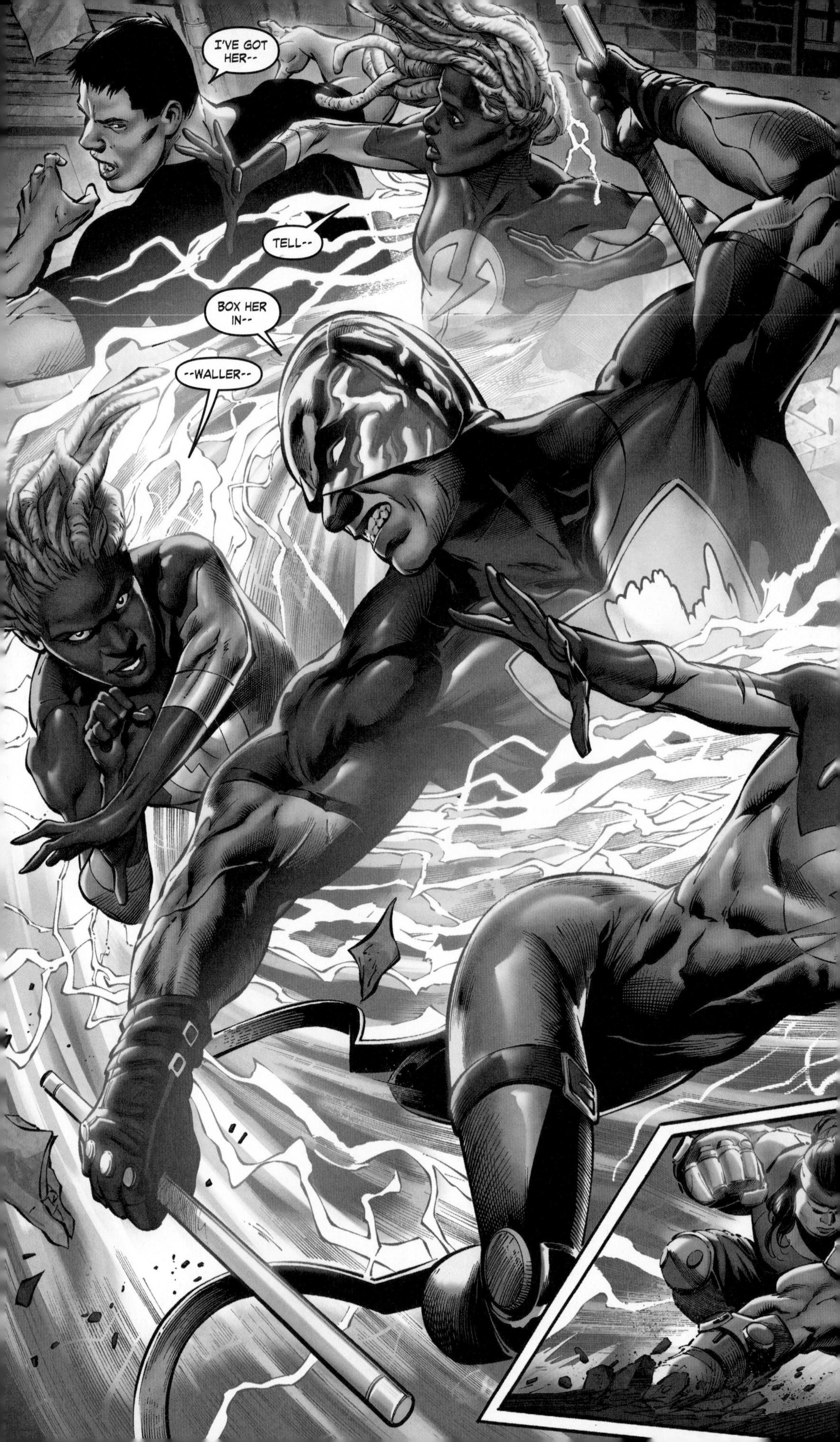
I'VE GOT HER--
TELL--
BOX HER IN--
--WALLER--

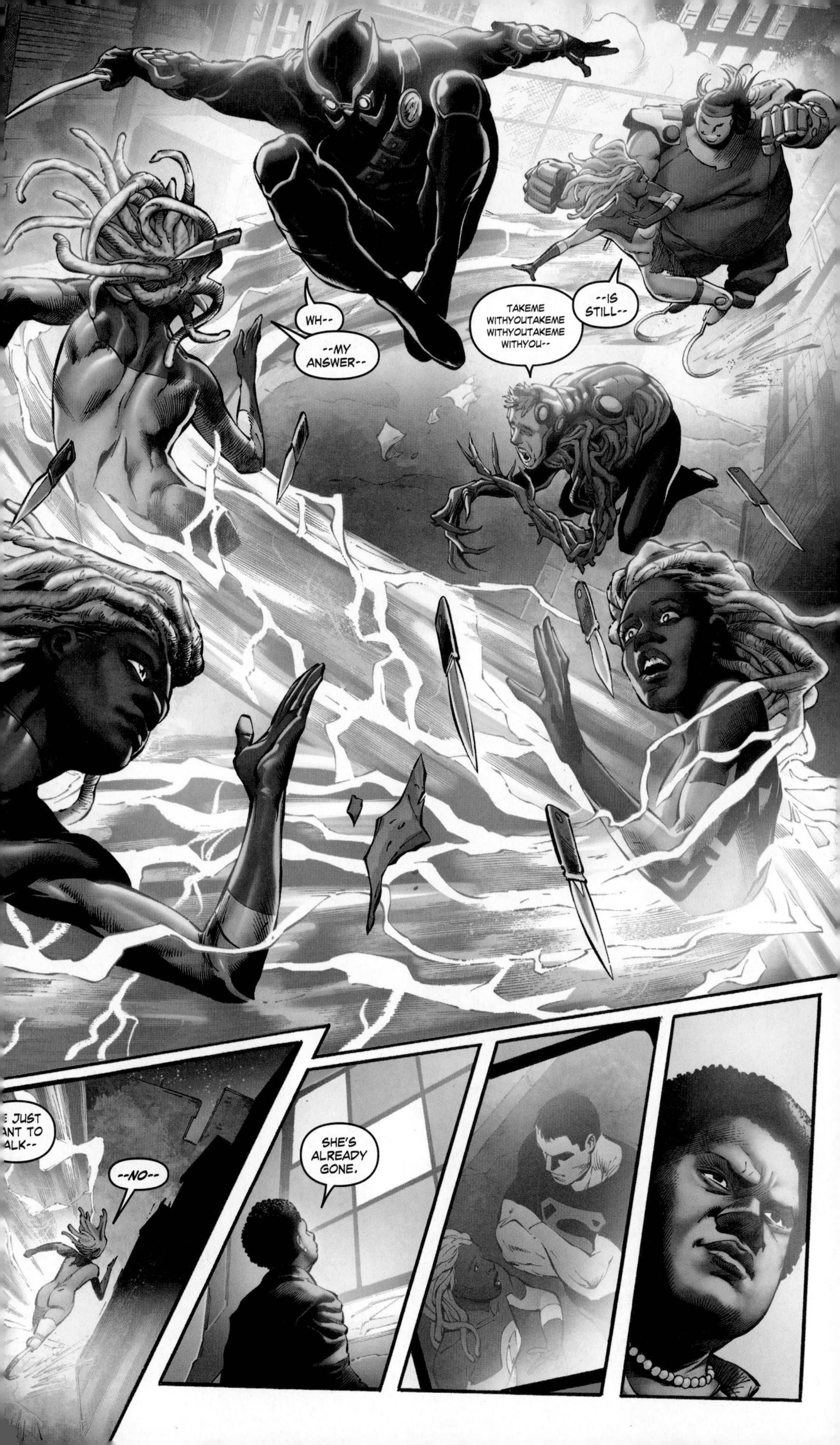
WH--
--MY ANSWER--
--IS STILL--
TAKEME WITHYOUTAKEME WITHYOUTAKEME WITHYOU--
E JUST ANT TO ALK--
--NO--
SHE'S ALREADY GONE.

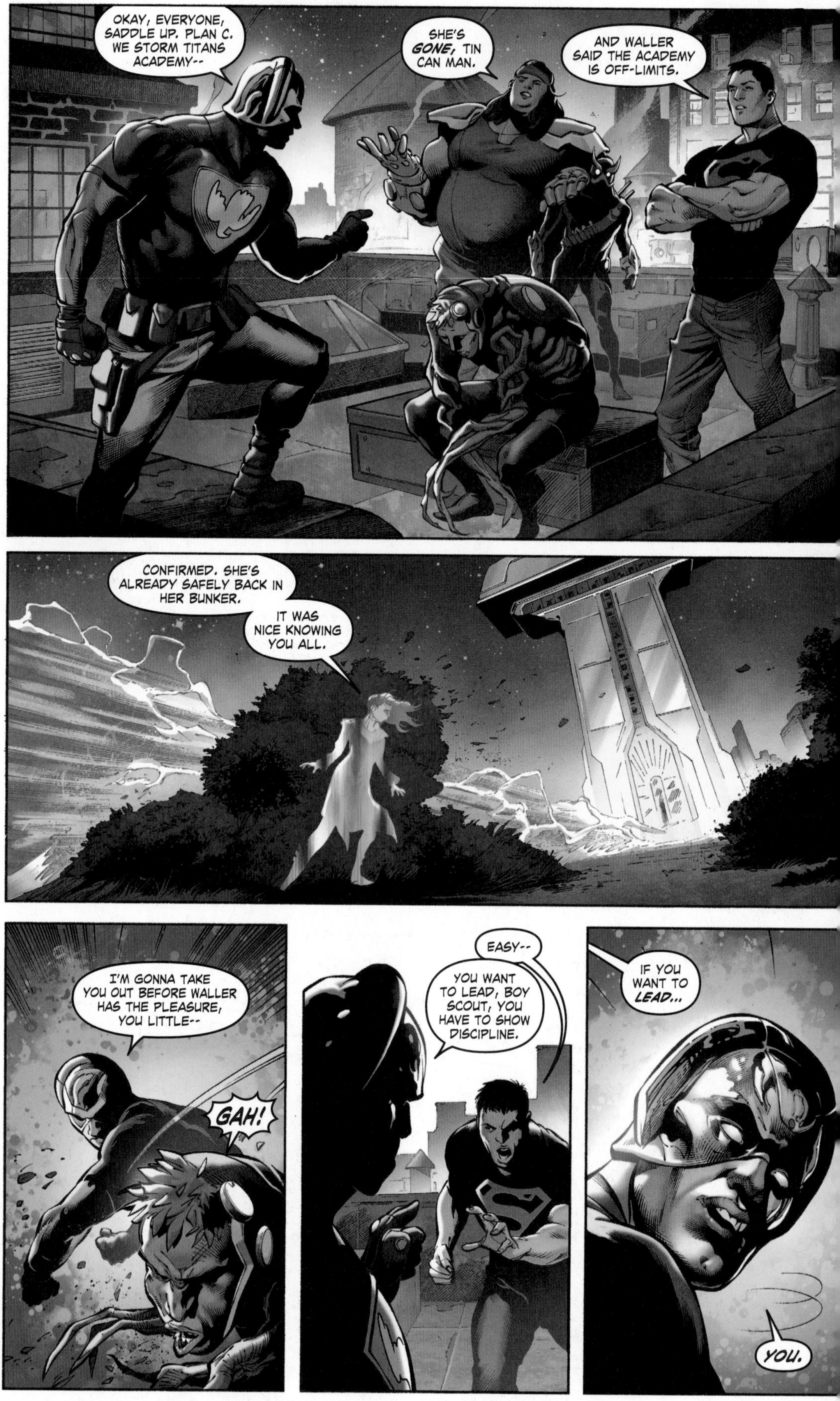
OKAY, EVERYONE, SADDLE UP. PLAN C. WE STORM TITANS ACADEMY--
SHE'S *GONE,* TIN CAN MAN.
AND WALLER SAID THE ACADEMY IS OFF-LIMITS.
CONFIRMED. SHE'S ALREADY SAFELY BACK IN HER BUNKER.
IT WAS NICE KNOWING YOU ALL.
I'M GONNA TAKE YOU OUT BEFORE WALLER HAS THE PLEASURE, YOU LITTLE--
GAH!
EASY--
YOU WANT TO LEAD, BOY SCOUT, YOU HAVE TO SHOW DISCIPLINE.
IF YOU WANT TO *LEAD...*
YOU.

...THEN YOU HAVE TO THINK NOT ONE...

...NOT TWO...

...BUT *THREE* STEPS AHEAD...

NOW, IF YOU *CIRCUS CLOWNS* WANT TO BREAK INTO TITANS ACADEMY...

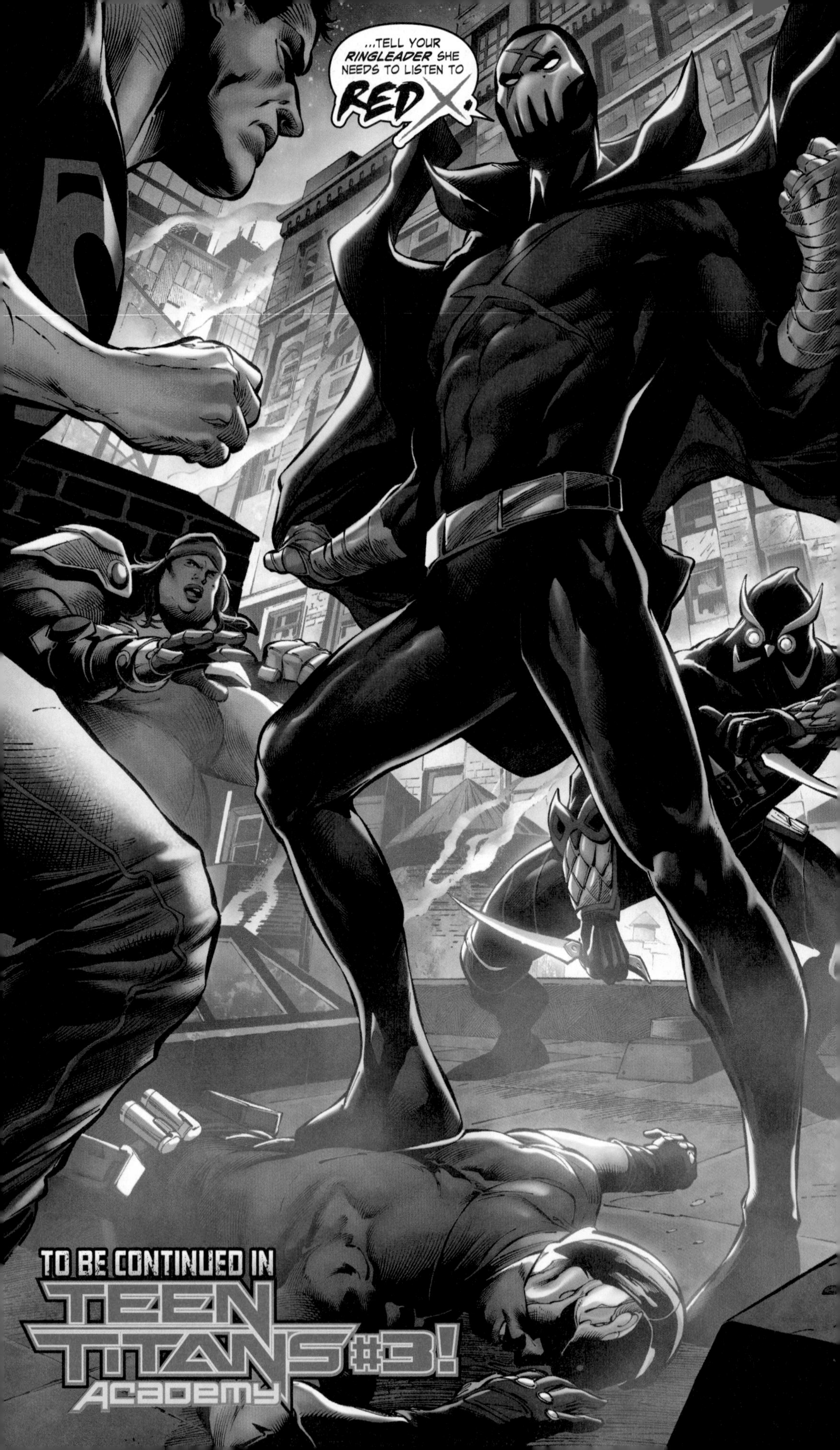
...TELL YOUR RINGLEADER SHE NEEDS TO LISTEN TO RED X.
TO BE CONTINUED IN TEEN TITANS ACADEMY #3!

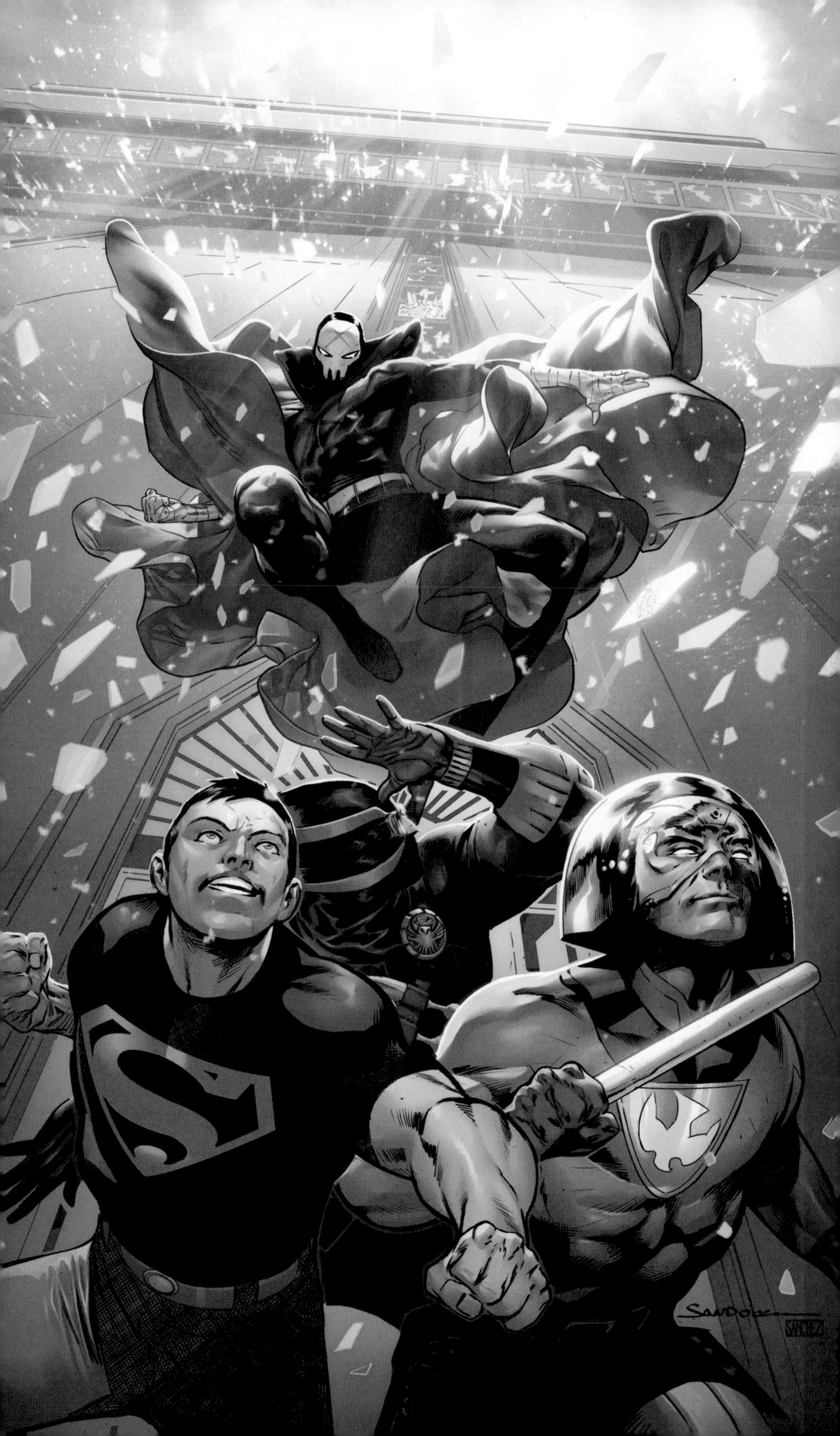
SANCHEZ

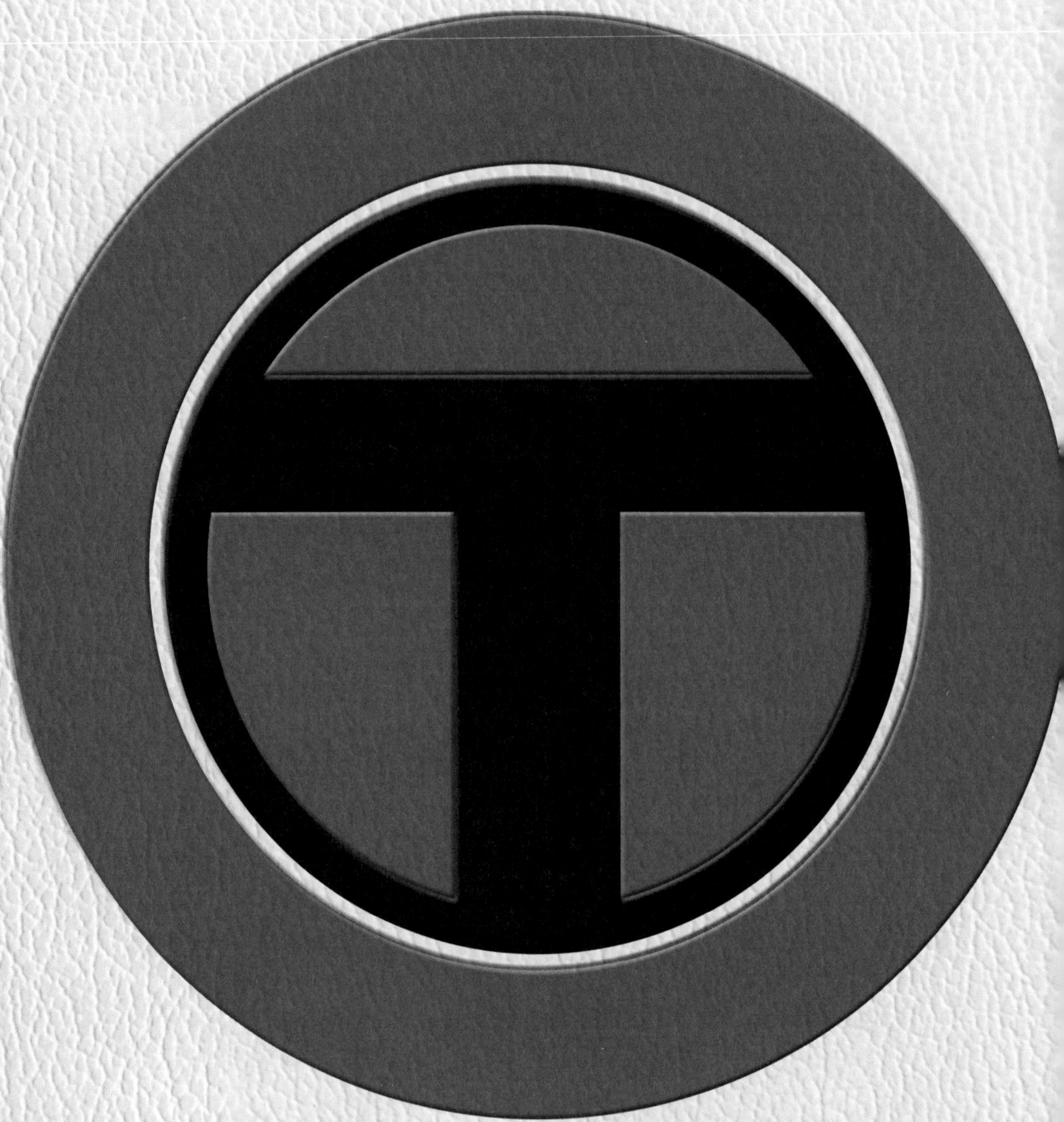

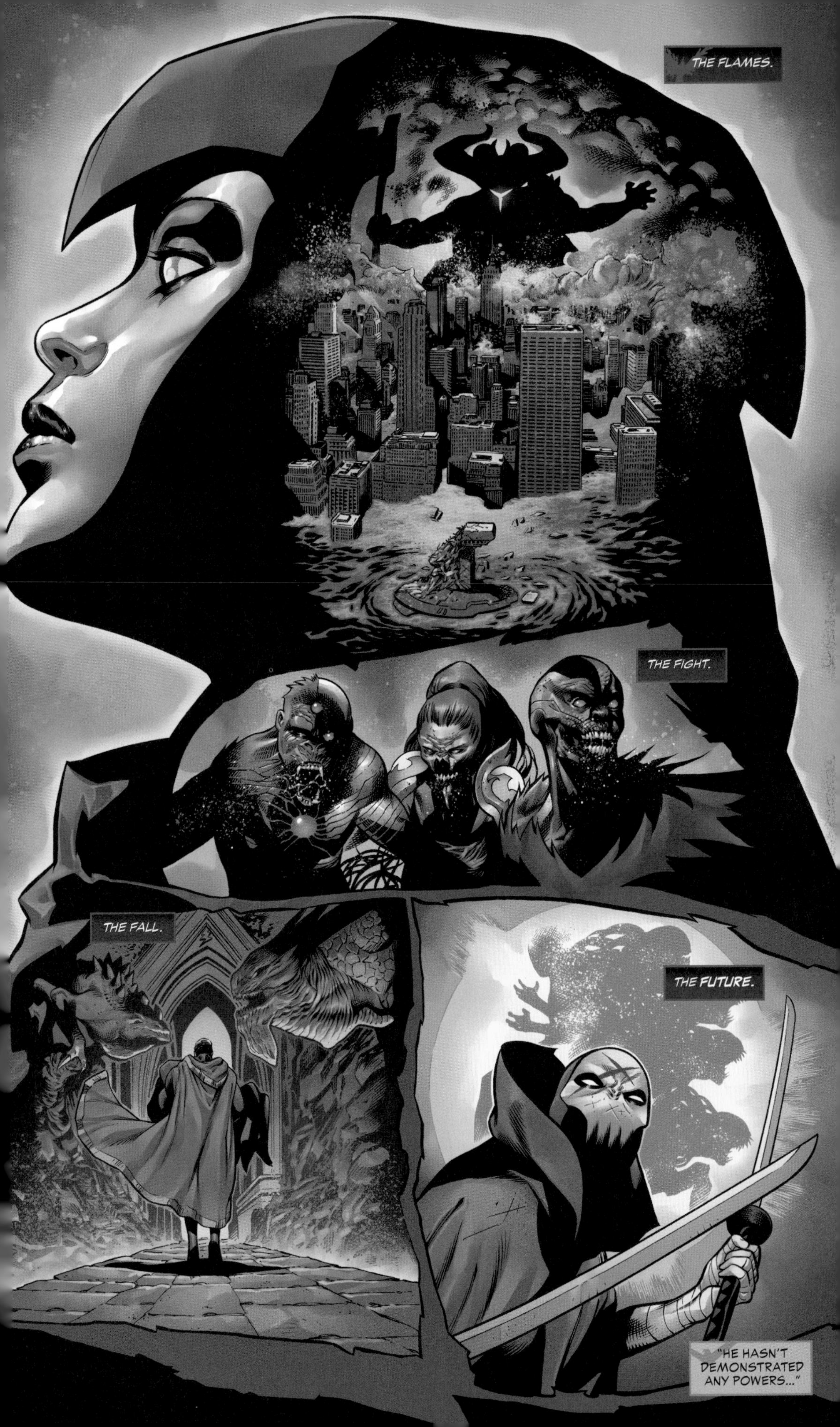
THE FLAMES.
THE FIGHT.
THE FALL.
THE FUTURE.
"HE HASN'T DEMONSTRATED ANY POWERS..."

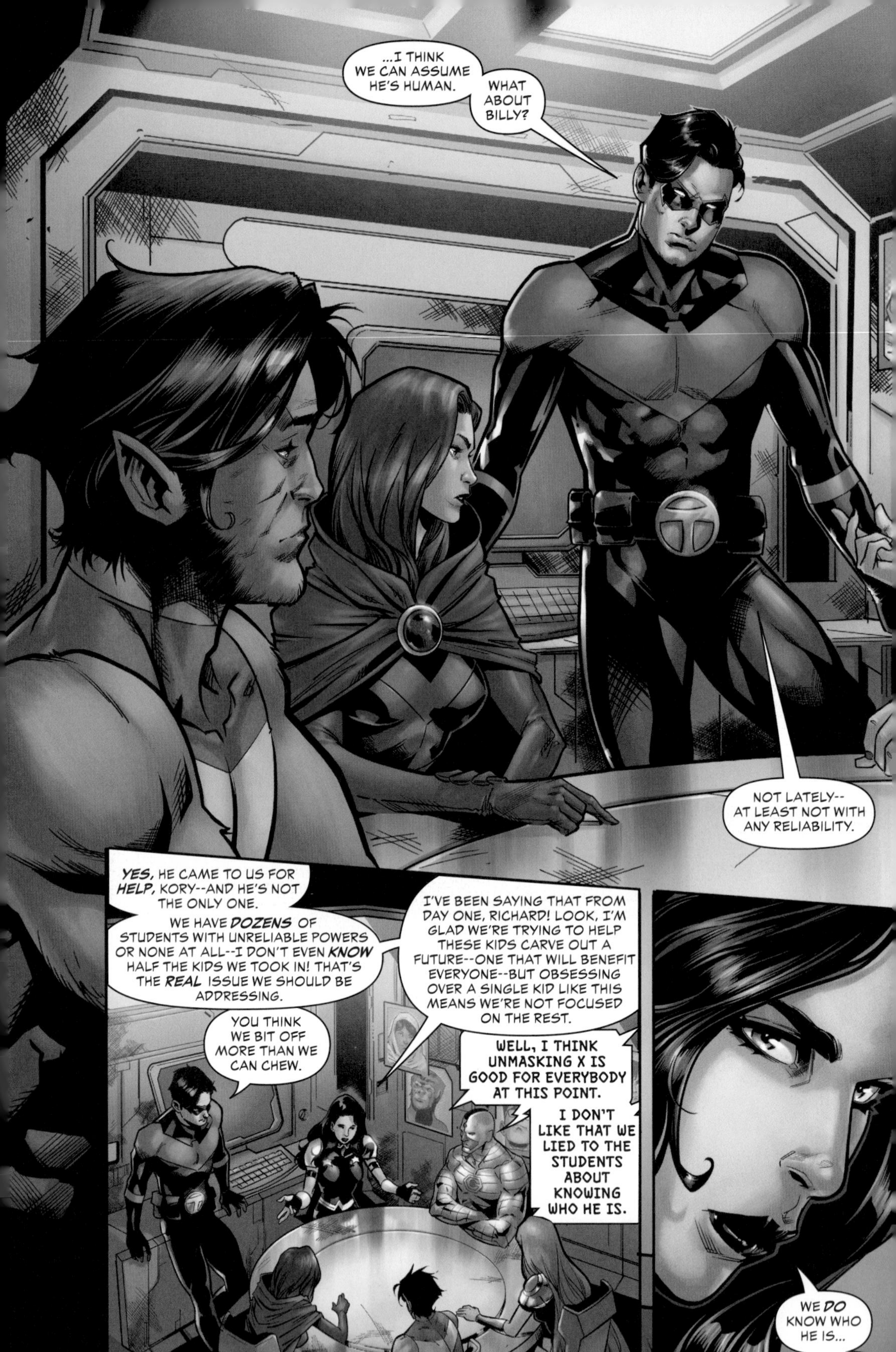

...I THINK WE CAN ASSUME HE'S HUMAN.
WHAT ABOUT BILLY?
NOT LATELY-- AT LEAST NOT WITH ANY RELIABILITY.
YES, HE CAME TO US FOR *HELP,* KORY--AND HE'S NOT THE ONLY ONE.
WE HAVE *DOZENS* OF STUDENTS WITH UNRELIABLE POWERS OR NONE AT ALL--I DON'T EVEN *KNOW* HALF THE KIDS WE TOOK IN! THAT'S THE *REAL* ISSUE WE SHOULD BE ADDRESSING.
YOU THINK WE BIT OFF MORE THAN WE CAN CHEW.
I'VE BEEN SAYING THAT FROM DAY ONE, RICHARD! LOOK, I'M GLAD WE'RE TRYING TO HELP THESE KIDS CARVE OUT A FUTURE--ONE THAT WILL BENEFIT EVERYONE--BUT OBSESSING OVER A SINGLE KID LIKE THIS MEANS WE'RE NOT FOCUSED ON THE REST.
WELL, I THINK UNMASKING X IS GOOD FOR EVERYBODY AT THIS POINT.
I DON'T LIKE THAT WE LIED TO THE STUDENTS ABOUT KNOWING WHO HE IS.
WE *DO* KNOW WHO HE IS...
HE'S *RED X.* THAT'S *ALL THAT MATTERS.*

Original Titans NIGHTWING, STARFIRE, RAVEN, DONNA TROY, CYBORG, and BEAST BOY reassemble to mentor the next generation of her
Now, TEEN TITANS ACADEMY opens its doors to a new crop of gifted youngsters eager to earn their place on the team's permane
roster, innocent of the many treacherous challenges they will face—in and out of school—over the months and years to com

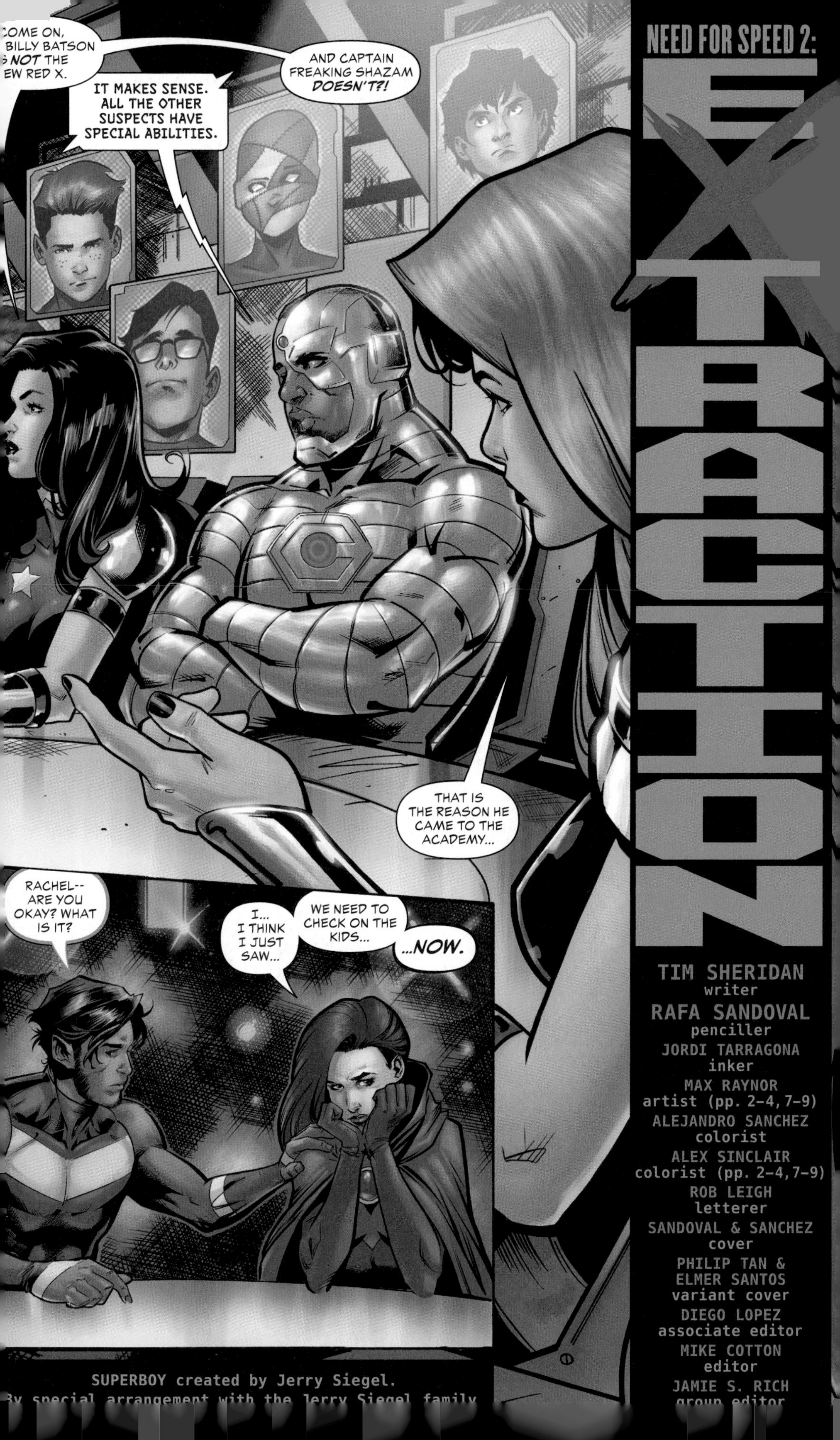
COME ON, BILLY BATSON S *NOT* THE EW RED X.
IT MAKES SENSE. ALL THE OTHER SUSPECTS HAVE SPECIAL ABILITIES.
AND CAPTAIN FREAKING SHAZAM *DOESN'T?!*
THAT IS THE REASON HE CAME TO THE ACADEMY...
RACHEL-- ARE YOU OKAY? WHAT IS IT?
I... I THINK I JUST SAW...
WE NEED TO CHECK ON THE KIDS...
...*NOW.*

NEED FOR SPEED 2:

EXTRACTION

TIM SHERIDAN
writer
RAFA SANDOVAL
penciller
JORDI TARRAGONA
inker
MAX RAYNOR
artist (pp. 2–4, 7–9)
ALEJANDRO SANCHEZ
colorist
ALEX SINCLAIR
colorist (pp. 2–4, 7–9)
ROB LEIGH
letterer
SANDOVAL & SANCHEZ
cover
PHILIP TAN & ELMER SANTOS
variant cover
DIEGO LOPEZ
associate editor
MIKE COTTON
editor
JAMIE S. RICH
group editor

SUPERBOY created by Jerry Siegel.
By special arrangement with the Jerry Siegel family

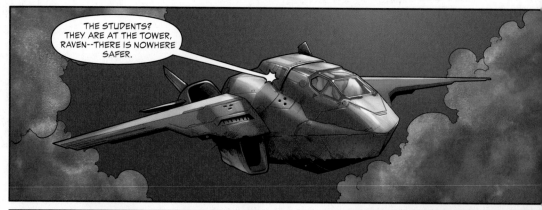

THE STUDENTS? THEY ARE AT THE TOWER, RAVEN--THERE IS NOWHERE SAFER.

IF RACHEL SAYS SHE SAW SOMETHING...

THEN THE *UPPERCLASSMEN* WILL HANDLE IT. WE LEFT THEM IN CHARGE--IT IS PART OF THEIR TRAINING.

IF THIS OPERATION IS A SUCCESS, WE'LL HAVE THE META-TEEN REFUGEES OUT OF MARKOVIA AND BACK HOME IN NINE HOURS MAX.

ARE WE REALLY GONNA SACRIFICE THOSE KIDS FOR ONE OF RAE'S LITTLE PREMONITIONS?

WHAT IS THAT SUPPOSED TO--

IT'S OKAY, GAR. HE'S RIGHT. AND I DON'T EVEN UNDERSTAND WHAT I SAW YET...NOT COMPLETELY. BUT...

I THINK SOMETHING'S COMING. SOMETHING *BIG*...AND *BAD*... AND I...

...I THINK... MAYBE *WE'RE* RESPONSIBLE.

COME ON, YOU NEED TO LIE DOWN.

THE KIDS ARE GONNA BE FINE. NO ONE CAN GET INSIDE THAT TOWER.

NO ONE?

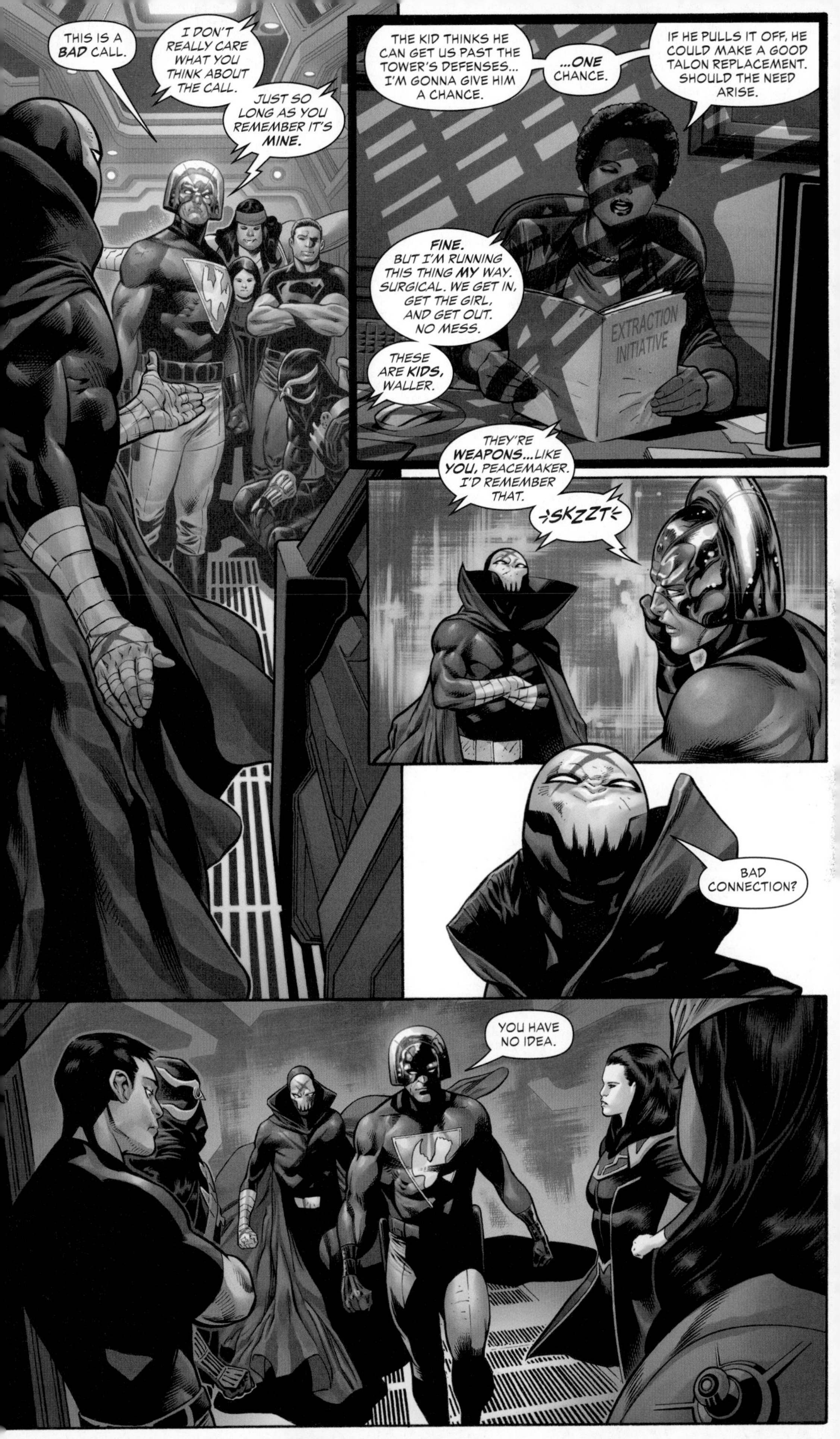
THIS IS A BAD CALL.
I DON'T REALLY CARE WHAT YOU THINK ABOUT THE CALL.
JUST SO LONG AS YOU REMEMBER IT'S MINE.
THE KID THINKS HE CAN GET US PAST THE TOWER'S DEFENSES... I'M GONNA GIVE HIM A CHANCE.
...ONE CHANCE.
IF HE PULLS IT OFF, HE COULD MAKE A GOOD TALON REPLACEMENT. SHOULD THE NEED ARISE.
FINE. BUT I'M RUNNING THIS THING MY WAY. SURGICAL. WE GET IN, GET THE GIRL, AND GET OUT. NO MESS.
THESE ARE KIDS, WALLER.
EXTRACTION INITIATIVE
THEY'RE WEAPONS...LIKE YOU, PEACEMAKER. I'D REMEMBER THAT.
SKZZT
BAD CONNECTION?
YOU HAVE NO IDEA.

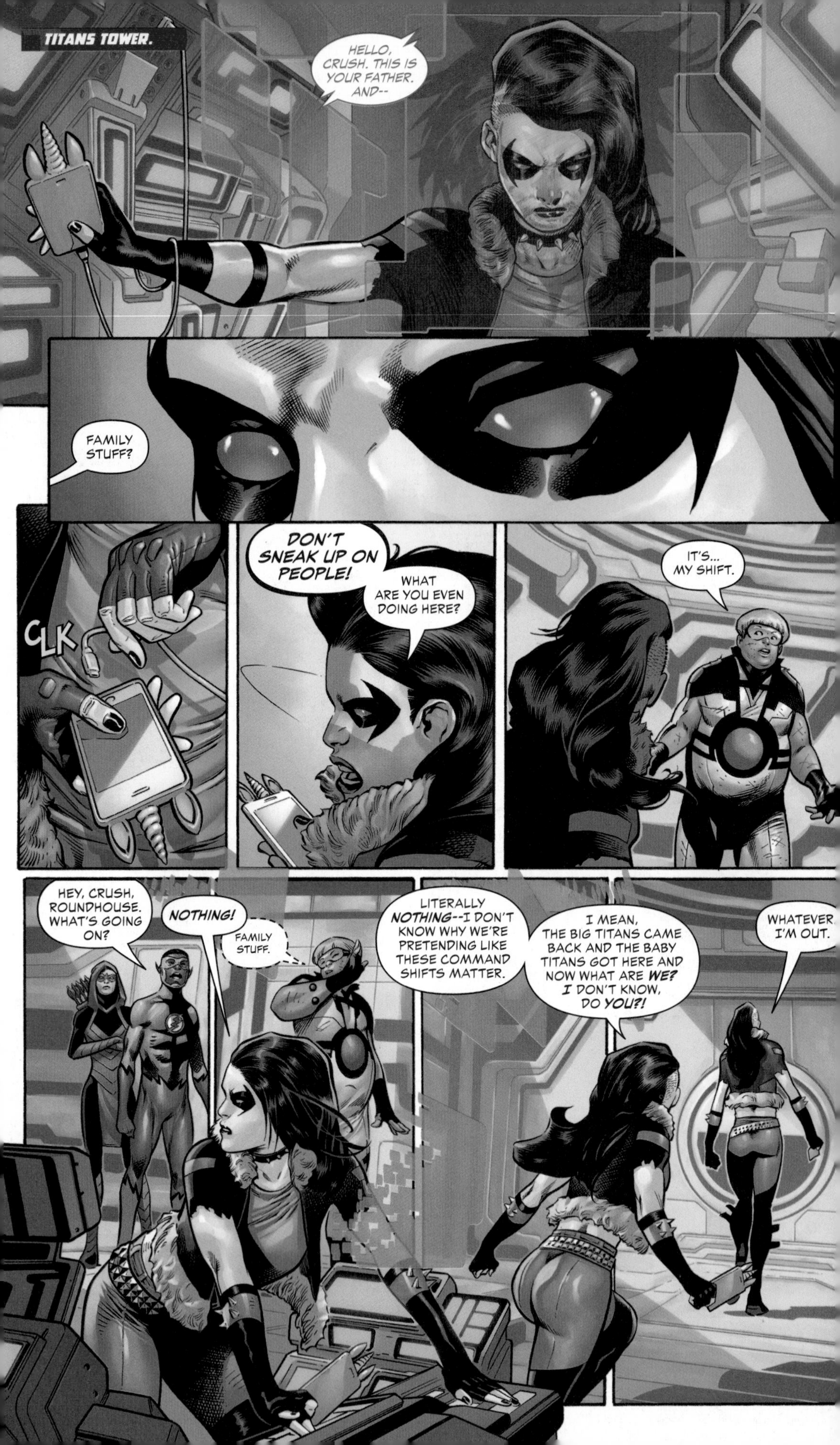
TITANS TOWER.
HELLO, CRUSH. THIS IS YOUR FATHER. AND--
FAMILY STUFF?
CLK
DON'T SNEAK UP ON PEOPLE!
WHAT ARE YOU EVEN DOING HERE?
IT'S... MY SHIFT.
HEY, CRUSH, ROUNDHOUSE. WHAT'S GOING ON?
NOTHING!
FAMILY STUFF.
LITERALLY NOTHING--I DON'T KNOW WHY WE'RE PRETENDING LIKE THESE COMMAND SHIFTS MATTER.
I MEAN, THE BIG TITANS CAME BACK AND THE BABY TITANS GOT HERE AND NOW WHAT ARE WE? I DON'T KNOW, DO YOU?!
WHATEVER I'M OUT.

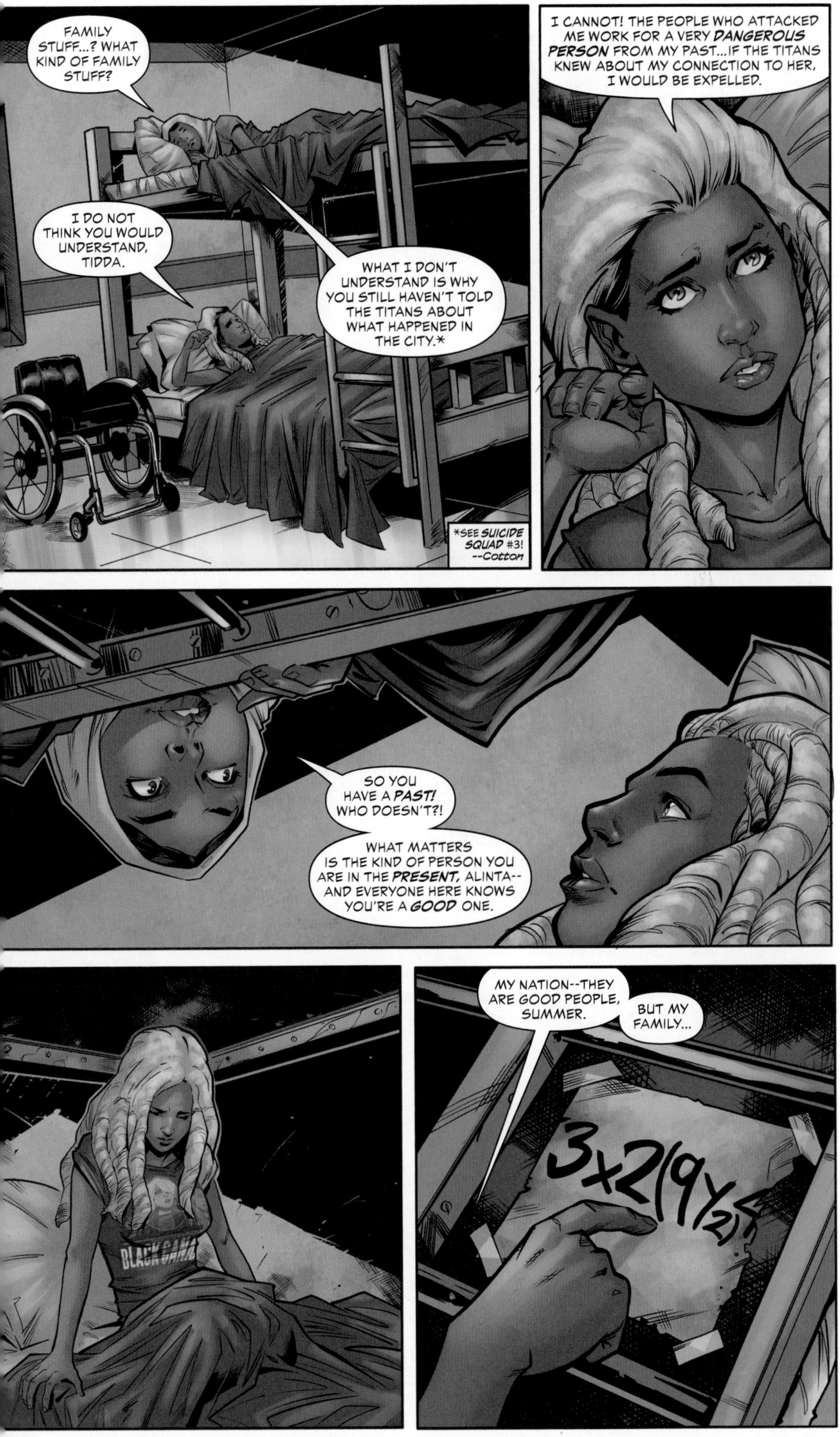
FAMILY STUFF...? WHAT KIND OF FAMILY STUFF?
I DO NOT THINK YOU WOULD UNDERSTAND, TIDDA.
WHAT I DON'T UNDERSTAND IS WHY YOU STILL HAVEN'T TOLD THE TITANS ABOUT WHAT HAPPENED IN THE CITY.*
*SEE SUICIDE SQUAD #3! --Cotton
I CANNOT! THE PEOPLE WHO ATTACKED ME WORK FOR A VERY DANGEROUS PERSON FROM MY PAST...IF THE TITANS KNEW ABOUT MY CONNECTION TO HER, I WOULD BE EXPELLED.
SO YOU HAVE A PAST! WHO DOESN'T?!
WHAT MATTERS IS THE KIND OF PERSON YOU ARE IN THE PRESENT, ALINTA--AND EVERYONE HERE KNOWS YOU'RE A GOOD ONE.
MY NATION--THEY ARE GOOD PEOPLE, SUMMER.
BUT MY FAMILY...

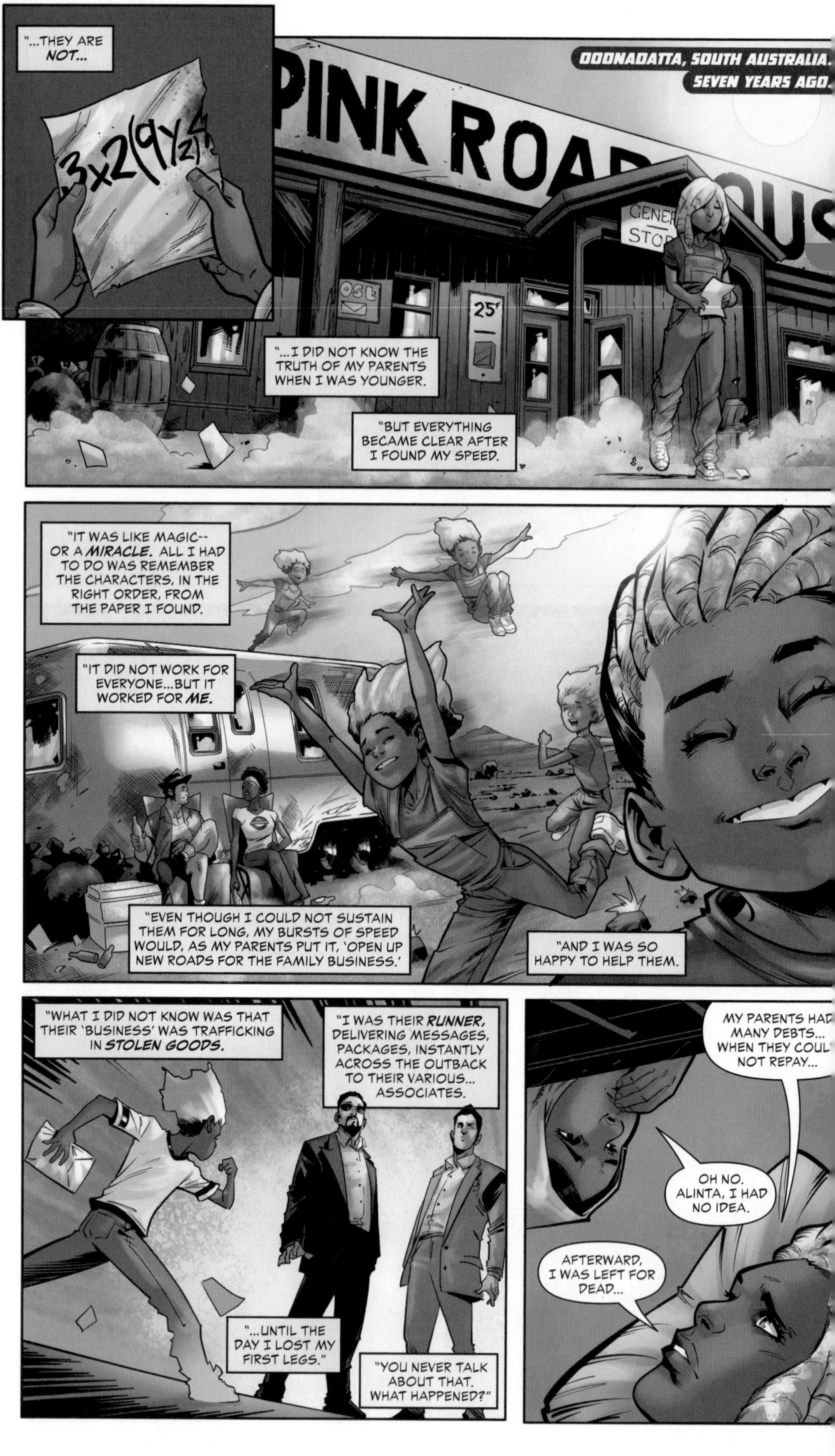
"...THEY ARE *NOT*...
3x2(9Y2)
PINK ROAD
GENER STO
25¢
OODNADATTA, SOUTH AUSTRALIA.
SEVEN YEARS AGO.
"...I DID NOT KNOW THE TRUTH OF MY PARENTS WHEN I WAS YOUNGER.
"BUT EVERYTHING BECAME CLEAR AFTER I FOUND MY SPEED.
"IT WAS LIKE MAGIC-- OR A *MIRACLE.* ALL I HAD TO DO WAS REMEMBER THE CHARACTERS, IN THE RIGHT ORDER, FROM THE PAPER I FOUND.
"IT DID NOT WORK FOR EVERYONE...BUT IT WORKED FOR *ME.*
"EVEN THOUGH I COULD NOT SUSTAIN THEM FOR LONG, MY BURSTS OF SPEED WOULD, AS MY PARENTS PUT IT, 'OPEN UP NEW ROADS FOR THE FAMILY BUSINESS.'
"AND I WAS SO HAPPY TO HELP THEM.
"WHAT I DID NOT KNOW WAS THAT THEIR 'BUSINESS' WAS TRAFFICKING IN *STOLEN GOODS.*
"I WAS THEIR *RUNNER,* DELIVERING MESSAGES, PACKAGES, INSTANTLY ACROSS THE OUTBACK TO THEIR VARIOUS... ASSOCIATES.
"...UNTIL THE DAY I LOST MY FIRST LEGS."
"YOU NEVER TALK ABOUT THAT. WHAT HAPPENED?"
MY PARENTS HAD MANY DEBTS... WHEN THEY COUL NOT REPAY...
OH NO. ALINTA, I HAD NO IDEA.
AFTERWARD, I WAS LEFT FOR DEAD...

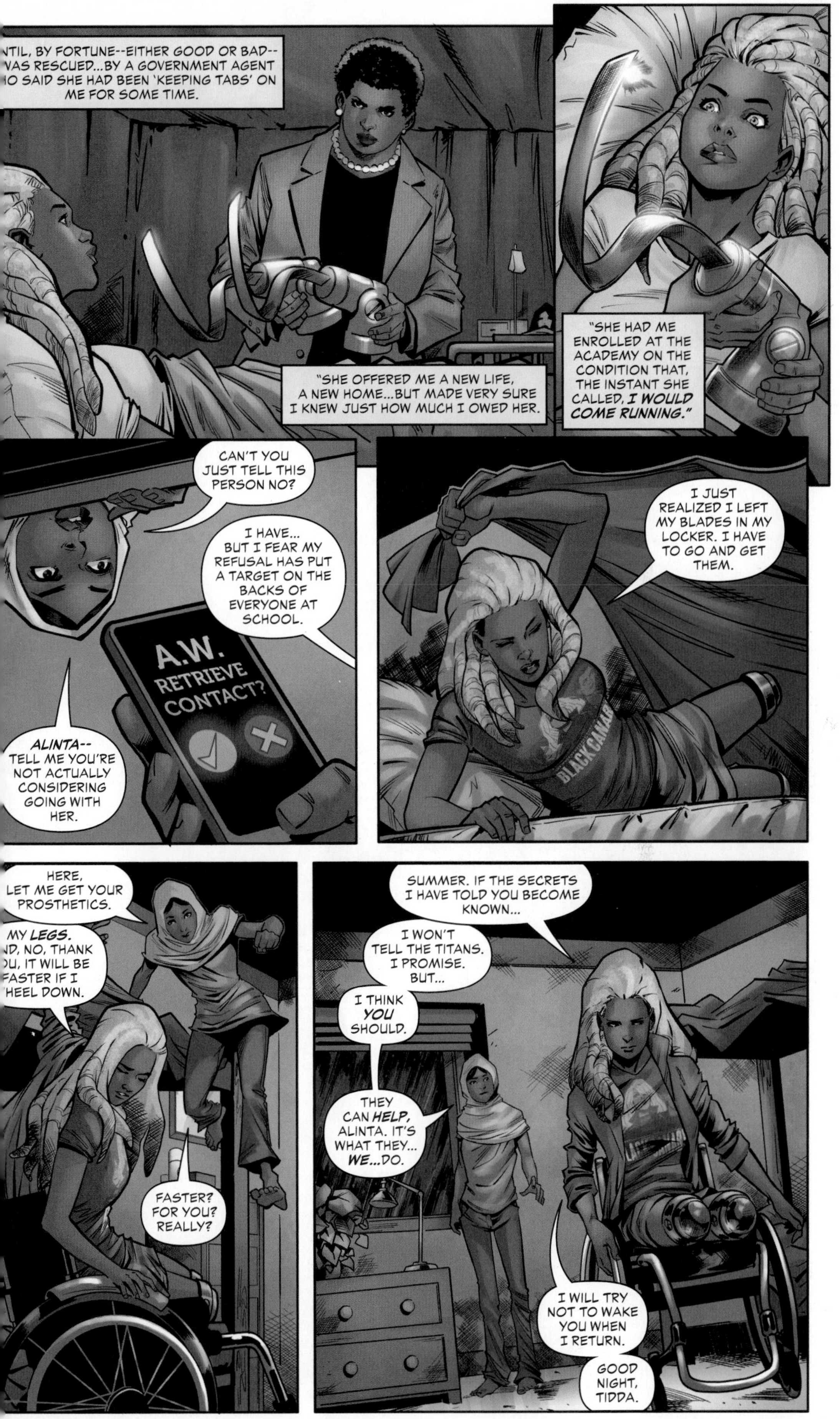
NTIL, BY FORTUNE--EITHER GOOD OR BAD--
VAS RESCUED...BY A GOVERNMENT AGENT
IO SAID SHE HAD BEEN 'KEEPING TABS' ON ME FOR SOME TIME.
"SHE OFFERED ME A NEW LIFE, A NEW HOME...BUT MADE VERY SURE I KNEW JUST HOW MUCH I OWED HER.
"SHE HAD ME ENROLLED AT THE ACADEMY ON THE CONDITION THAT, THE INSTANT SHE CALLED, I WOULD COME RUNNING."
CAN'T YOU JUST TELL THIS PERSON NO?
I HAVE... BUT I FEAR MY REFUSAL HAS PUT A TARGET ON THE BACKS OF EVERYONE AT SCHOOL.
A.W. RETRIEVE CONTACT?
ALINTA-- TELL ME YOU'RE NOT ACTUALLY CONSIDERING GOING WITH HER.
I JUST REALIZED I LEFT MY BLADES IN MY LOCKER. I HAVE TO GO AND GET THEM.
BLACK CANAR
HERE, LET ME GET YOUR PROSTHETICS.
MY LEGS.
ND, NO, THANK
OU, IT WILL BE
FASTER IF I
HEEL DOWN.
FASTER? FOR YOU? REALLY?
SUMMER. IF THE SECRETS I HAVE TOLD YOU BECOME KNOWN...
I WON'T TELL THE TITANS. I PROMISE. BUT...
I THINK YOU SHOULD.
THEY CAN HELP, ALINTA. IT'S WHAT THEY... WE...DO.
I WILL TRY NOT TO WAKE YOU WHEN I RETURN.
GOOD NIGHT, TIDDA.

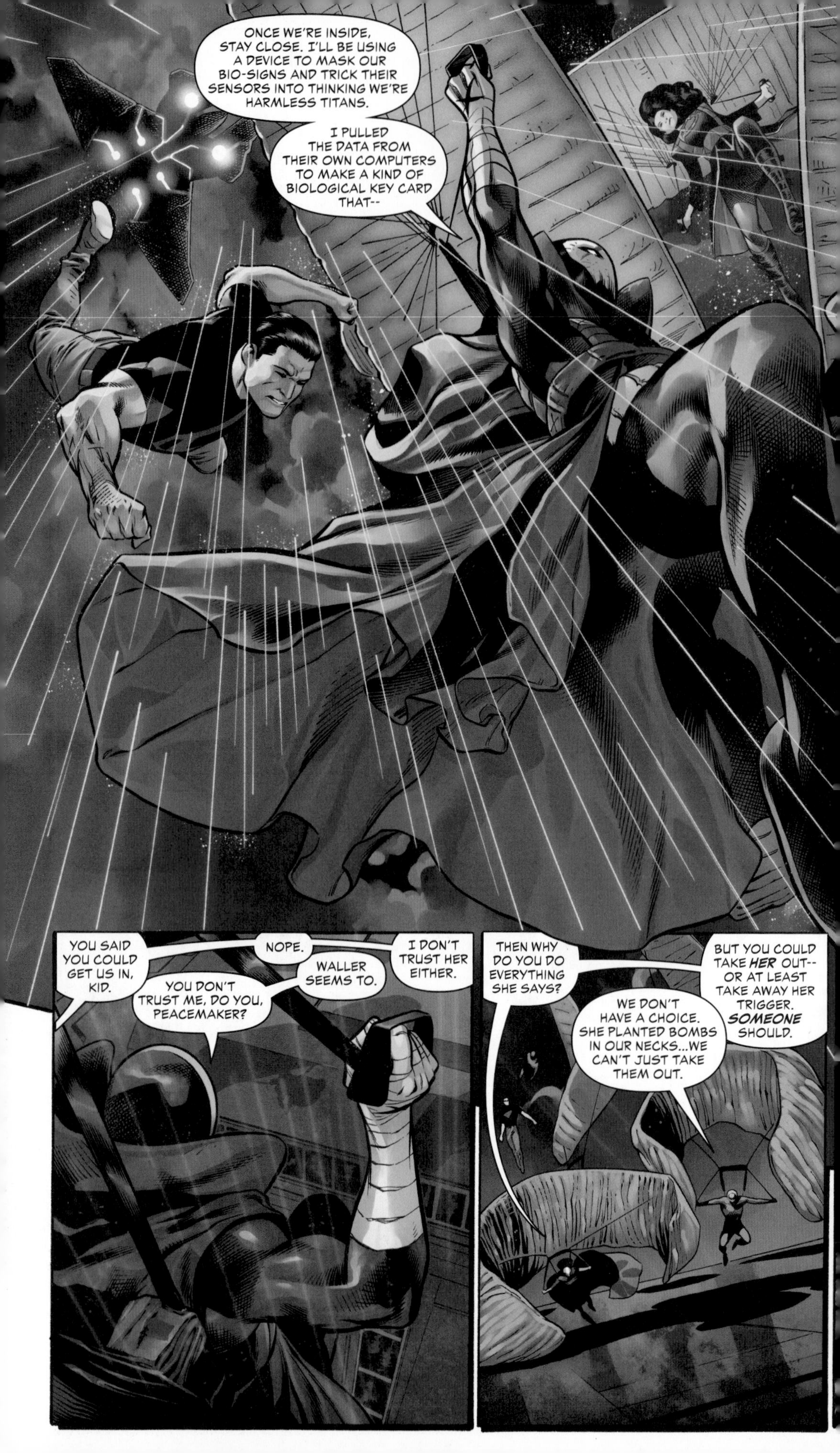
ONCE WE'RE INSIDE, STAY CLOSE. I'LL BE USING A DEVICE TO MASK OUR BIO-SIGNS AND TRICK THEIR SENSORS INTO THINKING WE'RE HARMLESS TITANS.
I PULLED THE DATA FROM THEIR OWN COMPUTERS TO MAKE A KIND OF BIOLOGICAL KEY CARD THAT--
YOU SAID YOU COULD GET US IN, KID.
YOU DON'T TRUST ME, DO YOU, PEACEMAKER?
NOPE.
WALLER SEEMS TO.
I DON'T TRUST HER EITHER.
THEN WHY DO YOU DO EVERYTHING SHE SAYS?
WE DON'T HAVE A CHOICE. SHE PLANTED BOMBS IN OUR NECKS...WE CAN'T JUST TAKE THEM OUT.
BUT YOU COULD TAKE *HER* OUT-- OR AT LEAST TAKE AWAY HER TRIGGER. ***SOMEONE*** SHOULD.

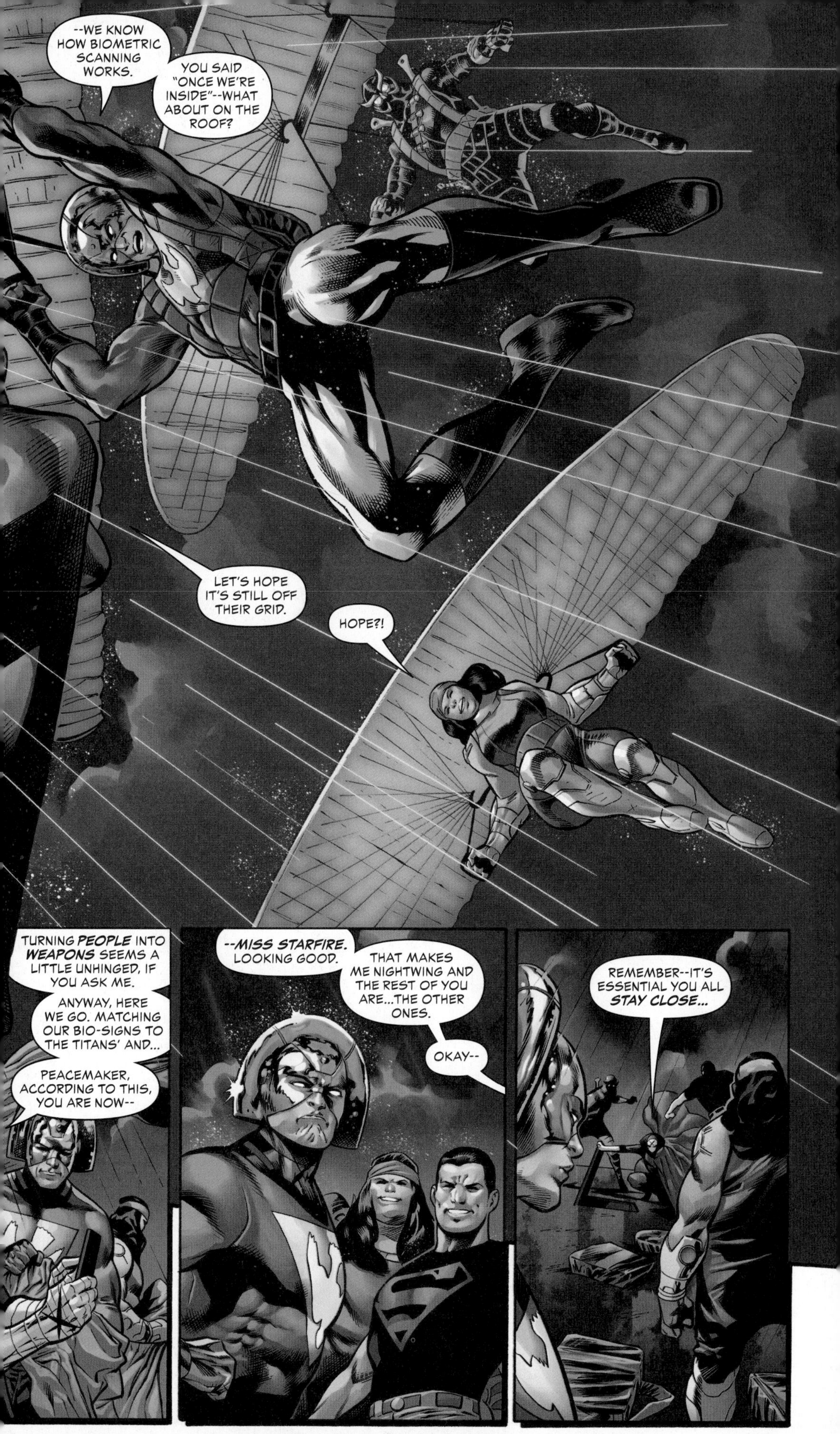
--WE KNOW HOW BIOMETRIC SCANNING WORKS.
YOU SAID "ONCE WE'RE INSIDE"--WHAT ABOUT ON THE ROOF?
LET'S HOPE IT'S STILL OFF THEIR GRID.
HOPE?!
TURNING *PEOPLE* INTO *WEAPONS* SEEMS A LITTLE UNHINGED, IF YOU ASK ME.
ANYWAY, HERE WE GO. MATCHING OUR BIO-SIGNS TO THE TITANS' AND...
PEACEMAKER, ACCORDING TO THIS, YOU ARE NOW--
--*MISS STARFIRE.* LOOKING GOOD.
THAT MAKES ME NIGHTWING AND THE REST OF YOU ARE...THE OTHER ONES.
OKAY--
REMEMBER--IT'S ESSENTIAL YOU ALL *STAY CLOSE...*

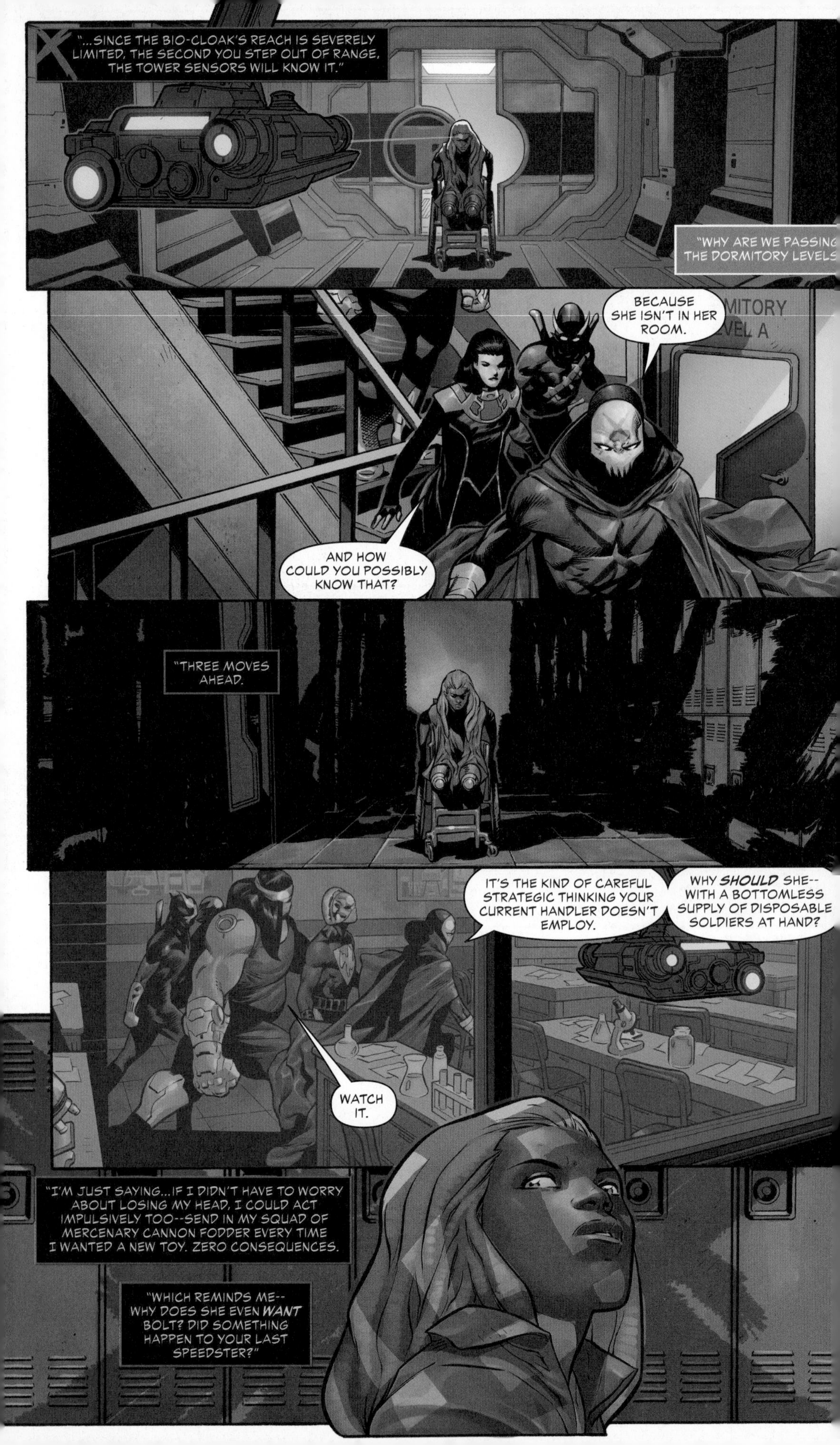
"...SINCE THE BIO-CLOAK'S REACH IS SEVERELY LIMITED, THE SECOND YOU STEP OUT OF RANGE, THE TOWER SENSORS WILL KNOW IT."
"WHY ARE WE PASSING THE DORMITORY LEVELS
BECAUSE SHE ISN'T IN HER ROOM.
AND HOW COULD YOU POSSIBLY KNOW THAT?
"THREE MOVES AHEAD.
IT'S THE KIND OF CAREFUL STRATEGIC THINKING YOUR CURRENT HANDLER DOESN'T EMPLOY.
WHY *SHOULD* SHE--WITH A BOTTOMLESS SUPPLY OF DISPOSABLE SOLDIERS AT HAND?
WATCH IT.
"I'M JUST SAYING...IF I DIDN'T HAVE TO WORRY ABOUT LOSING MY HEAD, I COULD ACT IMPULSIVELY TOO--SEND IN MY SQUAD OF MERCENARY CANNON FODDER EVERY TIME I WANTED A NEW TOY. ZERO CONSEQUENCES.
"WHICH REMINDS ME--WHY DOES SHE EVEN *WANT* BOLT? DID SOMETHING HAPPEN TO YOUR LAST SPEEDSTER?"

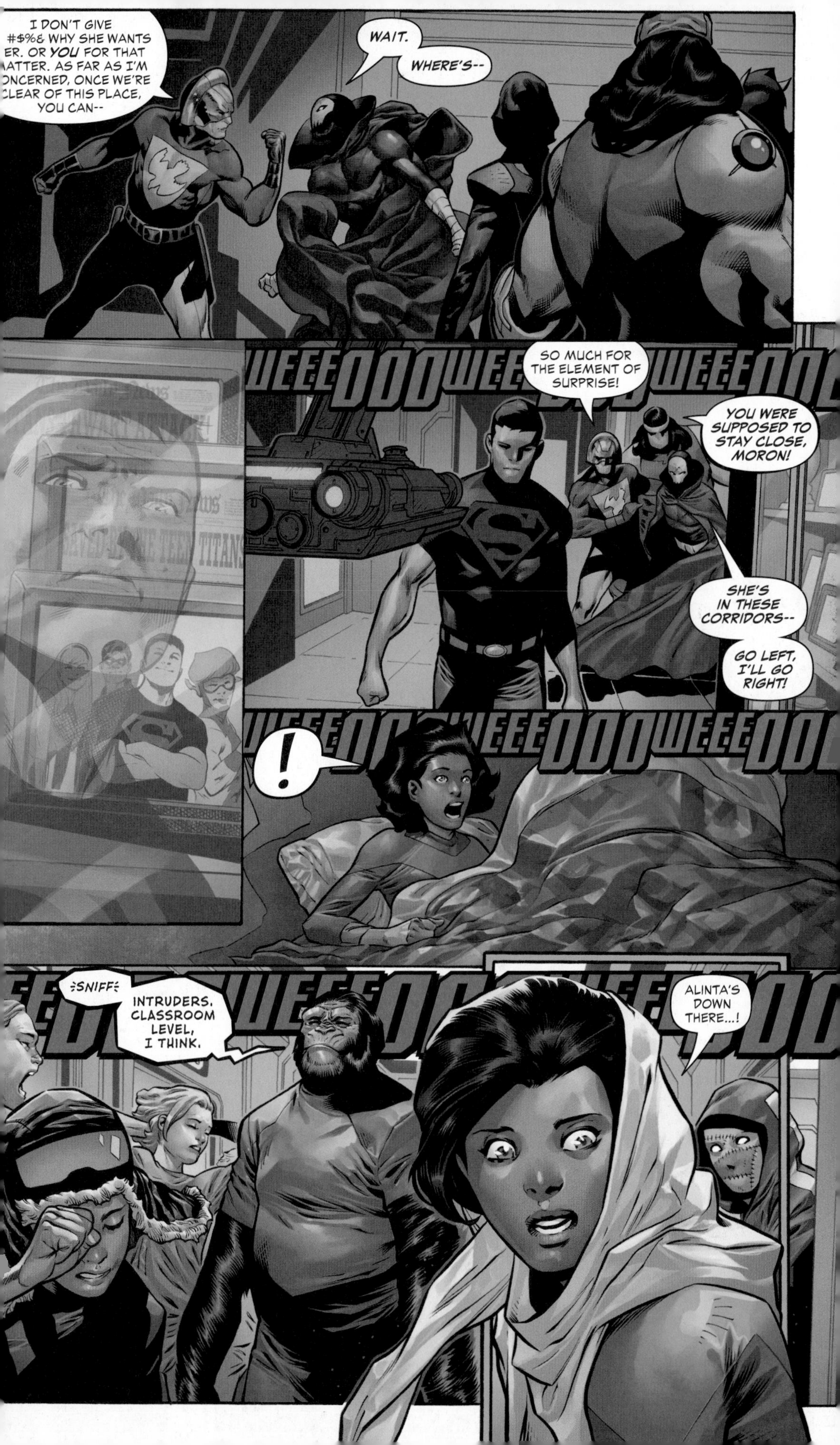
I DON'T GIVE #$%& WHY SHE WANTS ER. OR YOU FOR THAT ATTER. AS FAR AS I'M ONCERNED, ONCE WE'RE CLEAR OF THIS PLACE, YOU CAN--
WAIT.
WHERE'S--
WEEEOOOWEEEOOOWEEEOOOWEEEOOO
SO MUCH FOR THE ELEMENT OF SURPRISE!
YOU WERE SUPPOSED TO STAY CLOSE, MORON!
SHE'S IN THESE CORRIDORS--
GO LEFT, I'LL GO RIGHT!
SAVED BY THE TEEN TITANS
!
SNIFF
INTRUDERS. CLASSROOM LEVEL, I THINK.
ALINTA'S DOWN THERE...!

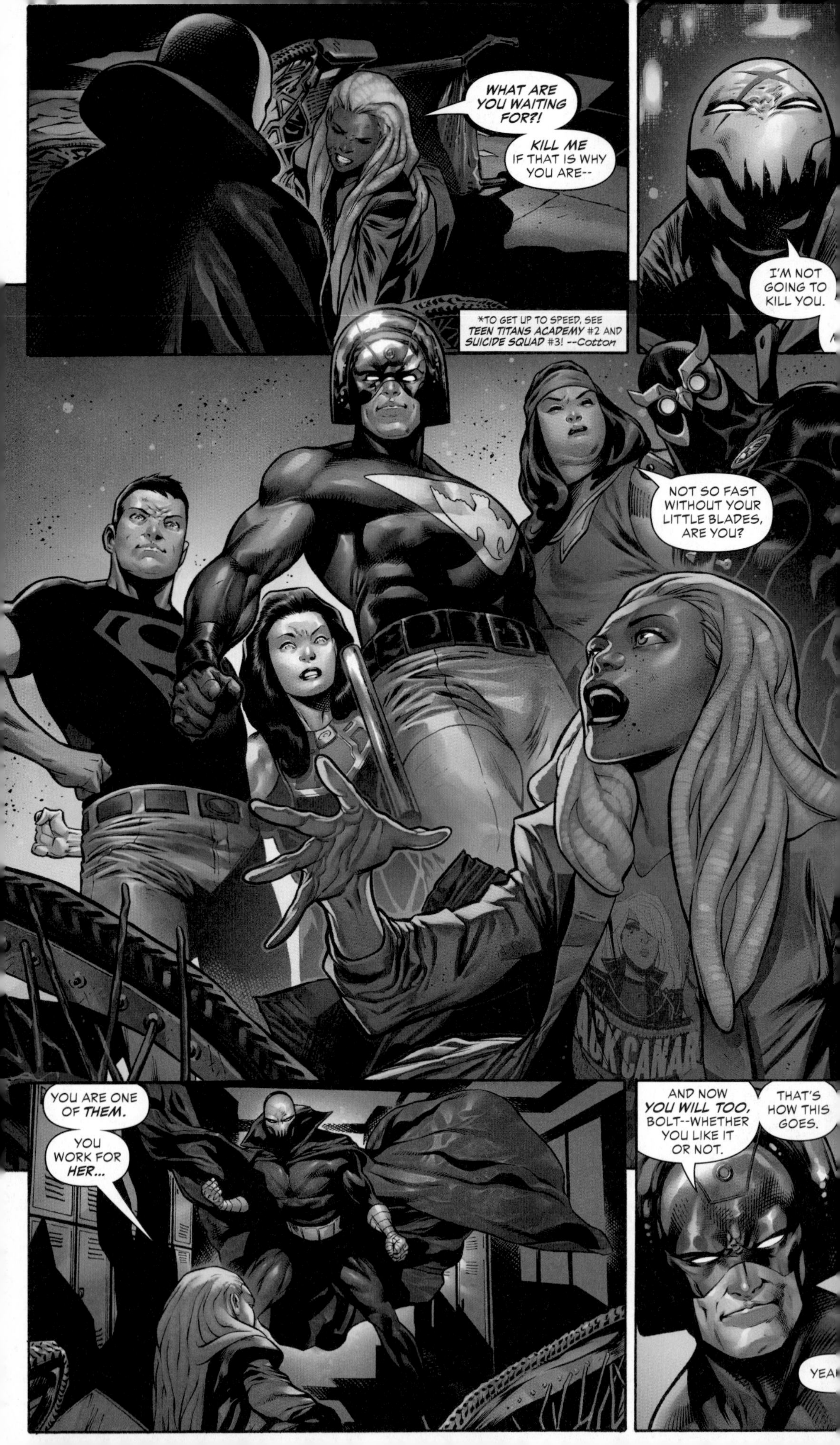
WHAT ARE YOU WAITING FOR?!
KILL ME IF THAT IS WHY YOU ARE--
I'M NOT GOING TO KILL YOU.
*TO GET UP TO SPEED, SEE TEEN TITANS ACADEMY #2 AND SUICIDE SQUAD #3! --Cotton
NOT SO FAST WITHOUT YOUR LITTLE BLADES, ARE YOU?
YOU ARE ONE OF THEM.
YOU WORK FOR HER...
AND NOW YOU WILL TOO, BOLT--WHETHER YOU LIKE IT OR NOT.
THAT'S HOW THIS GOES.

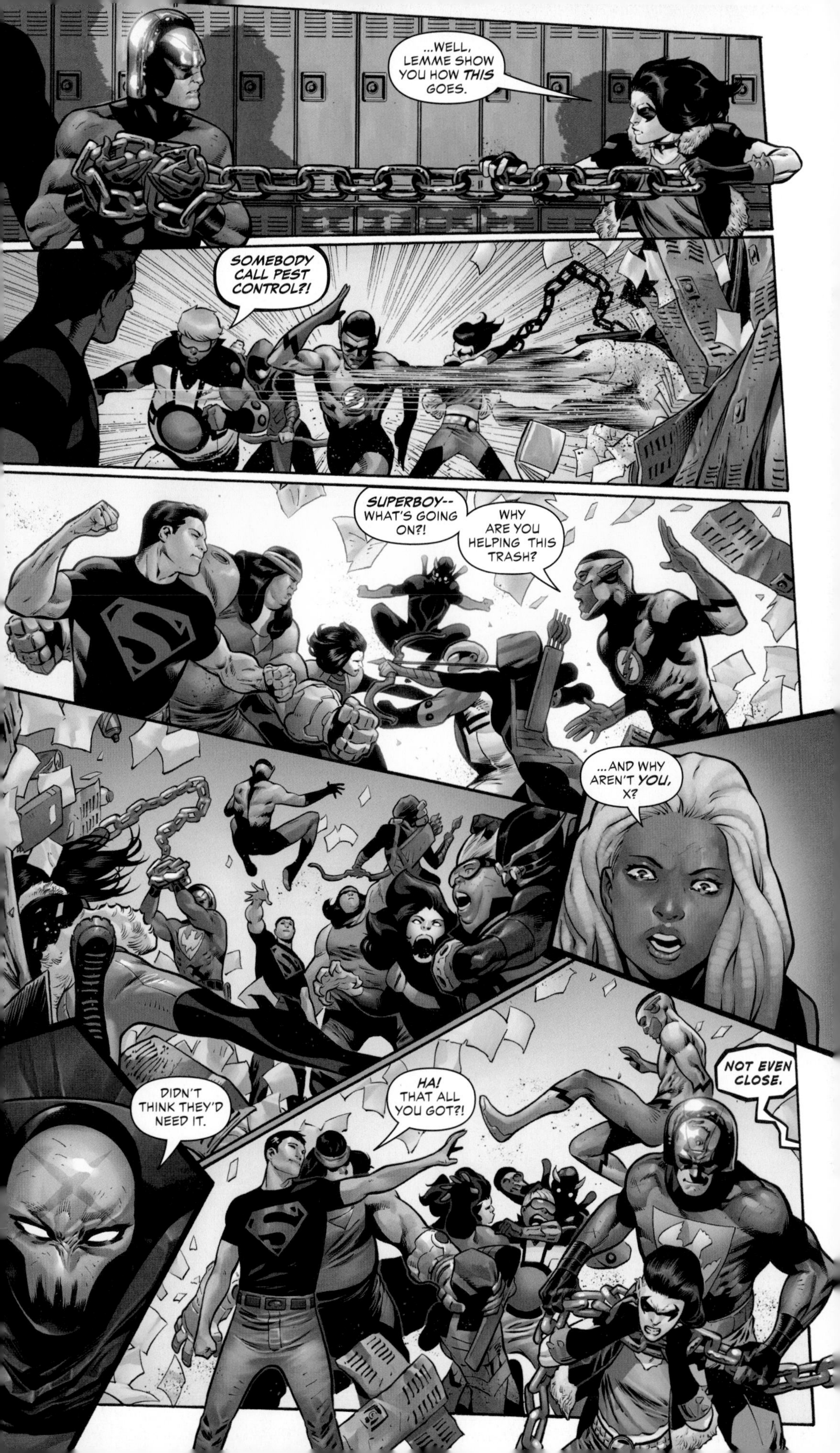
...WELL, LEMME SHOW YOU HOW THIS GOES.
SOMEBODY CALL PEST CONTROL?!
SUPERBOY-- WHAT'S GOING ON?!
WHY ARE YOU HELPING THIS TRASH?
...AND WHY AREN'T YOU, X?
DIDN'T THINK THEY'D NEED IT.
HA! THAT ALL YOU GOT?!
NOT EVEN CLOSE.

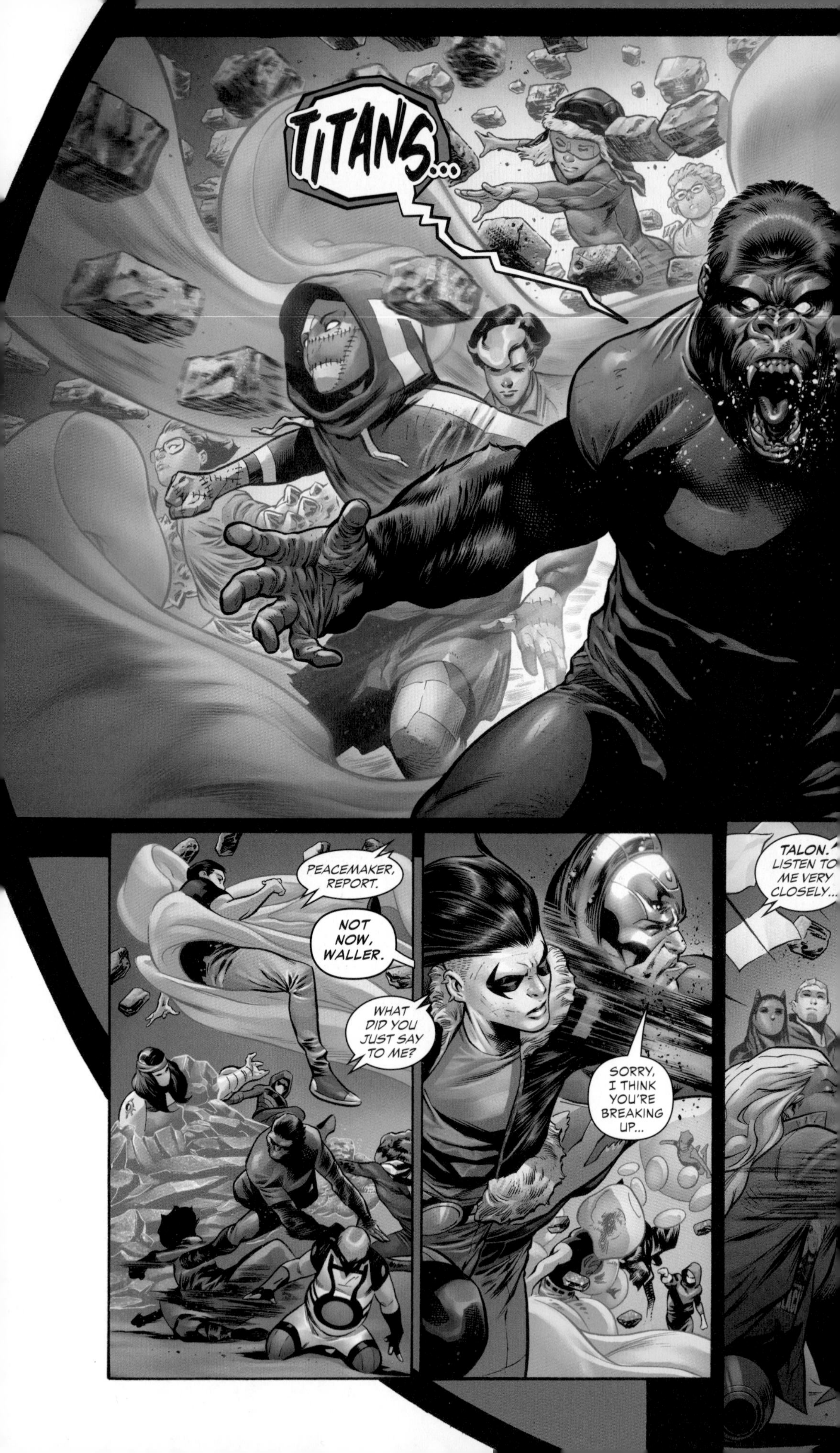
TITANS...
PEACEMAKER, REPORT.
NOT NOW, WALLER.
WHAT DID YOU JUST SAY TO ME?
SORRY, I THINK YOU'RE BREAKING UP...
TALON. LISTEN TO ME VERY CLOSELY...

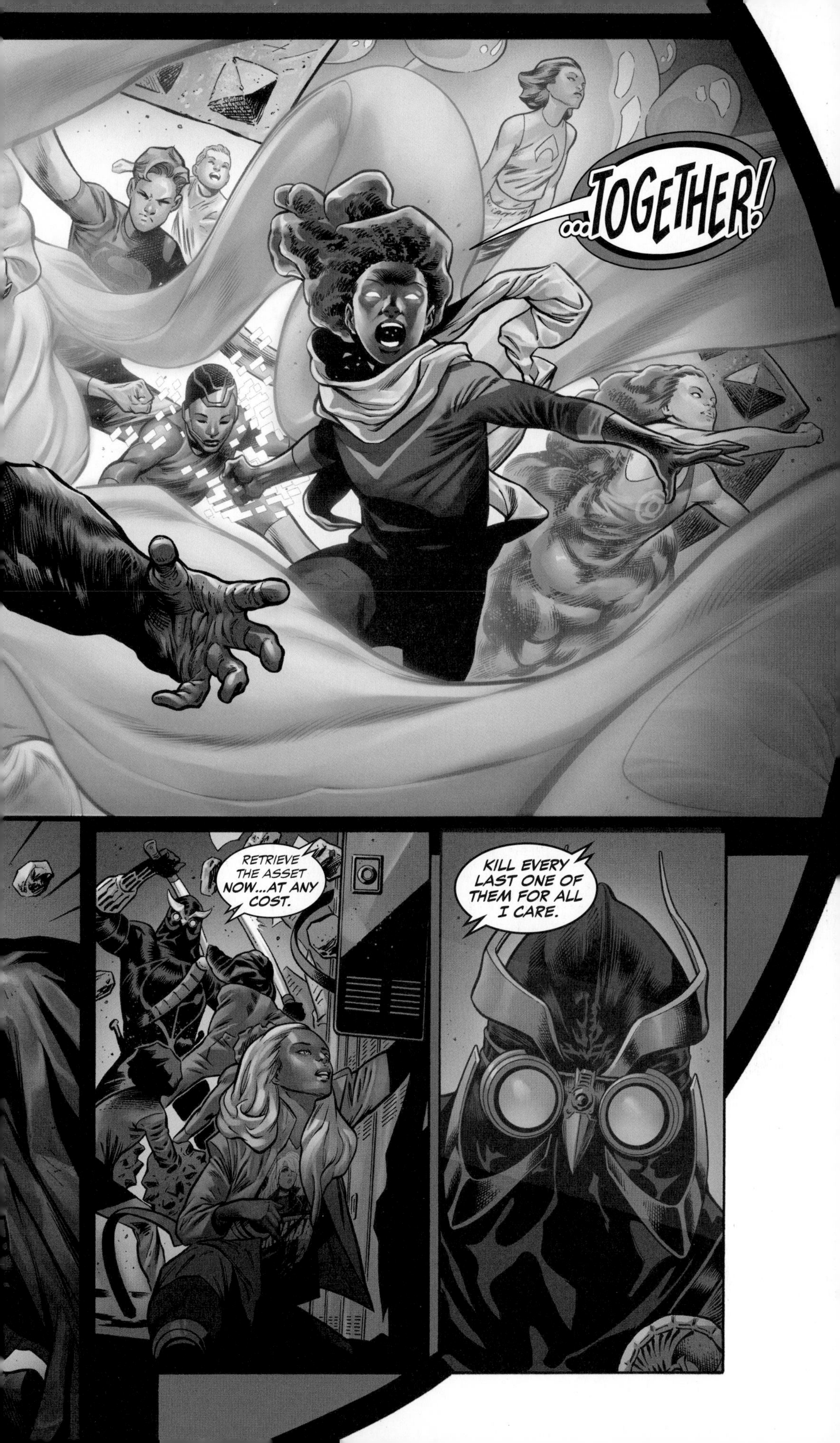
...TOGETHER!
RETRIEVE THE ASSET NOW...AT ANY COST.
KILL EVERY LAST ONE OF THEM FOR ALL I CARE.

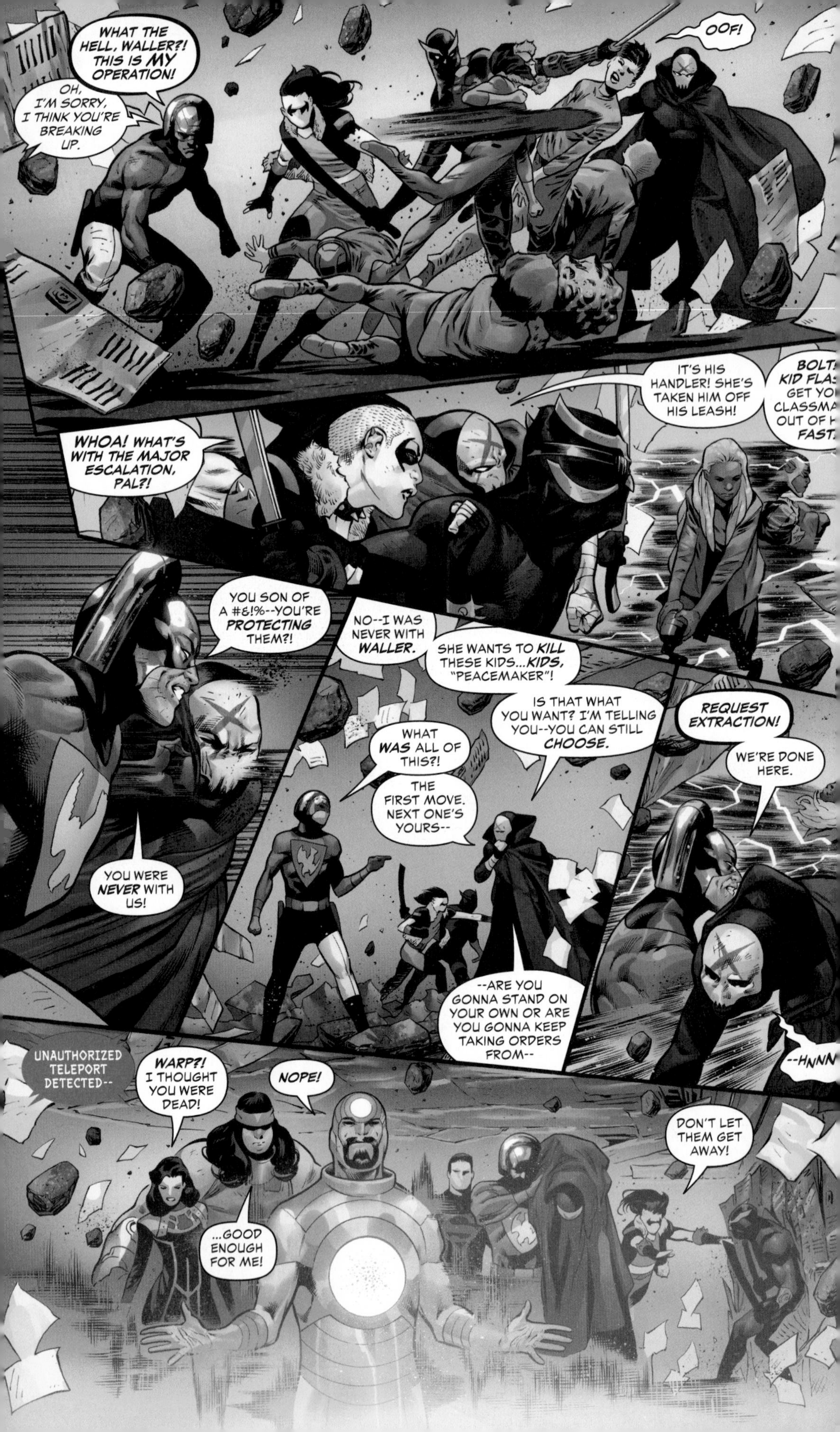
WHAT THE HELL, WALLER?! THIS IS MY OPERATION!
OH, I'M SORRY, I THINK YOU'RE BREAKING UP.
OOF!
WHOA! WHAT'S WITH THE MAJOR ESCALATION, PAL?!
IT'S HIS HANDLER! SHE'S TAKEN HIM OFF HIS LEASH!
BOLT! KID FLAS GET YO CLASSMA OUT OF H FAST!
YOU SON OF A #&!%--YOU'RE PROTECTING THEM?!
YOU WERE NEVER WITH US!
NO--I WAS NEVER WITH WALLER.
SHE WANTS TO KILL THESE KIDS...KIDS, "PEACEMAKER"!
IS THAT WHAT YOU WANT? I'M TELLING YOU--YOU CAN STILL CHOOSE.
WHAT WAS ALL OF THIS?!
THE FIRST MOVE. NEXT ONE'S YOURS--
--ARE YOU GONNA STAND ON YOUR OWN OR ARE YOU GONNA KEEP TAKING ORDERS FROM--
REQUEST EXTRACTION!
WE'RE DONE HERE.
--HNNN
UNAUTHORIZED TELEPORT DETECTED--
WARP?! I THOUGHT YOU WERE DEAD!
NOPE!
...GOOD ENOUGH FOR ME!
DON'T LET THEM GET AWAY!

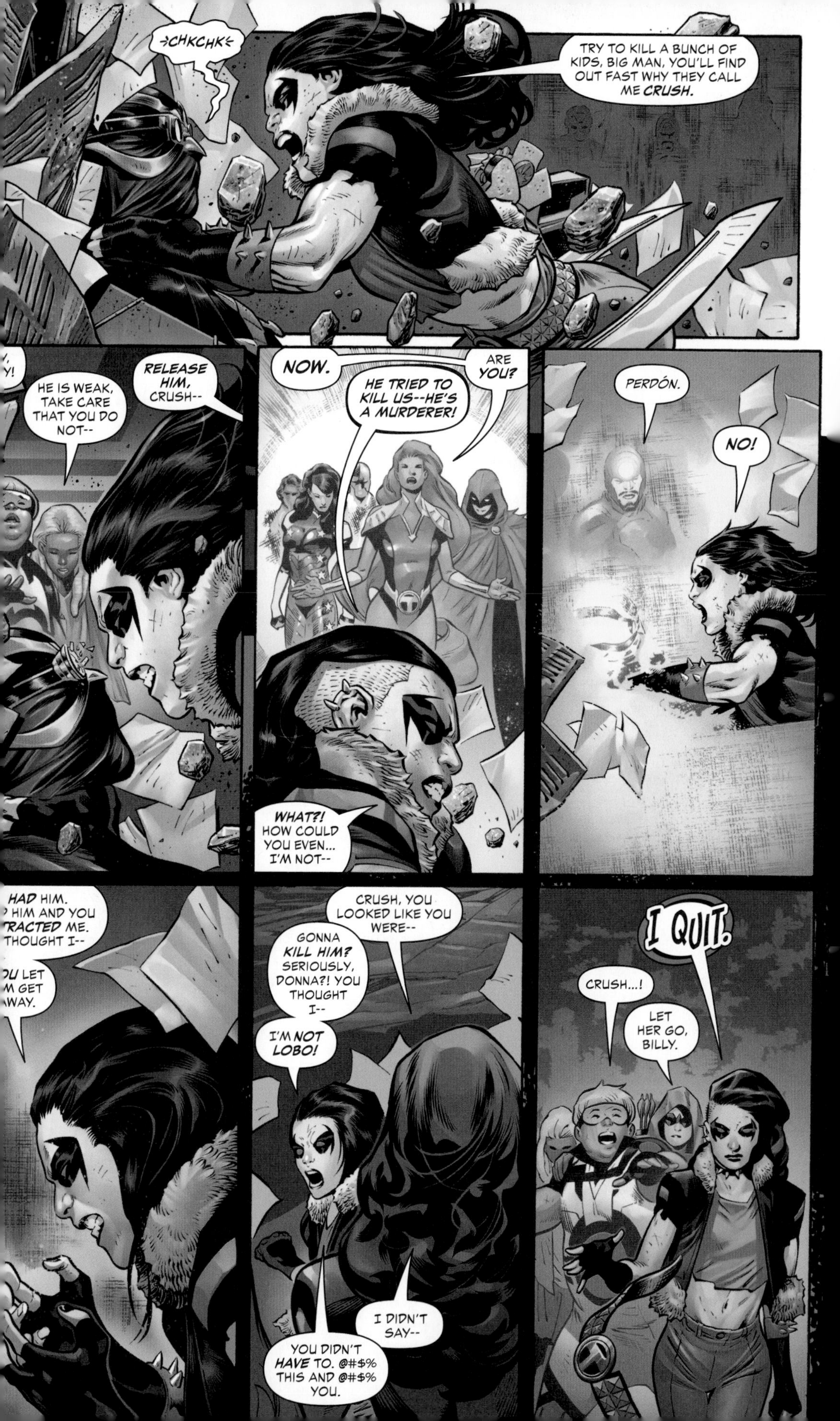

CHKCHK
TRY TO KILL A BUNCH OF KIDS, BIG MAN, YOU'LL FIND OUT FAST WHY THEY CALL ME CRUSH.
HE IS WEAK, TAKE CARE THAT YOU DO NOT--
RELEASE HIM, CRUSH--
NOW.
ARE YOU?
HE TRIED TO KILL US--HE'S A MURDERER!
WHAT?! HOW COULD YOU EVEN... I'M NOT--
PERDÓN.
NO!
HAD HIM.
HIM AND YOU
TRACTED ME.
THOUGHT I--
LET
GET
AWAY.
CRUSH, YOU LOOKED LIKE YOU WERE--
GONNA KILL HIM? SERIOUSLY, DONNA?! YOU THOUGHT I--
I'M NOT LOBO!
I DIDN'T SAY--
YOU DIDN'T HAVE TO. @#$% THIS AND @#$% YOU.
I QUIT.
CRUSH...!
LET HER GO, BILLY.

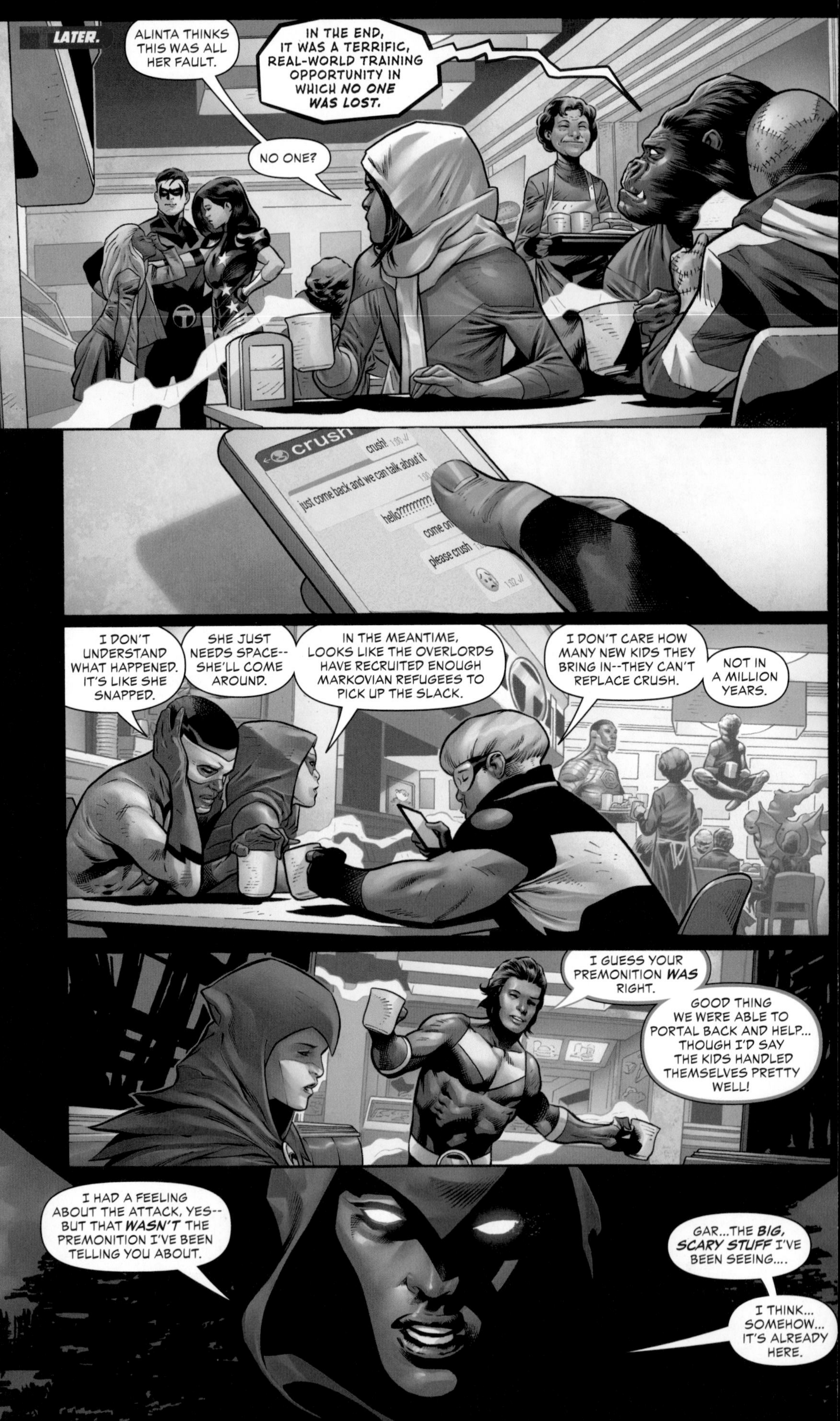

LATER.
ALINTA THINKS THIS WAS ALL HER FAULT.
IN THE END, IT WAS A TERRIFIC, REAL-WORLD TRAINING OPPORTUNITY IN WHICH NO ONE WAS LOST.
NO ONE?
crush
crush!
just come back and we can talk about it
hello??????????
come on
please crush
I DON'T UNDERSTAND WHAT HAPPENED. IT'S LIKE SHE SNAPPED.
SHE JUST NEEDS SPACE--SHE'LL COME AROUND.
IN THE MEANTIME, LOOKS LIKE THE OVERLORDS HAVE RECRUITED ENOUGH MARKOVIAN REFUGEES TO PICK UP THE SLACK.
I DON'T CARE HOW MANY NEW KIDS THEY BRING IN--THEY CAN'T REPLACE CRUSH.
NOT IN A MILLION YEARS.
I GUESS YOUR PREMONITION WAS RIGHT.
GOOD THING WE WERE ABLE TO PORTAL BACK AND HELP... THOUGH I'D SAY THE KIDS HANDLED THEMSELVES PRETTY WELL!
I HAD A FEELING ABOUT THE ATTACK, YES--BUT THAT WASN'T THE PREMONITION I'VE BEEN TELLING YOU ABOUT.
GAR...THE BIG, SCARY STUFF I'VE BEEN SEEING....
I THINK... SOMEHOW... IT'S ALREADY HERE.

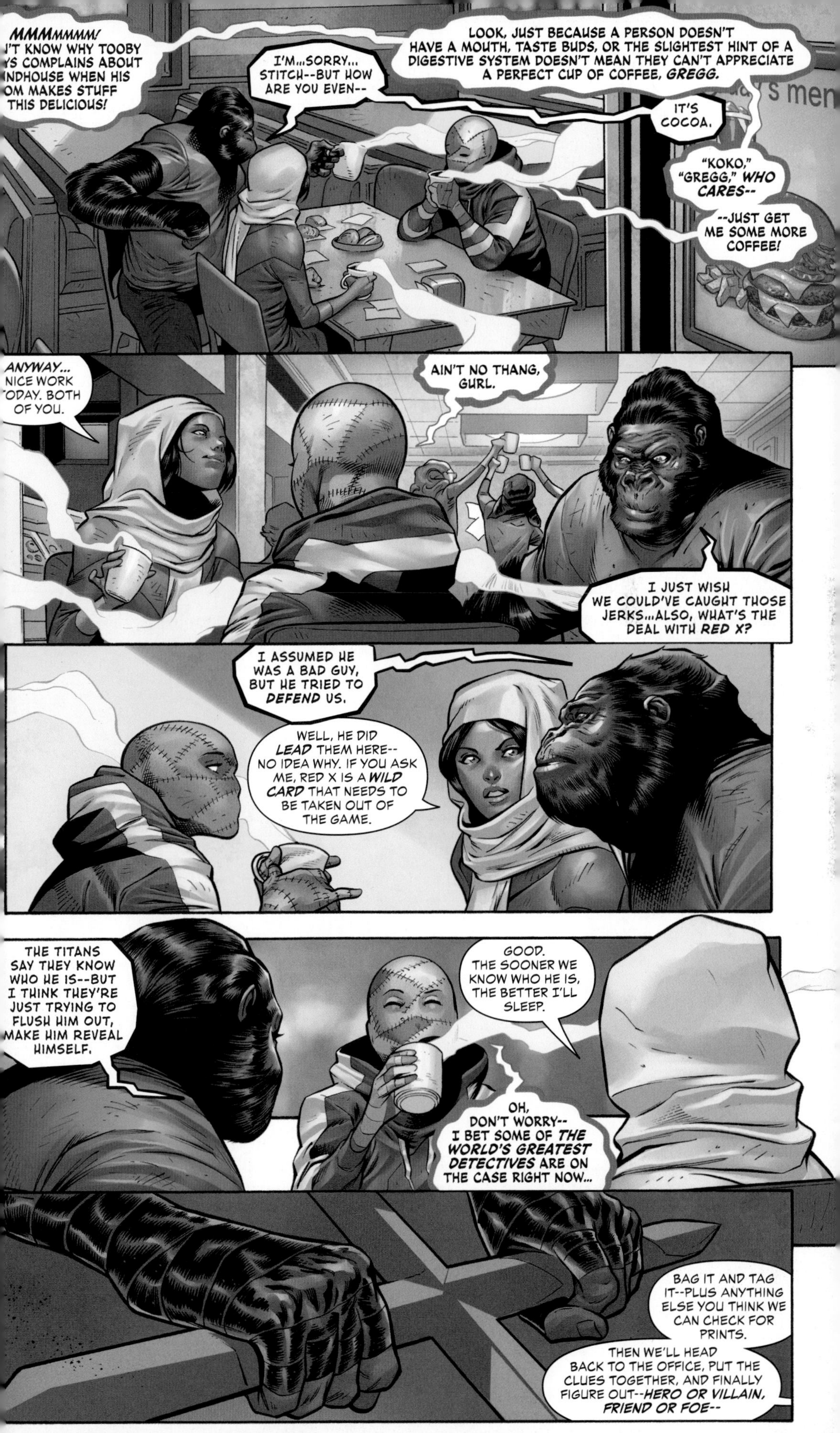
MMMMMMM! I'T KNOW WHY TOOBY YS COMPLAINS ABOUT NDHOUSE WHEN HIS OM MAKES STUFF THIS DELICIOUS!
I'M...SORRY... STITCH--BUT HOW ARE YOU EVEN--
LOOK, JUST BECAUSE A PERSON DOESN'T HAVE A MOUTH, TASTE BUDS, OR THE SLIGHTEST HINT OF A DIGESTIVE SYSTEM DOESN'T MEAN THEY CAN'T APPRECIATE A PERFECT CUP OF COFFEE, GREGG.
IT'S COCOA.
"KOKO," "GREGG," WHO CARES--
--JUST GET ME SOME MORE COFFEE!
ANYWAY... NICE WORK TODAY. BOTH OF YOU.
AIN'T NO THANG, GURL.
I JUST WISH WE COULD'VE CAUGHT THOSE JERKS...ALSO, WHAT'S THE DEAL WITH RED X?
I ASSUMED HE WAS A BAD GUY, BUT HE TRIED TO DEFEND US.
WELL, HE DID LEAD THEM HERE-- NO IDEA WHY. IF YOU ASK ME, RED X IS A WILD CARD THAT NEEDS TO BE TAKEN OUT OF THE GAME.
THE TITANS SAY THEY KNOW WHO HE IS--BUT I THINK THEY'RE JUST TRYING TO FLUSH HIM OUT, MAKE HIM REVEAL HIMSELF.
GOOD. THE SOONER WE KNOW WHO HE IS, THE BETTER I'LL SLEEP.
OH, DON'T WORRY-- I BET SOME OF THE WORLD'S GREATEST DETECTIVES ARE ON THE CASE RIGHT NOW...
BAG IT AND TAG IT--PLUS ANYTHING ELSE YOU THINK WE CAN CHECK FOR PRINTS.
THEN WE'LL HEAD BACK TO THE OFFICE, PUT THE CLUES TOGETHER, AND FINALLY FIGURE OUT--HERO OR VILLAIN, FRIEND OR FOE--

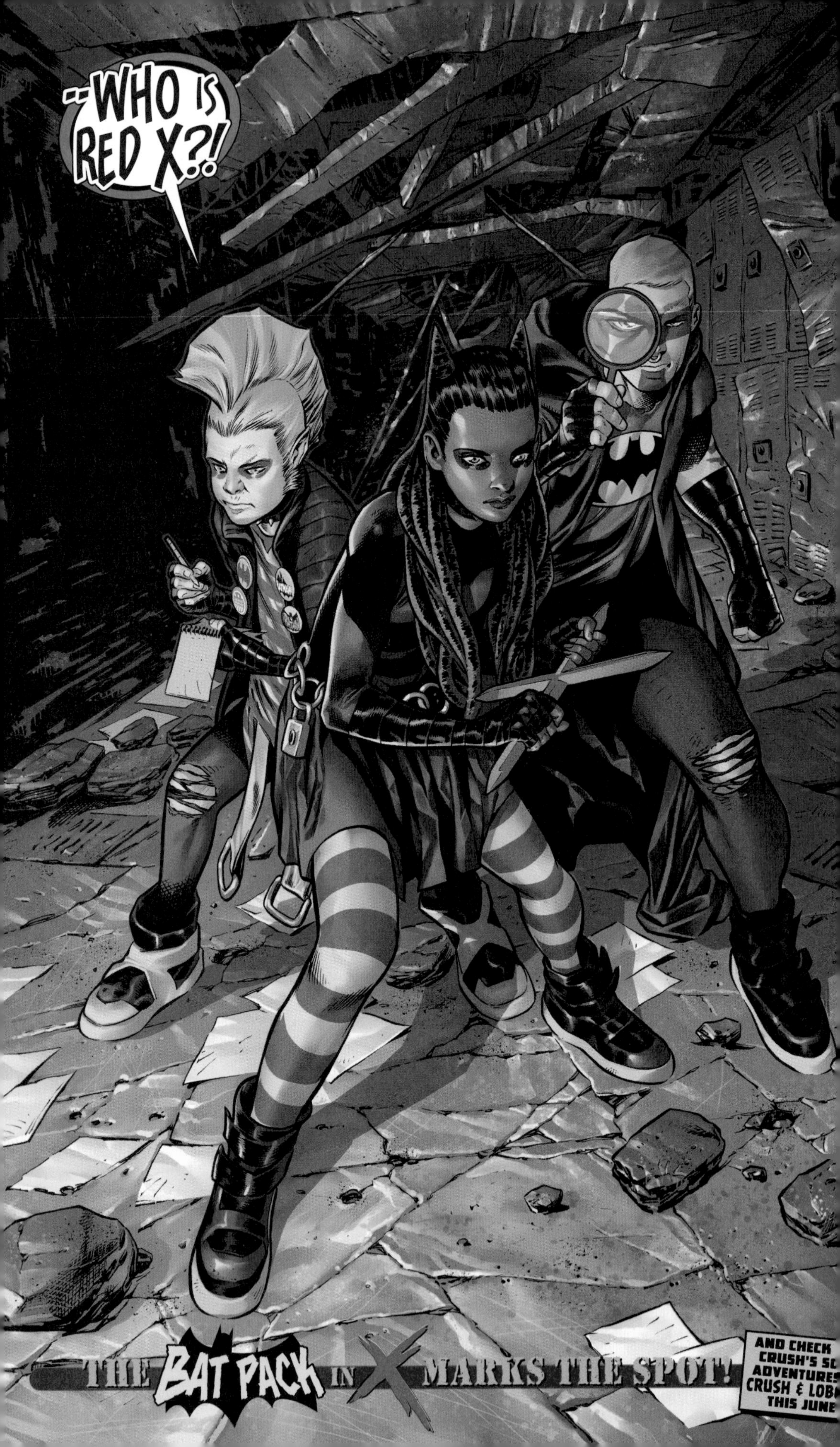
--WHO IS RED X?!
THE BAT PACK IN X MARKS THE SPOT!
AND CHECK
CRUSH'S SC
ADVENTURES
CRUSH & LOB
THIS JUNE

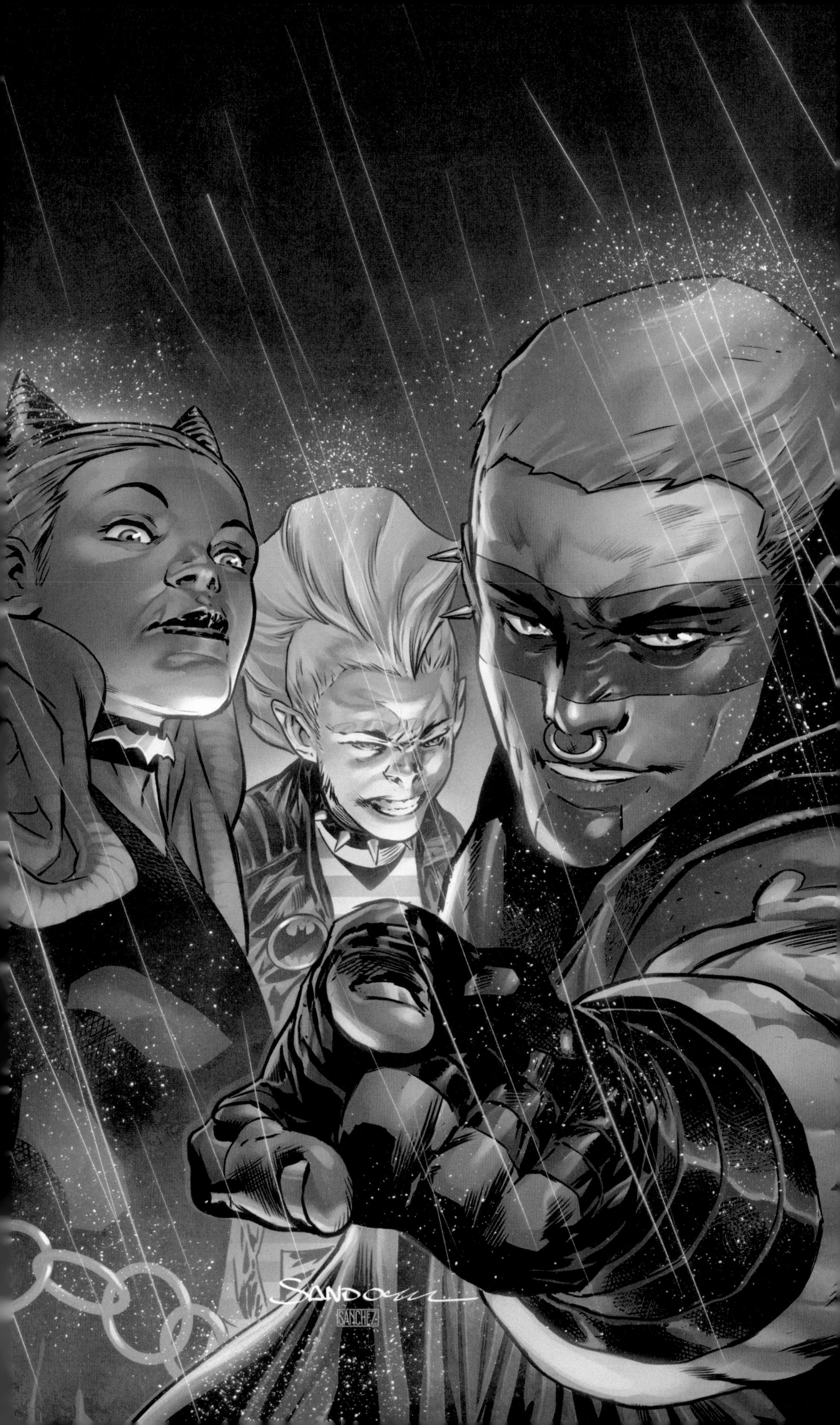
SANCHEZ

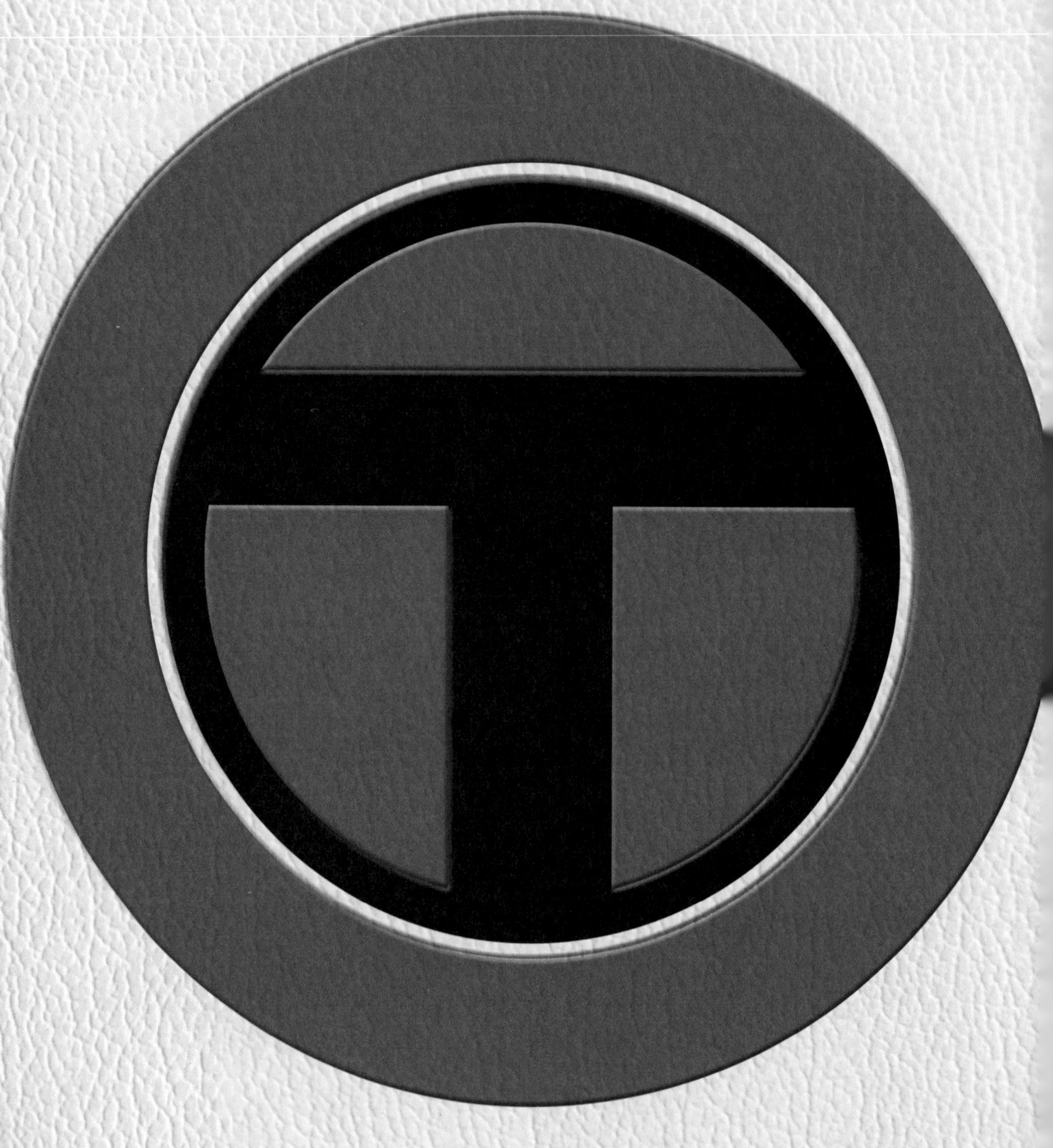

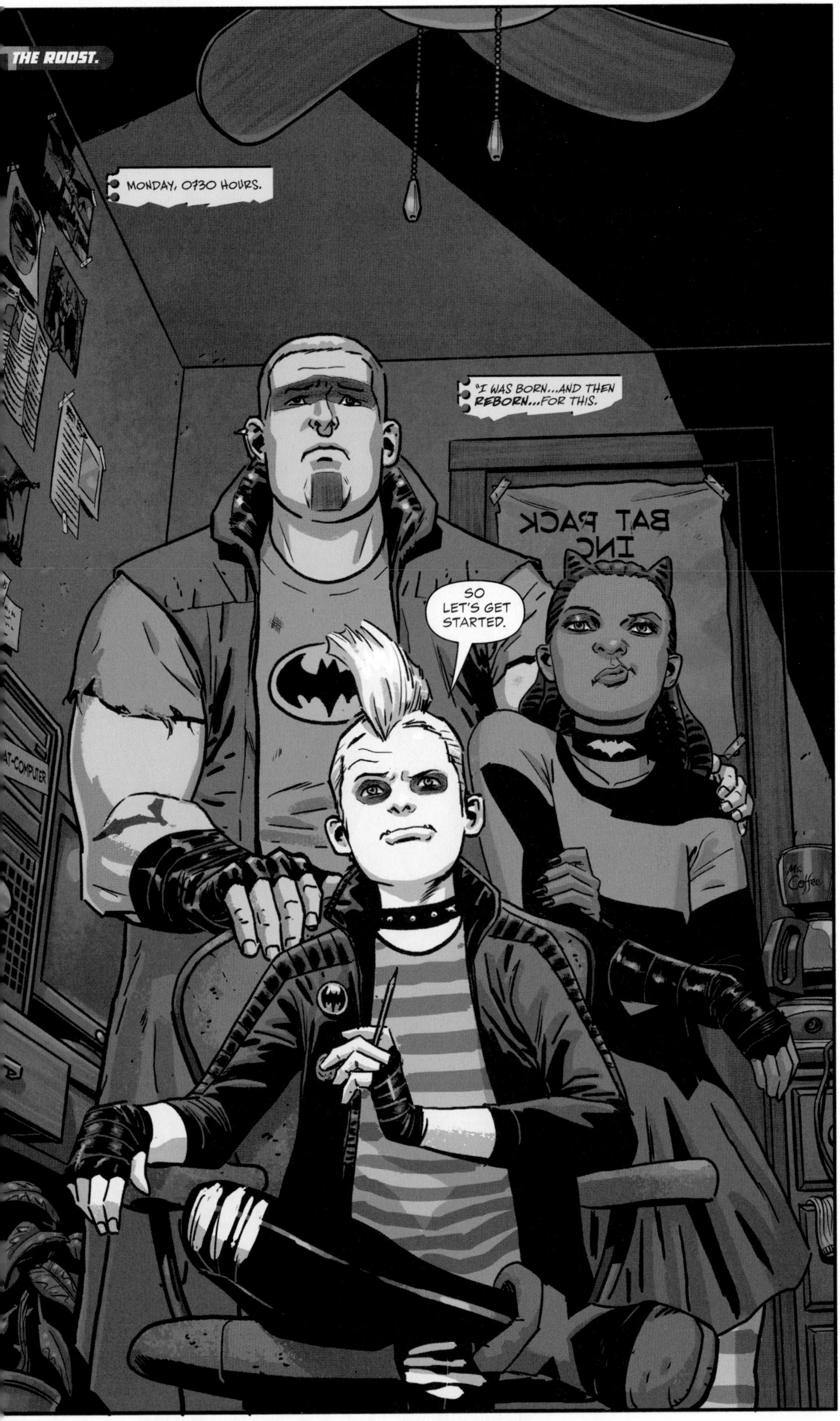
THE ROOST.
MONDAY, 0730 HOURS.
"I WAS BORN...AND THEN REBORN...FOR THIS.
BAT PACK INC
SO LET'S GET STARTED.
BAT-COMPUTER
Ms. Coffee

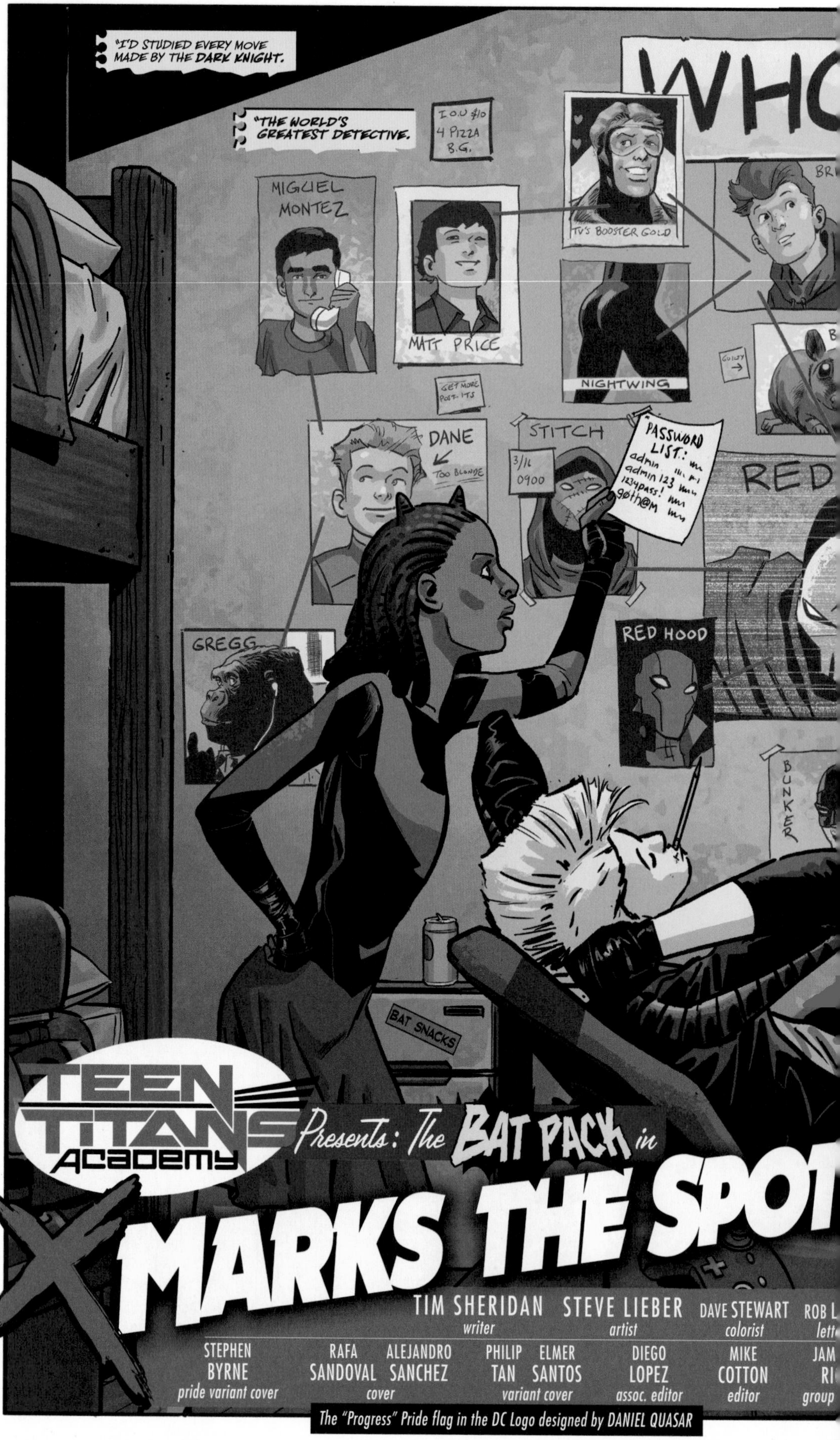

"I'D STUDIED EVERY MOVE MADE BY THE DARK KNIGHT.
"THE WORLD'S GREATEST DETECTIVE.
I.O.U $10 4 PIZZA B.G.
MIGUEL MONTEZ
MATT PRICE
TV'S BOOSTER GOLD
NIGHTWING
GET MORE POST-ITS
GUILTY →
DANE
TOO BLONDE
STITCH
3/16 0900
PASSWORD LIST: admin admin 123 1234pass! gøth@M
GREGG
RED HOOD
BUNKER
BAT SNACKS
TEEN TITANS ACADEMY Presents: The BAT PACK in
X MARKS THE SPOT
TIM SHERIDAN writer
STEVE LIEBER artist
DAVE STEWART colorist
STEPHEN BYRNE pride variant cover
RAFA SANDOVAL ALEJANDRO SANCHEZ cover
PHILIP TAN ELMER SANTOS variant cover
DIEGO LOPEZ assoc. editor
MIKE COTTON editor
The "Progress" Pride flag in the DC Logo designed by DANIEL QUASAR

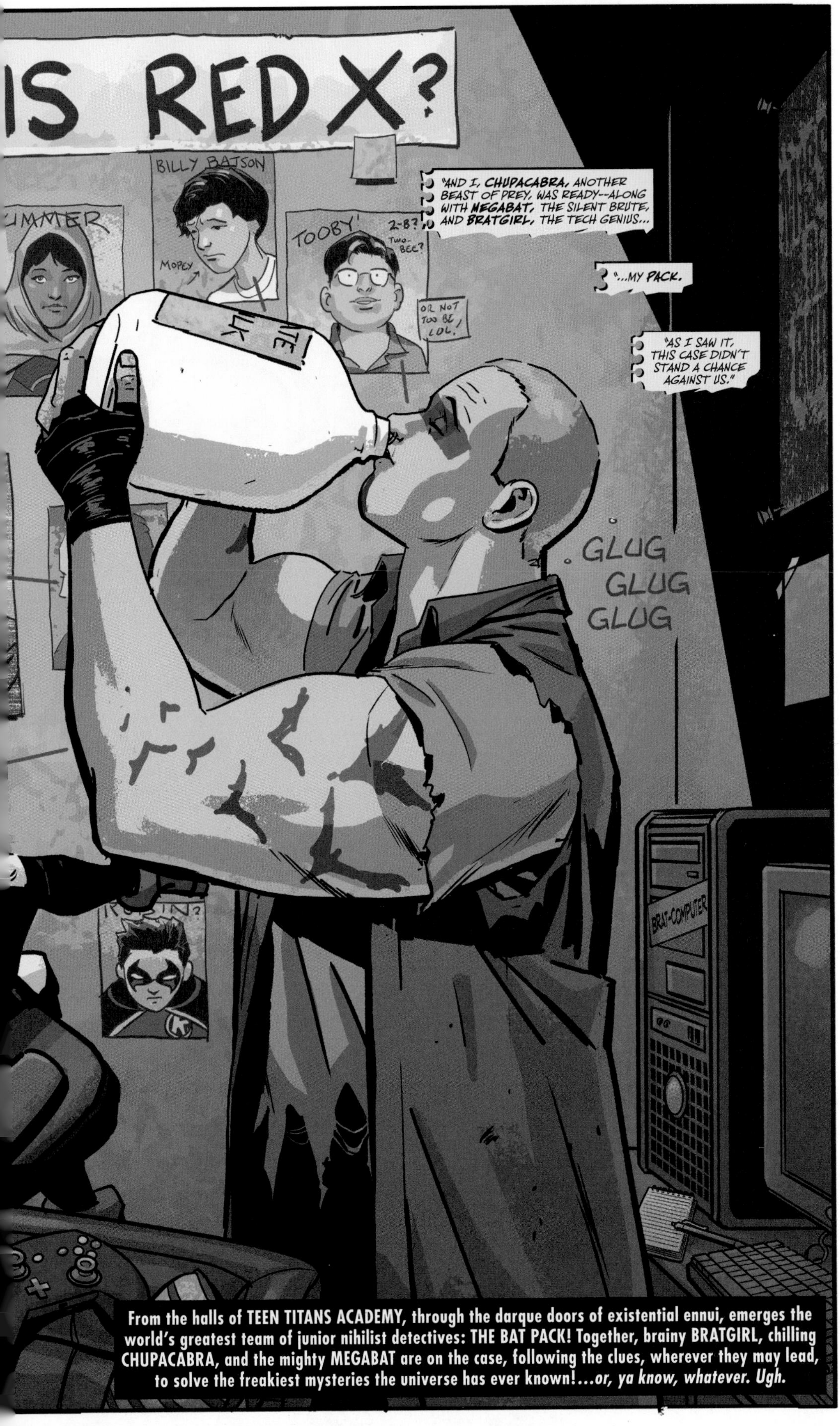
IS RED X?
BILLY BATSON
MOPEY
UMMER
TOOBY!
2-B?
TWO-BEE?
OR NOT TOO BE, LOL!
"AND I, CHUPACABRA, ANOTHER BEAST OF PREY, WAS READY--ALONG WITH MEGABAT, THE SILENT BRUTE, AND BRATGIRL, THE TECH GENIUS...
"...MY PACK.
"AS I SAW IT, THIS CASE DIDN'T STAND A CHANCE AGAINST US."
GLUG GLUG GLUG
BRAT-COMPUTER
From the halls of TEEN TITANS ACADEMY, through the darque doors of existential ennui, emerges the world's greatest team of junior nihilist detectives: THE BAT PACK! Together, brainy BRATGIRL, chilling CHUPACABRA, and the mighty MEGABAT are on the case, following the clues, wherever they may lead, to solve the freakiest mysteries the universe has ever known!...or, ya know, whatever. Ugh.

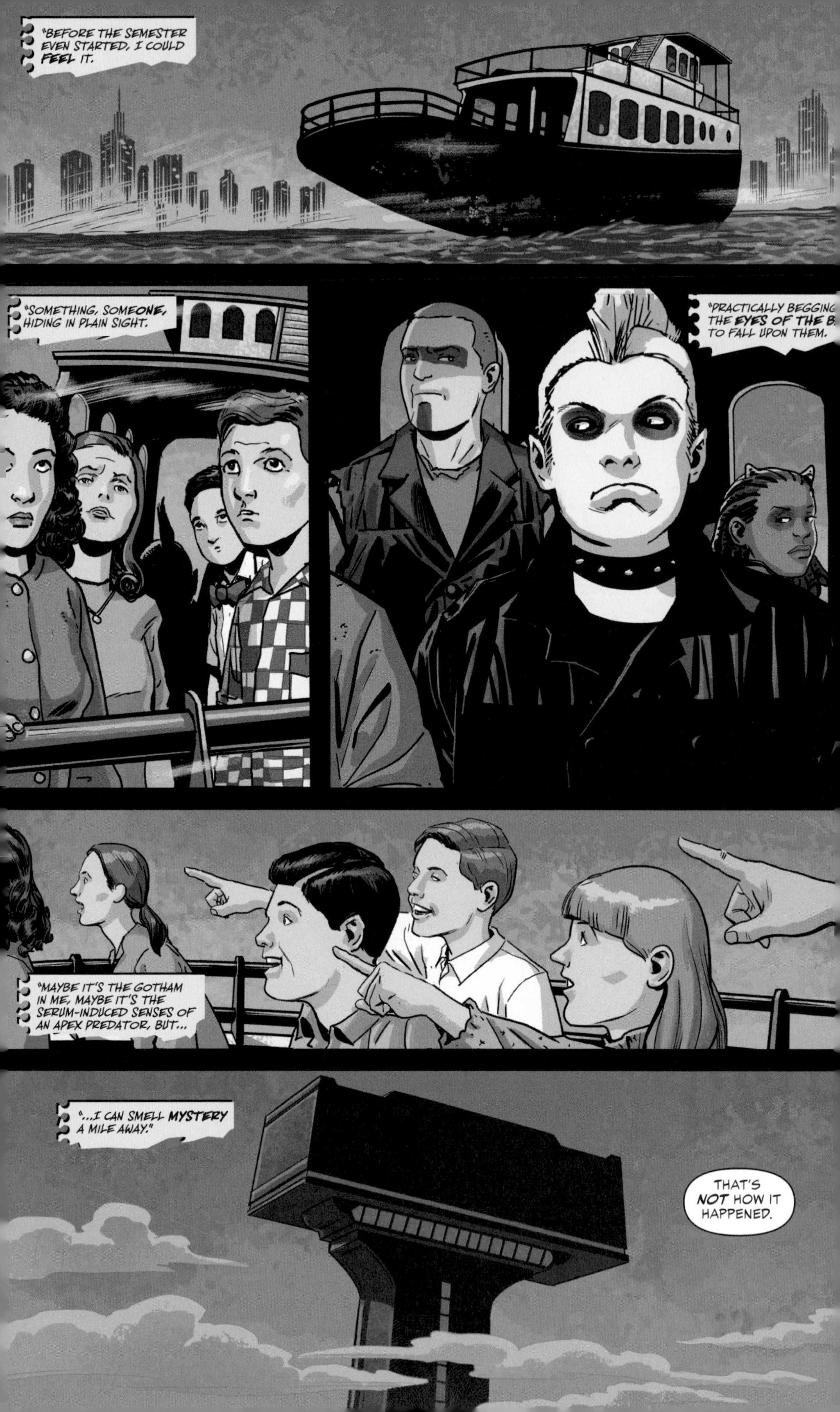
"BEFORE THE SEMESTER EVEN STARTED, I COULD FEEL IT.
"SOMETHING, SOMEONE, HIDING IN PLAIN SIGHT.
"PRACTICALLY BEGGING THE EYES OF THE B
TO FALL UPON THEM.
"MAYBE IT'S THE GOTHAM IN ME, MAYBE IT'S THE SERUM-INDUCED SENSES OF AN APEX PREDATOR, BUT...
"...I CAN SMELL MYSTERY A MILE AWAY."
THAT'S NOT HOW IT HAPPENED.

THE ONLY THING YOU WERE SMELLING IN THAT FERRY WAS YOUR OWN PUKE SPEWING OFF THE PORT BOW.

IF YOU'RE GONNA TELL THE STORY, *DIEGO,* TELL IT RIGHT.

IT'S CALLED *LICENCIA POÉTICA,* MERISSA!

NOW WHERE WAS I?

OH YEAH-- *MYSTERY...*

"...THE ROY HARPER TITANS ACADEMY WAS TEEMING WITH IT.

"AND AT ITS CENTER WAS THE MAN WHO'D BROUGHT US, THREE ORPHANS AND WARDS OF THE STATE, ALL THE WAY HERE FROM GOTHAM CITY..."

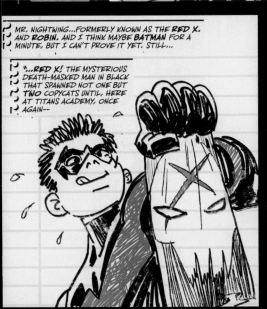

MR. NIGHTWING...FORMERLY KNOWN AS THE *RED X,* AND *ROBIN,* AND I THINK MAYBE *BATMAN* FOR A MINUTE, BUT I CAN'T PROVE IT YET. STILL...

"...*RED X!* THE MYSTERIOUS DEATH-MASKED MAN IN BLACK THAT SPAWNED NOT ONE BUT *TWO* COPYCATS UNTIL, HERE AT TITANS ACADEMY, ONCE AGAIN--

"--THE *RED X* WAS REBORN!

TOTAL BUTTHOLE

"THIS ONE'S IDENTITY, LIKE THE LAST TWO, WAS A CAREFULLY SHROUDED SECRET...ONE TOO TEMPTING TO RESIST.

SERIOUSLY

"WE ROUNDED UP THE USUAL SUSPECTS...

"WHICH WASN'T HARD. BAD GUYS CRUMBLE FAST IF YOU CAN STRIKE FEAR IN THEIR HEARTS. AND THAT'S *THE BAT PACK'S* SPECIALTY...!

"WELL, THAT AND *INTERROGATION.*

"OR, AS I CALL IT--"

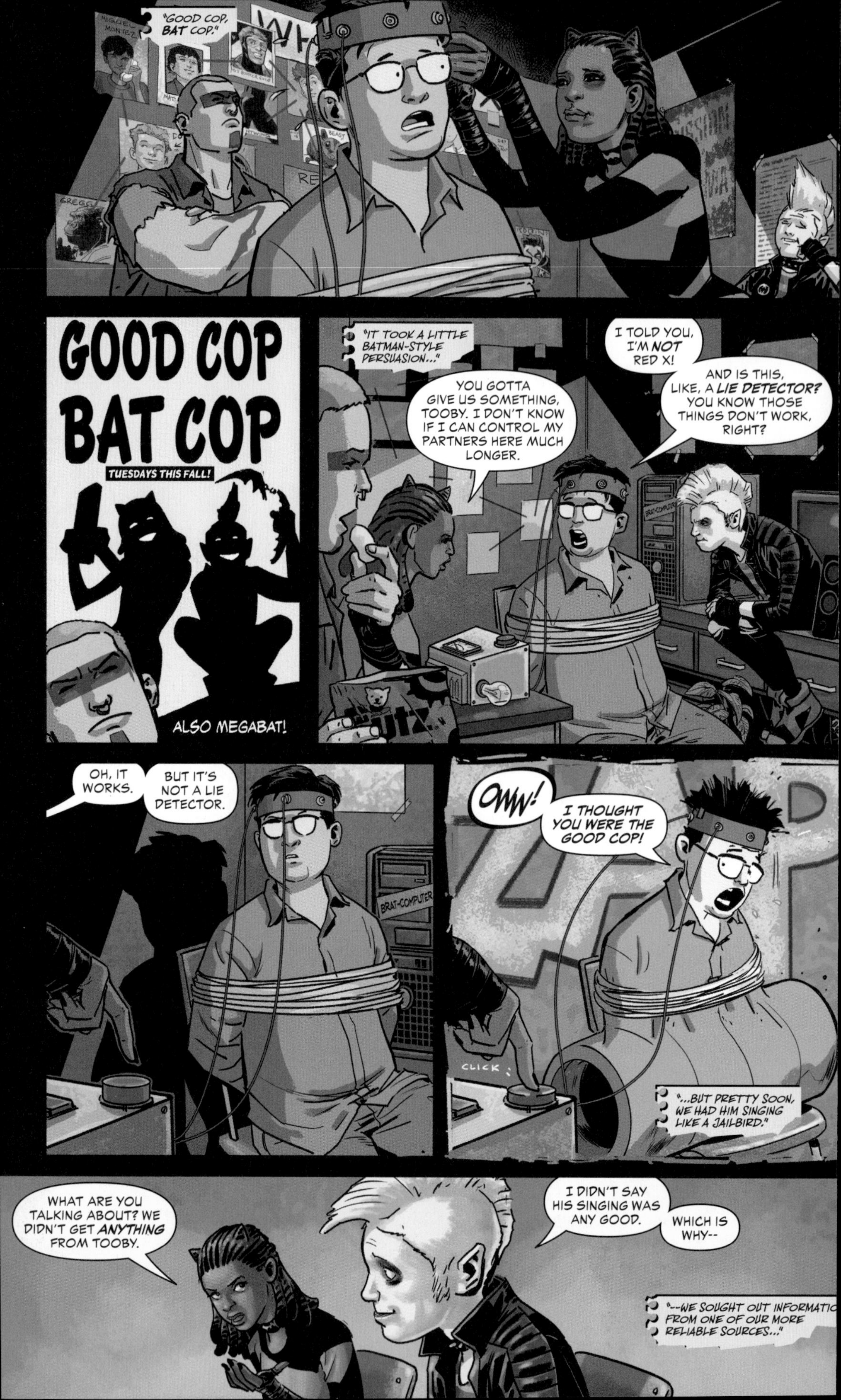
"GOOD COP, BAT COP."
GOOD COP BAT COP
TUESDAYS THIS FALL!
ALSO MEGABAT!
"IT TOOK A LITTLE BATMAN-STYLE PERSUASION..."
YOU GOTTA GIVE US SOMETHING, TOOBY. I DON'T KNOW IF I CAN CONTROL MY PARTNERS HERE MUCH LONGER.
I TOLD YOU, I'M NOT RED X!
AND IS THIS, LIKE, A LIE DETECTOR? YOU KNOW THOSE THINGS DON'T WORK, RIGHT?
BRAT-COMPUTER
OH, IT WORKS.
BUT IT'S NOT A LIE DETECTOR.
BRAT-COMPUTER
OWW!
I THOUGHT YOU WERE THE GOOD COP!
CLICK
"...BUT PRETTY SOON, WE HAD HIM SINGING LIKE A JAILBIRD."
WHAT ARE YOU TALKING ABOUT? WE DIDN'T GET ANYTHING FROM TOOBY.
I DIDN'T SAY HIS SINGING WAS ANY GOOD.
WHICH IS WHY--
"--WE SOUGHT OUT INFORMATIO FROM ONE OF OUR MORE RELIABLE SOURCES..."

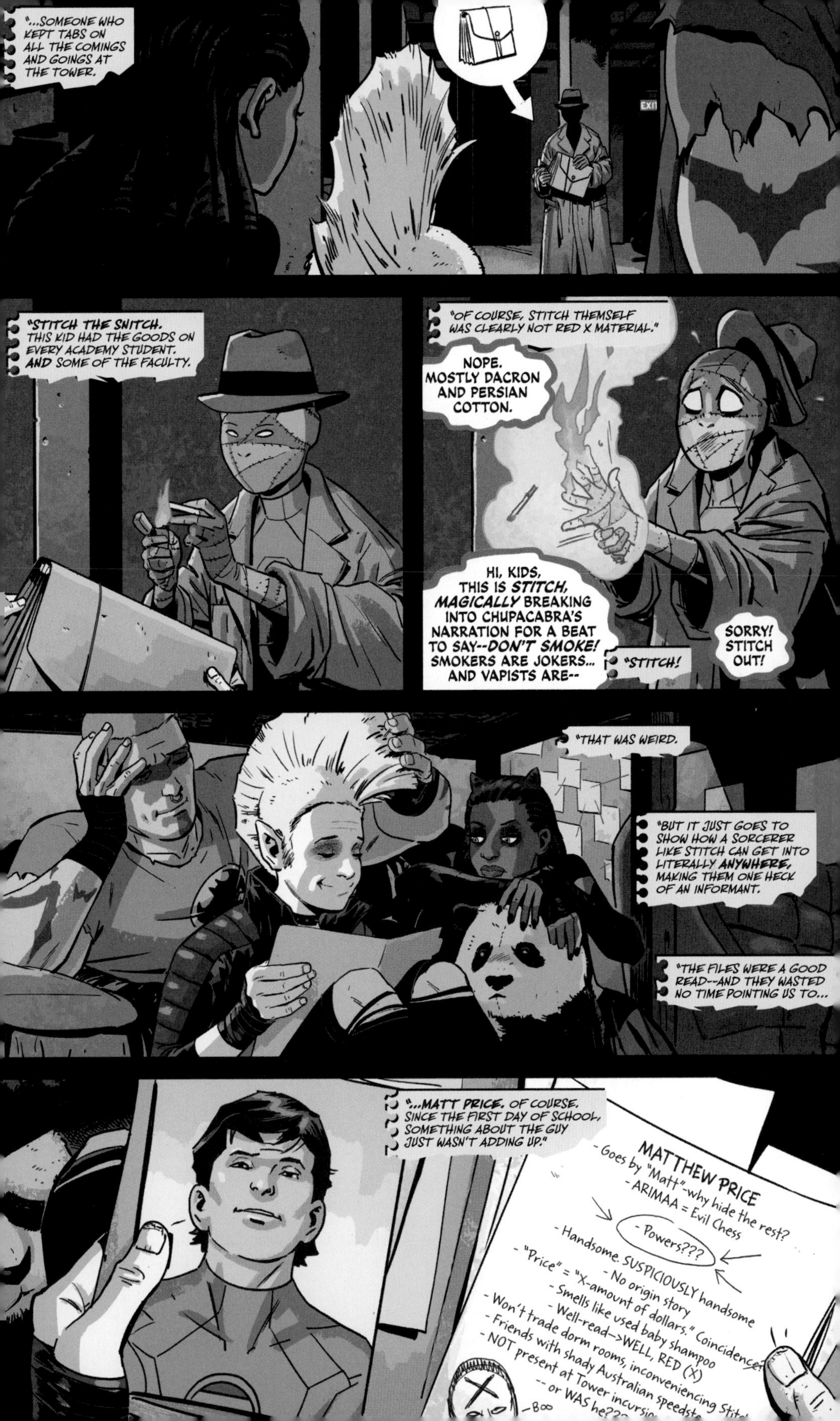
"...SOMEONE WHO KEPT TABS ON ALL THE COMINGS AND GOINGS AT THE TOWER.
EXIT
"STITCH THE SNITCH. THIS KID HAD THE GOODS ON EVERY ACADEMY STUDENT. AND SOME OF THE FACULTY.
"OF COURSE, STITCH THEMSELF WAS CLEARLY NOT RED X MATERIAL."
NOPE. MOSTLY DACRON AND PERSIAN COTTON.
HI, KIDS, THIS IS STITCH, MAGICALLY BREAKING INTO CHUPACABRA'S NARRATION FOR A BEAT TO SAY--DON'T SMOKE! SMOKERS ARE JOKERS... AND VAPISTS ARE--
"STITCH!
SORRY! STITCH OUT!
"THAT WAS WEIRD.
"BUT IT JUST GOES TO SHOW HOW A SORCERER LIKE STITCH CAN GET INTO LITERALLY ANYWHERE, MAKING THEM ONE HECK OF AN INFORMANT.
"THE FILES WERE A GOOD READ--AND THEY WASTED NO TIME POINTING US TO...
"...MATT PRICE, OF COURSE. SINCE THE FIRST DAY OF SCHOOL, SOMETHING ABOUT THE GUY JUST WASN'T ADDING UP."
MATTHEW PRICE
- Goes by "Matt"-why hide the rest?
- ARIMAA = Evil Chess
- Powers???
- Handsome. SUSPICIOUSLY handsome
- No origin story
- "Price" = "X-amount of dollars." Coincidence?
- Smells like used baby shampoo
- Well-read->WELL, RED (X)
- Won't trade dorm rooms, inconveniencing Stit
- Friends with shady Australian speedst
- NOT present at Tower incursi
-- or WAS he??
-Boo

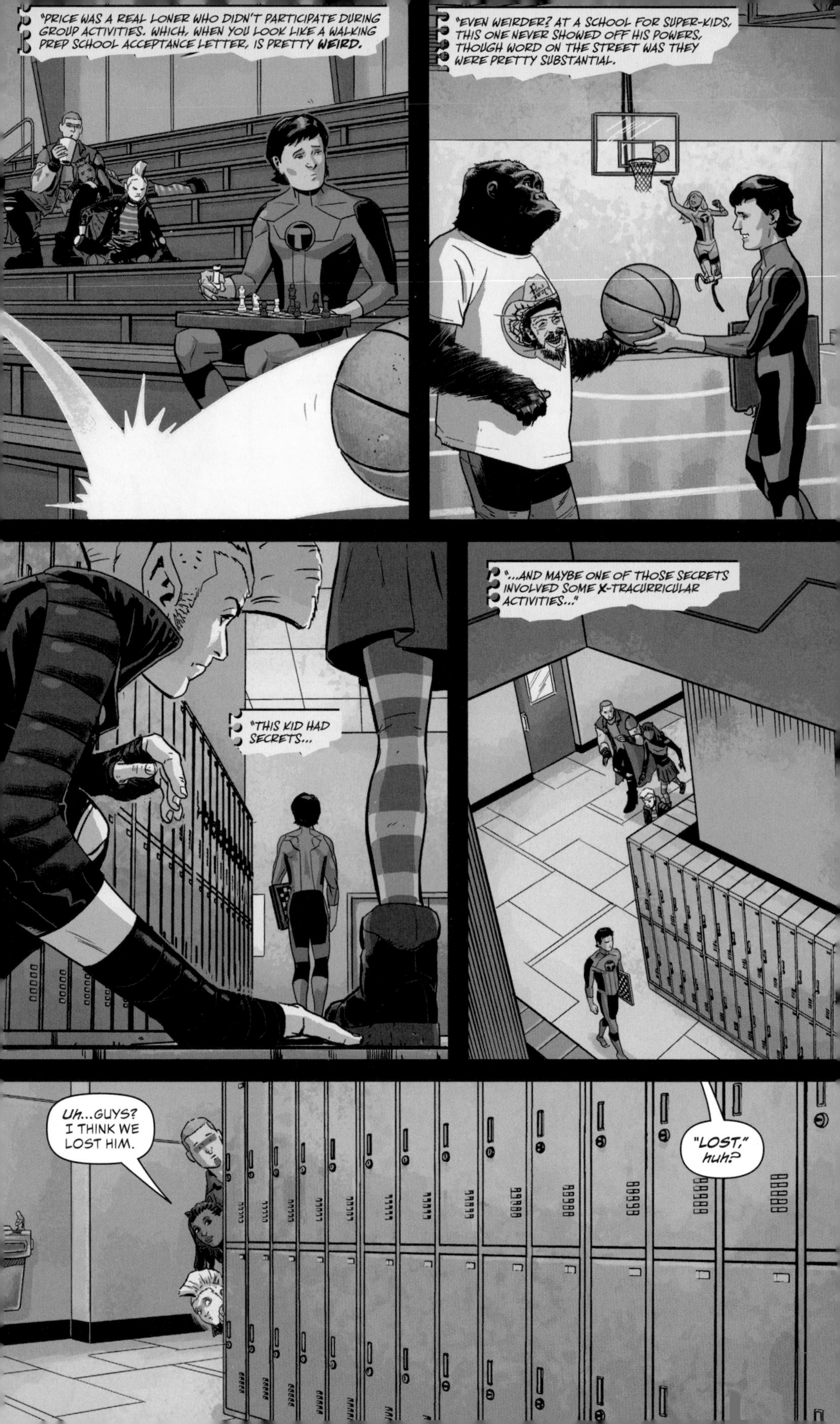
"PRICE WAS A REAL LONER WHO DIDN'T PARTICIPATE DURING GROUP ACTIVITIES. WHICH, WHEN YOU LOOK LIKE A WALKING PREP SCHOOL ACCEPTANCE LETTER, IS PRETTY WEIRD.
"EVEN WEIRDER? AT A SCHOOL FOR SUPER-KIDS, THIS ONE NEVER SHOWED OFF HIS POWERS, THOUGH WORD ON THE STREET WAS THEY WERE PRETTY SUBSTANTIAL.
"THIS KID HAD SECRETS...
"...AND MAYBE ONE OF THOSE SECRETS INVOLVED SOME X-TRACURRICULAR ACTIVITIES..."
Uh...GUYS? I THINK WE LOST HIM.
"LOST," huh?

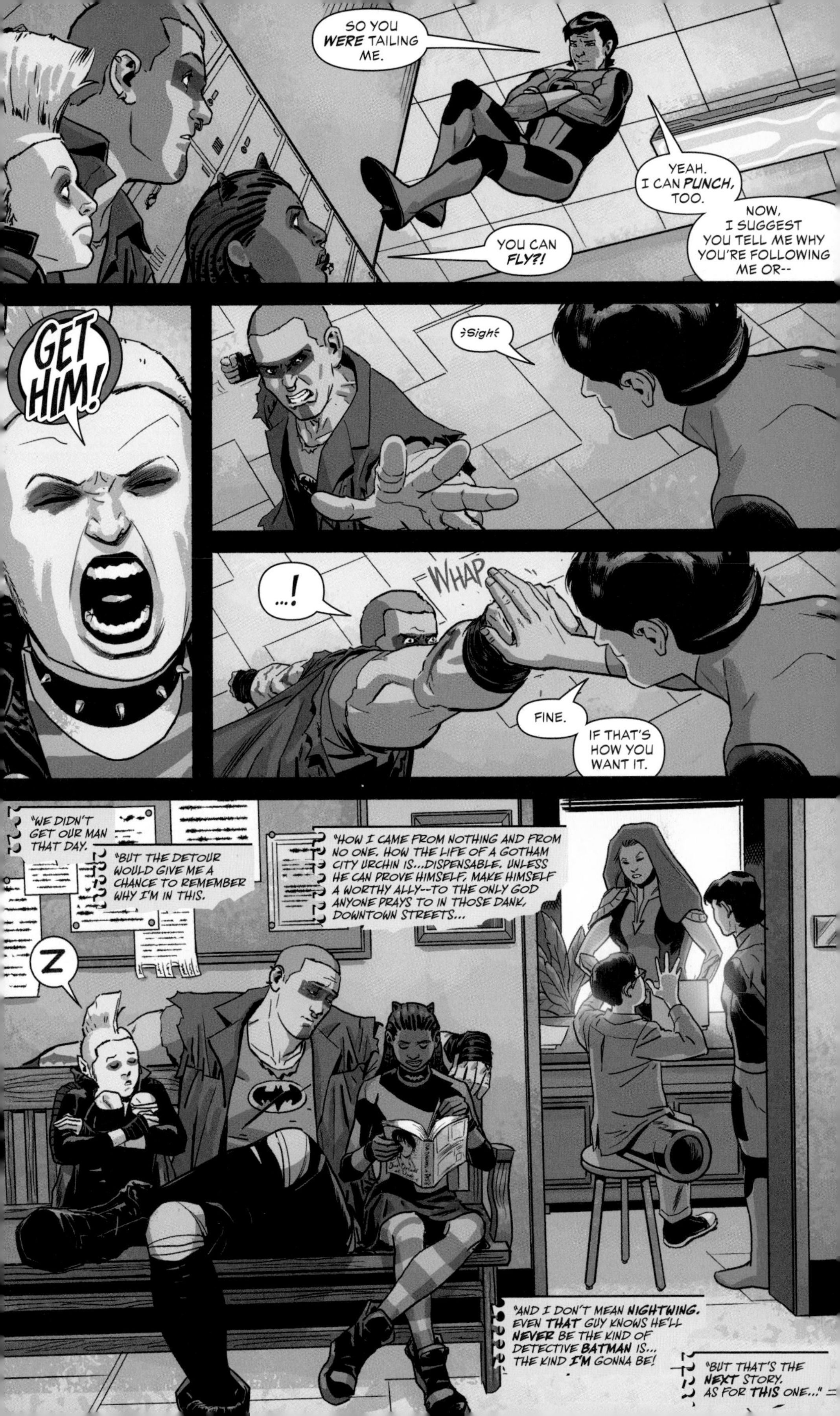

SO YOU WERE TAILING ME.
YOU CAN FLY?!
YEAH. I CAN PUNCH, TOO.
NOW, I SUGGEST YOU TELL ME WHY YOU'RE FOLLOWING ME OR--
GET HIM!
Sigh
...!
WHAP
FINE.
IF THAT'S HOW YOU WANT IT.
"WE DIDN'T GET OUR MAN THAT DAY.
"BUT THE DETOUR WOULD GIVE ME A CHANCE TO REMEMBER WHY I'M IN THIS.
"HOW I CAME FROM NOTHING AND FROM NO ONE. HOW THE LIFE OF A GOTHAM CITY URCHIN IS...DISPENSABLE. UNLESS HE CAN PROVE HIMSELF, MAKE HIMSELF A WORTHY ALLY--TO THE ONLY GOD ANYONE PRAYS TO IN THOSE DANK, DOWNTOWN STREETS...
Z
"AND I DON'T MEAN NIGHTWING. EVEN THAT GUY KNOWS HE'LL NEVER BE THE KIND OF DETECTIVE BATMAN IS... THE KIND I'M GONNA BE!
"BUT THAT'S THE NEXT STORY. AS FOR THIS ONE..."

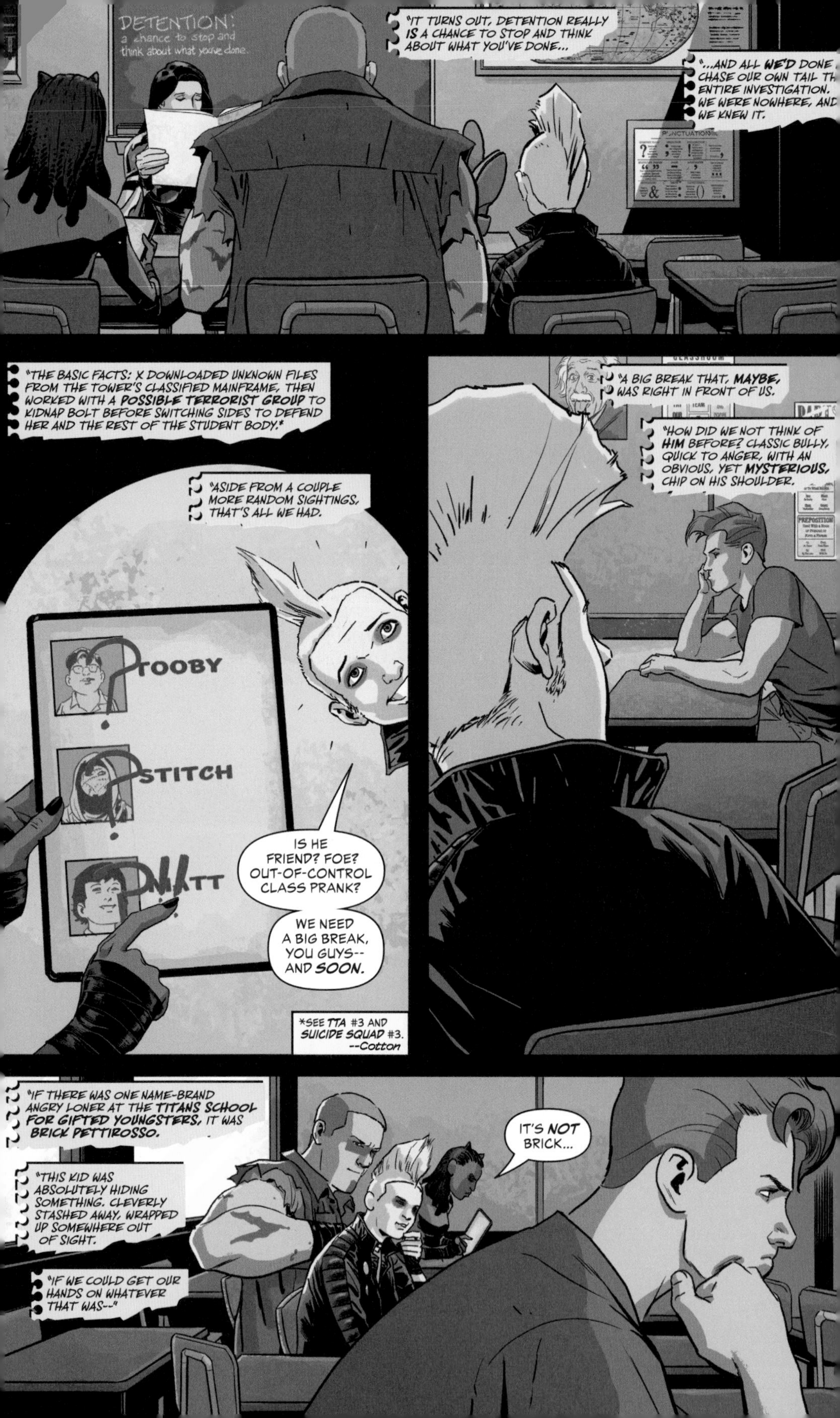
DETENTION: a chance to stop and think about what you've done.
"IT TURNS OUT, DETENTION REALLY IS A CHANCE TO STOP AND THINK ABOUT WHAT YOU'VE DONE...
"...AND ALL WE'D DONE CHASE OUR OWN TAIL TH ENTIRE INVESTIGATION. WE WERE NOWHERE, AND WE KNEW IT.
PUNCTUATION
"THE BASIC FACTS: X DOWNLOADED UNKNOWN FILES FROM THE TOWER'S CLASSIFIED MAINFRAME, THEN WORKED WITH A POSSIBLE TERRORIST GROUP TO KIDNAP BOLT BEFORE SWITCHING SIDES TO DEFEND HER AND THE REST OF THE STUDENT BODY.*
"ASIDE FROM A COUPLE MORE RANDOM SIGHTINGS, THAT'S ALL WE HAD.
TOOBY
STITCH
IS HE FRIEND? FOE? OUT-OF-CONTROL CLASS PRANK?
WE NEED A BIG BREAK, YOU GUYS-- AND SOON.
*SEE TTA #3 AND SUICIDE SQUAD #3. --Cotton
"A BIG BREAK THAT, MAYBE, WAS RIGHT IN FRONT OF US.
"HOW DID WE NOT THINK OF HIM BEFORE? CLASSIC BULLY, QUICK TO ANGER, WITH AN OBVIOUS, YET MYSTERIOUS, CHIP ON HIS SHOULDER.
PREPOSITION
"IF THERE WAS ONE NAME-BRAND ANGRY LONER AT THE TITANS SCHOOL FOR GIFTED YOUNGSTERS, IT WAS BRICK PETTIROSSO.
"THIS KID WAS ABSOLUTELY HIDING SOMETHING. CLEVERLY STASHED AWAY, WRAPPED UP SOMEWHERE OUT OF SIGHT.
"IF WE COULD GET OUR HANDS ON WHATEVER THAT WAS--"
IT'S NOT BRICK...

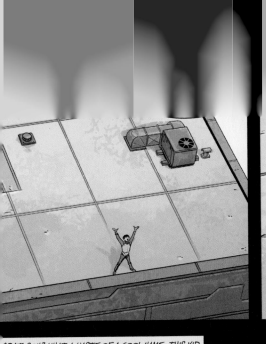

"BAT-SON? WHAT A WASTE OF A COOL NAME. THIS KID HAD NO SKILLS, NO POWERS OR SECRET IDENTITIES TO SPEAK OF. WHAT MADE HIM ACADEMY MATERIAL? NO ONE KNEW.
"IN FACT, NO ONE KNEW MUCH OF ANYTHING ABOUT BILLY BATSON..."
LOOK AT THIS VIDEO OF X FROM TWO MONTHS AGO.
COULD BE THE SAME GUY.
GO BACK TO THE LIVE FEED...
LET'S SEE IF WE CAN READ BILLY'S LIPS, FIGURE OUT WHAT HE'S--
THAT'S ODD.
FSSSSSHHH
VISUAL'S DOWN--SOME KIND OF SUDDEN ELECTRICAL INTERFERENCE...
WHAT THE HECK IS HAPPENING UP THERE?!

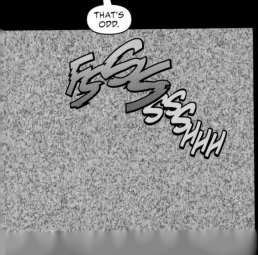

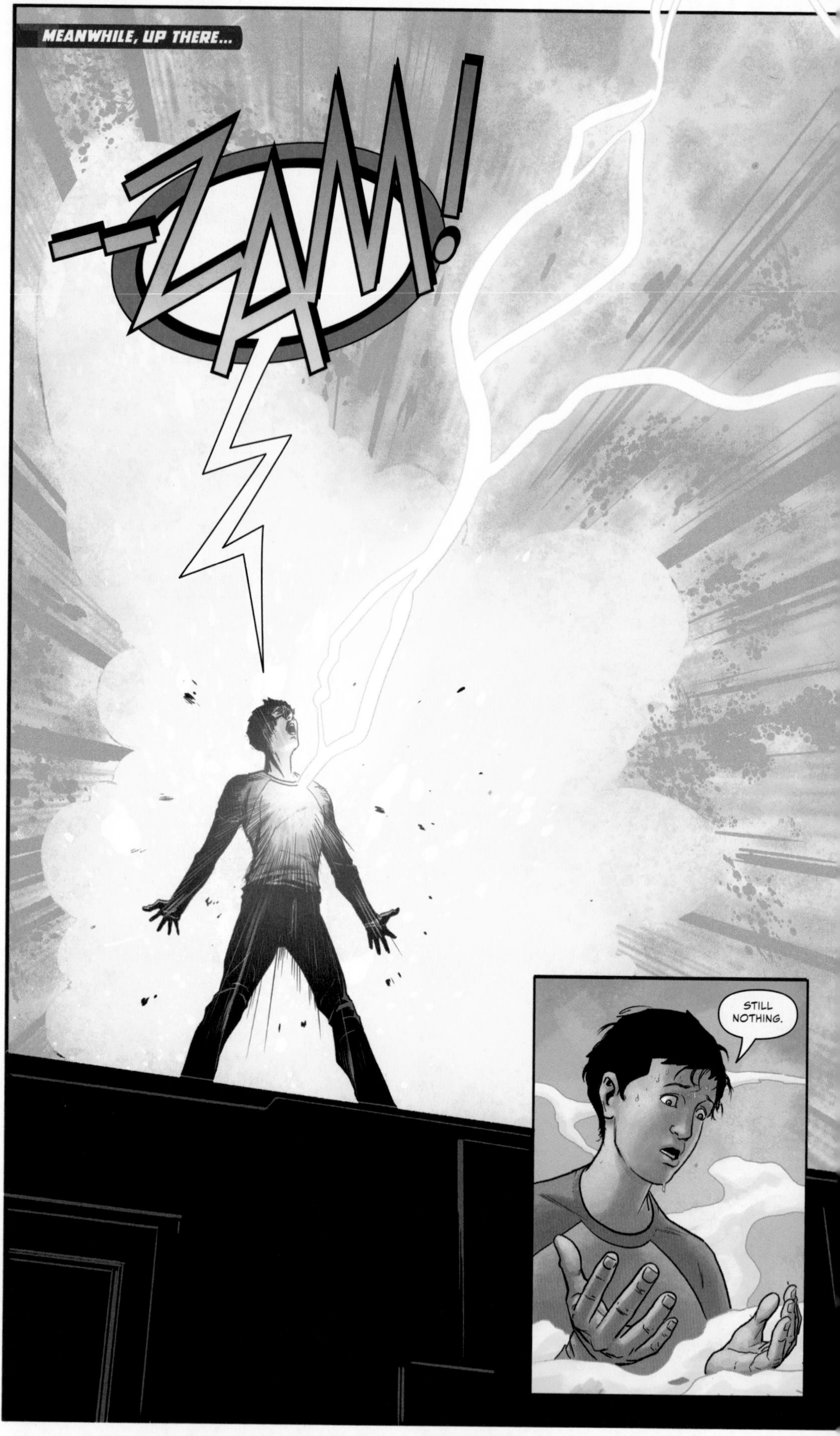
MEANWHILE, UP THERE...
--ZAM!
STILL NOTHING.

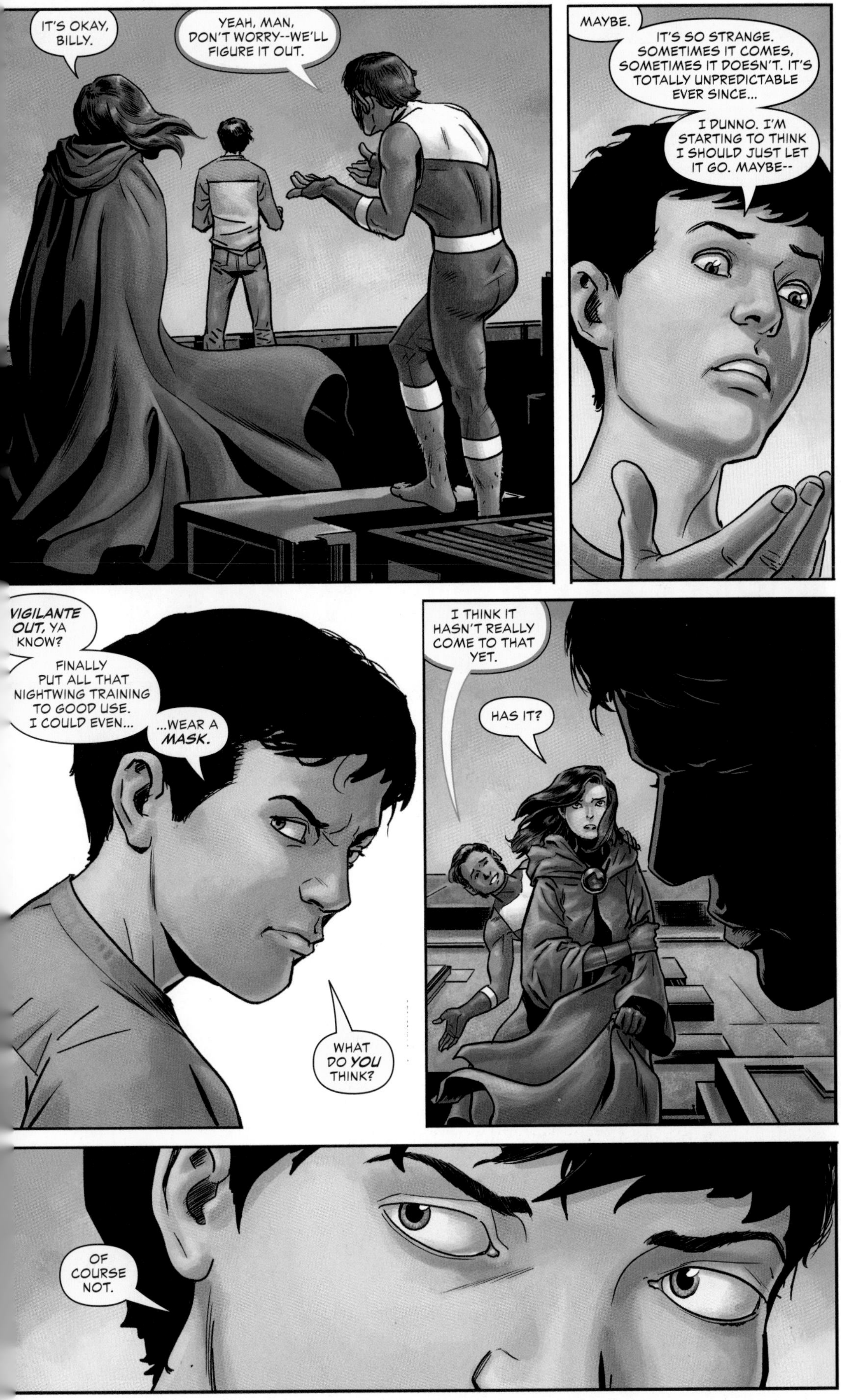
IT'S OKAY, BILLY.
YEAH, MAN, DON'T WORRY--WE'LL FIGURE IT OUT.
MAYBE.
IT'S SO STRANGE. SOMETIMES IT COMES, SOMETIMES IT DOESN'T. IT'S TOTALLY UNPREDICTABLE EVER SINCE...
I DUNNO. I'M STARTING TO THINK I SHOULD JUST LET IT GO. MAYBE--
VIGILANTE OUT, YA KNOW?
FINALLY PUT ALL THAT NIGHTWING TRAINING TO GOOD USE. I COULD EVEN...
...WEAR A MASK.
WHAT DO YOU THINK?
I THINK IT HASN'T REALLY COME TO THAT YET.
HAS IT?
OF COURSE NOT.

"SINCE BRATGIRL COULDN'T REESTABLISH THE VISUAL LINK TO THE ROOF, WE HAD ABSOLUTELY NO IDEA WHAT HAPPENED UP THERE."

"SO AFTER DETENTION, WE PAID A VISIT TO BILLY'S PLACE, WHERE WE MET ONE *MIGUEL MONTEZ.*"

B. BATSON
M. MONTEZ

NO, I UNDERSTAND COMPLETELY. YOU THREE WANT TO SEARCH OUR ROOM AS PART OF SOME TOP SECRET UNDERGROUND INVESTIGATION YOU'RE CONDUCTING.

GOT IT.

B. BATSON
M. MONTEZ

SLAM

B. BATSON
M. MONTEZ

YIKES.

THE DOOR WASN'T OPEN LONG ENOUGH TO COMPLETE MY SCAN.

B. BATSON
M. MONTEZ

YOU CAN SCAN *MY* STUFF IF YOU WANT.

M. RADLEY
B. PETTIROSSO

I MEAN, LIKE, IF IT'S FOR SCIENCE, OR WHATEVER.

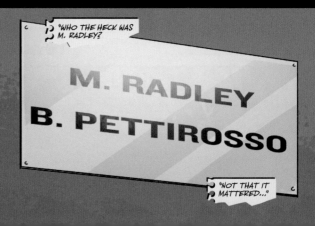

"WHO THE HECK WAS M. RADLEY?

M. RADLEY
B. PETTIROSSO

"NOT THAT IT MATTERED..."

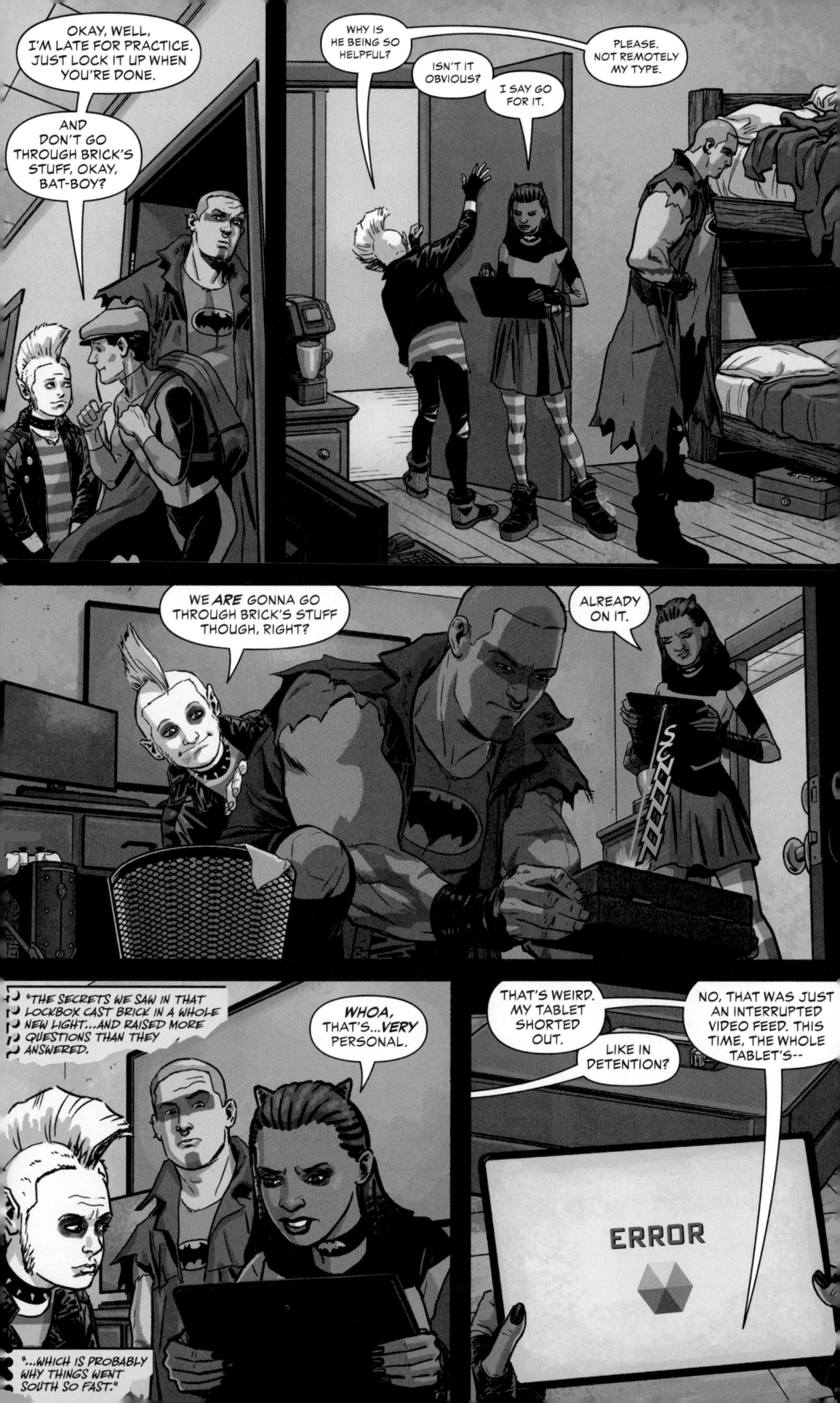
OKAY, WELL, I'M LATE FOR PRACTICE. JUST LOCK IT UP WHEN YOU'RE DONE.
AND DON'T GO THROUGH BRICK'S STUFF, OKAY, BAT-BOY?
WHY IS HE BEING SO HELPFUL?
PLEASE. NOT REMOTELY MY TYPE.
ISN'T IT OBVIOUS?
I SAY GO FOR IT.
WE ARE GONNA GO THROUGH BRICK'S STUFF THOUGH, RIGHT?
ALREADY ON IT.
SCHNNNN
"THE SECRETS WE SAW IN THAT LOCKBOX CAST BRICK IN A WHOLE NEW LIGHT...AND RAISED MORE QUESTIONS THAN THEY ANSWERED.
WHOA, THAT'S...VERY PERSONAL.
"...WHICH IS PROBABLY WHY THINGS WENT SOUTH SO FAST."
THAT'S WEIRD. MY TABLET SHORTED OUT.
LIKE IN DETENTION?
NO, THAT WAS JUST AN INTERRUPTED VIDEO FEED. THIS TIME, THE WHOLE TABLET'S--
ERROR

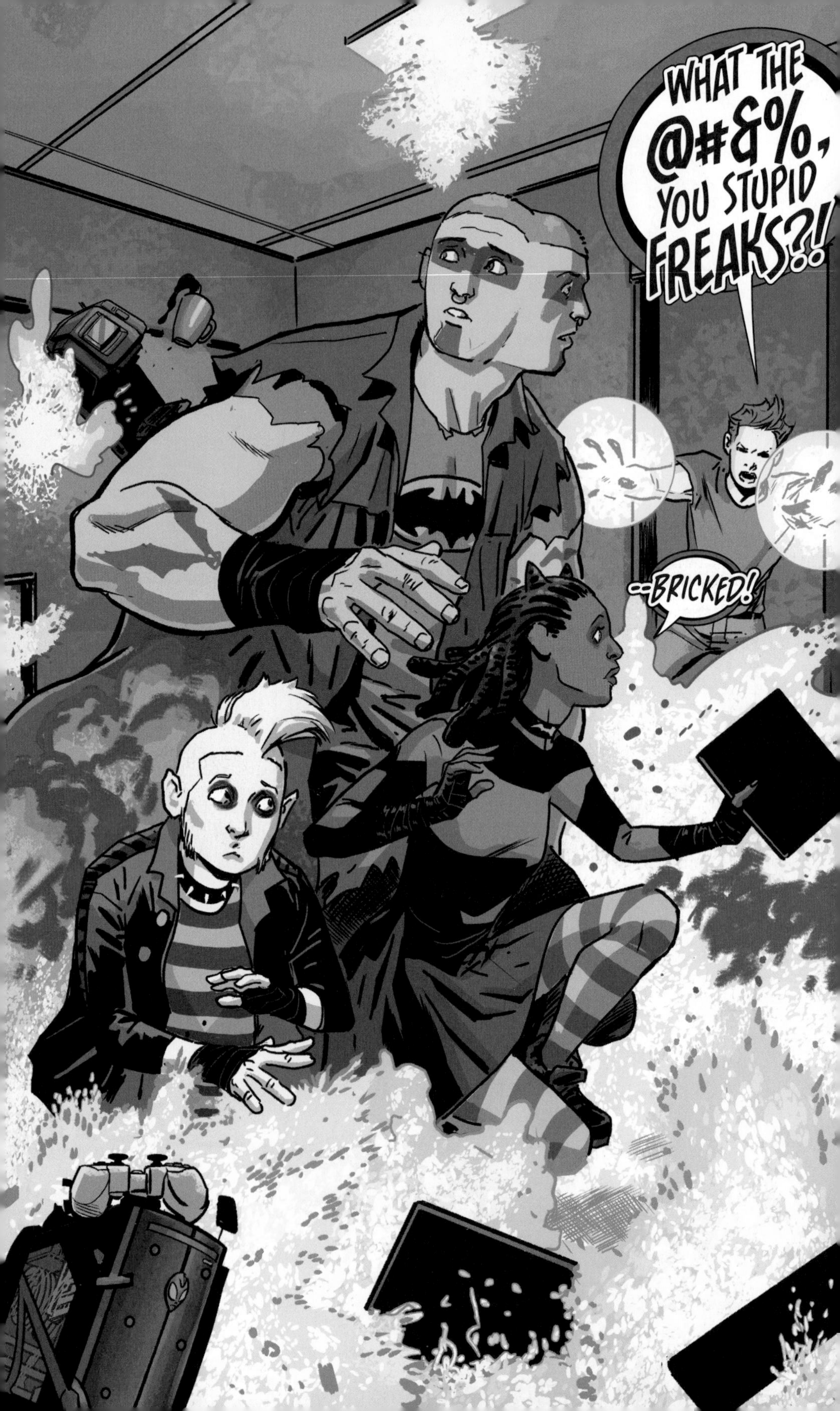
WHAT THE @#&%, YOU STUPID FREAKS?!
--BRICKED!

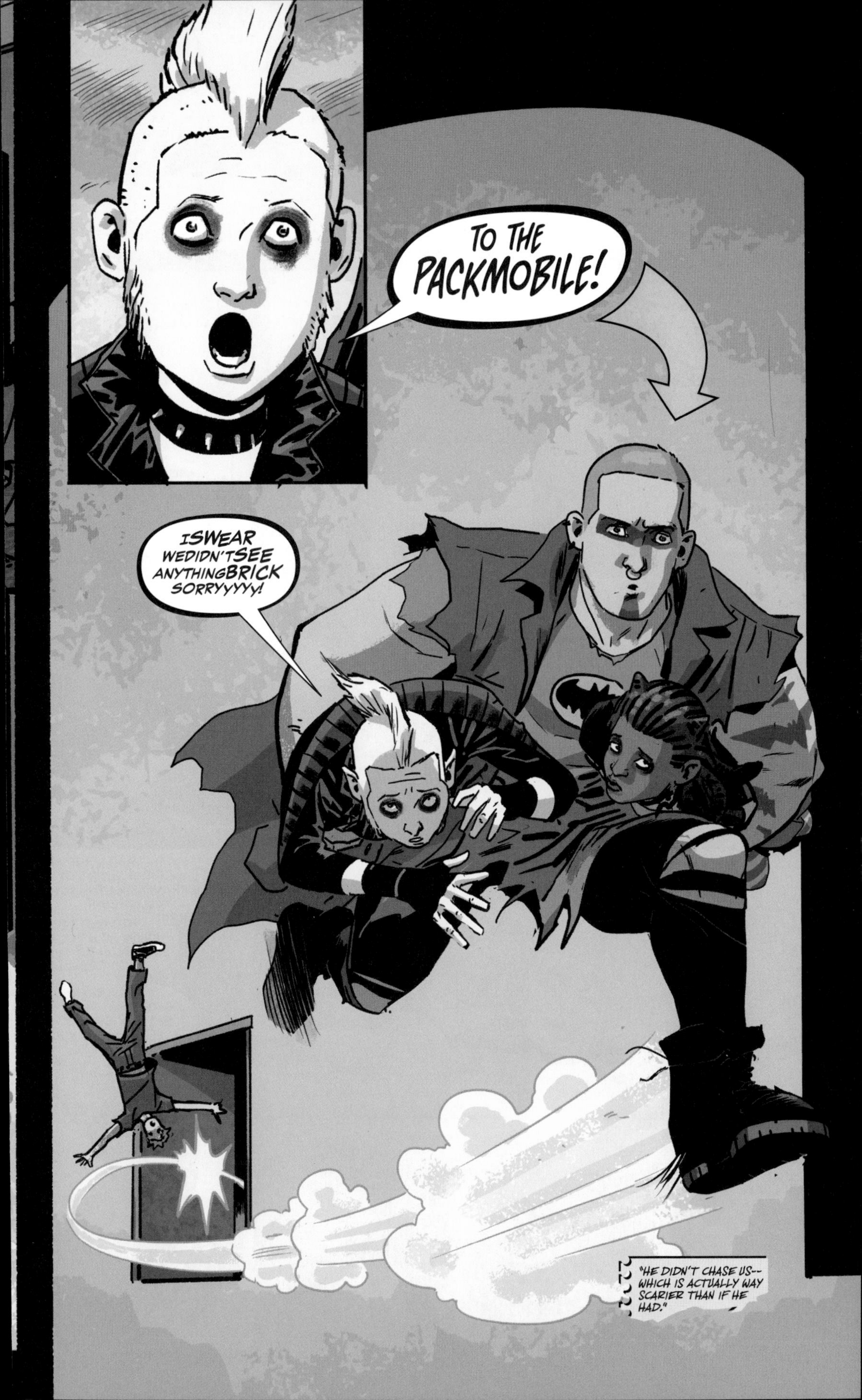
TO THE PACKMOBILE!
ISWEAR WEDIDN'TSEE ANYTHINGBRICK SORRYYYYY!
"HE DIDN'T CHASE US--WHICH IS ACTUALLY WAY SCARIER THAN IF HE HAD."

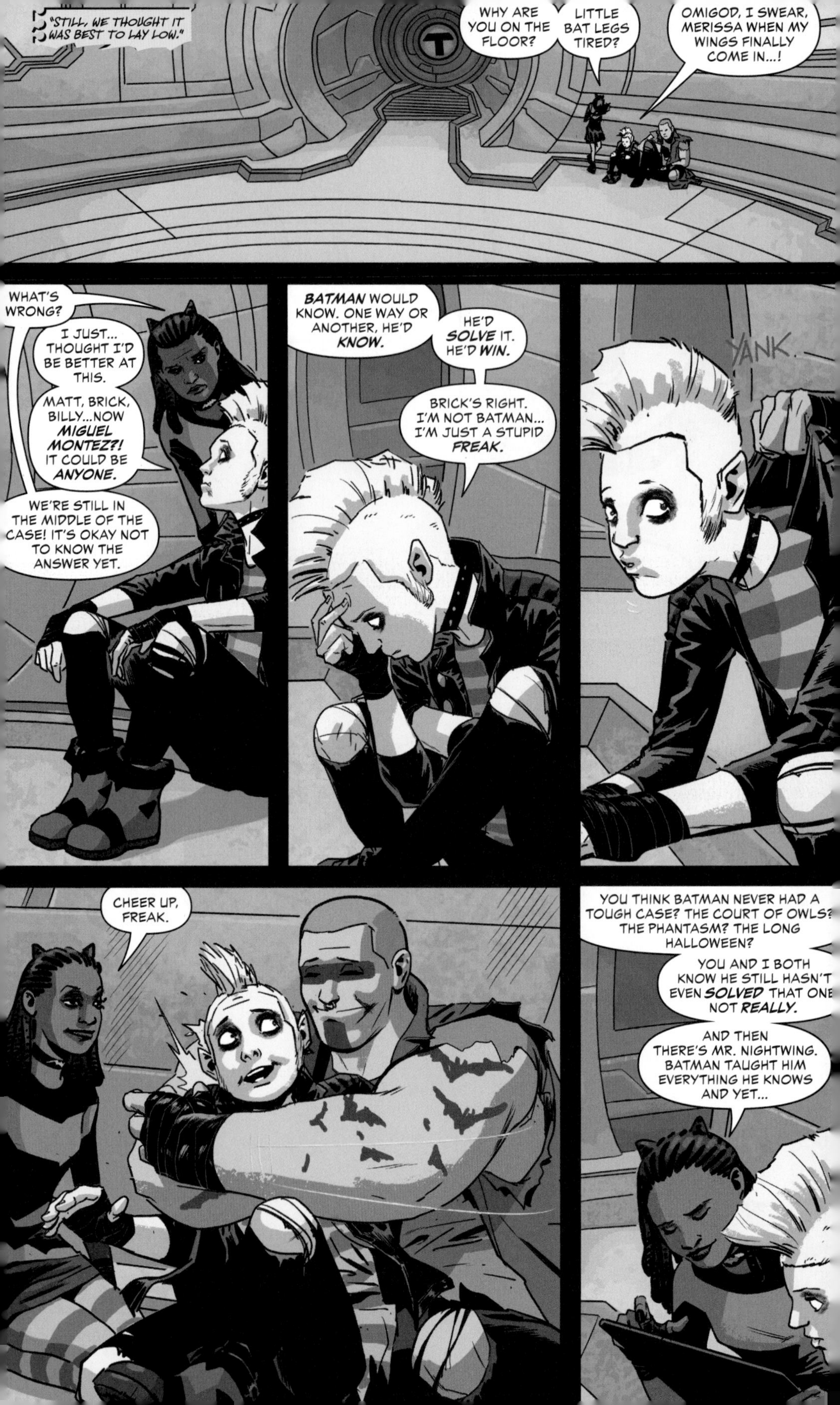

"STILL, WE THOUGHT IT WAS BEST TO LAY LOW."
WHY ARE YOU ON THE FLOOR?
LITTLE BAT LEGS TIRED?
OMIGOD, I SWEAR, MERISSA WHEN MY WINGS FINALLY COME IN...!
WHAT'S WRONG?
I JUST... THOUGHT I'D BE BETTER AT THIS.
MATT, BRICK, BILLY...NOW MIGUEL MONTEZ?! IT COULD BE ANYONE.
WE'RE STILL IN THE MIDDLE OF THE CASE! IT'S OKAY NOT TO KNOW THE ANSWER YET.
BATMAN WOULD KNOW. ONE WAY OR ANOTHER, HE'D KNOW.
HE'D SOLVE IT. HE'D WIN.
BRICK'S RIGHT. I'M NOT BATMAN... I'M JUST A STUPID FREAK.
YANK
CHEER UP, FREAK.
YOU THINK BATMAN NEVER HAD A TOUGH CASE? THE COURT OF OWLS? THE PHANTASM? THE LONG HALLOWEEN?
YOU AND I BOTH KNOW HE STILL HASN'T EVEN SOLVED THAT ONE NOT REALLY.
AND THEN THERE'S MR. NIGHTWING. BATMAN TAUGHT HIM EVERYTHING HE KNOWS AND YET...

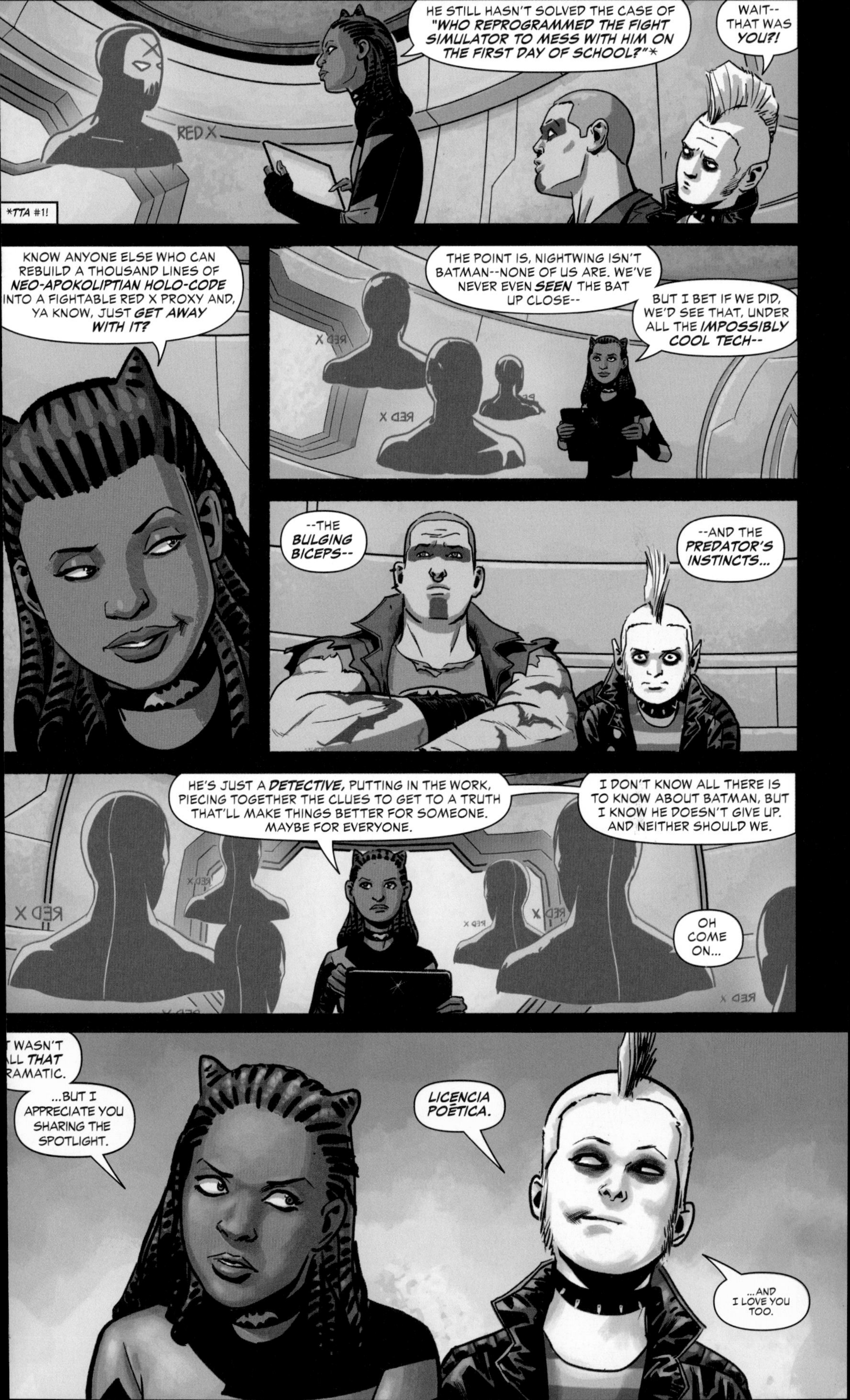
HE STILL HASN'T SOLVED THE CASE OF "WHO REPROGRAMMED THE FIGHT SIMULATOR TO MESS WITH HIM ON THE FIRST DAY OF SCHOOL?"*
WAIT-- THAT WAS YOU?!
RED X
*TTA #1!
KNOW ANYONE ELSE WHO CAN REBUILD A THOUSAND LINES OF NEO-APOKOLIPTIAN HOLO-CODE INTO A FIGHTABLE RED X PROXY AND, YA KNOW, JUST GET AWAY WITH IT?
THE POINT IS, NIGHTWING ISN'T BATMAN--NONE OF US ARE. WE'VE NEVER EVEN SEEN THE BAT UP CLOSE--
BUT I BET IF WE DID, WE'D SEE THAT, UNDER ALL THE IMPOSSIBLY COOL TECH--
--THE BULGING BICEPS--
--AND THE PREDATOR'S INSTINCTS...
HE'S JUST A DETECTIVE, PUTTING IN THE WORK, PIECING TOGETHER THE CLUES TO GET TO A TRUTH THAT'LL MAKE THINGS BETTER FOR SOMEONE. MAYBE FOR EVERYONE.
I DON'T KNOW ALL THERE IS TO KNOW ABOUT BATMAN, BUT I KNOW HE DOESN'T GIVE UP. AND NEITHER SHOULD WE.
OH COME ON...
T WASN'T LL THAT RAMATIC.
...BUT I APPRECIATE YOU SHARING THE SPOTLIGHT.
LICENCIA POÉTICA.
...AND I LOVE YOU TOO.

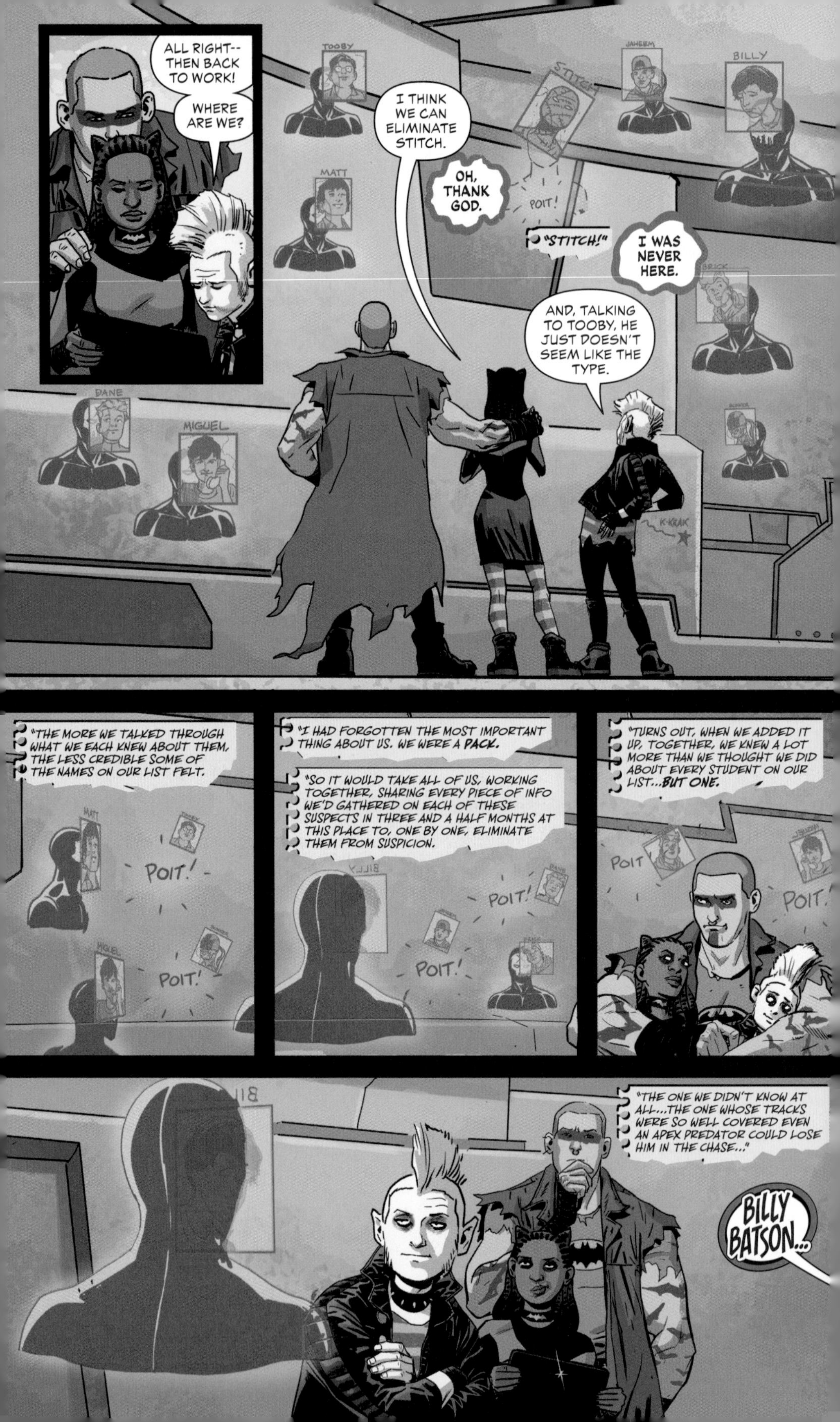
ALL RIGHT-- THEN BACK TO WORK!
WHERE ARE WE?
TOOBY
JAHEEM
BILLY
STITCH
MATT
I THINK WE CAN ELIMINATE STITCH.
OH, THANK GOD.
POIT!
"STITCH!"
I WAS NEVER HERE.
BRICK
AND, TALKING TO TOOBY, HE JUST DOESN'T SEEM LIKE THE TYPE.
DANE
MIGUEL
K-KRAK
"THE MORE WE TALKED THROUGH WHAT WE EACH KNEW ABOUT THEM, THE LESS CREDIBLE SOME OF THE NAMES ON OUR LIST FELT.
POIT!
POIT!
"I HAD FORGOTTEN THE MOST IMPORTANT THING ABOUT US. WE WERE A PACK.
"SO IT WOULD TAKE ALL OF US, WORKING TOGETHER, SHARING EVERY PIECE OF INFO WE'D GATHERED ON EACH OF THESE SUSPECTS IN THREE AND A HALF MONTHS AT THIS PLACE TO, ONE BY ONE, ELIMINATE THEM FROM SUSPICION.
POIT!
POIT!
"TURNS OUT, WHEN WE ADDED IT UP, TOGETHER, WE KNEW A LOT MORE THAN WE THOUGHT WE DID ABOUT EVERY STUDENT ON OUR LIST...BUT ONE.
POIT
POIT.
"THE ONE WE DIDN'T KNOW AT ALL...THE ONE WHOSE TRACKS WERE SO WELL COVERED EVEN AN APEX PREDATOR COULD LOSE HIM IN THE CHASE..."
BILLY BATSON...

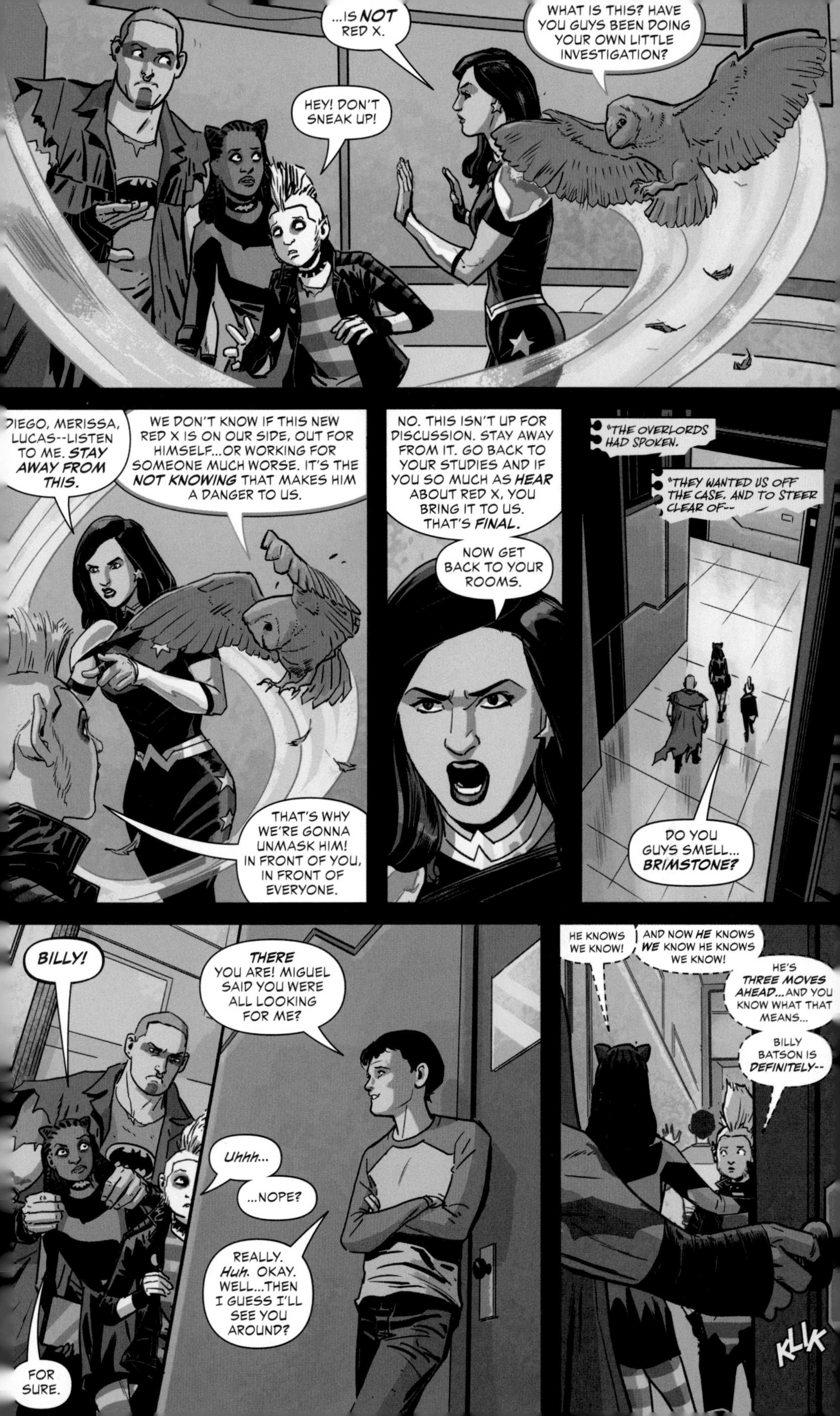

...IS **NOT** RED X.
WHAT IS THIS? HAVE YOU GUYS BEEN DOING YOUR OWN LITTLE INVESTIGATION?
HEY! DON'T SNEAK UP!
DIEGO, MERISSA, LUCAS--LISTEN TO ME. ***STAY AWAY FROM THIS.***
WE DON'T KNOW IF THIS NEW RED X IS ON OUR SIDE, OUT FOR HIMSELF...OR WORKING FOR SOMEONE MUCH WORSE. IT'S THE ***NOT KNOWING*** THAT MAKES HIM A DANGER TO US.
THAT'S WHY WE'RE GONNA UNMASK HIM! IN FRONT OF YOU, IN FRONT OF EVERYONE.
NO. THIS ISN'T UP FOR DISCUSSION. STAY AWAY FROM IT. GO BACK TO YOUR STUDIES AND IF YOU SO MUCH AS ***HEAR*** ABOUT RED X, YOU BRING IT TO US. THAT'S ***FINAL.***
NOW GET BACK TO YOUR ROOMS.
"THE OVERLORDS HAD SPOKEN.
"THEY WANTED US OFF THE CASE. AND TO STEER CLEAR OF--
DO YOU GUYS SMELL... **BRIMSTONE?**
BILLY!
THERE YOU ARE! MIGUEL SAID YOU WERE ALL LOOKING FOR ME?
Uhhh...
...NOPE?
REALLY. *Huh.* OKAY. WELL...THEN I GUESS I'LL SEE YOU AROUND?
FOR SURE.
HE KNOWS WE KNOW!
AND NOW ***HE*** KNOWS ***WE*** KNOW HE KNOWS WE KNOW!
HE'S ***THREE MOVES AHEAD...*** AND YOU KNOW WHAT THAT MEANS...
BILLY BATSON IS ***DEFINITELY--***
KLIK

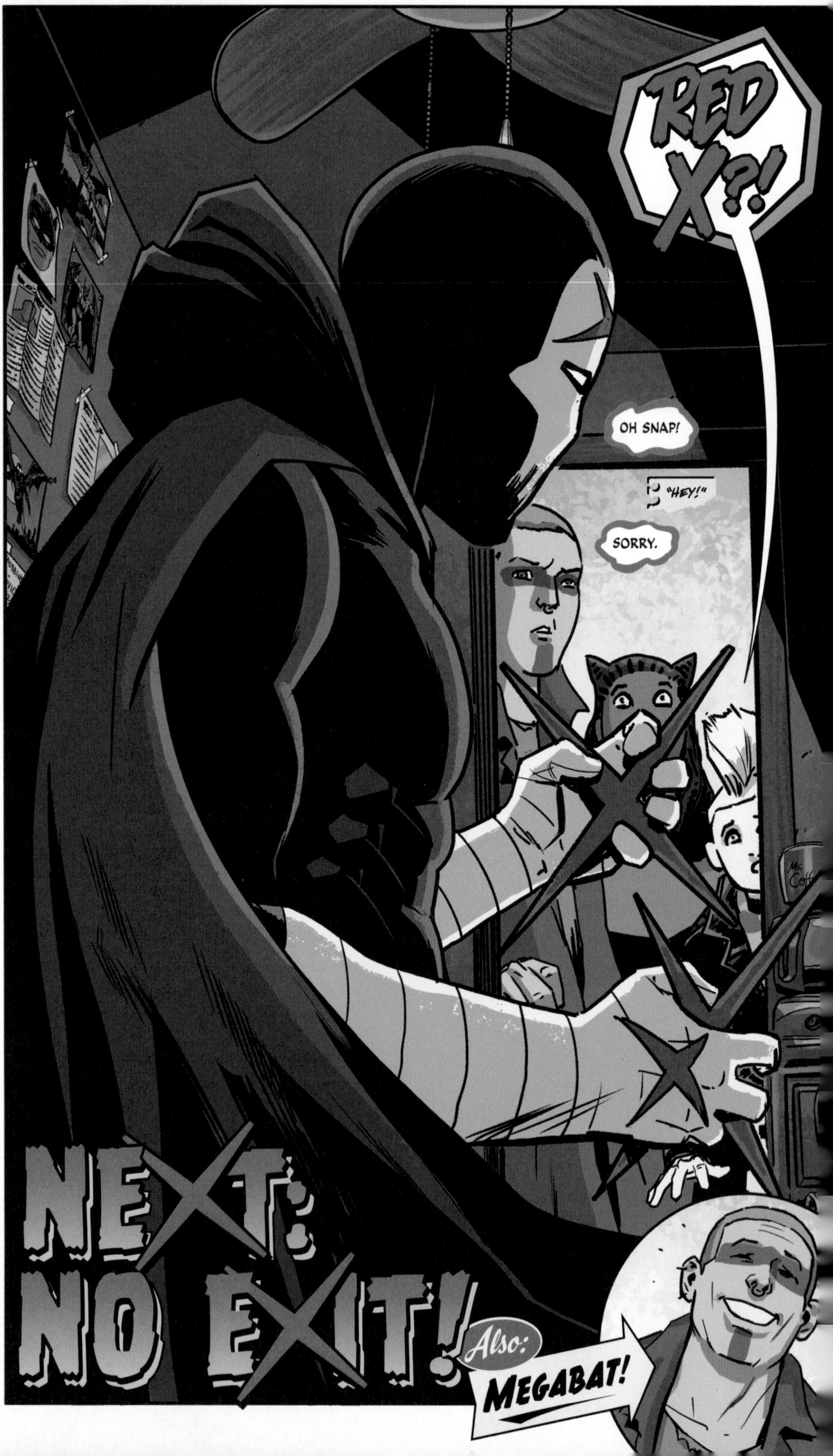

RED X?!
OH SNAP!
"HEY!"
SORRY.
NEXT: NO EXIT!
Also: MEGABAT!

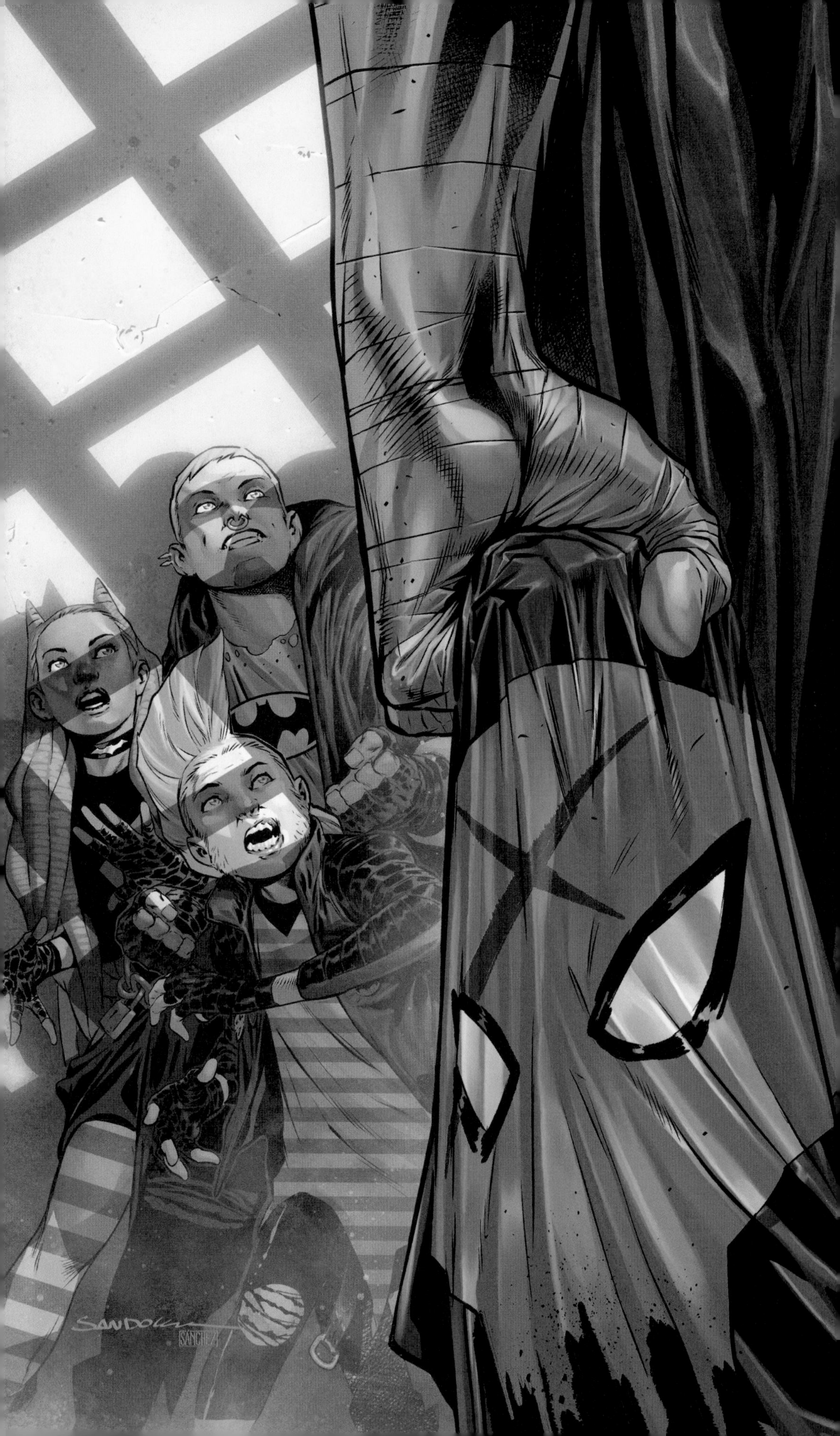

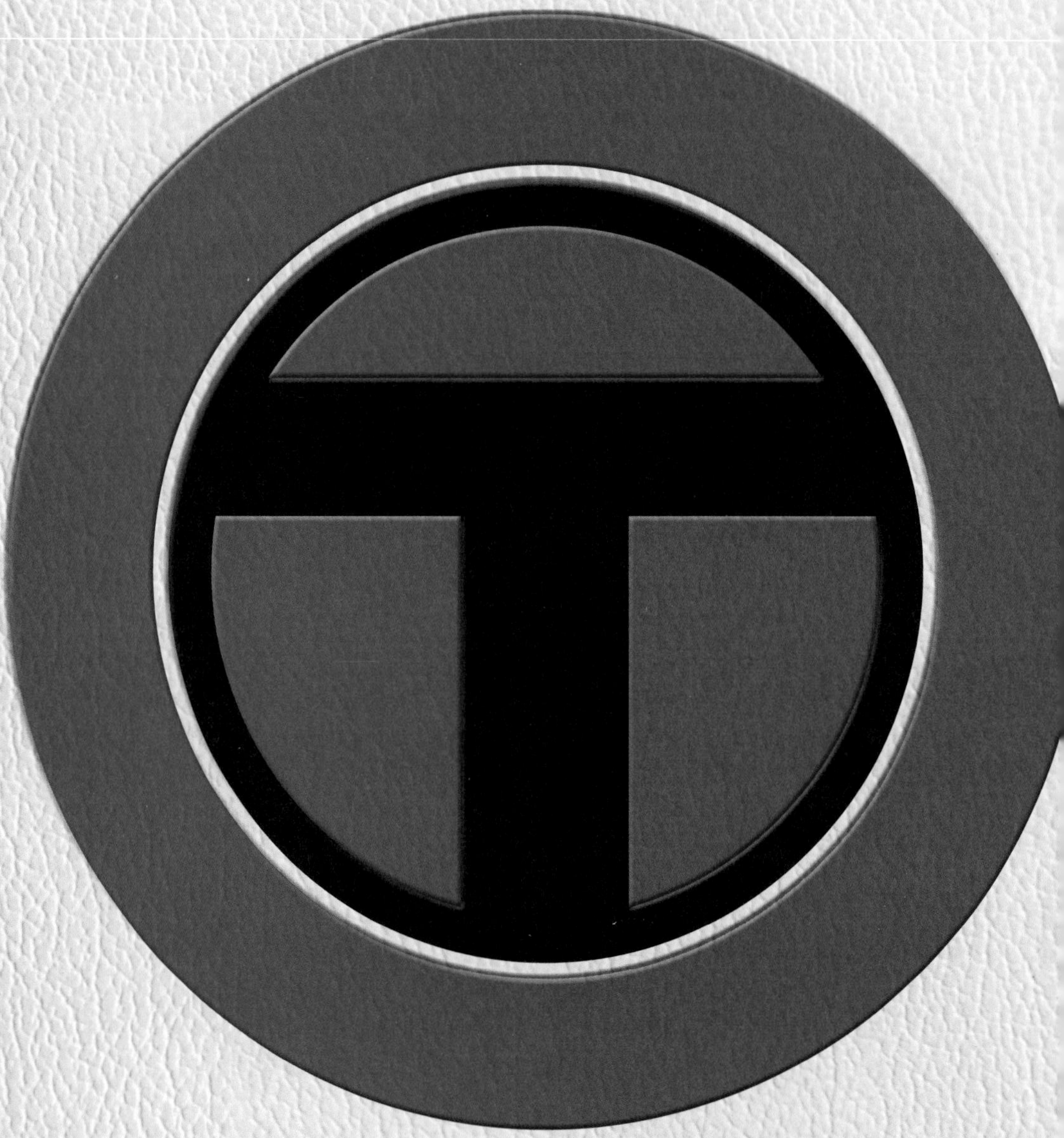

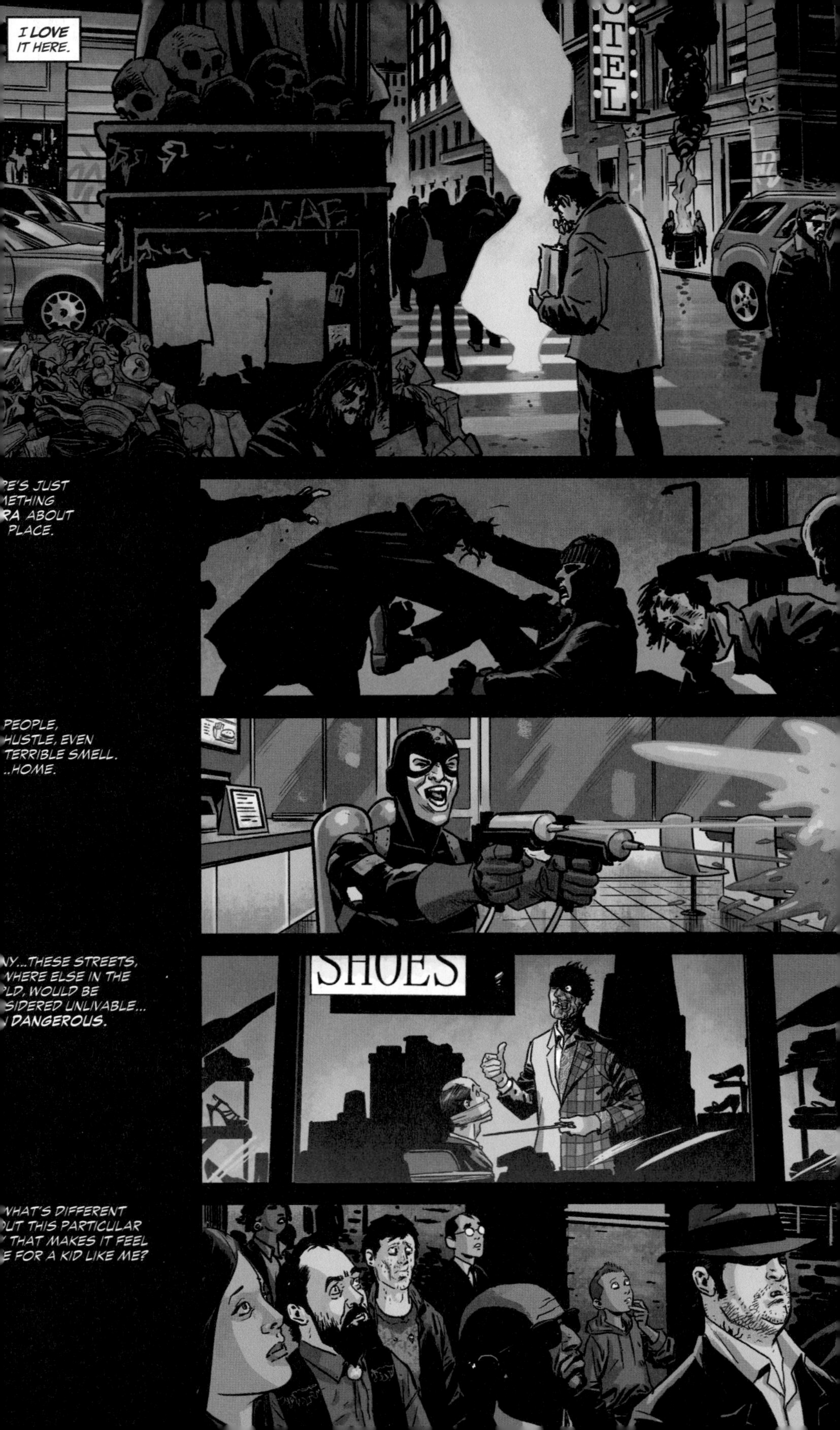
I LOVE IT HERE.
HOTEL
'E'S JUST
IETHING
RA ABOUT
PLACE.
PEOPLE,
HUSTLE, EVEN
TERRIBLE SMELL.
..HOME.
NY...THESE STREETS,
WHERE ELSE IN THE
LD, WOULD BE
SIDERED UNLIVABLE...
DANGEROUS.
SHOES
WHAT'S DIFFERENT
UT THIS PARTICULAR
THAT MAKES IT FEEL
E FOR A KID LIKE ME?

ON'T KNOW.

TEEN TITANS ACADEMY PRESENTS: THE BAT PACK in

NO EXIT!

| TIM **SHERIDAN** writer | STEVE **LIEBER** artist | DAVE **STEWART** colorist | ROB **LEIGH** letterer | RAFA **SANDOVAL** | ALEJANDRO **SANCHEZ** cover | PHILIP **TAN** | ELMER **SANTOS** variant cover | DIEGO **LOPEZ** assoc. editor | C |

From the halls of **TEEN TITANS ACADEMY**, through the darque doors of existential ennui, emerges the world's greatest team of junior nihilist detectives: **THE BAT PACK!** Together, brainy **BRATGIRL**, chilling CHUPACARRA, and the mighty MEGARAT are on the case, following the clues, wherever they may lead

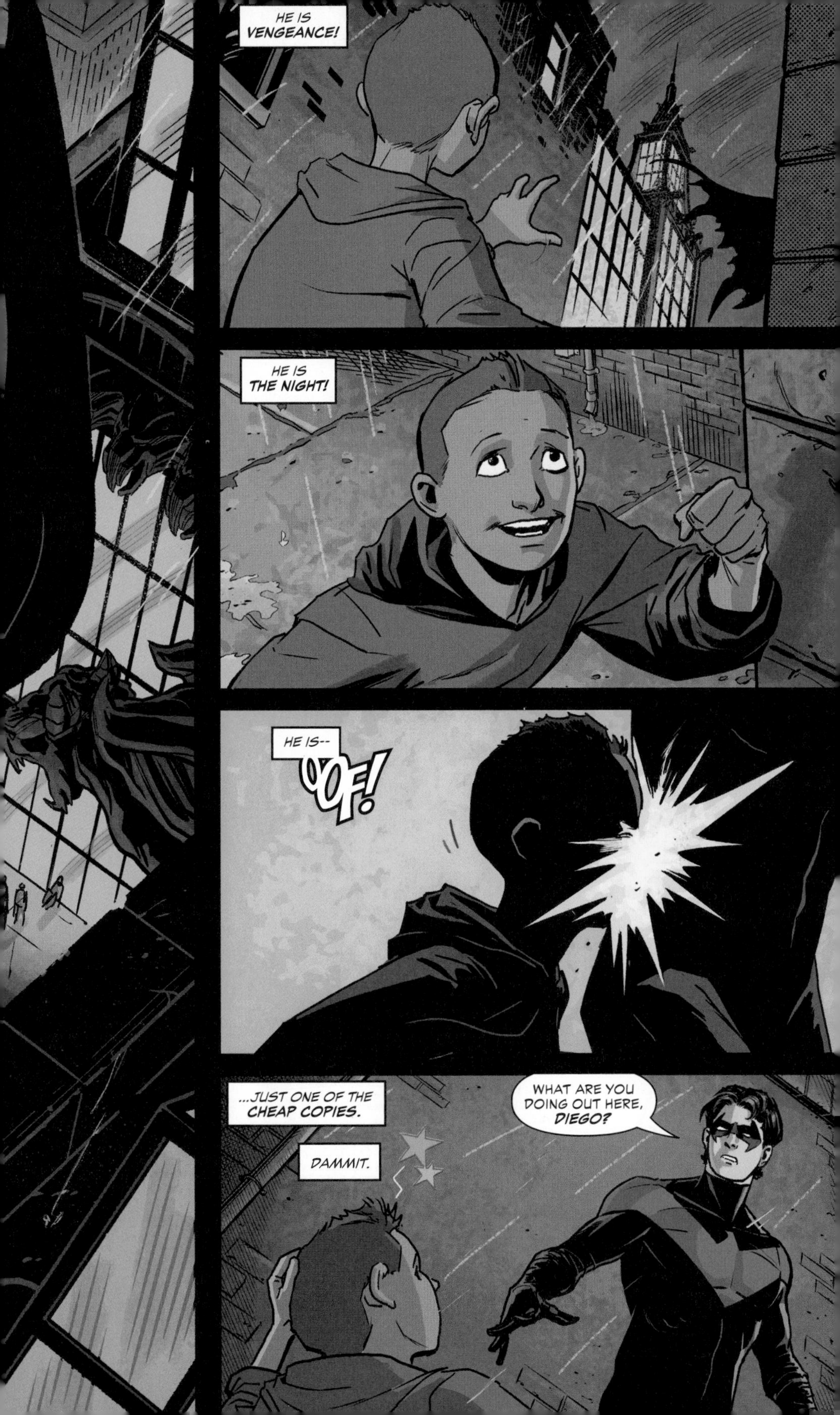
HE IS VENGEANCE!
HE IS THE NIGHT!
HE IS--
OOF!
...JUST ONE OF THE CHEAP COPIES.
DAMMIT.
WHAT ARE YOU DOING OUT HERE, DIEGO?

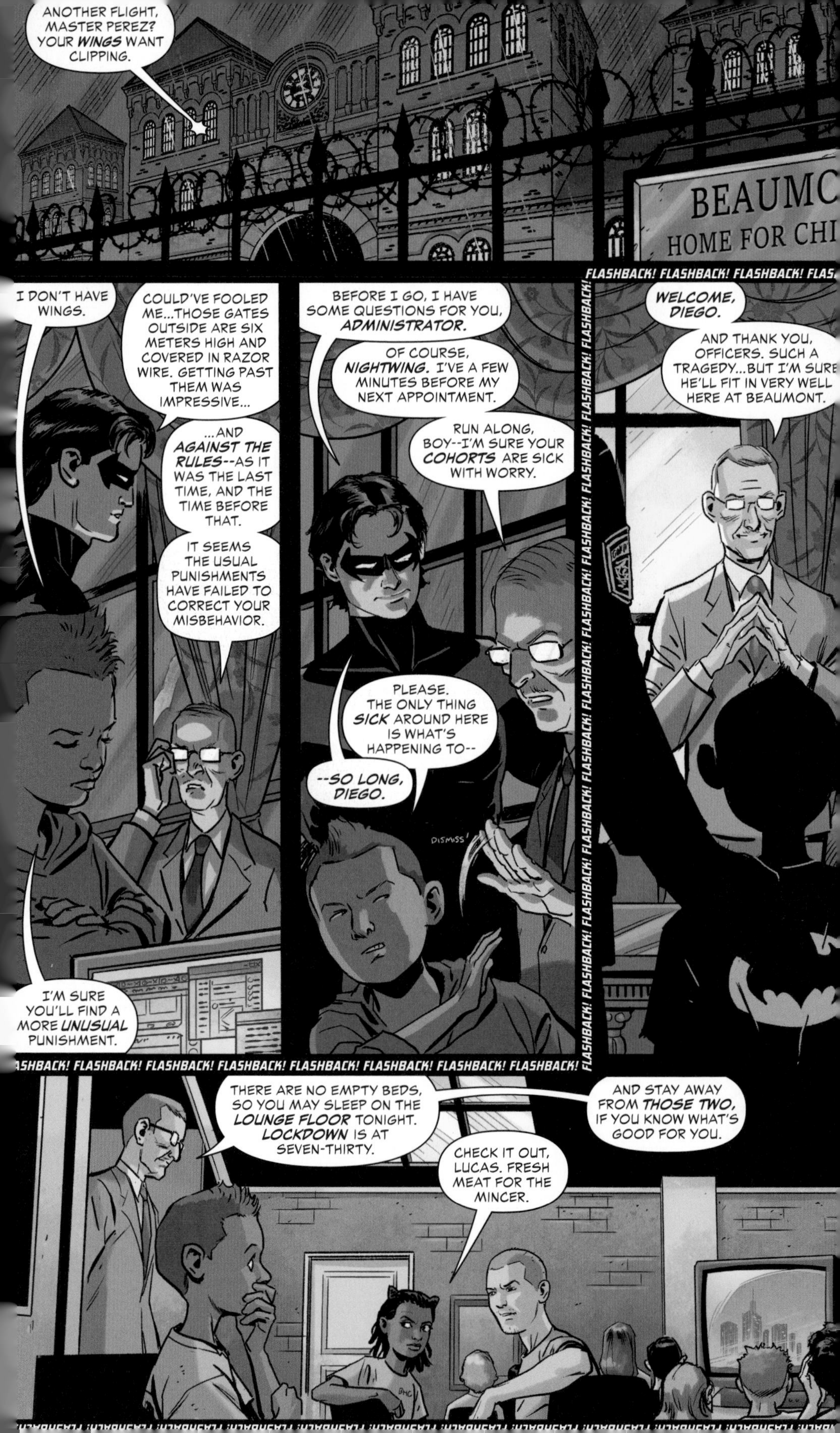
ANOTHER FLIGHT, MASTER PEREZ? YOUR WINGS WANT CLIPPING.
BEAUMC
HOME FOR CHI
FLASHBACK! FLASHBACK! FLASHBACK! FLAS
I DON'T HAVE WINGS.
COULD'VE FOOLED ME...THOSE GATES OUTSIDE ARE SIX METERS HIGH AND COVERED IN RAZOR WIRE. GETTING PAST THEM WAS IMPRESSIVE...
...AND AGAINST THE RULES--AS IT WAS THE LAST TIME, AND THE TIME BEFORE THAT.
IT SEEMS THE USUAL PUNISHMENTS HAVE FAILED TO CORRECT YOUR MISBEHAVIOR.
I'M SURE YOU'LL FIND A MORE UNUSUAL PUNISHMENT.
BEFORE I GO, I HAVE SOME QUESTIONS FOR YOU, ADMINISTRATOR.
OF COURSE, NIGHTWING. I'VE A FEW MINUTES BEFORE MY NEXT APPOINTMENT.
RUN ALONG, BOY--I'M SURE YOUR COHORTS ARE SICK WITH WORRY.
PLEASE. THE ONLY THING SICK AROUND HERE IS WHAT'S HAPPENING TO--
--SO LONG, DIEGO.
DISMISS'
WELCOME, DIEGO.
AND THANK YOU, OFFICERS. SUCH A TRAGEDY...BUT I'M SURE HE'LL FIT IN VERY WELL HERE AT BEAUMONT.
FLASHBACK! FLASHBACK! FLASHBACK! FLASHBACK! FLASHBACK! FLASHBACK! FLASHBACK! FLASHBACK!
THERE ARE NO EMPTY BEDS, SO YOU MAY SLEEP ON THE LOUNGE FLOOR TONIGHT. LOCKDOWN IS AT SEVEN-THIRTY.
AND STAY AWAY FROM THOSE TWO, IF YOU KNOW WHAT'S GOOD FOR YOU.
CHECK IT OUT, LUCAS. FRESH MEAT FOR THE MINCER.
BHC

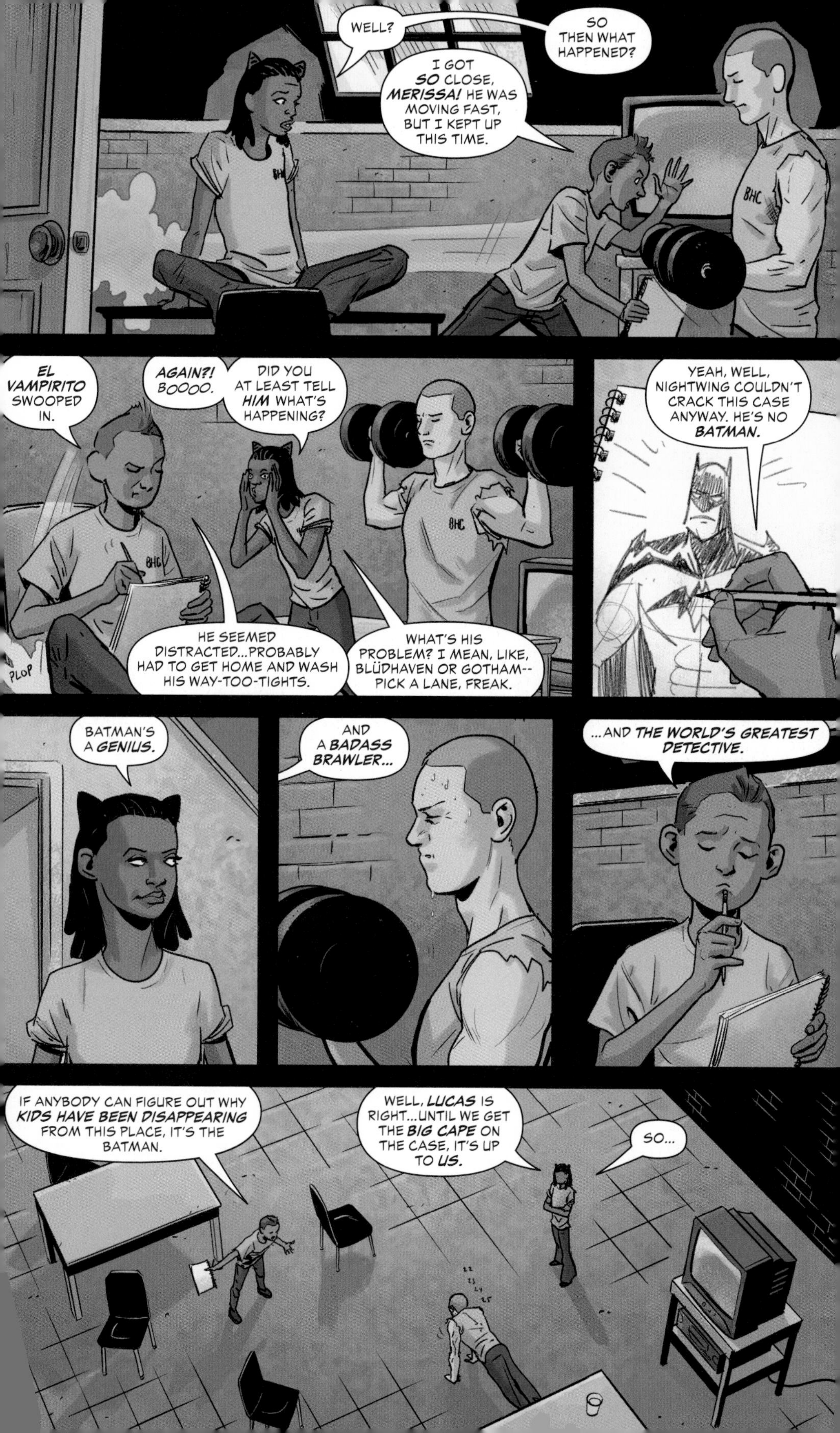
WELL?
SO THEN WHAT HAPPENED?
I GOT SO CLOSE, MERISSA! HE WAS MOVING FAST, BUT I KEPT UP THIS TIME.
EL VAMPIRITO SWOOPED IN.
AGAIN?! BOOOO.
DID YOU AT LEAST TELL HIM WHAT'S HAPPENING?
HE SEEMED DISTRACTED...PROBABLY HAD TO GET HOME AND WASH HIS WAY-TOO-TIGHTS.
WHAT'S HIS PROBLEM? I MEAN, LIKE, BLÜDHAVEN OR GOTHAM--PICK A LANE, FREAK.
PLOP
YEAH, WELL, NIGHTWING COULDN'T CRACK THIS CASE ANYWAY. HE'S NO BATMAN.
BATMAN'S A GENIUS.
AND A BADASS BRAWLER...
...AND THE WORLD'S GREATEST DETECTIVE.
IF ANYBODY CAN FIGURE OUT WHY KIDS HAVE BEEN DISAPPEARING FROM THIS PLACE, IT'S THE BATMAN.
WELL, LUCAS IS RIGHT...UNTIL WE GET THE BIG CAPE ON THE CASE, IT'S UP TO US.
SO...

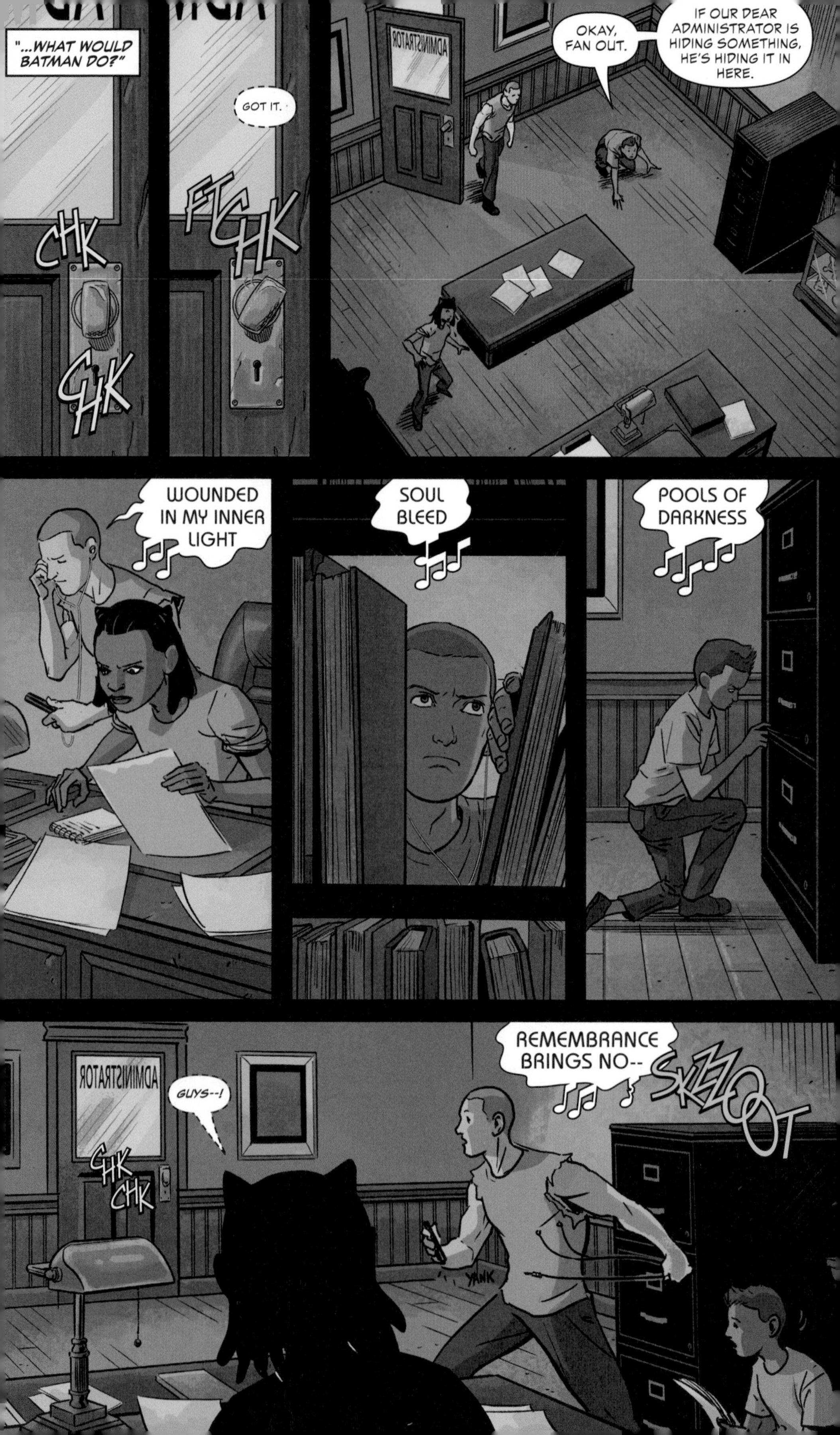
"...WHAT WOULD BATMAN DO?"
CHK
CHK
GOT IT.
FTCHK
ADMINISTRATOR
OKAY, FAN OUT.
IF OUR DEAR ADMINISTRATOR IS HIDING SOMETHING, HE'S HIDING IT IN HERE.
WOUNDED IN MY INNER LIGHT
SOUL BLEED
POOLS OF DARKNESS
ADMINISTRATOR
GUYS--!
CHK CHK
REMEMBRANCE BRINGS NO--
SKZZOOT
YANK

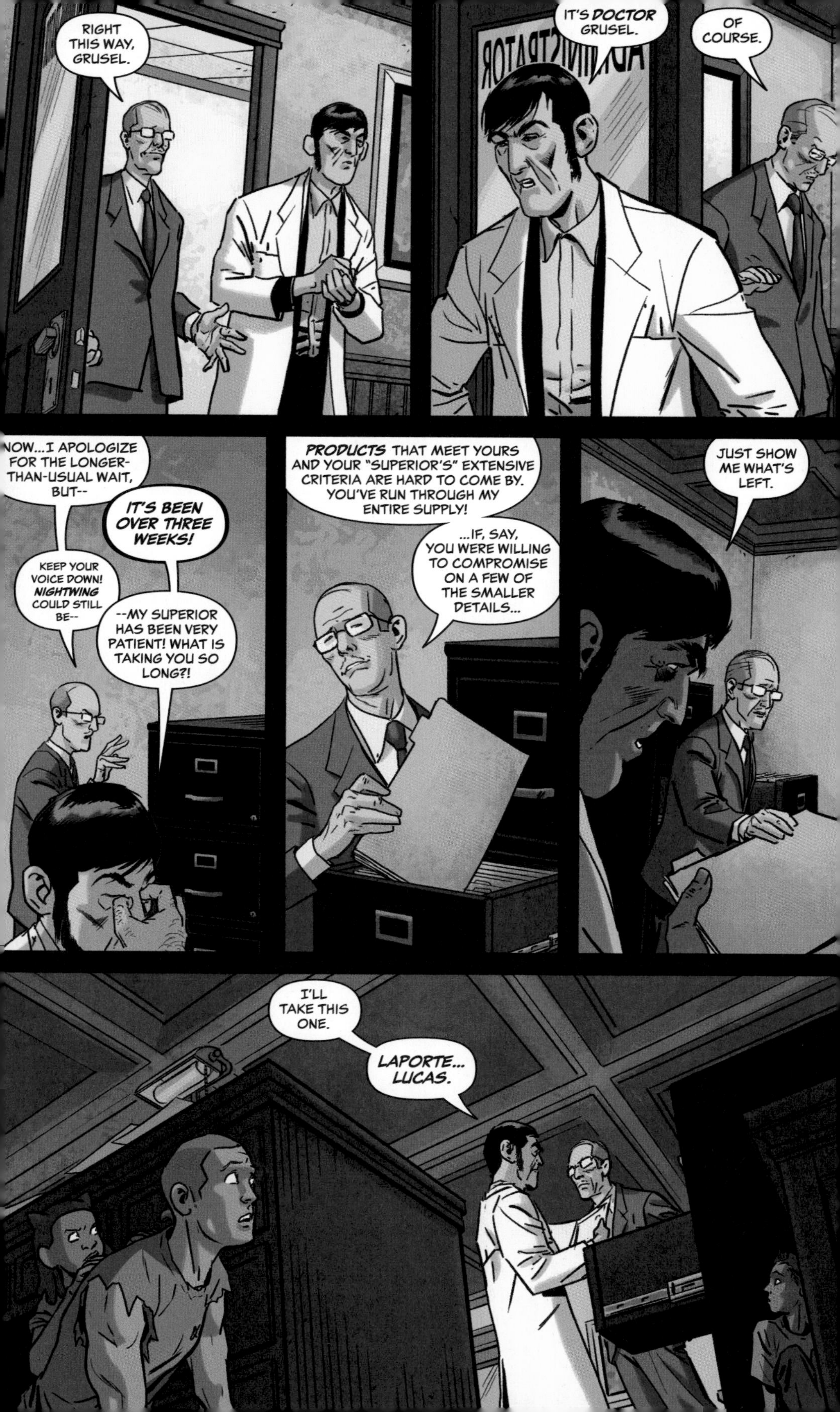
RIGHT THIS WAY, GRUSEL.
IT'S DOCTOR GRUSEL.
OF COURSE.
NOW...I APOLOGIZE FOR THE LONGER-THAN-USUAL WAIT, BUT--
IT'S BEEN OVER THREE WEEKS!
KEEP YOUR VOICE DOWN! NIGHTWING COULD STILL BE--
--MY SUPERIOR HAS BEEN VERY PATIENT! WHAT IS TAKING YOU SO LONG?!
PRODUCTS THAT MEET YOURS AND YOUR "SUPERIOR'S" EXTENSIVE CRITERIA ARE HARD TO COME BY. YOU'VE RUN THROUGH MY ENTIRE SUPPLY!
...IF, SAY, YOU WERE WILLING TO COMPROMISE ON A FEW OF THE SMALLER DETAILS...
JUST SHOW ME WHAT'S LEFT.
I'LL TAKE THIS ONE.
LAPORTE... LUCAS.

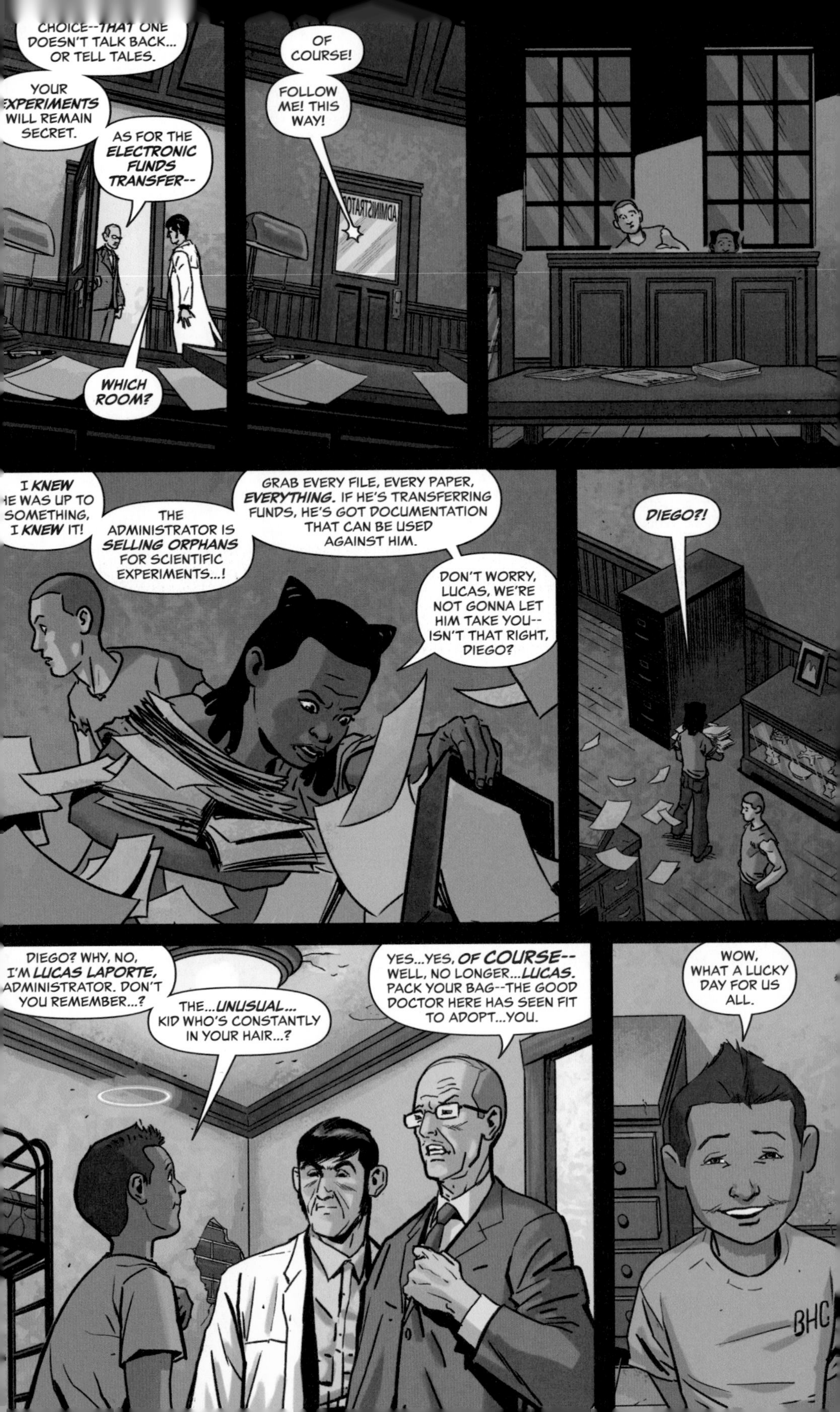
CHOICE--THAT ONE DOESN'T TALK BACK... OR TELL TALES.
YOUR EXPERIMENTS WILL REMAIN SECRET.
AS FOR THE ELECTRONIC FUNDS TRANSFER--
WHICH ROOM?
OF COURSE!
FOLLOW ME! THIS WAY!
ADMINISTRATOR
I KNEW HE WAS UP TO SOMETHING, I KNEW IT!
THE ADMINISTRATOR IS SELLING ORPHANS FOR SCIENTIFIC EXPERIMENTS...!
GRAB EVERY FILE, EVERY PAPER, EVERYTHING. IF HE'S TRANSFERRING FUNDS, HE'S GOT DOCUMENTATION THAT CAN BE USED AGAINST HIM.
DON'T WORRY, LUCAS, WE'RE NOT GONNA LET HIM TAKE YOU--ISN'T THAT RIGHT, DIEGO?
DIEGO?!
DIEGO? WHY, NO, I'M LUCAS LAPORTE, ADMINISTRATOR. DON'T YOU REMEMBER...?
THE...UNUSUAL... KID WHO'S CONSTANTLY IN YOUR HAIR...?
YES...YES, OF COURSE--WELL, NO LONGER...LUCAS. PACK YOUR BAG--THE GOOD DOCTOR HERE HAS SEEN FIT TO ADOPT...YOU.
WOW, WHAT A LUCKY DAY FOR US ALL.
BHC

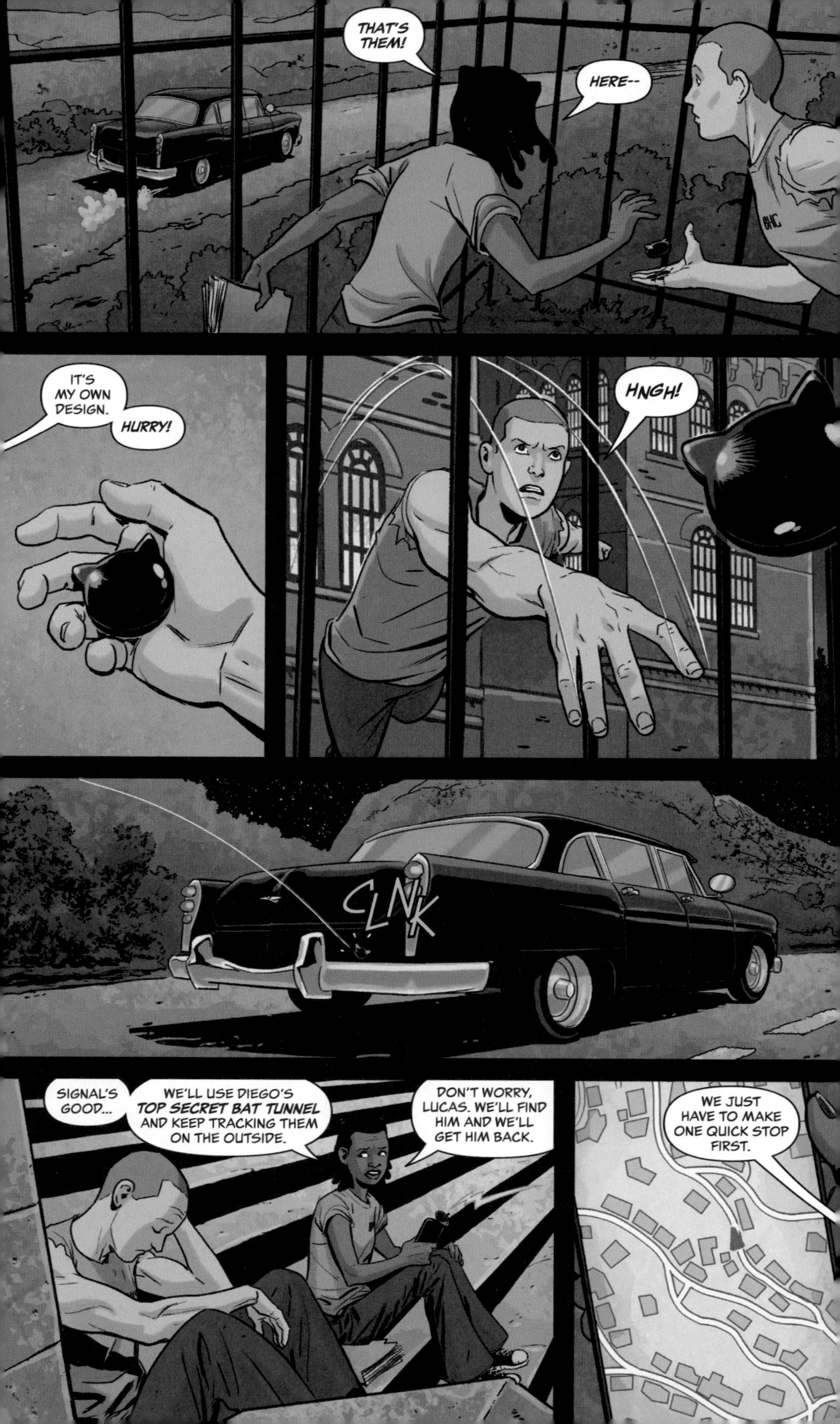
THAT'S THEM!
HERE--
IT'S MY OWN DESIGN.
HURRY!
HNGH!
CLNK
SIGNAL'S GOOD...
WE'LL USE DIEGO'S TOP SECRET BAT TUNNEL AND KEEP TRACKING THEM ON THE OUTSIDE.
DON'T WORRY, LUCAS. WE'LL FIND HIM AND WE'LL GET HIM BACK.
WE JUST HAVE TO MAKE ONE QUICK STOP FIRST.

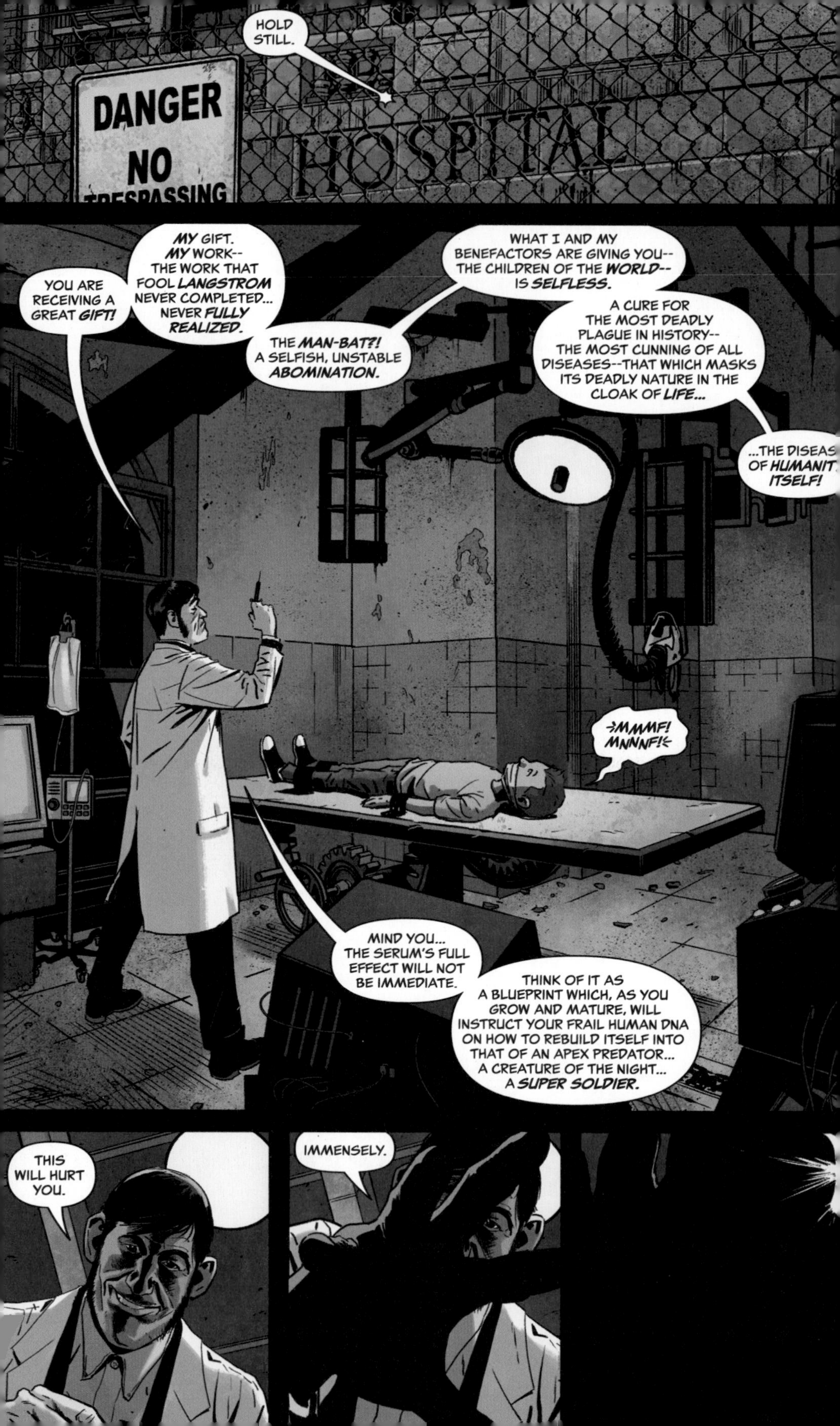

HOLD STILL.
DANGER NO TRESPASSING
HOSPITAL
YOU ARE RECEIVING A GREAT GIFT!
MY GIFT. MY WORK-- THE WORK THAT FOOL LANGSTROM NEVER COMPLETED... NEVER FULLY REALIZED.
THE MAN-BAT?! A SELFISH, UNSTABLE ABOMINATION.
WHAT I AND MY BENEFACTORS ARE GIVING YOU-- THE CHILDREN OF THE WORLD-- IS SELFLESS.
A CURE FOR THE MOST DEADLY PLAGUE IN HISTORY-- THE MOST CUNNING OF ALL DISEASES--THAT WHICH MASKS ITS DEADLY NATURE IN THE CLOAK OF LIFE...
...THE DISEAS OF HUMANIT ITSELF!
MMMF! MNNNF!
MIND YOU... THE SERUM'S FULL EFFECT WILL NOT BE IMMEDIATE.
THINK OF IT AS A BLUEPRINT WHICH, AS YOU GROW AND MATURE, WILL INSTRUCT YOUR FRAIL HUMAN DNA ON HOW TO REBUILD ITSELF INTO THAT OF AN APEX PREDATOR... A CREATURE OF THE NIGHT... A SUPER SOLDIER.
THIS WILL HURT YOU.
IMMENSELY.

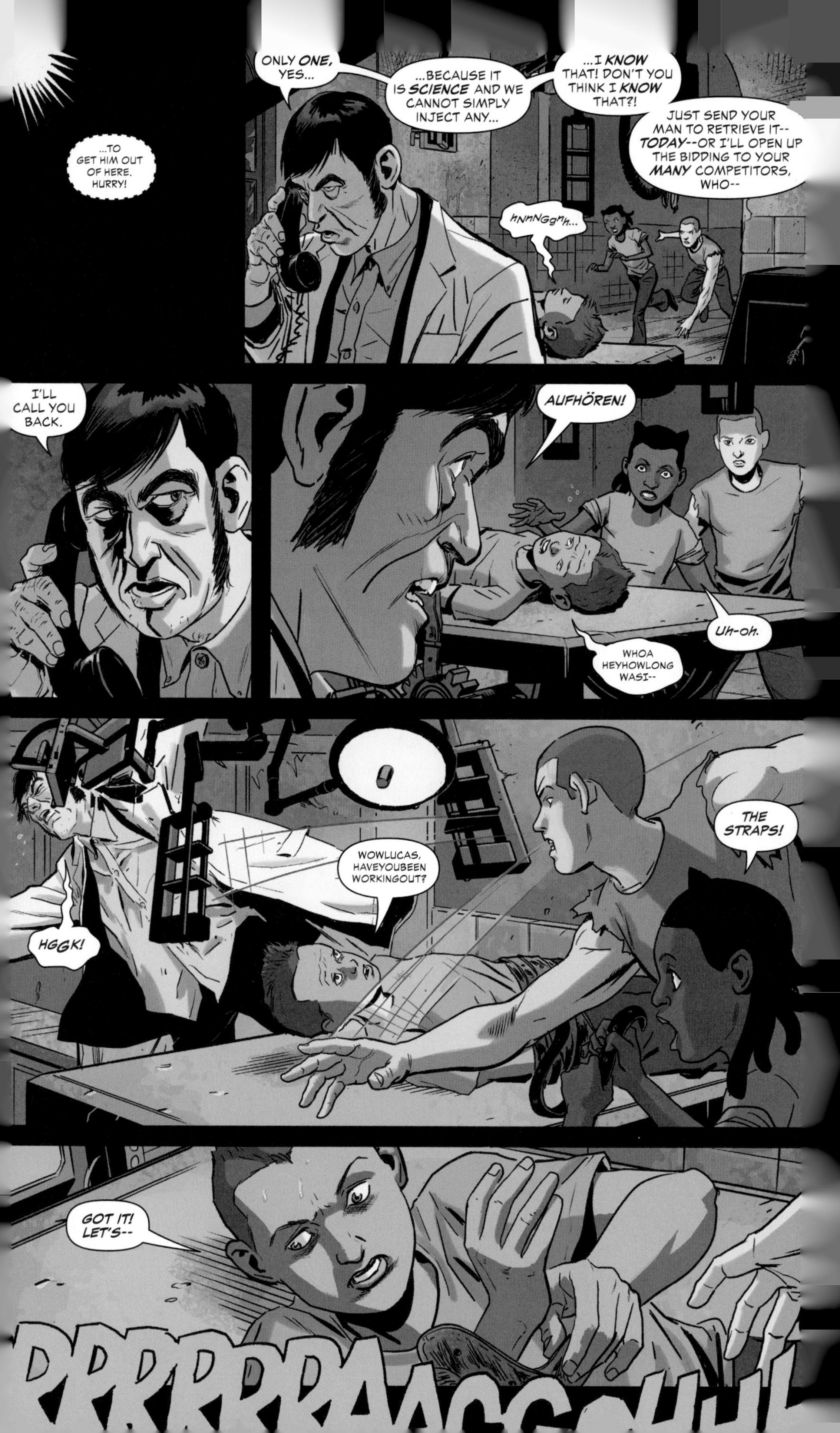
...TO GET HIM OUT OF HERE. HURRY!
ONLY ONE, YES...
...BECAUSE IT IS SCIENCE AND WE CANNOT SIMPLY INJECT ANY...
...I KNOW THAT! DON'T YOU THINK I KNOW THAT?!
JUST SEND YOUR MAN TO RETRIEVE IT-- TODAY--OR I'LL OPEN UP THE BIDDING TO YOUR MANY COMPETITORS, WHO--
hnnNGgnh...
I'LL CALL YOU BACK.
AUFHÖREN!
Uh-oh.
WHOA HEYHOWLONG WASI--
THE STRAPS!
WOWLUCAS, HAVEYOUBEEN WORKINGOUT?
HGGK!
GOT IT! LET'S--

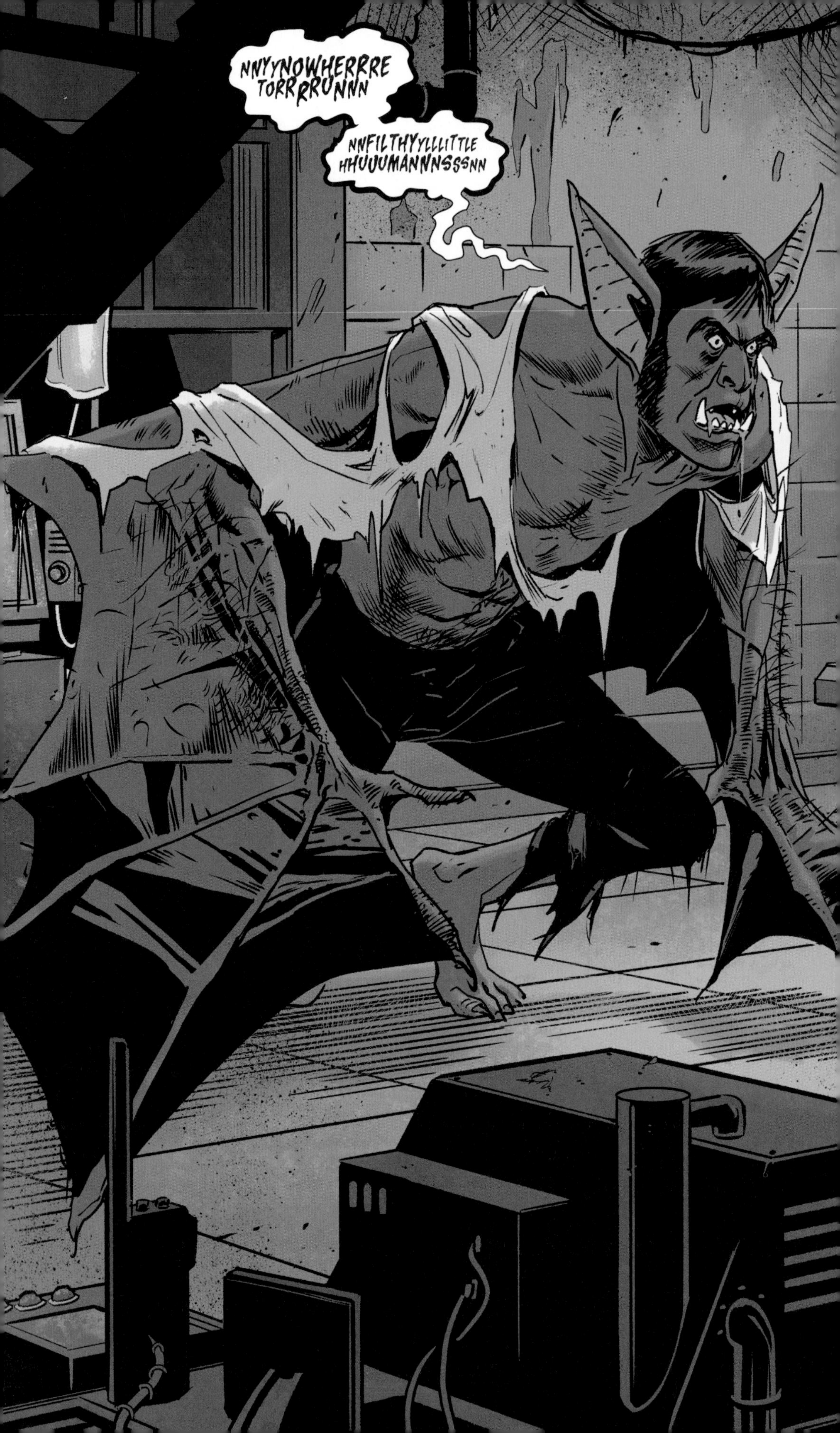
NNYYNOWHERRRE TORRRRUNNN
NNFILTHYYLLLITTLE HHUUUMANNNSSSNN

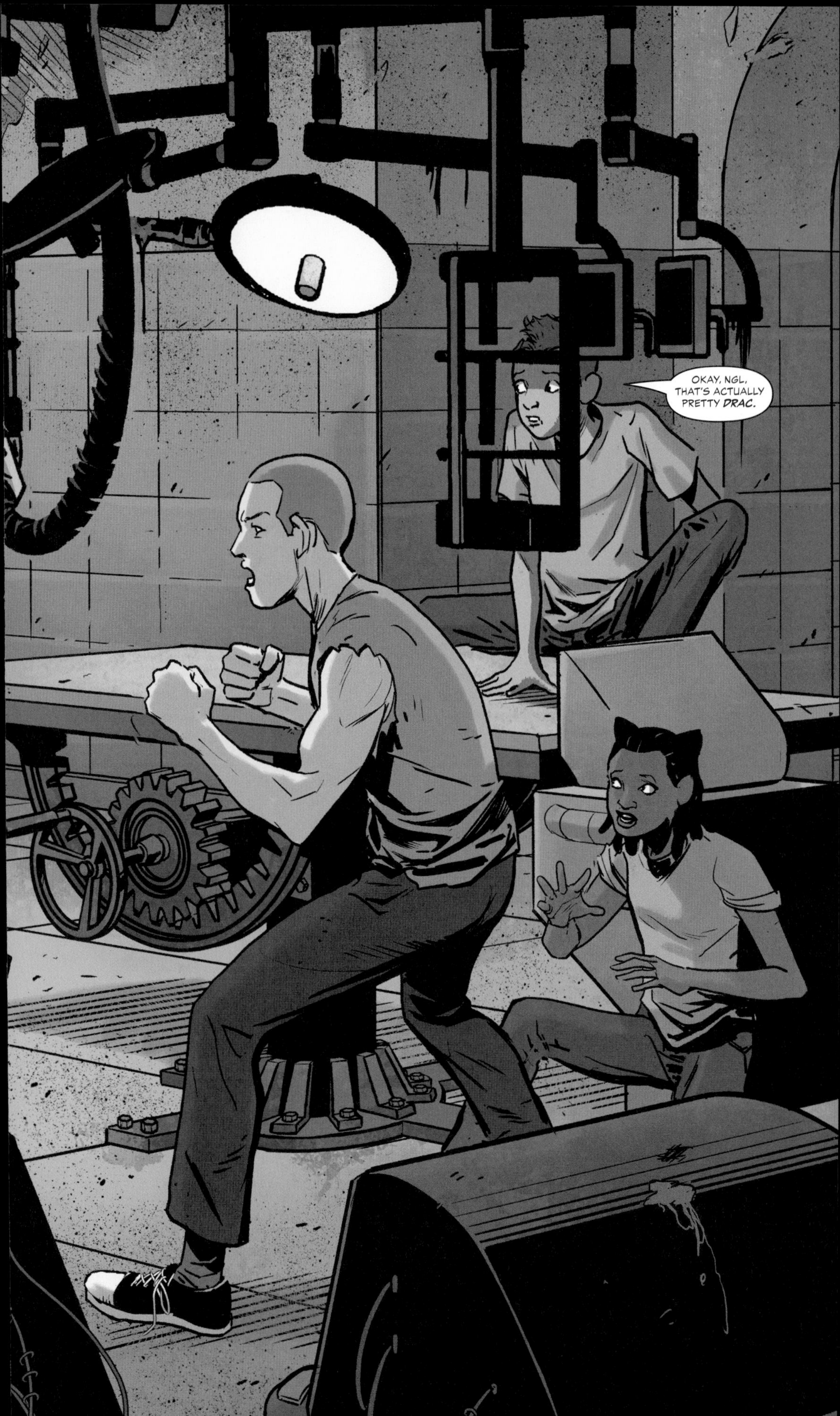
OKAY, NGL, THAT'S ACTUALLY PRETTY DRAC.

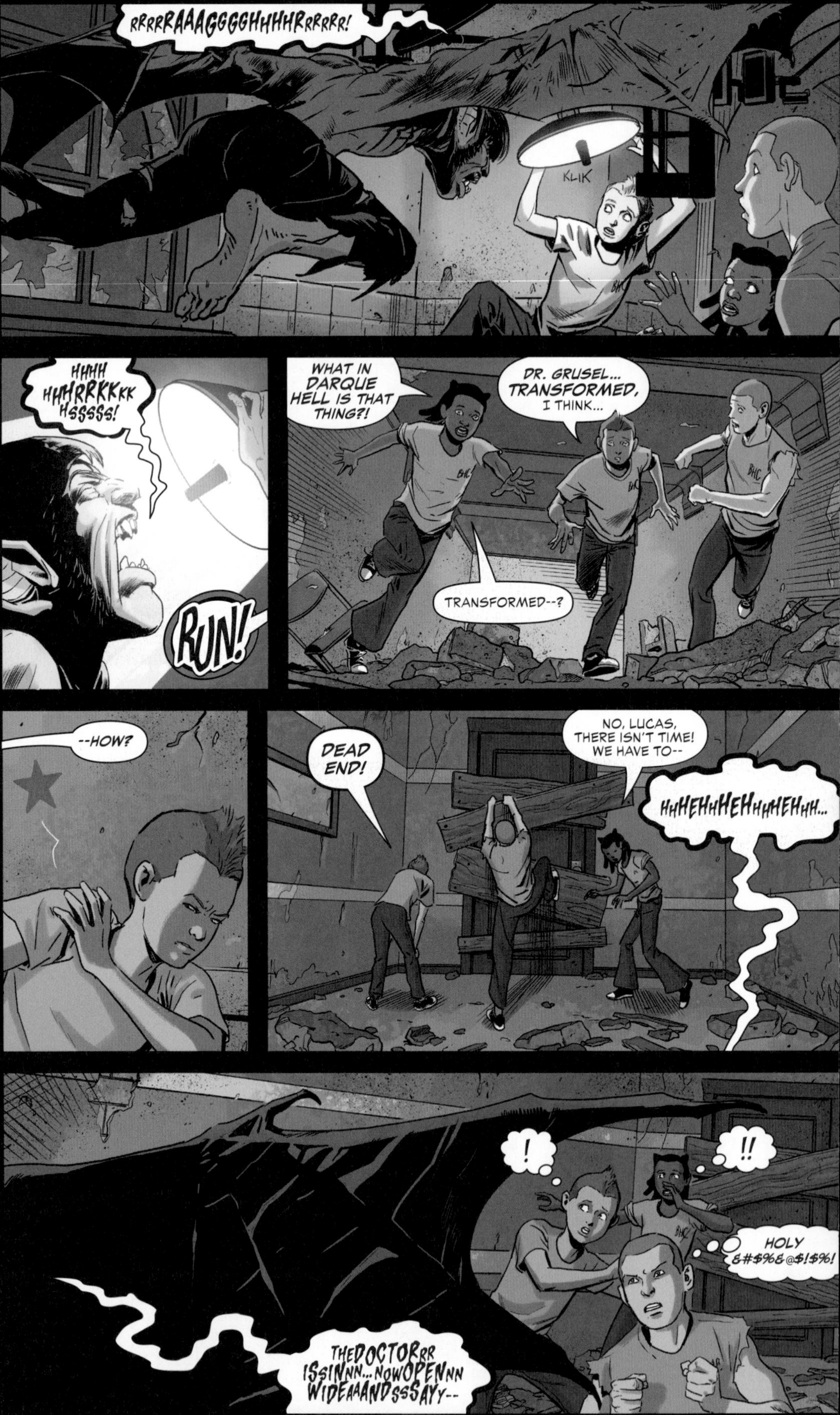

RRRRRAAAGGGGHHHHRRRRRR!
KLIK
HHHH HHHRRKKKKK HSSSSS!
RUN!
WHAT IN DARQUE HELL IS THAT THING?!
DR. GRUSEL... TRANSFORMED, I THINK...
TRANSFORMED--?
--HOW?
DEAD END!
NO, LUCAS, THERE ISN'T TIME! WE HAVE TO--
HHHEHHHEHHHHEHHH...
!
!!
HOLY &#$%&@$!$%!
THEDOCTORRR ISSINNN... NOWOPENNN WIDEAAANDSSSAYY--

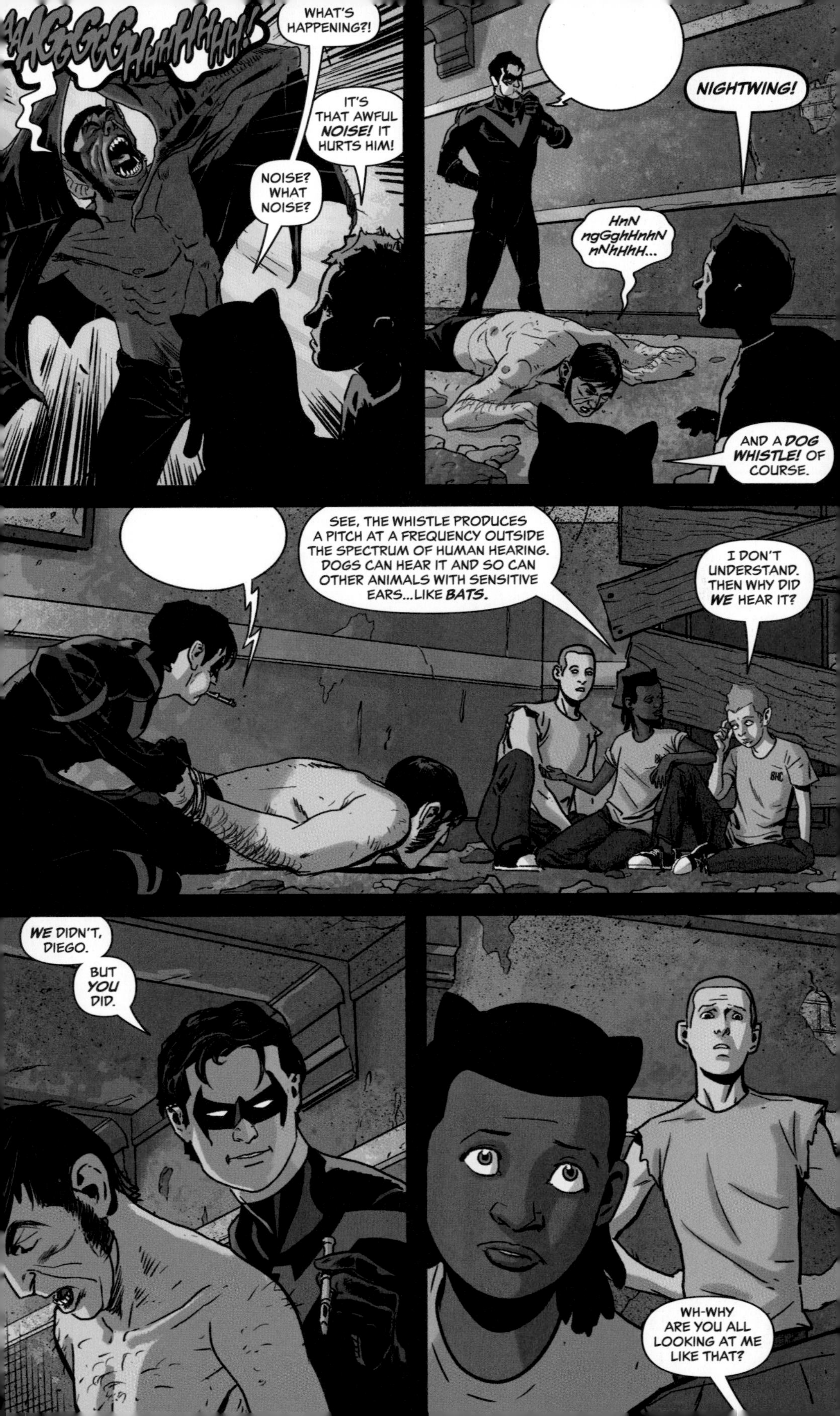
AAAGGGGHHHHHHH!
WHAT'S HAPPENING?!
IT'S THAT AWFUL NOISE! IT HURTS HIM!
NOISE? WHAT NOISE?
NIGHTWING!
HnN ngGghHnhN nNhHHH...
AND A DOG WHISTLE! OF COURSE.
SEE, THE WHISTLE PRODUCES A PITCH AT A FREQUENCY OUTSIDE THE SPECTRUM OF HUMAN HEARING. DOGS CAN HEAR IT AND SO CAN OTHER ANIMALS WITH SENSITIVE EARS...LIKE BATS.
I DON'T UNDERSTAND. THEN WHY DID WE HEAR IT?
WE DIDN'T, DIEGO.
BUT YOU DID.
WH-WHY ARE YOU ALL LOOKING AT ME LIKE THAT?

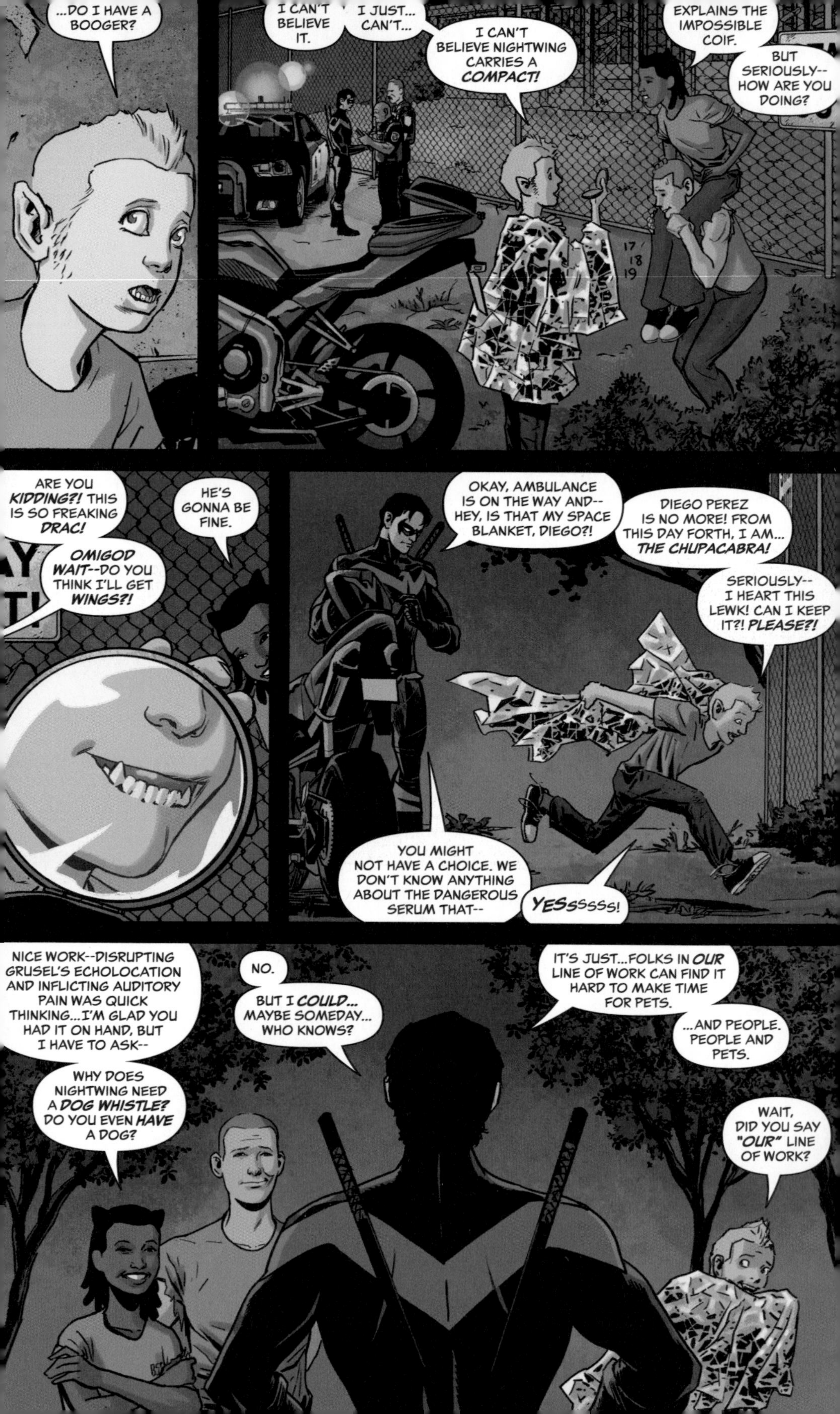
...DO I HAVE A BOOGER?
I CAN'T BELIEVE IT.
I JUST... CAN'T...
I CAN'T BELIEVE NIGHTWING CARRIES A COMPACT!
EXPLAINS THE IMPOSSIBLE COIF.
BUT SERIOUSLY--HOW ARE YOU DOING?
ARE YOU KIDDING?! THIS IS SO FREAKING DRAC!
OMIGOD WAIT--DO YOU THINK I'LL GET WINGS?!
HE'S GONNA BE FINE.
OKAY, AMBULANCE IS ON THE WAY AND--HEY, IS THAT MY SPACE BLANKET, DIEGO?!
DIEGO PEREZ IS NO MORE! FROM THIS DAY FORTH, I AM... THE CHUPACABRA!
SERIOUSLY--I HEART THIS LEWK! CAN I KEEP IT?! PLEASE?!
YOU MIGHT NOT HAVE A CHOICE. WE DON'T KNOW ANYTHING ABOUT THE DANGEROUS SERUM THAT--
YESsssss!
NICE WORK--DISRUPTING GRUSEL'S ECHOLOCATION AND INFLICTING AUDITORY PAIN WAS QUICK THINKING...I'M GLAD YOU HAD IT ON HAND, BUT I HAVE TO ASK--
WHY DOES NIGHTWING NEED A DOG WHISTLE? DO YOU EVEN HAVE A DOG?
NO.
BUT I COULD... MAYBE SOMEDAY... WHO KNOWS?
IT'S JUST...FOLKS IN OUR LINE OF WORK CAN FIND IT HARD TO MAKE TIME FOR PETS.
...AND PEOPLE. PEOPLE AND PETS.
WAIT, DID YOU SAY "OUR" LINE OF WORK?

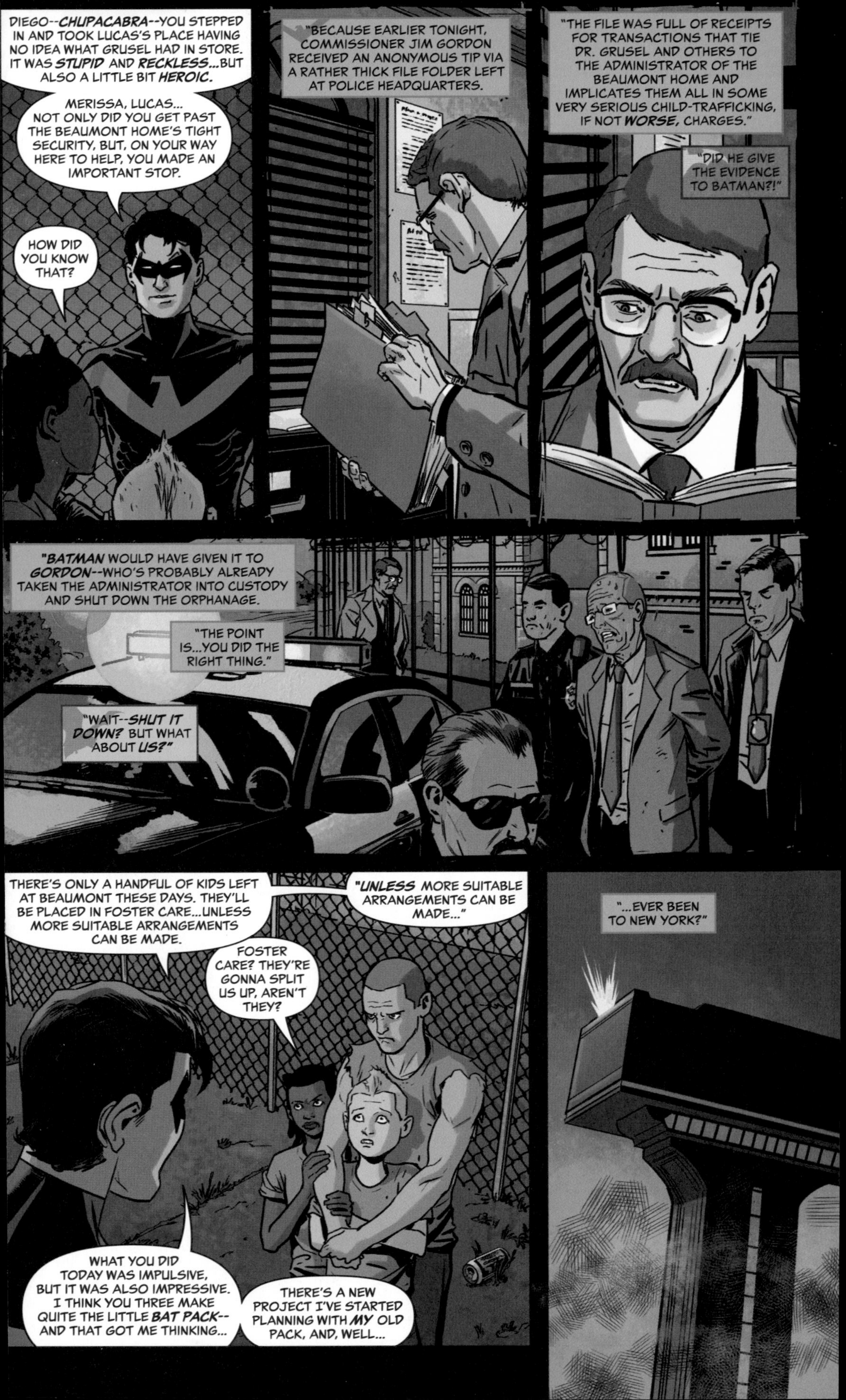
DIEGO--CHUPACABRA--YOU STEPPED IN AND TOOK LUCAS'S PLACE HAVING NO IDEA WHAT GRUSEL HAD IN STORE. IT WAS STUPID AND RECKLESS...BUT ALSO A LITTLE BIT HEROIC.
MERISSA, LUCAS... NOT ONLY DID YOU GET PAST THE BEAUMONT HOME'S TIGHT SECURITY, BUT, ON YOUR WAY HERE TO HELP, YOU MADE AN IMPORTANT STOP.
HOW DID YOU KNOW THAT?
"BECAUSE EARLIER TONIGHT, COMMISSIONER JIM GORDON RECEIVED AN ANONYMOUS TIP VIA A RATHER THICK FILE FOLDER LEFT AT POLICE HEADQUARTERS.
"THE FILE WAS FULL OF RECEIPTS FOR TRANSACTIONS THAT TIE DR. GRUSEL AND OTHERS TO THE ADMINISTRATOR OF THE BEAUMONT HOME AND IMPLICATES THEM ALL IN SOME VERY SERIOUS CHILD-TRAFFICKING, IF NOT WORSE, CHARGES."
"DID HE GIVE THE EVIDENCE TO BATMAN?!"
"BATMAN WOULD HAVE GIVEN IT TO GORDON--WHO'S PROBABLY ALREADY TAKEN THE ADMINISTRATOR INTO CUSTODY AND SHUT DOWN THE ORPHANAGE.
"THE POINT IS...YOU DID THE RIGHT THING."
"WAIT--SHUT IT DOWN? BUT WHAT ABOUT US?"
THERE'S ONLY A HANDFUL OF KIDS LEFT AT BEAUMONT THESE DAYS. THEY'LL BE PLACED IN FOSTER CARE...UNLESS MORE SUITABLE ARRANGEMENTS CAN BE MADE.
FOSTER CARE? THEY'RE GONNA SPLIT US UP, AREN'T THEY?
WHAT YOU DID TODAY WAS IMPULSIVE, BUT IT WAS ALSO IMPRESSIVE. I THINK YOU THREE MAKE QUITE THE LITTLE BAT PACK-- AND THAT GOT ME THINKING...
THERE'S A NEW PROJECT I'VE STARTED PLANNING WITH MY OLD PACK, AND, WELL...
"UNLESS MORE SUITABLE ARRANGEMENTS CAN BE MADE..."
"...EVER BEEN TO NEW YORK?"

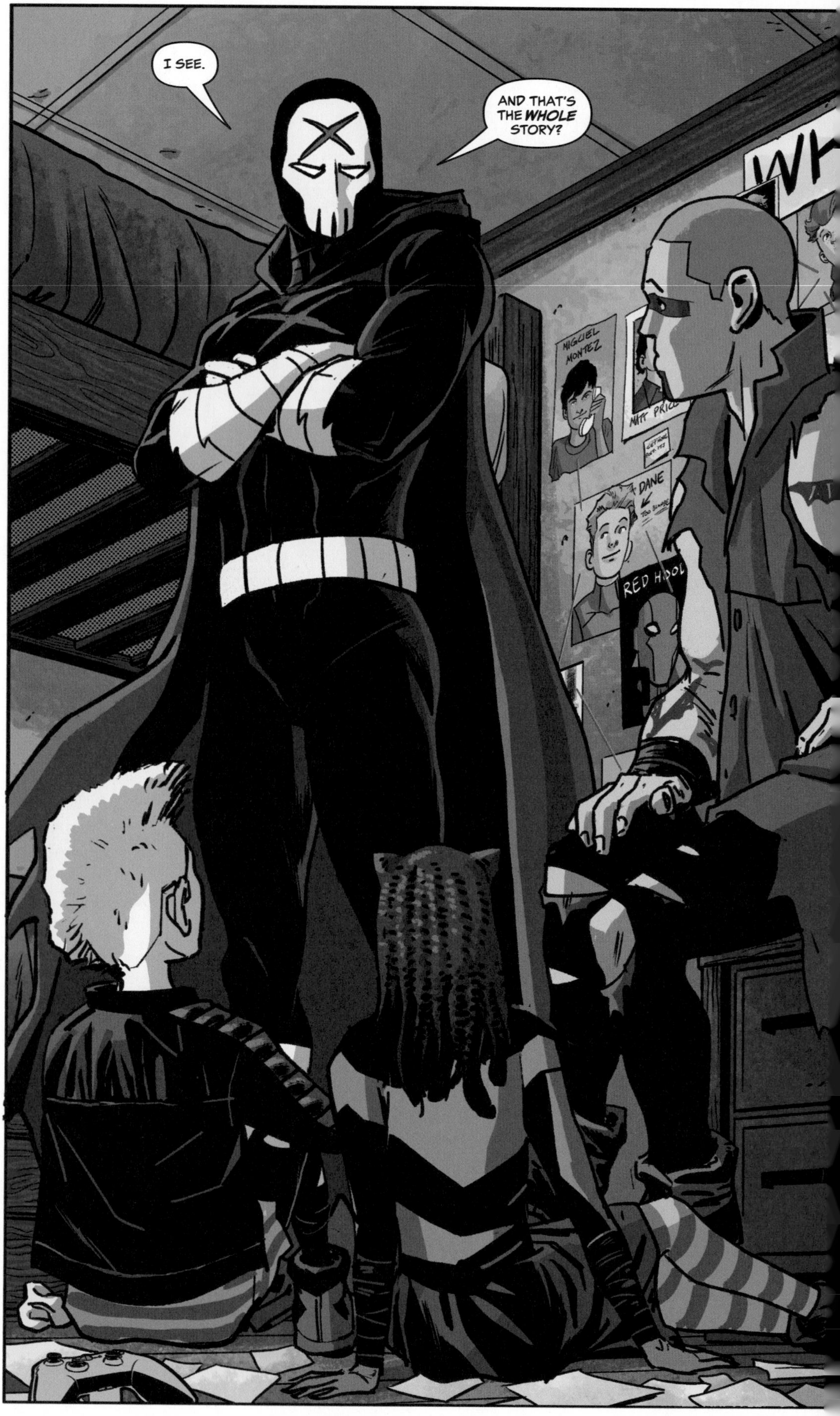
I SEE.
AND THAT'S THE *WHOLE* STORY?
MIGUEL MONTEZ
DANE

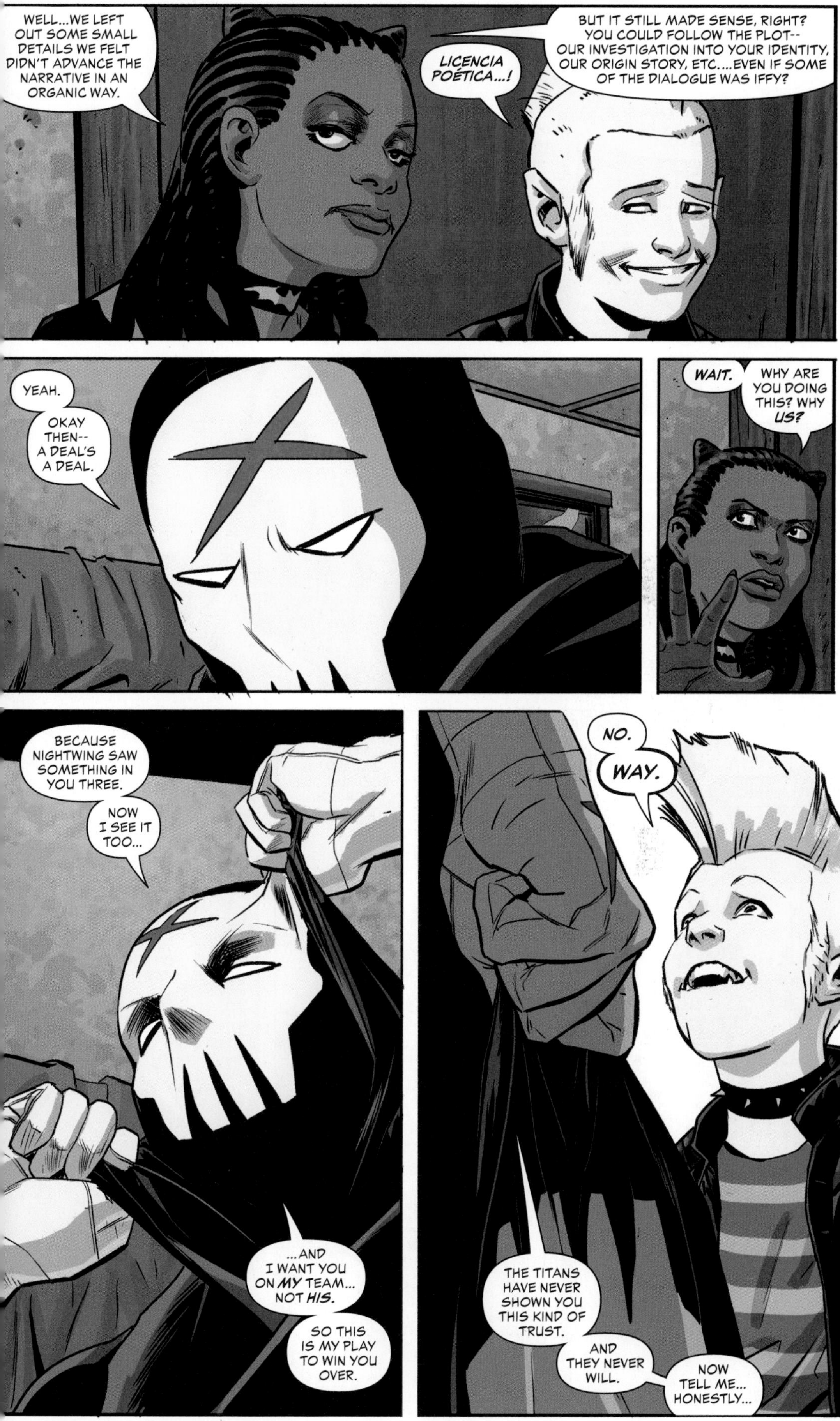
WELL...WE LEFT OUT SOME SMALL DETAILS WE FELT DIDN'T ADVANCE THE NARRATIVE IN AN ORGANIC WAY.
LICENCIA POÉTICA...!
BUT IT STILL MADE SENSE, RIGHT? YOU COULD FOLLOW THE PLOT-- OUR INVESTIGATION INTO YOUR IDENTITY, OUR ORIGIN STORY, ETC....EVEN IF SOME OF THE DIALOGUE WAS IFFY?
YEAH.
OKAY THEN-- A DEAL'S A DEAL.
WAIT.
WHY ARE YOU DOING THIS? WHY US?
BECAUSE NIGHTWING SAW SOMETHING IN YOU THREE.
NOW I SEE IT TOO...
...AND I WANT YOU ON MY TEAM... NOT HIS.
SO THIS IS MY PLAY TO WIN YOU OVER.
NO.
WAY.
THE TITANS HAVE NEVER SHOWN YOU THIS KIND OF TRUST.
AND THEY NEVER WILL.
NOW TELL ME... HONESTLY...

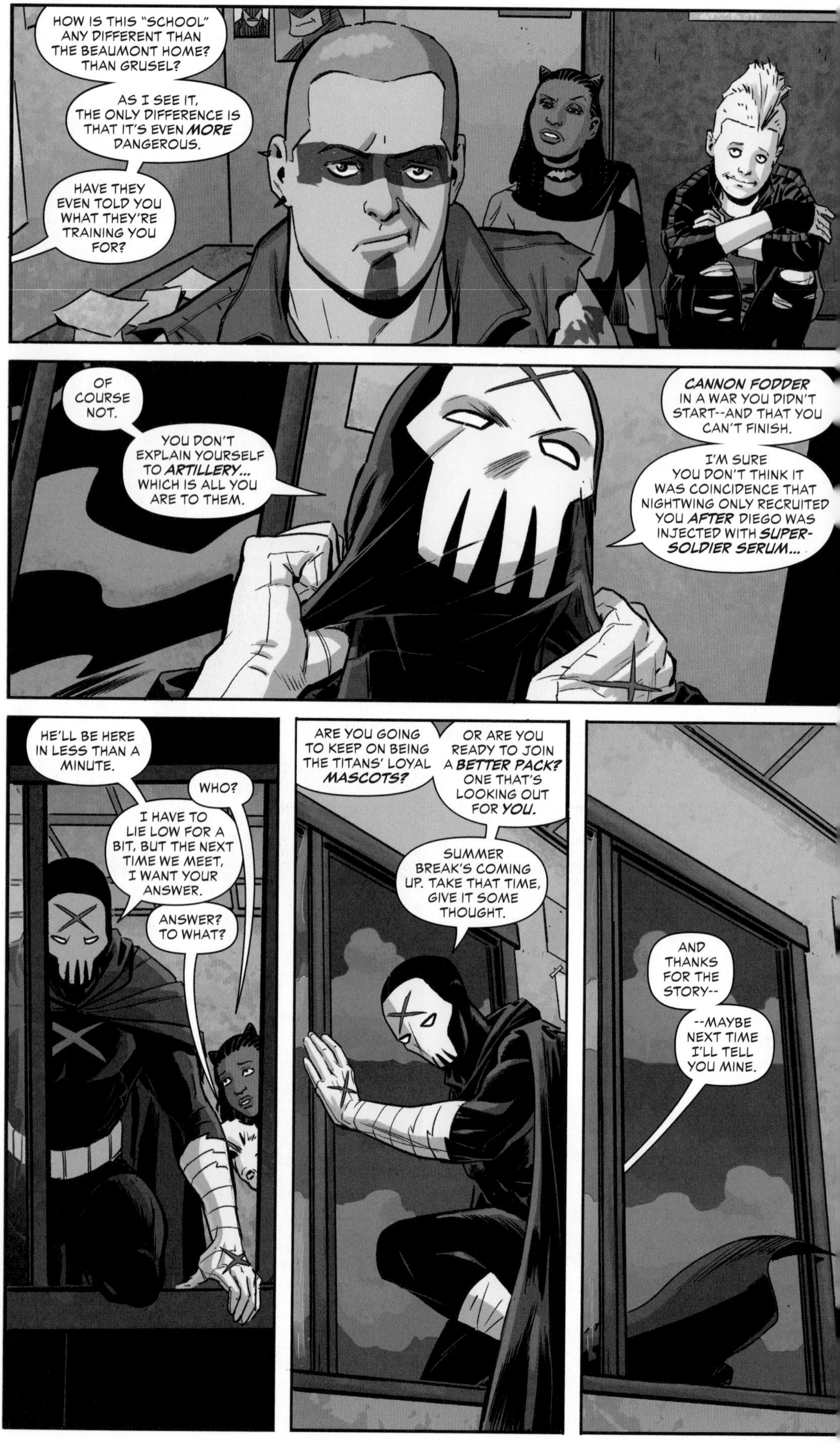
HOW IS THIS "SCHOOL" ANY DIFFERENT THAN THE BEAUMONT HOME? THAN GRUSEL?
AS I SEE IT, THE ONLY DIFFERENCE IS THAT IT'S EVEN *MORE* DANGEROUS.
HAVE THEY EVEN TOLD YOU WHAT THEY'RE TRAINING YOU FOR?
OF COURSE NOT.
YOU DON'T EXPLAIN YOURSELF TO *ARTILLERY...* WHICH IS ALL YOU ARE TO THEM.
CANNON FODDER IN A WAR YOU DIDN'T START--AND THAT YOU CAN'T FINISH.
I'M SURE YOU DON'T THINK IT WAS COINCIDENCE THAT NIGHTWING ONLY RECRUITED YOU *AFTER* DIEGO WAS INJECTED WITH *SUPER-SOLDIER SERUM...*
HE'LL BE HERE IN LESS THAN A MINUTE.
WHO?
I HAVE TO LIE LOW FOR A BIT, BUT THE NEXT TIME WE MEET, I WANT YOUR ANSWER.
ANSWER? TO WHAT?
ARE YOU GOING TO KEEP ON BEING THE TITANS' LOYAL *MASCOTS?*
OR ARE YOU READY TO JOIN A *BETTER PACK?* ONE THAT'S LOOKING OUT FOR *YOU.*
SUMMER BREAK'S COMING UP. TAKE THAT TIME, GIVE IT SOME THOUGHT.
AND THANKS FOR THE STORY--
--MAYBE NEXT TIME I'LL TELL YOU MINE.

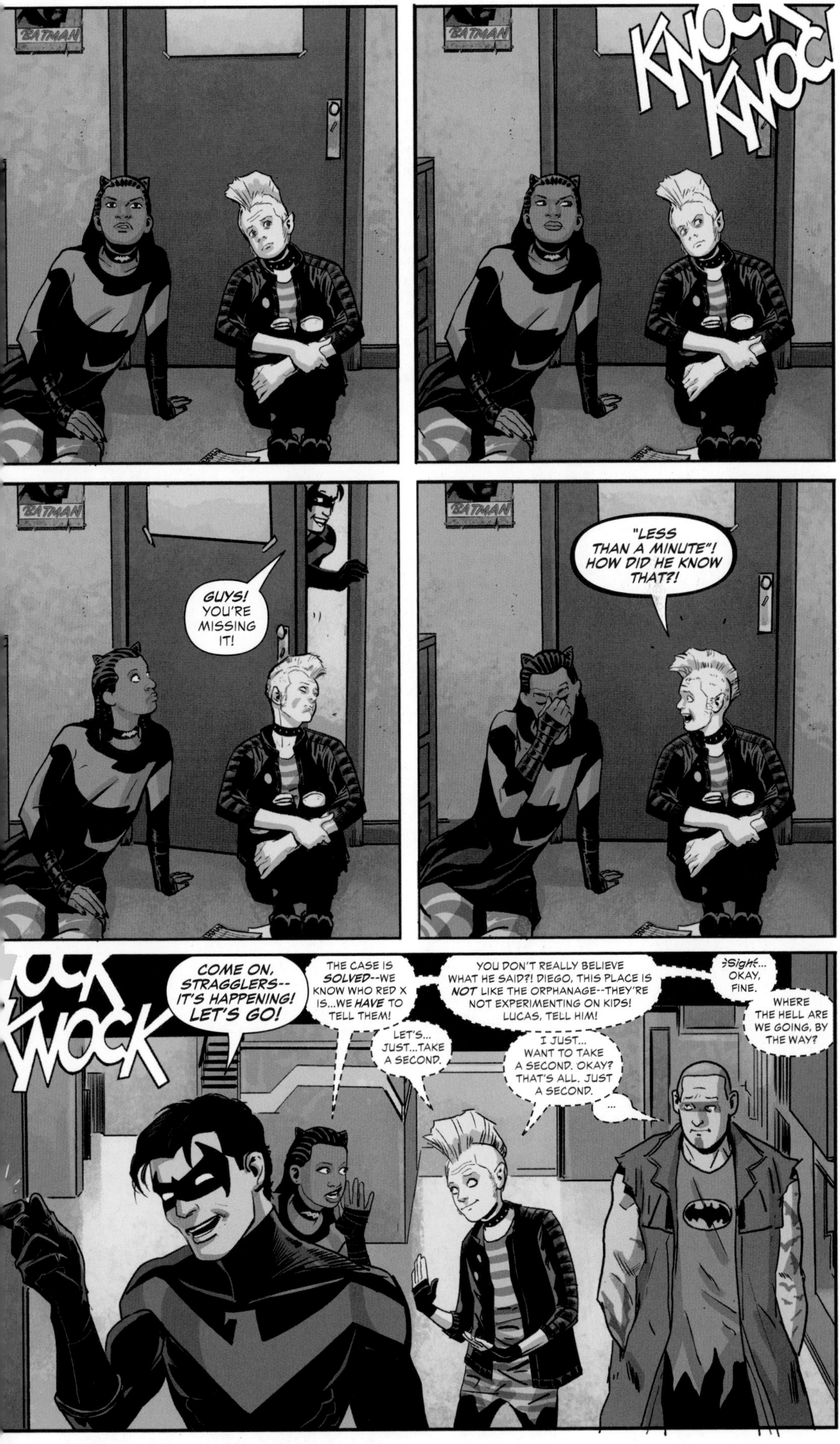
BATMAN
KNOCK KNOCK
GUYS! YOU'RE MISSING IT!
"LESS THAN A MINUTE"! HOW DID HE KNOW THAT?!
COME ON, STRAGGLERS--IT'S HAPPENING! LET'S GO!
THE CASE IS SOLVED--WE KNOW WHO RED X IS...WE HAVE TO TELL THEM!
LET'S... JUST...TAKE A SECOND.
YOU DON'T REALLY BELIEVE WHAT HE SAID?! DIEGO, THIS PLACE IS NOT LIKE THE ORPHANAGE--THEY'RE NOT EXPERIMENTING ON KIDS! LUCAS, TELL HIM!
I JUST... WANT TO TAKE A SECOND. OKAY? THAT'S ALL. JUST A SECOND.
...
Sigh... OKAY, FINE.
WHERE THE HELL ARE WE GOING, BY THE WAY?

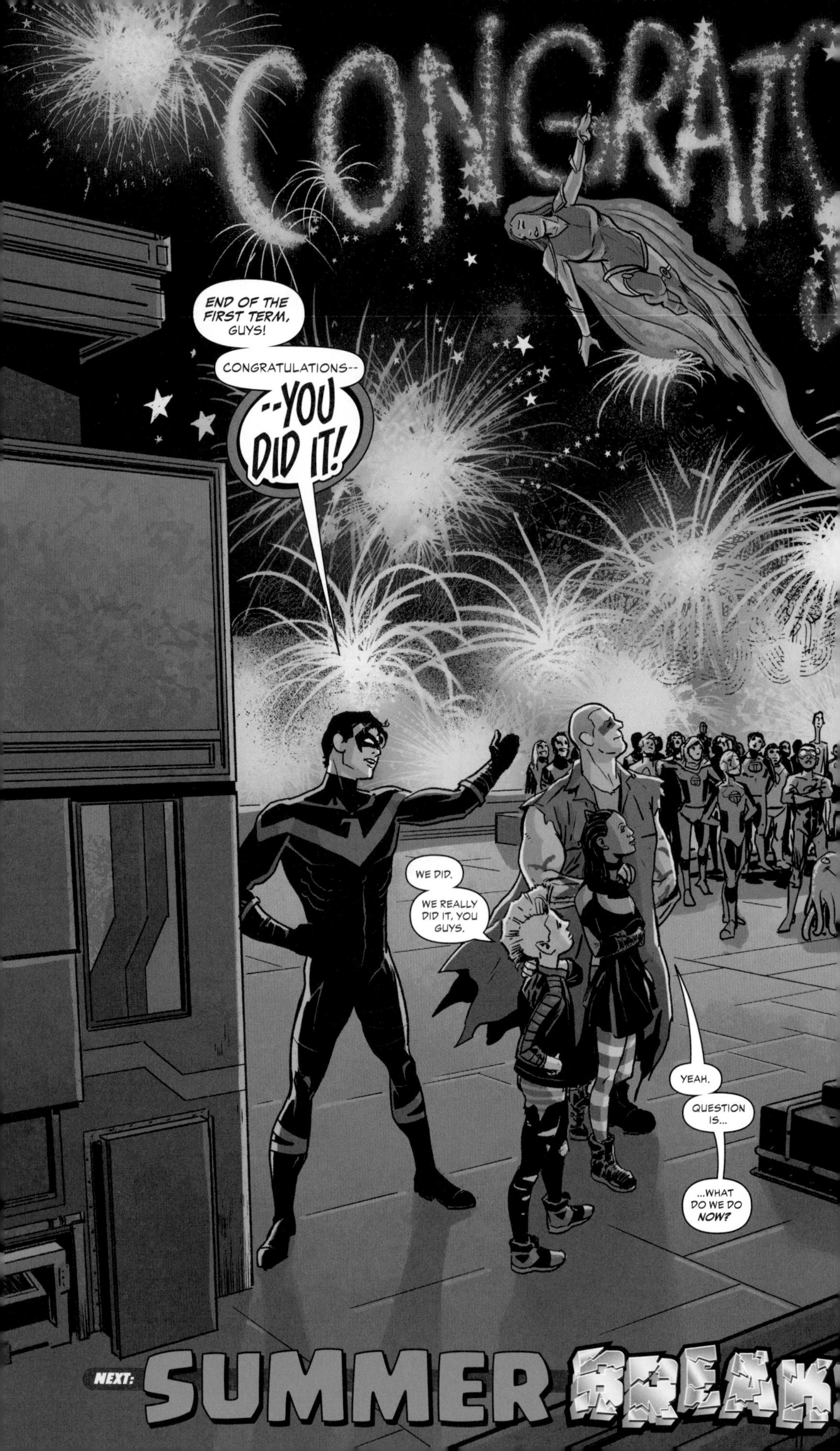

CONGRATS
END OF THE FIRST TERM, GUYS!
CONGRATULATIONS--
--YOU DID IT!
WE DID.
WE REALLY DID IT, YOU GUYS.
YEAH.
QUESTION IS...
...WHAT DO WE DO NOW?
NEXT: SUMMER BREAK

TEEN TITANS ACADEMY

2021 YEARBOOK

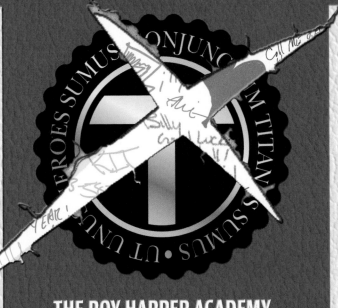

**THE ROY HARPER ACADEMY
INAUGURAL CLASS**

Contents

2021 RETROSPECTIVE
IN MEMORIAM: ROY HARPER
FACULTY BIOGRAPHIES
SENIOR CLASS PORTRAITS
CANDID CAMPUS
INAUGURAL CLASS SUPERLATIVES
PHOTO ESSAY: THE SHOW CHOIR'S
ORIGINAL PRODUCTION:
"THE JUDAS CONTRACT ON ICE"
BOOSTERS & CORPORATE SPONSORS
UNDERCLASSMEN PORTRAITS
CLUBS & ORGANIZATIONS

...21

...arbook Staff

...OR: Gorilla Gregg
...OGRAPHER: Billy Batson
...ARCH: Diego Perez
...GN: Wallace West
...PPORT: Merissa Cooper
...LTY ADVISOR: Mr. Beast Boy

A LETTER FROM *The Class President*

Dear Members of the Inaugural Class of the
ROY HARPER TITANS ACADEMY,

A **JOURNEY** is about growth and change. And I don't mean all that physical growth and change so many of you, especially the boys and girls, are experiencing. Let's keep that crap in Health class where it belongs! I mean a much bigger journey—the kind our faithful teachers, the "classic" Titans, undertook. Theirs is the story of humble sidekicks who carved a path to their own identities, independent of the heroes they served. A path that started in a big T-shaped building in San Francisco and led all the way to...another big T-shaped building in New York City.

And so, as you leaf through this book, turning the page from memory to memory, call to mind the incredible journeys of those that came before us to open the doors of this school, so that one day, we could walk through them...

...as we begin journeys of our own.

BOOM. Nailed it,

PRESIDENT STITCH
(They/Them)

Go Ape this Summer! Gregg ☺

Billy

TITANS together! -Jooby!

You're one of the reasons I left! -CRUSH

Good Luck this Summer Miguel

KIT ↓ STITCH

ROUNDHOUSE

Love you mean it Emiko☾

BEEP Runny

...EG ya DAVE.

-Kid FLASH ☺

Gotham 4 EVER! -The BAT PACK!

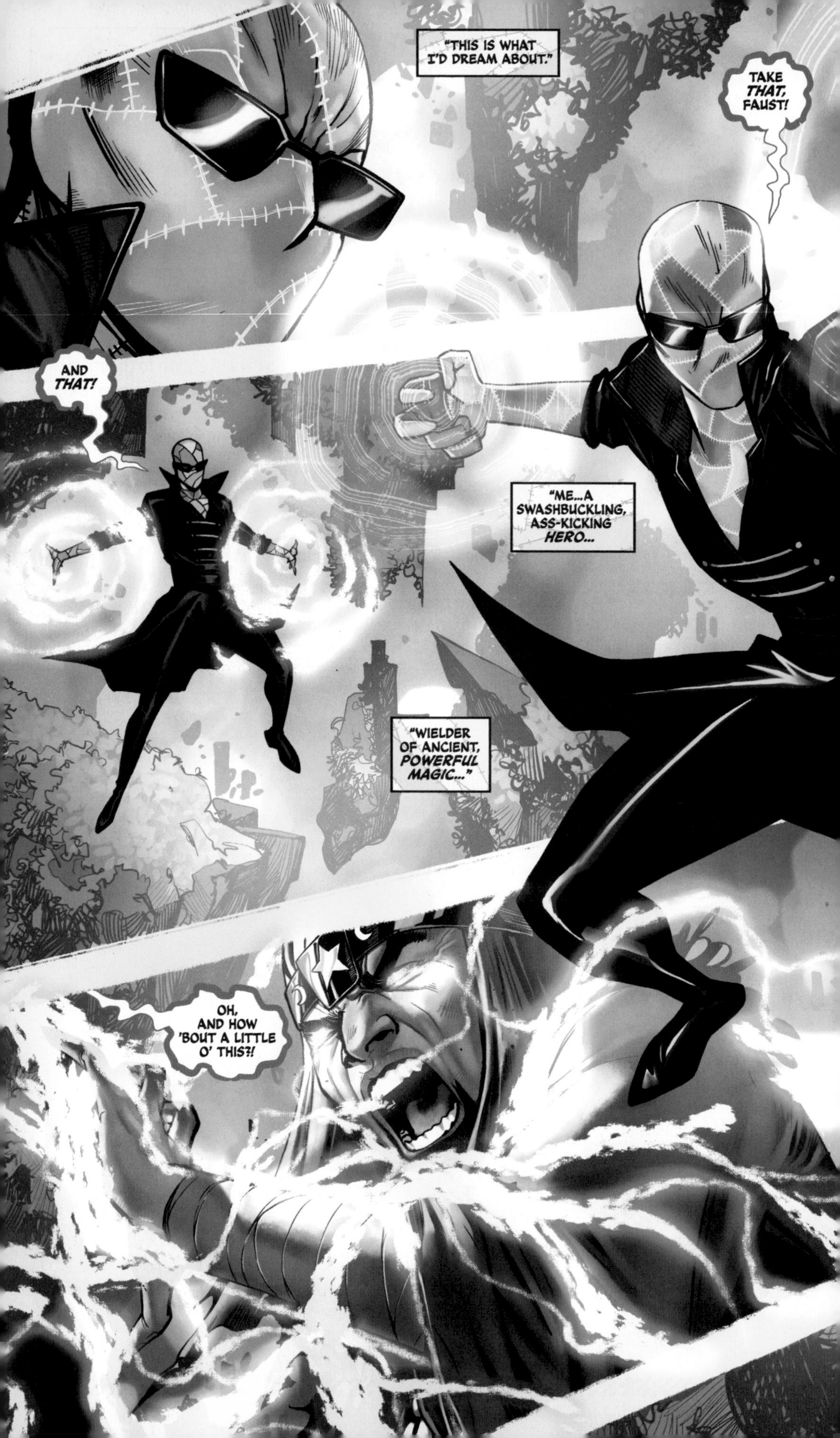
"THIS IS WHAT I'D DREAM ABOUT."
TAKE *THAT,* FAUST!
AND *THAT!*
"ME...A SWASHBUCKLING, ASS-KICKING *HERO*...
"WIELDER OF ANCIENT, *POWERFUL* MAGIC..."
OH, AND HOW 'BOUT A LITTLE O' THIS?!

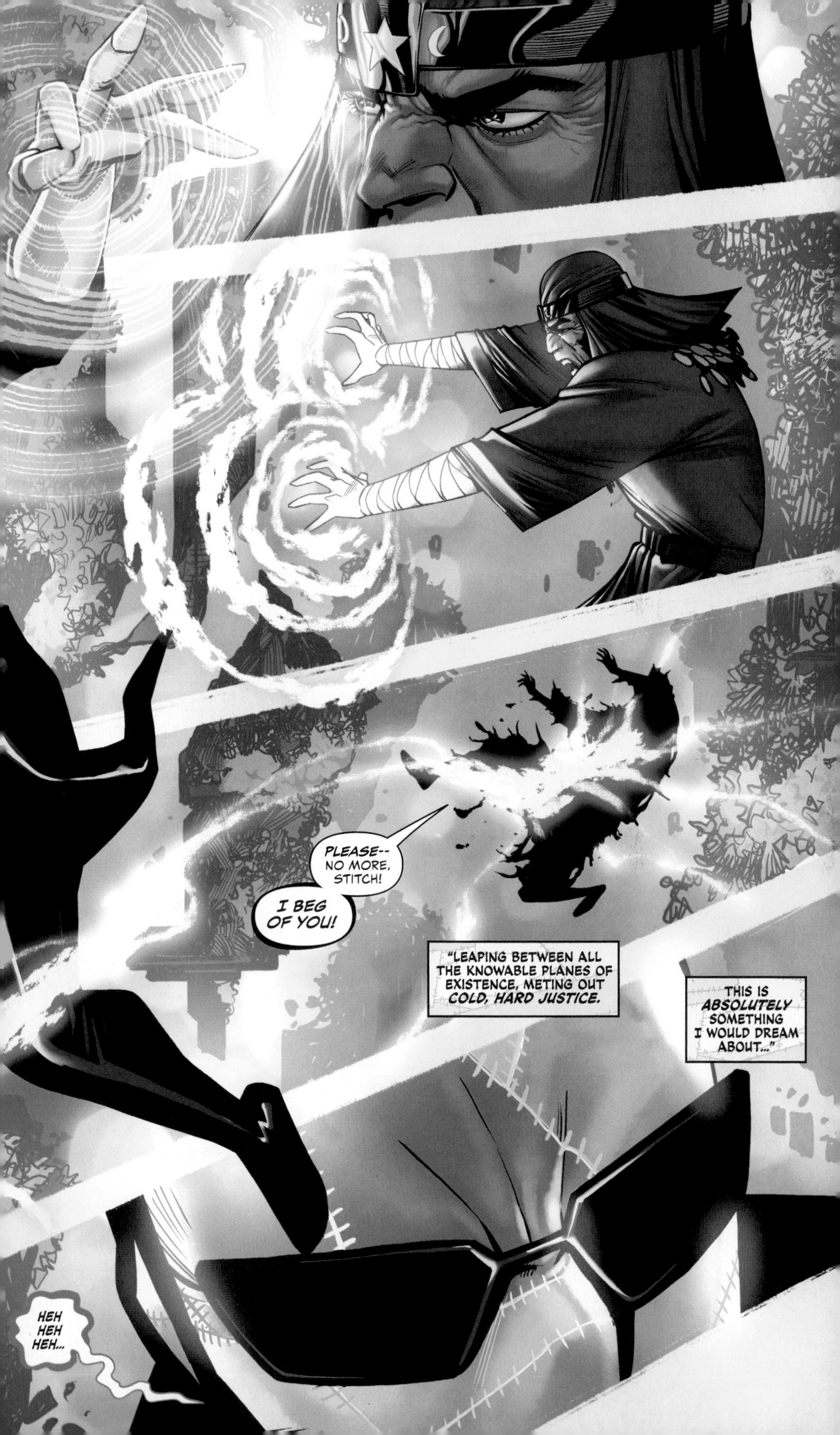
PLEASE-- NO MORE, STITCH!
I BEG OF YOU!
"LEAPING BETWEEN ALL THE KNOWABLE PLANES OF EXISTENCE, METING OUT COLD, HARD JUSTICE.
THIS IS ABSOLUTELY SOMETHING I WOULD DREAM ABOUT..."
HEH HEH HEH...

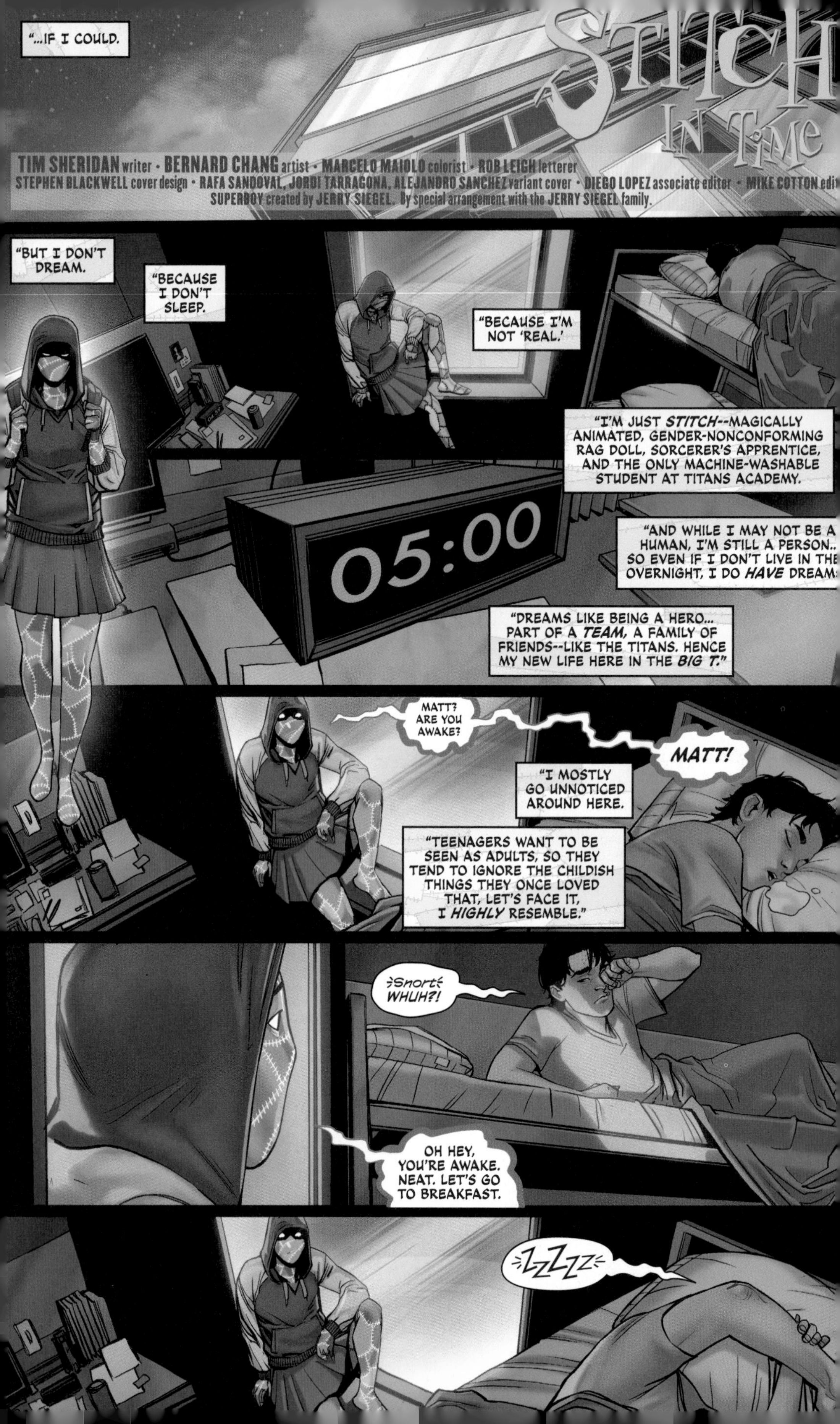
"...IF I COULD.
STITCH IN TIME
TIM SHERIDAN writer • BERNARD CHANG artist • MARCELO MAIOLO colorist • ROB LEIGH letterer
STEPHEN BLACKWELL cover design • RAFA SANDOVAL, JORDI TARRAGONA, ALEJANDRO SANCHEZ variant cover • DIEGO LOPEZ associate editor • MIKE COTTON edi
SUPERBOY created by JERRY SIEGEL. By special arrangement with the JERRY SIEGEL family.
"BUT I DON'T DREAM.
"BECAUSE I DON'T SLEEP.
"BECAUSE I'M NOT 'REAL.'
"I'M JUST *STITCH*--MAGICALLY ANIMATED, GENDER-NONCONFORMING RAG DOLL, SORCERER'S APPRENTICE, AND THE ONLY MACHINE-WASHABLE STUDENT AT TITANS ACADEMY.
05:00
"AND WHILE I MAY NOT BE A HUMAN, I'M STILL A PERSON... SO EVEN IF I DON'T LIVE IN THE OVERNIGHT, I DO *HAVE* DREAMS
"DREAMS LIKE BEING A HERO... PART OF A *TEAM*, A FAMILY OF FRIENDS--LIKE THE TITANS. HENCE MY NEW LIFE HERE IN THE *BIG T*."
MATT? ARE YOU AWAKE?
MATT!
"I MOSTLY GO UNNOTICED AROUND HERE.
"TEENAGERS WANT TO BE SEEN AS ADULTS, SO THEY TEND TO IGNORE THE CHILDISH THINGS THEY ONCE LOVED THAT, LET'S FACE IT, I *HIGHLY* RESEMBLE."
Snort WHUH?!
OH HEY, YOU'RE AWAKE. NEAT. LET'S GO TO BREAKFAST.
ZZZZZ

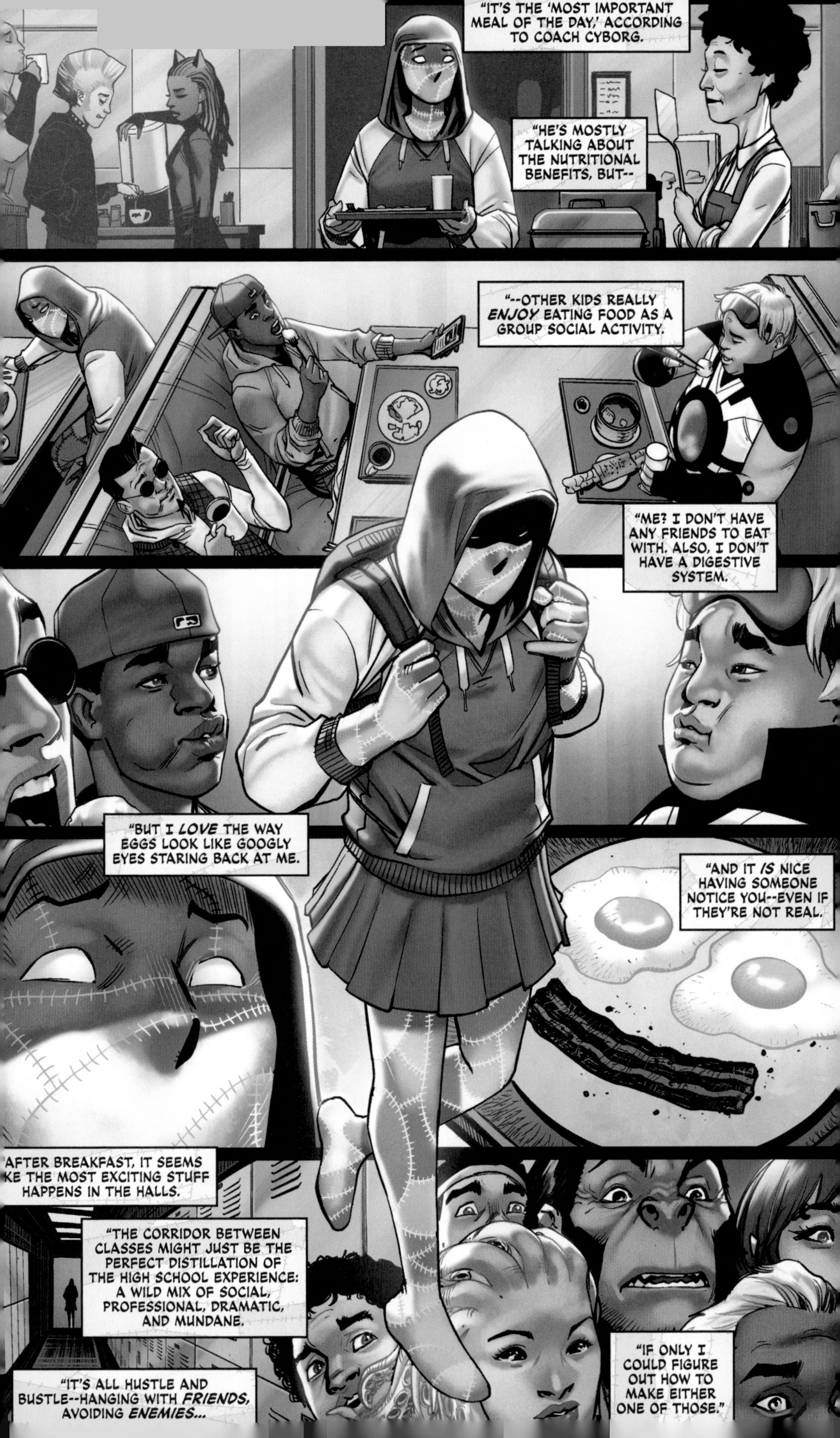
"IT'S THE 'MOST IMPORTANT MEAL OF THE DAY,' ACCORDING TO COACH CYBORG.
"HE'S MOSTLY TALKING ABOUT THE NUTRITIONAL BENEFITS, BUT--
"--OTHER KIDS REALLY ENJOY EATING FOOD AS A GROUP SOCIAL ACTIVITY.
"ME? I DON'T HAVE ANY FRIENDS TO EAT WITH. ALSO, I DON'T HAVE A DIGESTIVE SYSTEM.
"BUT I LOVE THE WAY EGGS LOOK LIKE GOOGLY EYES STARING BACK AT ME.
"AND IT IS NICE HAVING SOMEONE NOTICE YOU--EVEN IF THEY'RE NOT REAL.
AFTER BREAKFAST, IT SEEMS KE THE MOST EXCITING STUFF HAPPENS IN THE HALLS.
"THE CORRIDOR BETWEEN CLASSES MIGHT JUST BE THE PERFECT DISTILLATION OF THE HIGH SCHOOL EXPERIENCE: A WILD MIX OF SOCIAL, PROFESSIONAL, DRAMATIC, AND MUNDANE.
"IT'S ALL HUSTLE AND BUSTLE--HANGING WITH FRIENDS, AVOIDING ENEMIES...
"IF ONLY I COULD FIGURE OUT HOW TO MAKE EITHER ONE OF THOSE."

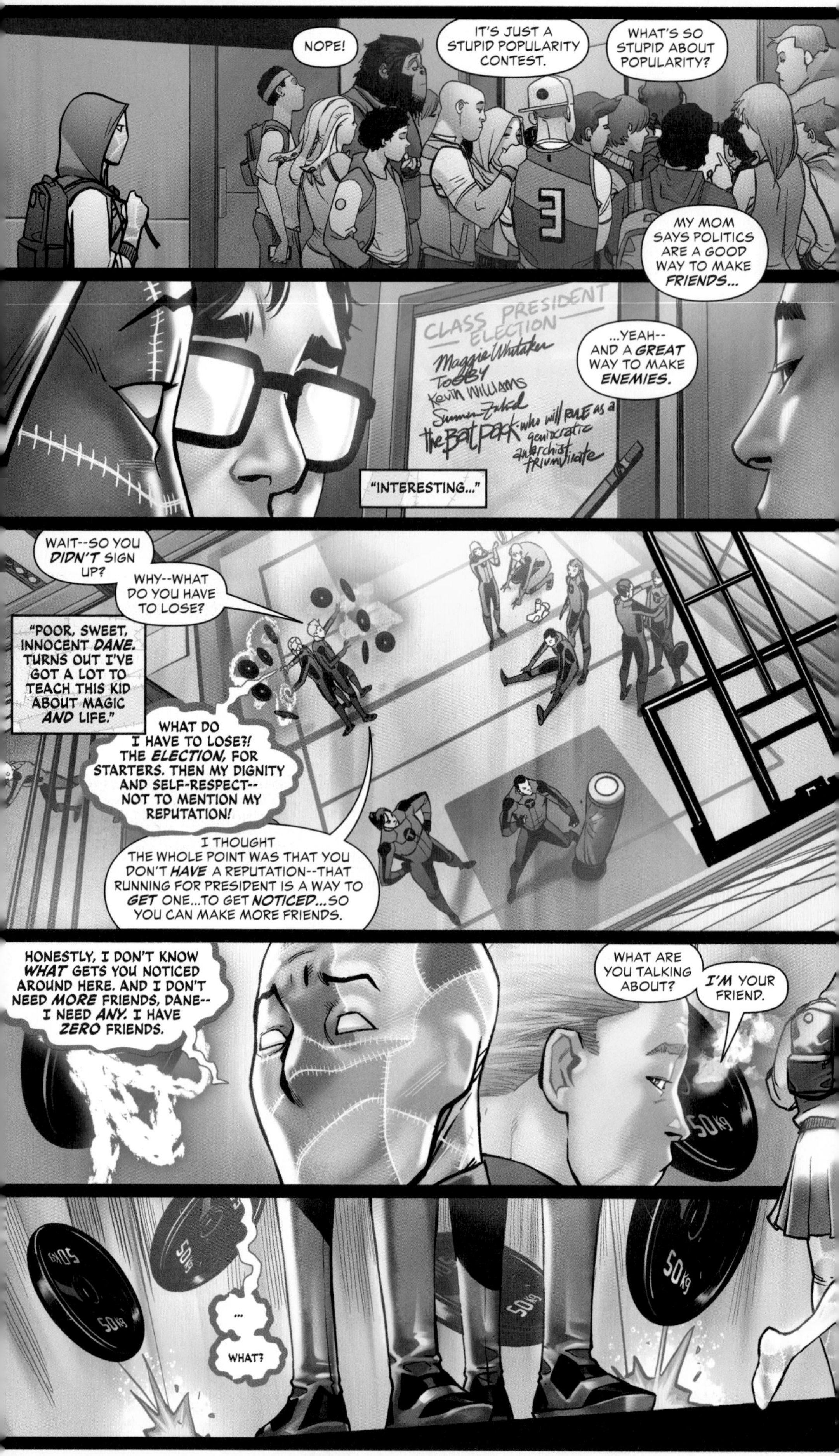
NOPE!
IT'S JUST A STUPID POPULARITY CONTEST.
WHAT'S SO STUPID ABOUT POPULARITY?
MY MOM SAYS POLITICS ARE A GOOD WAY TO MAKE FRIENDS...
CLASS PRESIDENT ELECTION
Maggie Whitaker
Toby
Kevin Williams
Summer Zahid
the Bat Pack - who will RULE as a geniocratic anarchist triumvirate
...YEAH-- AND A GREAT WAY TO MAKE ENEMIES.
"INTERESTING..."
WAIT--SO YOU DIDN'T SIGN UP?
WHY--WHAT DO YOU HAVE TO LOSE?
"POOR, SWEET, INNOCENT DANE. TURNS OUT I'VE GOT A LOT TO TEACH THIS KID ABOUT MAGIC AND LIFE."
WHAT DO I HAVE TO LOSE?! THE ELECTION, FOR STARTERS. THEN MY DIGNITY AND SELF-RESPECT-- NOT TO MENTION MY REPUTATION!
I THOUGHT THE WHOLE POINT WAS THAT YOU DON'T HAVE A REPUTATION--THAT RUNNING FOR PRESIDENT IS A WAY TO GET ONE...TO GET NOTICED...SO YOU CAN MAKE MORE FRIENDS.
HONESTLY, I DON'T KNOW WHAT GETS YOU NOTICED AROUND HERE. AND I DON'T NEED MORE FRIENDS, DANE-- I NEED ANY. I HAVE ZERO FRIENDS.
WHAT ARE YOU TALKING ABOUT?
I'M YOUR FRIEND.
50kg
...
WHAT?

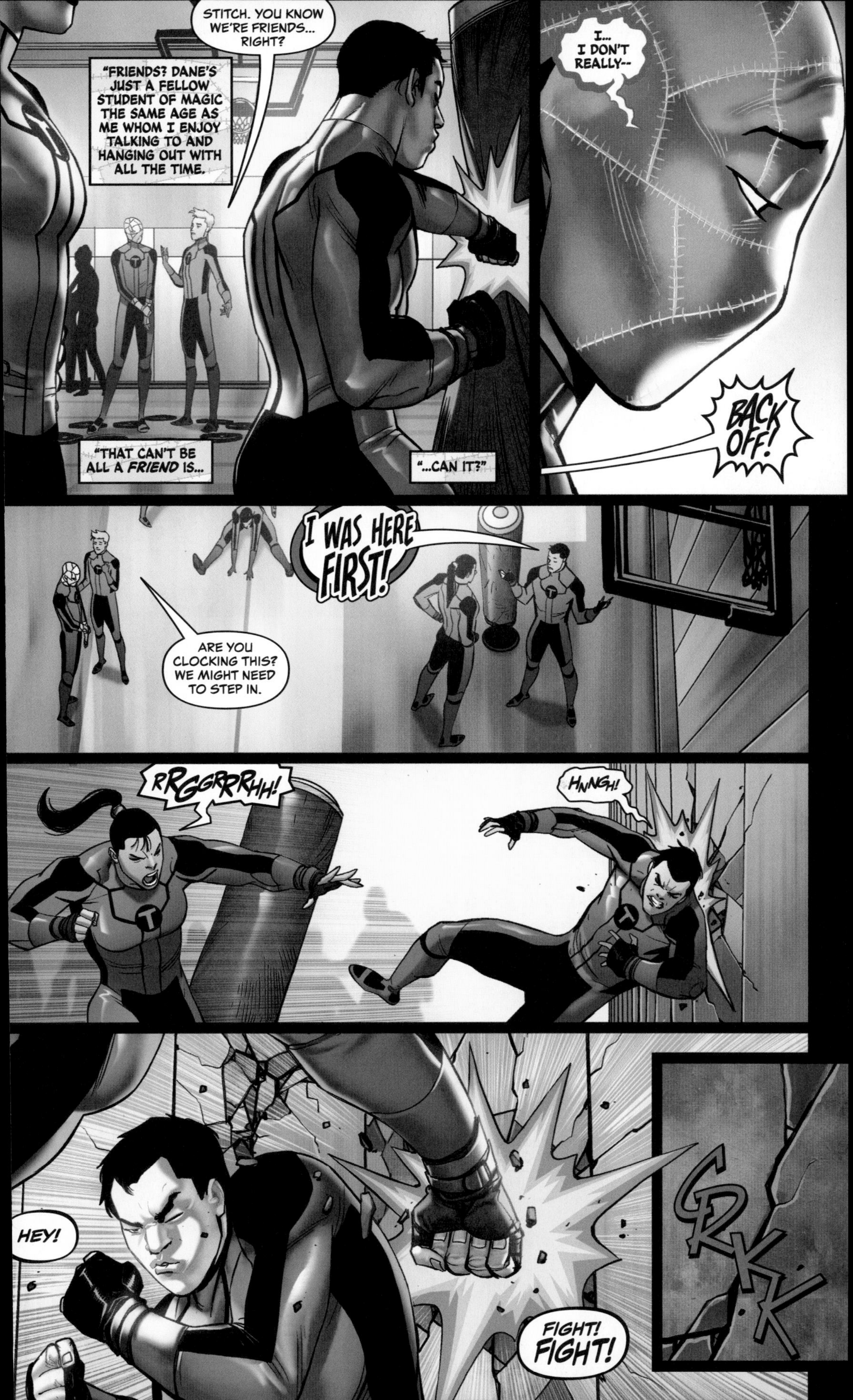

"FRIENDS? DANE'S JUST A FELLOW STUDENT OF MAGIC THE SAME AGE AS ME WHOM I ENJOY TALKING TO AND HANGING OUT WITH ALL THE TIME.
STITCH. YOU KNOW WE'RE FRIENDS... RIGHT?
"THAT CAN'T BE ALL A *FRIEND* IS...
"...CAN IT?"
I... I DON'T REALLY--
BACK OFF!
I WAS HERE FIRST!
ARE YOU CLOCKING THIS? WE MIGHT NEED TO STEP IN.
RRGGRRRHH!
HNNGH!
HEY!
FIGHT! FIGHT!
CRKKK

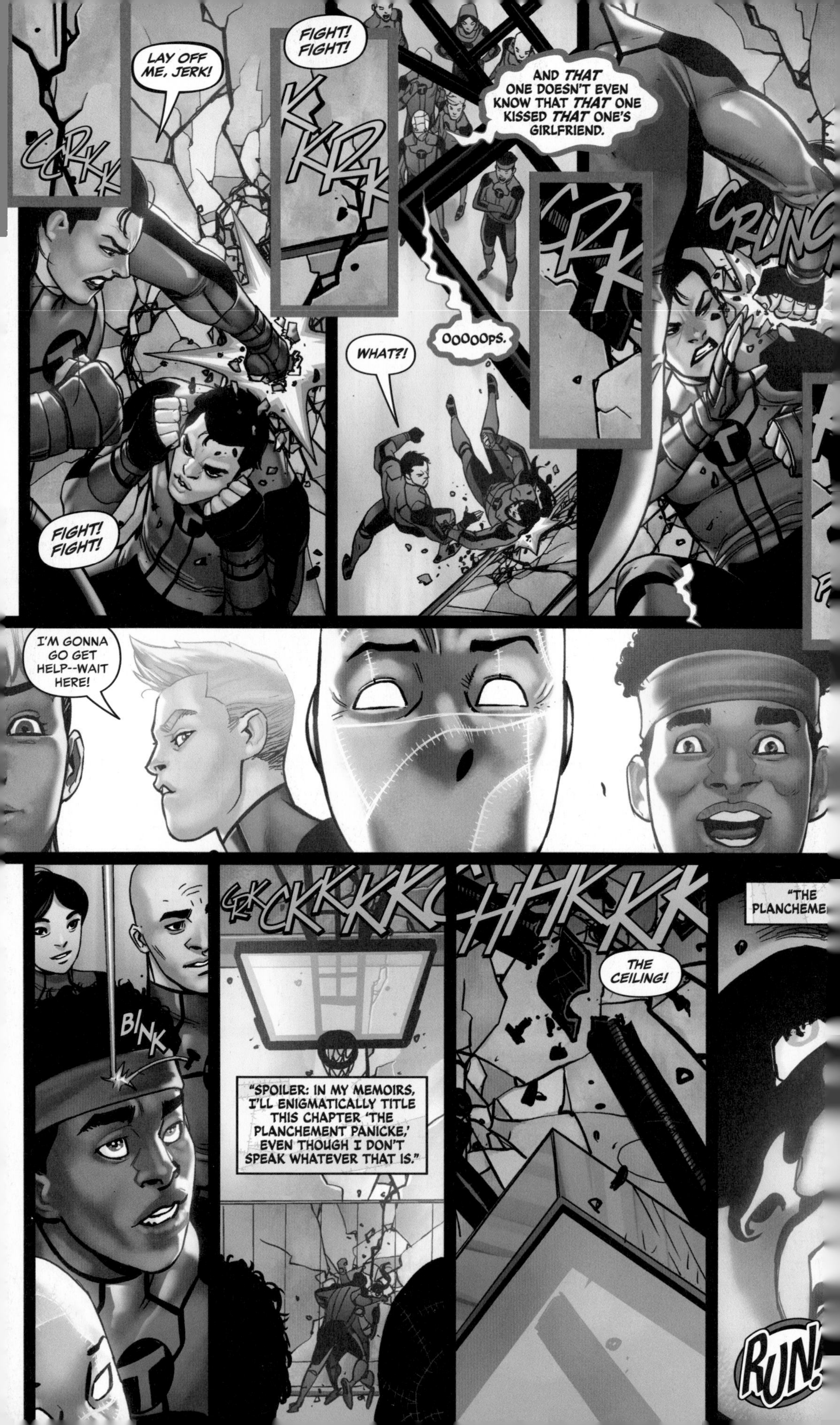
CRKK
LAY OFF ME, JERK!
FIGHT! FIGHT!
KKRK
FIGHT! FIGHT!
AND THAT ONE DOESN'T EVEN KNOW THAT THAT ONE KISSED THAT ONE'S GIRLFRIEND.
WHAT?!
OOOOOPS.
CRK
CRUNC
I'M GONNA GO GET HELP--WAIT HERE!
BINK
CRKCKKKKCHHKKK
"SPOILER: IN MY MEMOIRS, I'LL ENIGMATICALLY TITLE THIS CHAPTER 'THE PLANCHEMENT PANICKE,' EVEN THOUGH I DON'T SPEAK WHATEVER THAT IS."
THE CEILING!
"THE PLANCHEME
RUN!

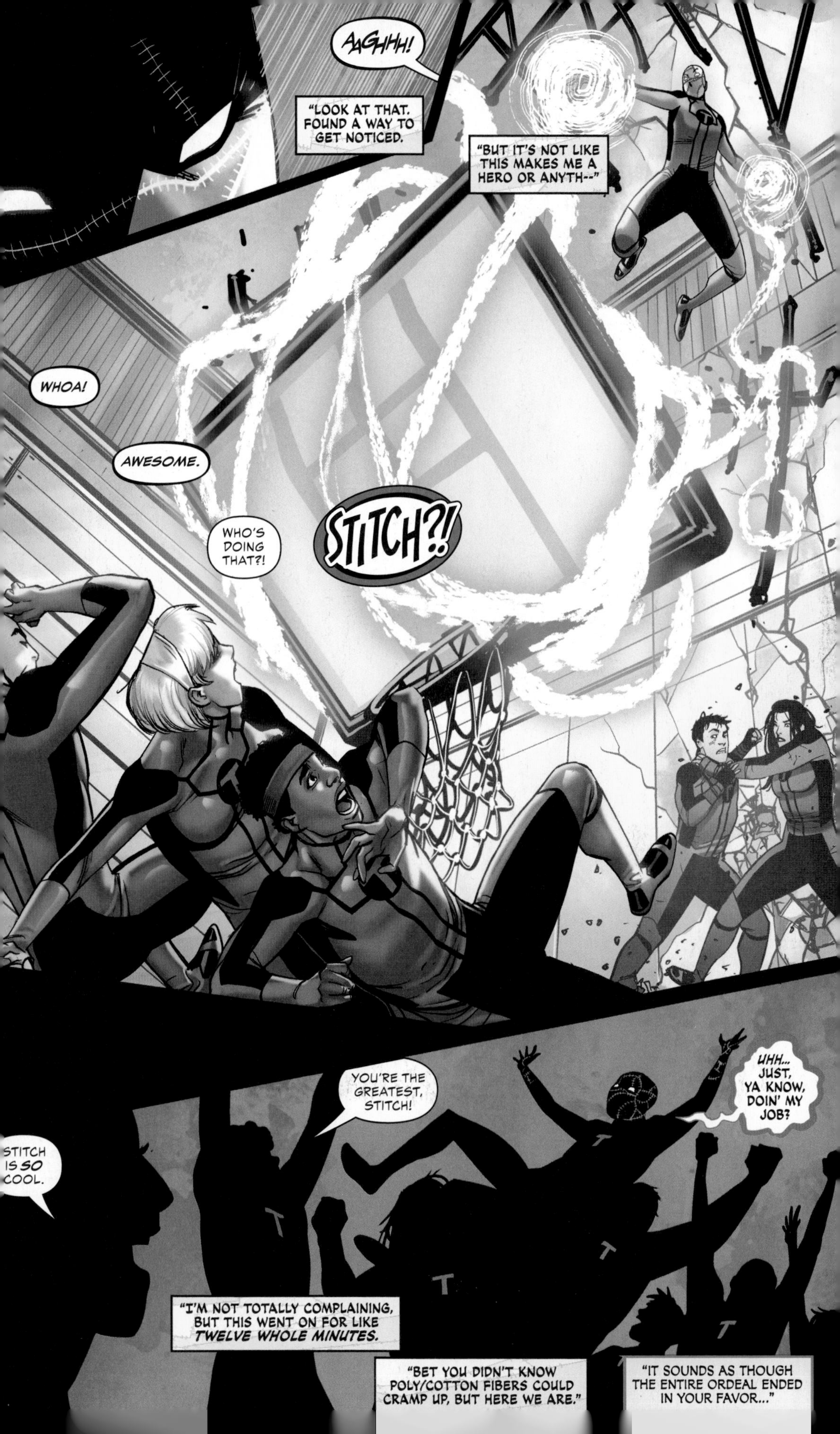
AAGHHH!
"LOOK AT THAT. FOUND A WAY TO GET NOTICED.
"BUT IT'S NOT LIKE THIS MAKES ME A HERO OR ANYTH--"
WHOA!
AWESOME.
WHO'S DOING THAT?!
STITCH?!
YOU'RE THE GREATEST, STITCH!
UHH... JUST, YA KNOW, DOIN' MY JOB?
STITCH IS SO COOL.
"I'M NOT TOTALLY COMPLAINING, BUT THIS WENT ON FOR LIKE TWELVE WHOLE MINUTES.
"BET YOU DIDN'T KNOW POLY/COTTON FIBERS COULD CRAMP UP, BUT HERE WE ARE."
"IT SOUNDS AS THOUGH THE ENTIRE ORDEAL ENDED IN YOUR FAVOR..."

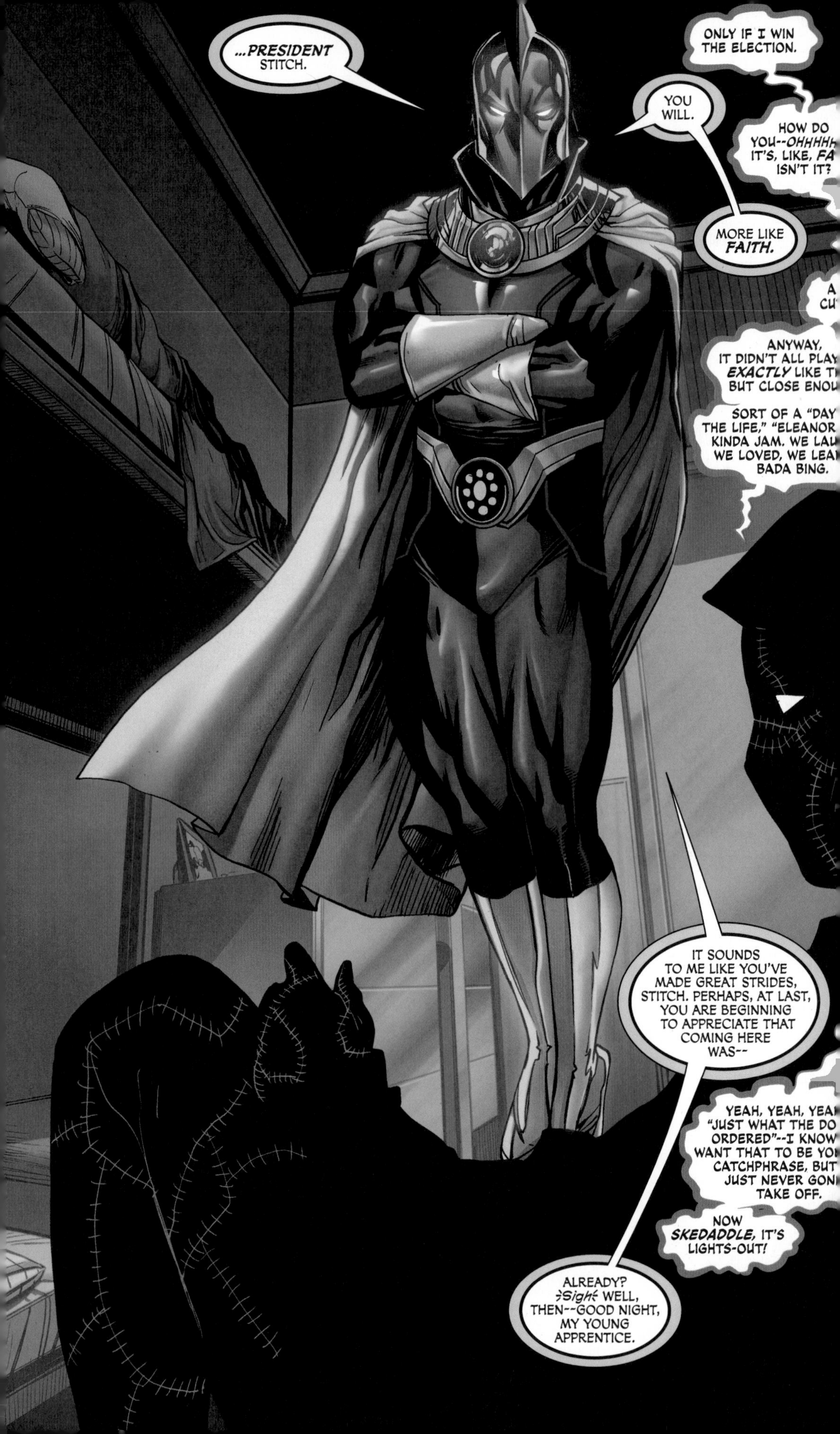

...*PRESIDENT* STITCH.
ONLY IF I WIN THE ELECTION.
YOU WILL.
HOW DO YOU--*OHHHHH* IT'S, LIKE, *FA* ISN'T IT?
MORE LIKE *FAITH.*
A CU
ANYWAY, IT DIDN'T ALL PLAY *EXACTLY* LIKE T BUT CLOSE ENOU
SORT OF A "DAY THE LIFE," "ELEANOR KINDA JAM. WE LAU WE LOVED, WE LEA BADA BING.
IT SOUNDS TO ME LIKE YOU'VE MADE GREAT STRIDES, STITCH. PERHAPS, AT LAST, YOU ARE BEGINNING TO APPRECIATE THAT COMING HERE WAS--
YEAH, YEAH, YEA "JUST WHAT THE DO ORDERED"--I KNOW WANT THAT TO BE YO CATCHPHRASE, BUT JUST NEVER GON TAKE OFF.
NOW *SKEDADDLE,* IT'S LIGHTS-OUT!
ALREADY? *Sigh* WELL, THEN--GOOD NIGHT, MY YOUNG APPRENTICE.

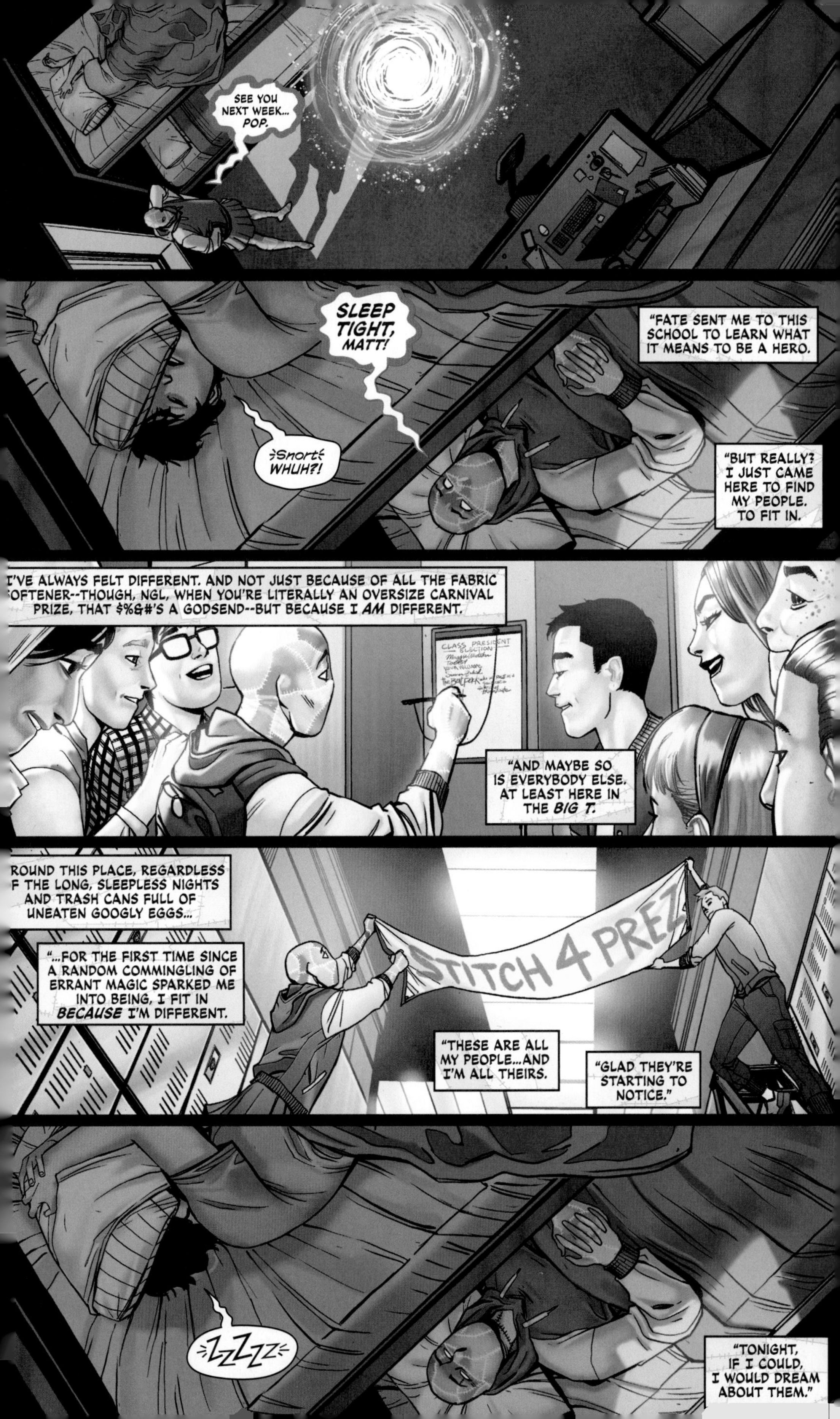
SEE YOU NEXT WEEK... POP.
SLEEP TIGHT, MATT!
"FATE SENT ME TO THIS SCHOOL TO LEARN WHAT IT MEANS TO BE A HERO.
Snort WHUH?!
"BUT REALLY? I JUST CAME HERE TO FIND MY PEOPLE. TO FIT IN.
I'VE ALWAYS FELT DIFFERENT. AND NOT JUST BECAUSE OF ALL THE FABRIC SOFTENER--THOUGH, NGL, WHEN YOU'RE LITERALLY AN OVERSIZE CARNIVAL PRIZE, THAT $%&#'S A GODSEND--BUT BECAUSE I AM DIFFERENT.
CLASS PRESIDENT ELECTION
"AND MAYBE SO IS EVERYBODY ELSE. AT LEAST HERE IN THE BIG T.
ROUND THIS PLACE, REGARDLESS F THE LONG, SLEEPLESS NIGHTS AND TRASH CANS FULL OF UNEATEN GOOGLY EGGS...
"...FOR THE FIRST TIME SINCE A RANDOM COMMINGLING OF ERRANT MAGIC SPARKED ME INTO BEING, I FIT IN BECAUSE I'M DIFFERENT.
STITCH 4 PREZ
"THESE ARE ALL MY PEOPLE...AND I'M ALL THEIRS.
"GLAD THEY'RE STARTING TO NOTICE."
ZZZZZ
"TONIGHT, IF I COULD, I WOULD DREAM ABOUT THEM."

IN *Memoriam*

This yearbook is dedicated to the memory and enduring legacy of ROY W. HARPER JR. a.k.a. "Mr. Arsenal" a.k.a. "Mr. Red Arrow (1)", a.k.a. "Mr. Speedy."

We, the students of the Roy Harper Titans Academy, wish to honor Mr. Speedy's heroic actions and sacrifice by posthumously naming him an HONORARY ADVISOR TO THE INAUGURAL CLASS.

"Sometimes an Outsider, forever a Titan, always in our hearts. Wherever you are, may you be at peace..."

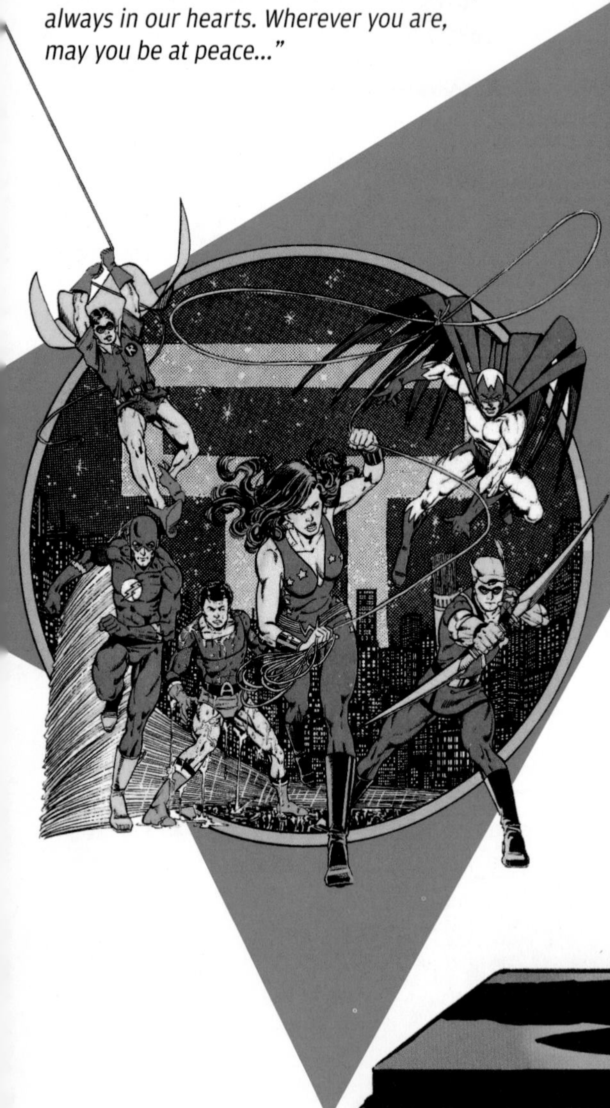

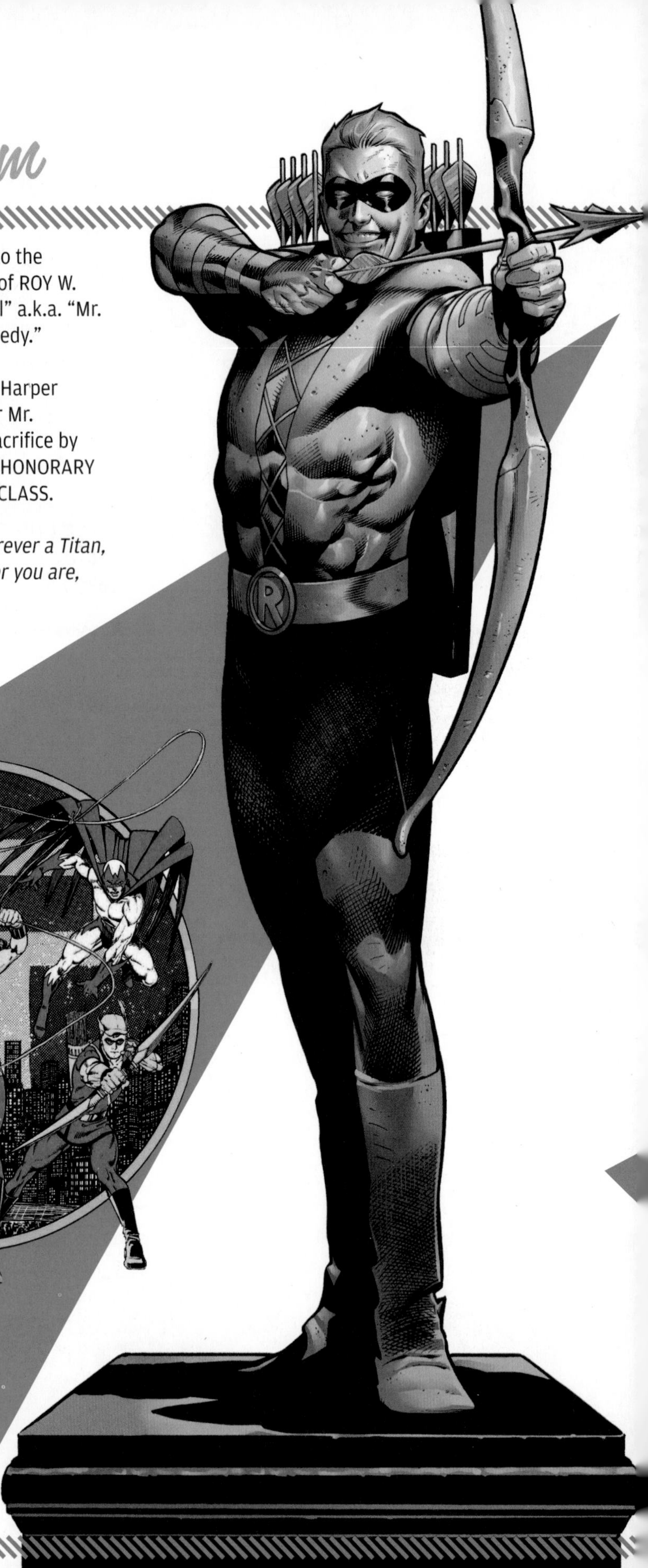

HTWING

t approved before deadline.

DONNA TROY

Ms. Troy's origins seem as complicated as her History of the Multiverse class, but it's in her Armed Combat Work-shop that we learned the simplest lesson of all —that a REAL hero offers their foe a hand before offering a fist.

CYBORG

Part man, part machine, all heart. Students in Coach Cyborg's Home Ec class know how much of a softie this metric ton of steel and muscle can be. Whether calling plays or cooling pies, he's taught us there's no substitute for hard work and a little seasoning.

BEAST BOY

No instructor makes us laugh more than Mr. Beast Boy! And even if many of us struggle in his Intro to Acting class, who can forget his... interesting...one-man production of *Animal Farm*?

RAVEN

Our counselor and confidant, magical Ms. Raven helps shine a light in the darkness that can come with being a super teen in a super weird world. She always finds a moment to help a stu-dent in need, even if it means literally stopping time to do it...

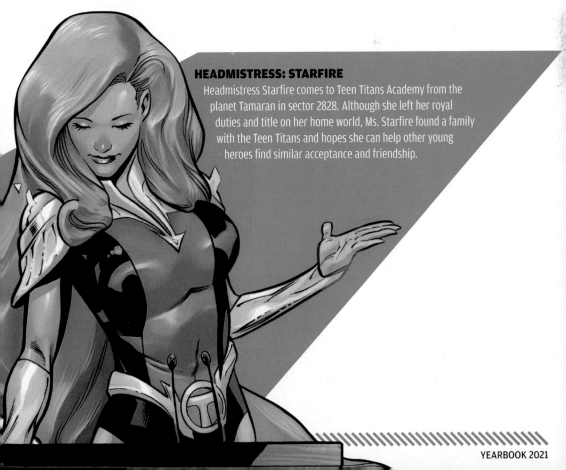

HEADMISTRESS: STARFIRE

Headmistress Starfire comes to Teen Titans Academy from the planet Tamaran in sector 2828. Although she left her royal duties and title on her home world, Ms. Starfire found a family with the Teen Titans and hopes she can help other young heroes find similar acceptance and friendship.

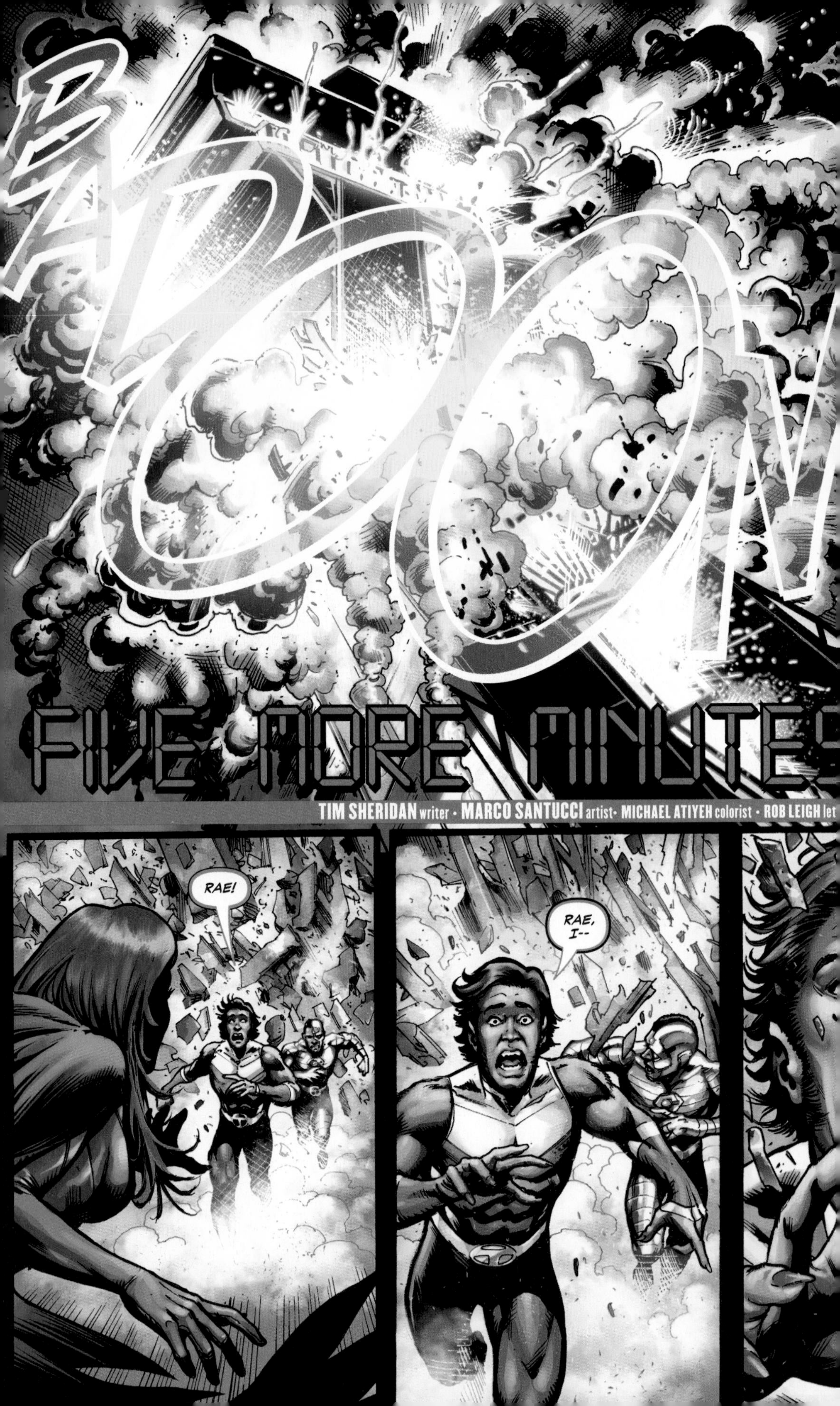
BADOOOM
FIVE MORE MINUTES
TIM SHERIDAN writer · MARCO SANTUCCI artist · MICHAEL ATIYEH colorist · ROB LEIGH let
RAE!
RAE, I--

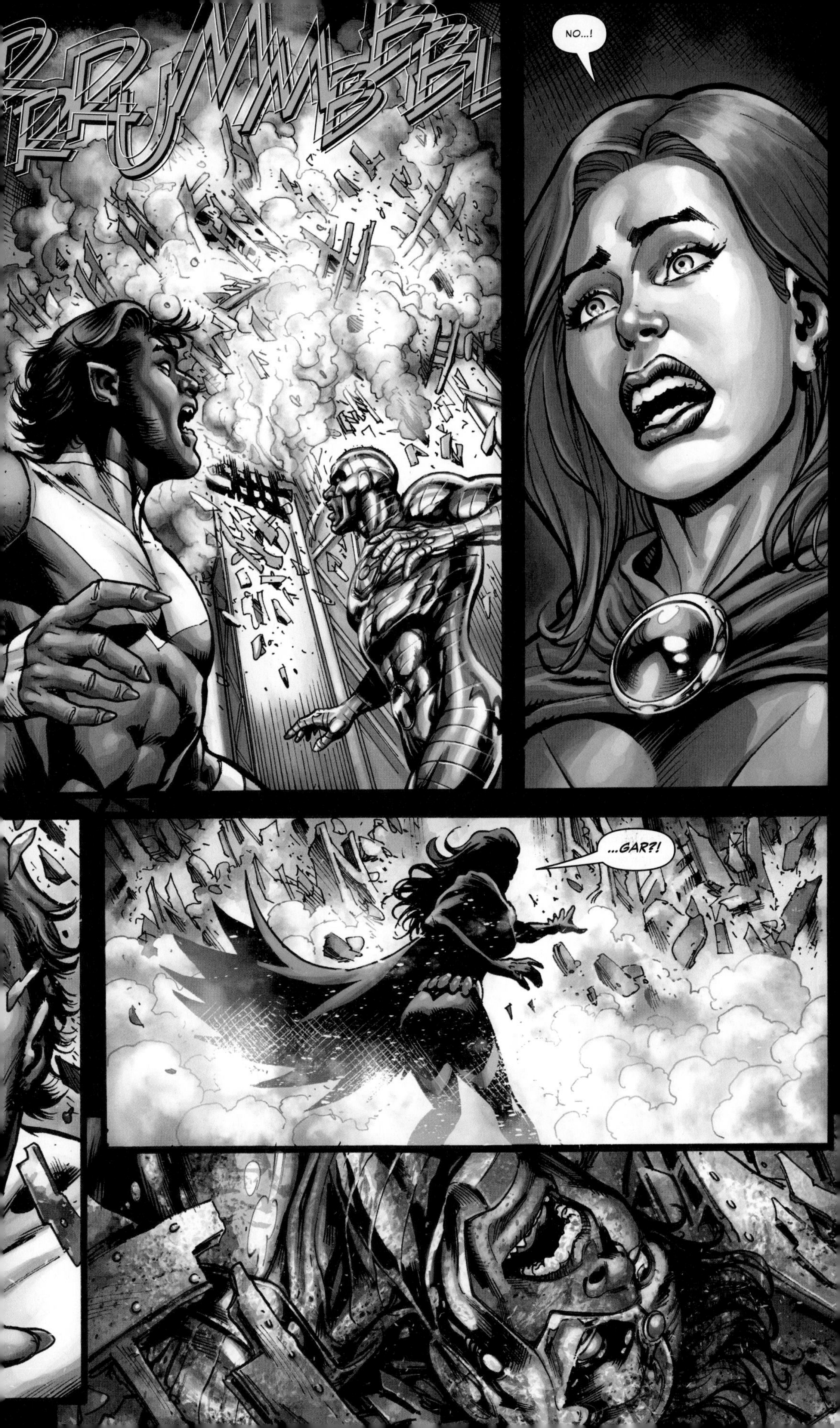
NO...!
...GAR?!

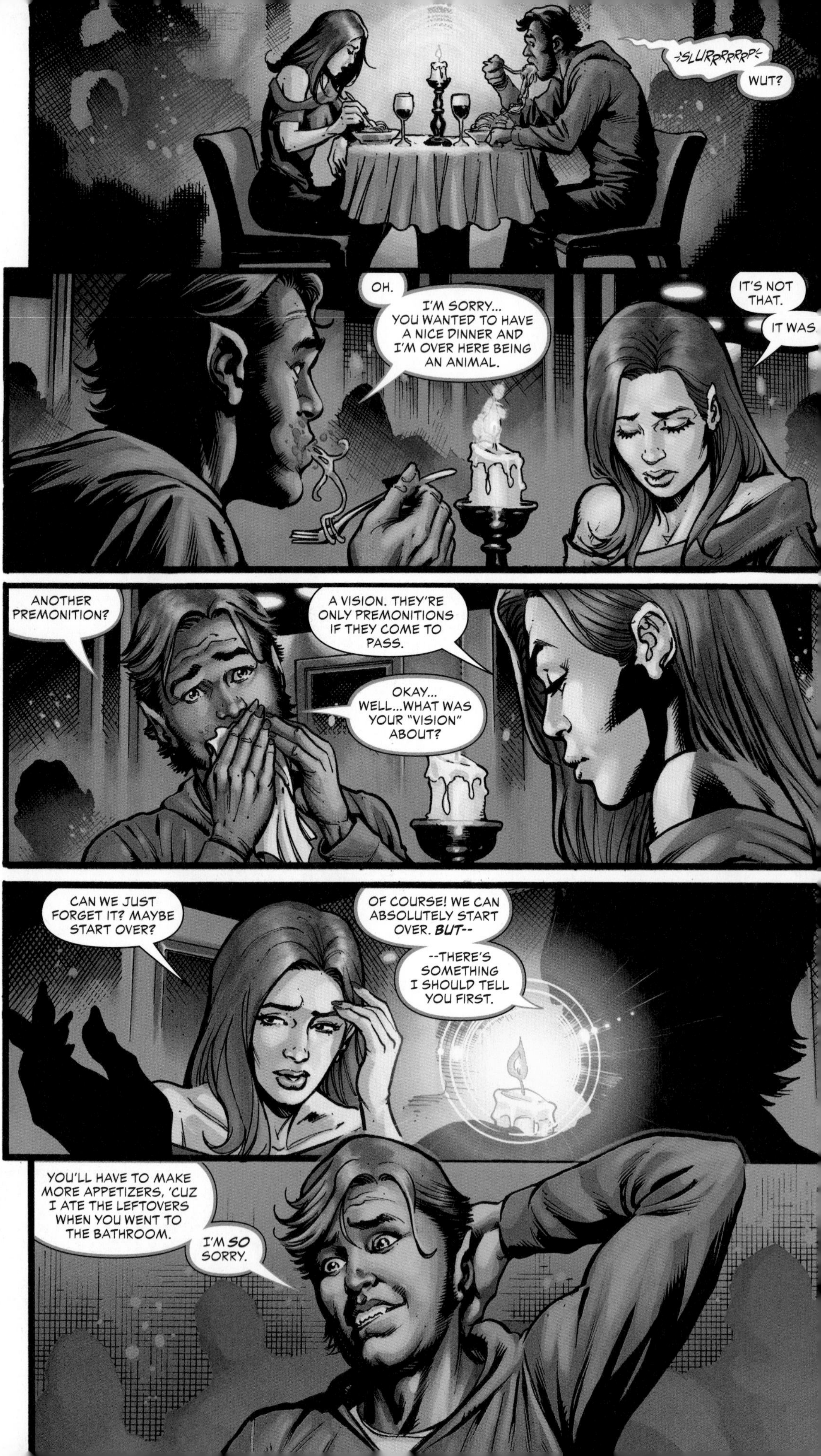

SLURRRRRP
WUT?
OH.
I'M SORRY... YOU WANTED TO HAVE A NICE DINNER AND I'M OVER HERE BEING AN ANIMAL.
IT'S NOT THAT.
IT WAS
ANOTHER PREMONITION?
A VISION. THEY'RE ONLY PREMONITIONS IF THEY COME TO PASS.
OKAY... WELL...WHAT WAS YOUR "VISION" ABOUT?
CAN WE JUST FORGET IT? MAYBE START OVER?
OF COURSE! WE CAN ABSOLUTELY START OVER. BUT--
--THERE'S SOMETHING I SHOULD TELL YOU FIRST.
YOU'LL HAVE TO MAKE MORE APPETIZERS, 'CUZ I ATE THE LEFTOVERS WHEN YOU WENT TO THE BATHROOM.
I'M SO SORRY.

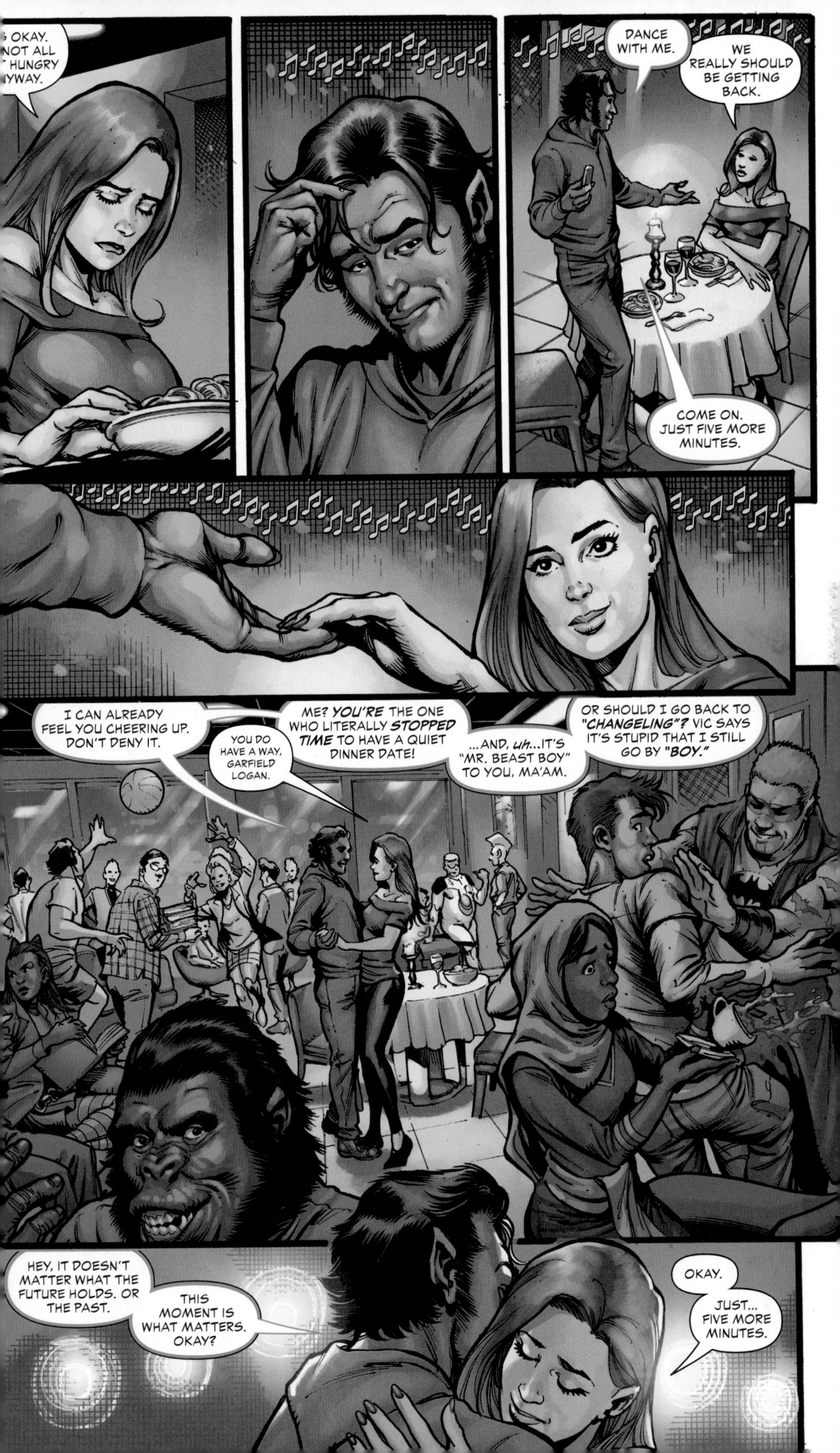

S OKAY. NOT ALL HUNGRY YWAY.
DANCE WITH ME.
WE REALLY SHOULD BE GETTING BACK.
COME ON. JUST FIVE MORE MINUTES.
I CAN ALREADY FEEL YOU CHEERING UP. DON'T DENY IT.
YOU DO HAVE A WAY, GARFIELD LOGAN.
ME? *YOU'RE* THE ONE WHO LITERALLY ***STOPPED TIME*** TO HAVE A QUIET DINNER DATE!
...AND, *uh*...IT'S "MR. BEAST BOY" TO YOU, MA'AM.
OR SHOULD I GO BACK TO ***"CHANGELING"?*** VIC SAYS IT'S STUPID THAT I STILL GO BY ***"BOY."***
HEY, IT DOESN'T MATTER WHAT THE FUTURE HOLDS. OR THE PAST.
THIS MOMENT IS WHAT MATTERS. OKAY?
OKAY.
JUST... FIVE MORE MINUTES.

CANDID *Campus*

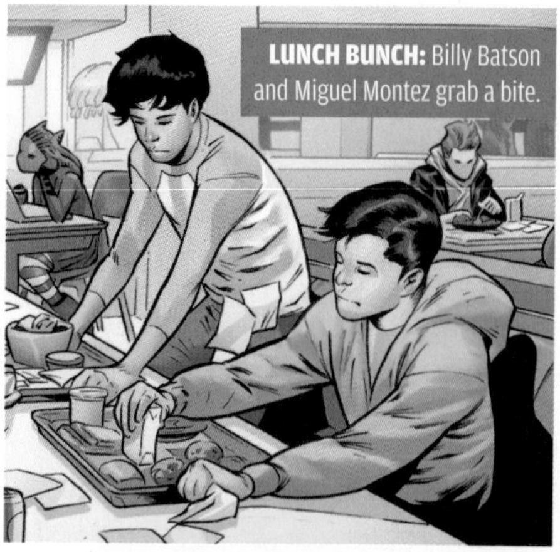

LUNCH BUNCH: Billy Batson and Miguel Montez grab a bite.

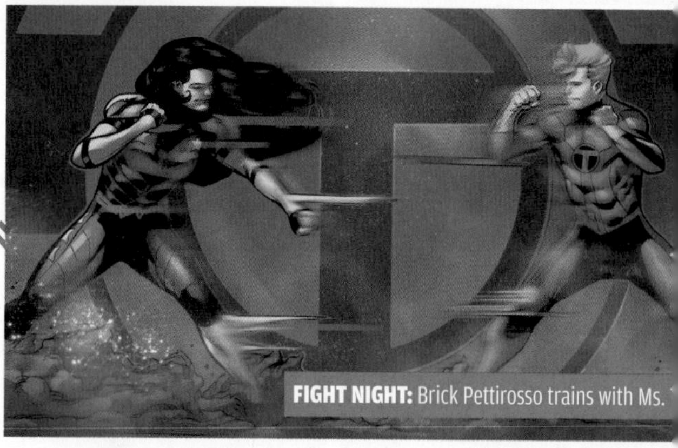

FIGHT NIGHT: Brick Pettirosso trains with Ms.

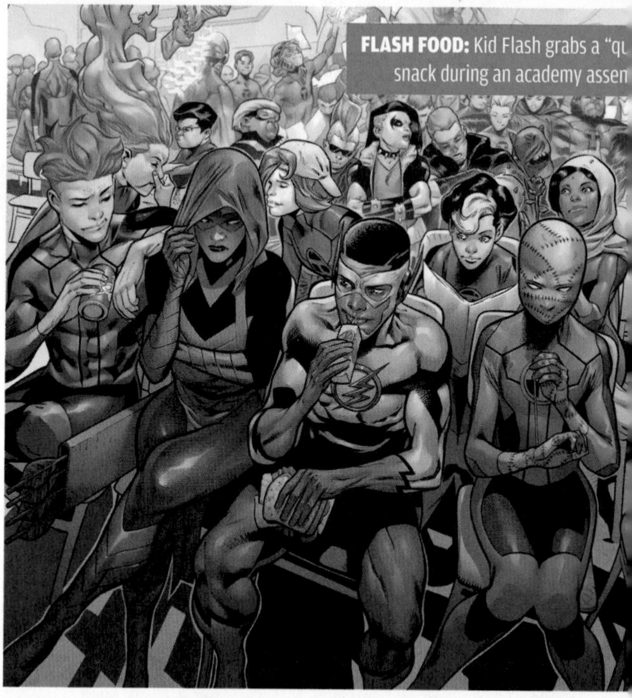

FLASH FOOD: Kid Flash grabs a "qu snack during an academy assem

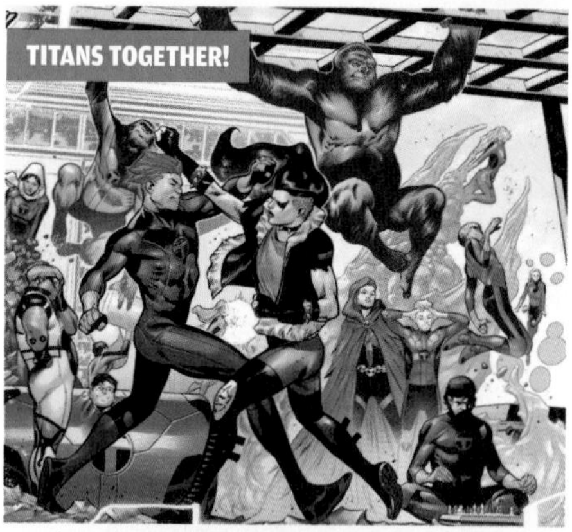

TITANS TOGETHER!

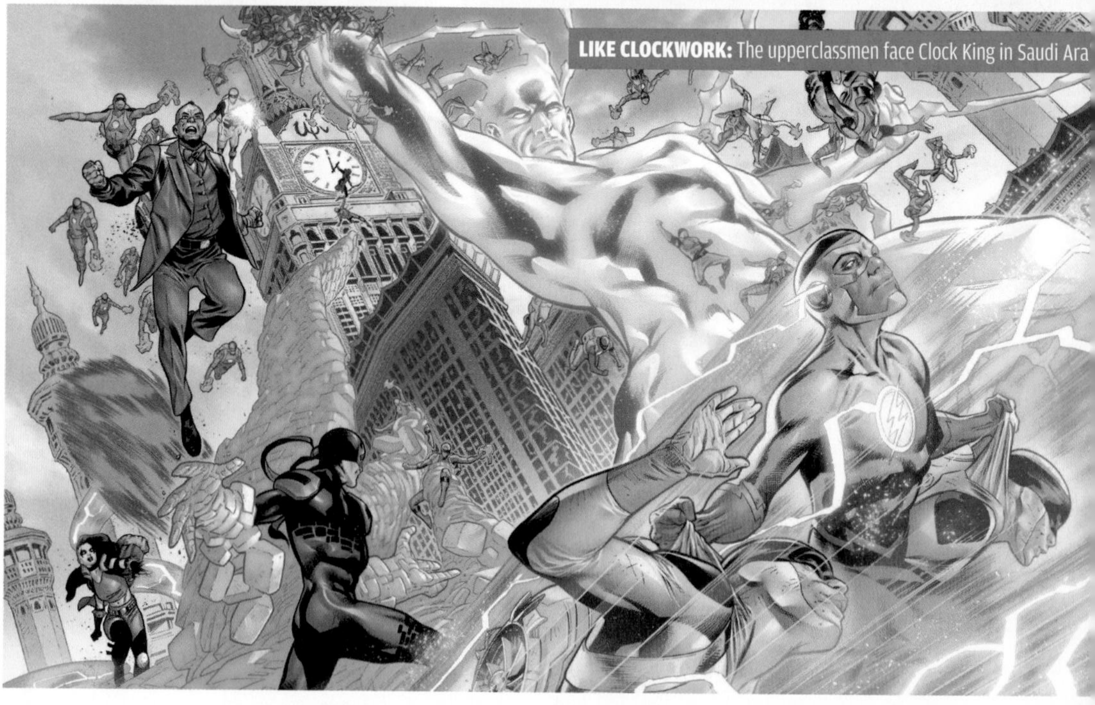

LIKE CLOCKWORK: The upperclassmen face Clock King in Saudi Ara

CLASS Superlatives

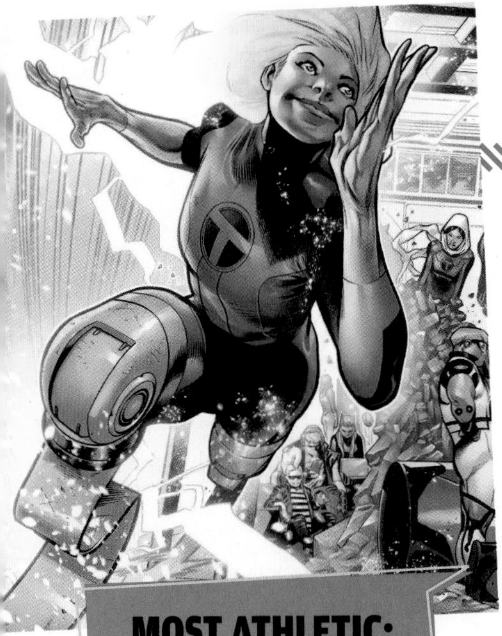

MOST ATHLETIC:
Bolt

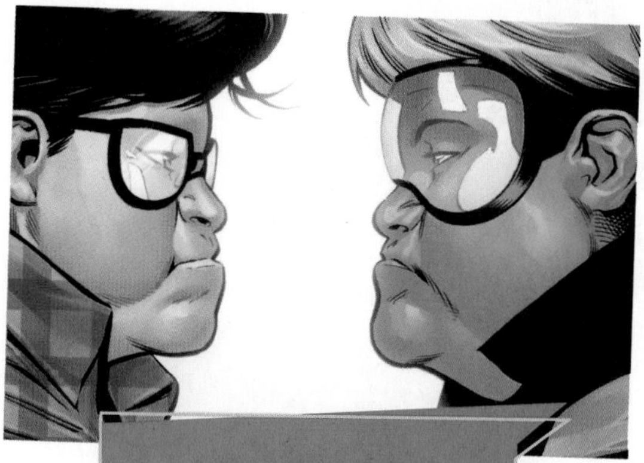

FRIENDS 'TILL THE END:
Tooby & Roundhouse

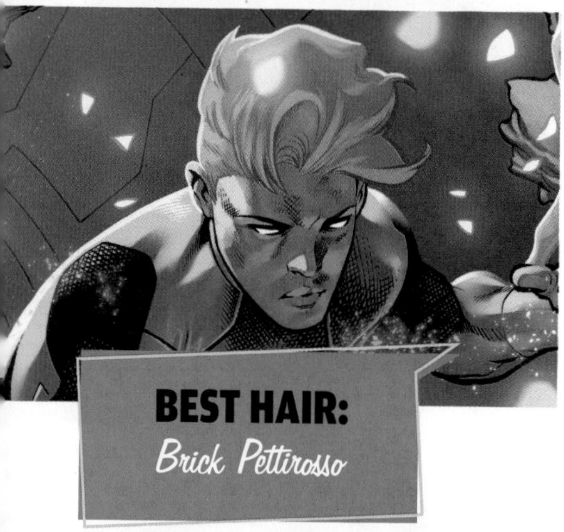

BEST HAIR:
Brick Pettirosso

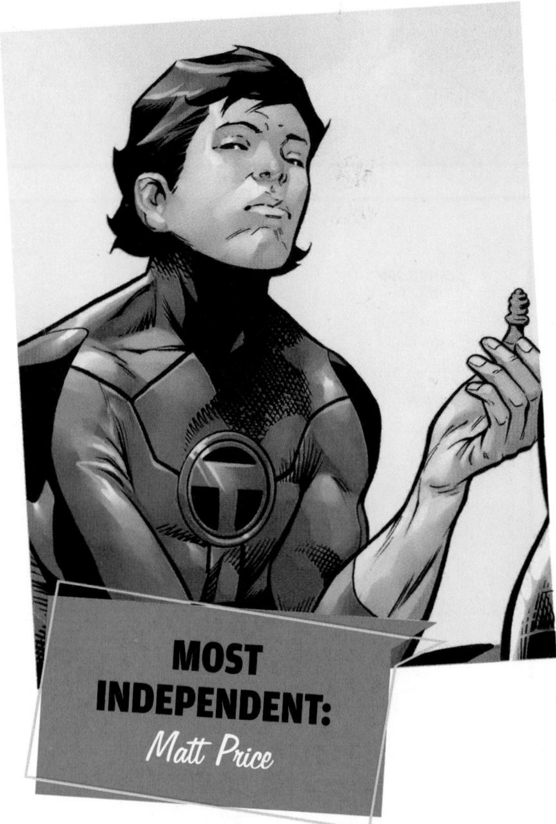

MOST INDEPENDENT:
Matt Price

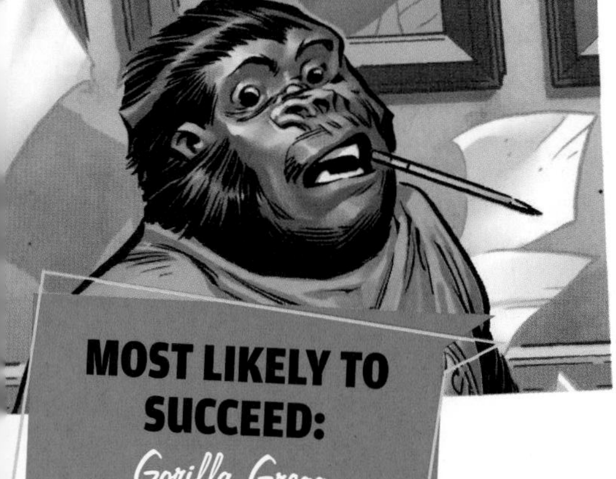

MOST LIKELY TO SUCCEED:
Gorilla Gregg

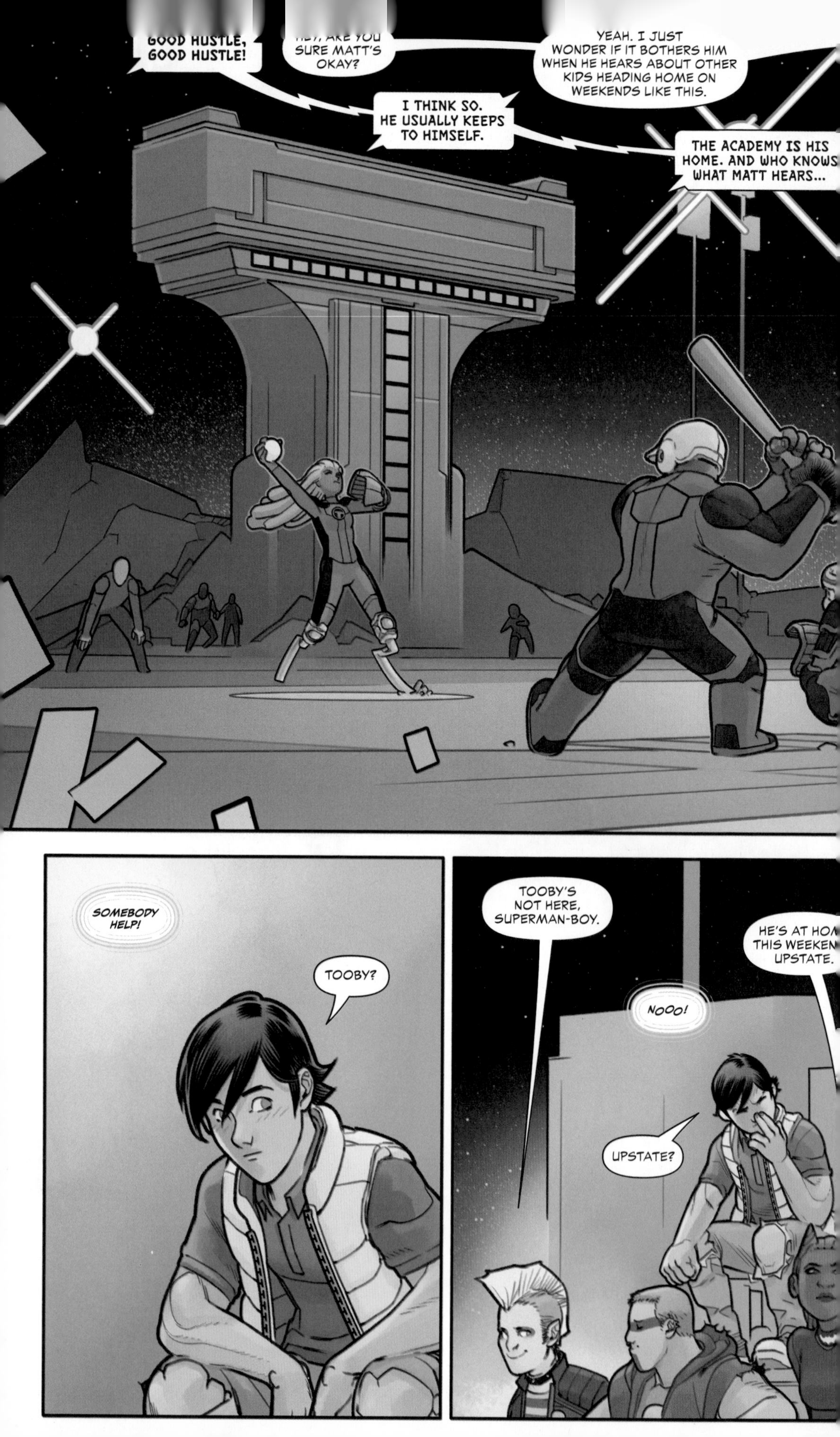
GOOD HUSTLE, GOOD HUSTLE!
SURE MATT'S OKAY?
I THINK SO. HE USUALLY KEEPS TO HIMSELF.
YEAH. I JUST WONDER IF IT BOTHERS HIM WHEN HE HEARS ABOUT OTHER KIDS HEADING HOME ON WEEKENDS LIKE THIS.
THE ACADEMY IS HIS HOME. AND WHO KNOWS WHAT MATT HEARS...
SOMEBODY HELP!
TOOBY?
TOOBY'S NOT HERE, SUPERMAN-BOY.
HE'S AT HO THIS WEEKEN UPSTATE.
NOOO!
UPSTATE?

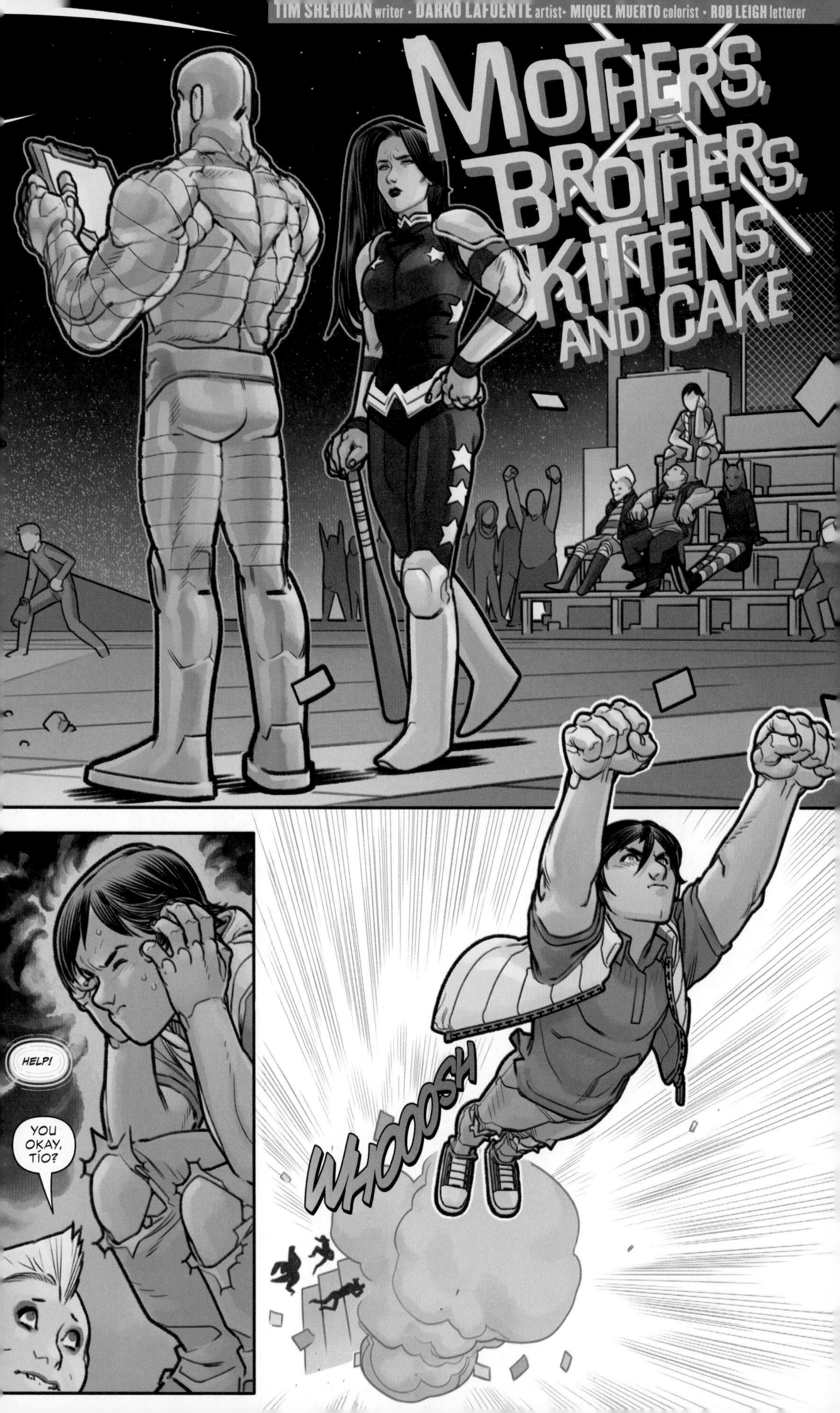
TIM SHERIDAN writer • DARKO LAFUENTE artist • MIQUEL MUERTO colorist • ROB LEIGH letterer
MOTHERS, BROTHERS, KITTENS, AND CAKE
HELP!
YOU OKAY, TÍO?
WHOOOSH

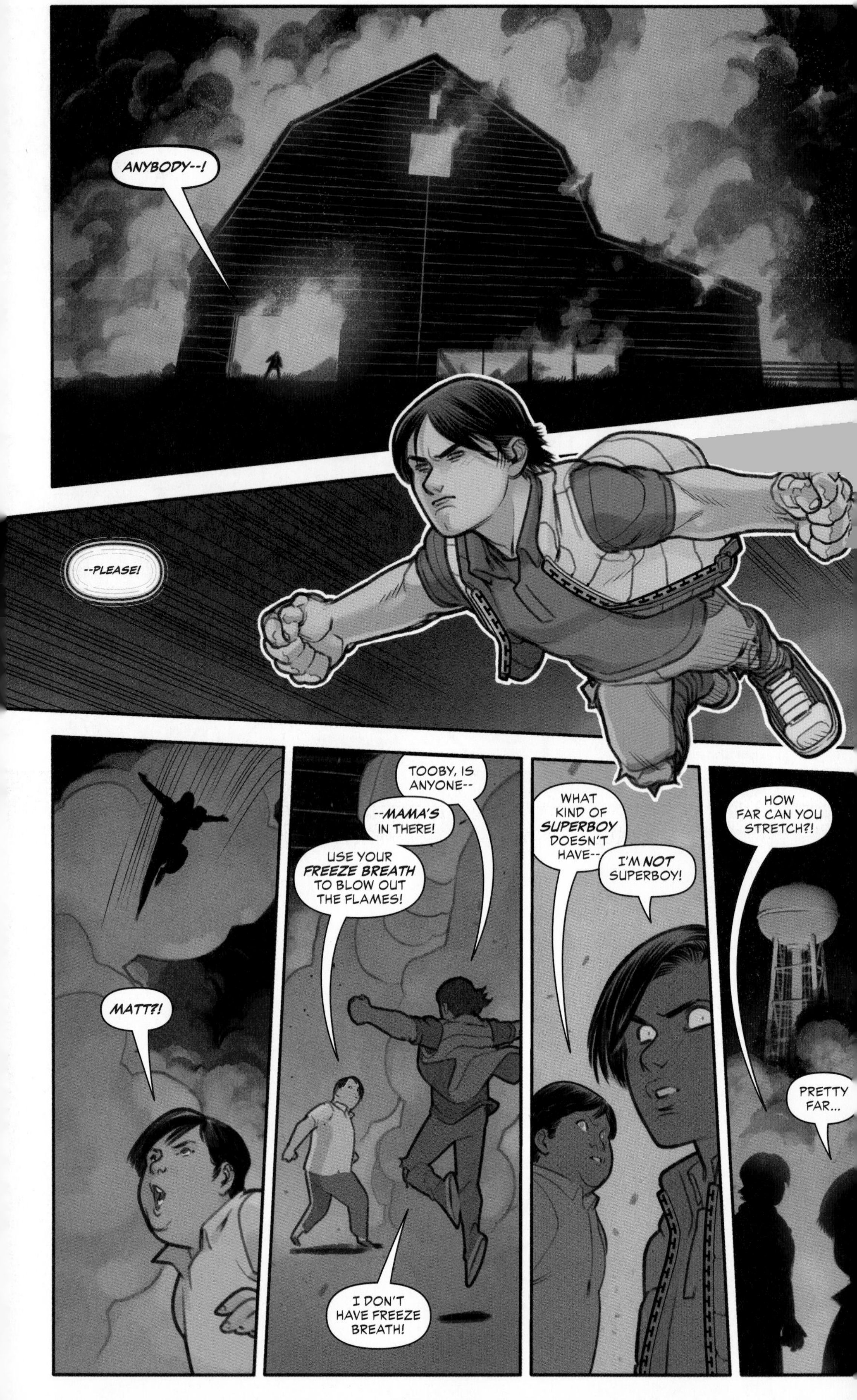
ANYBODY--!
--PLEASE!
MATT?!
TOOBY, IS ANYONE--
--MAMA'S IN THERE!
USE YOUR FREEZE BREATH TO BLOW OUT THE FLAMES!
I DON'T HAVE FREEZE BREATH!
WHAT KIND OF SUPERBOY DOESN'T HAVE--
I'M NOT SUPERBOY!
HOW FAR CAN YOU STRETCH?!
PRETTY FAR...

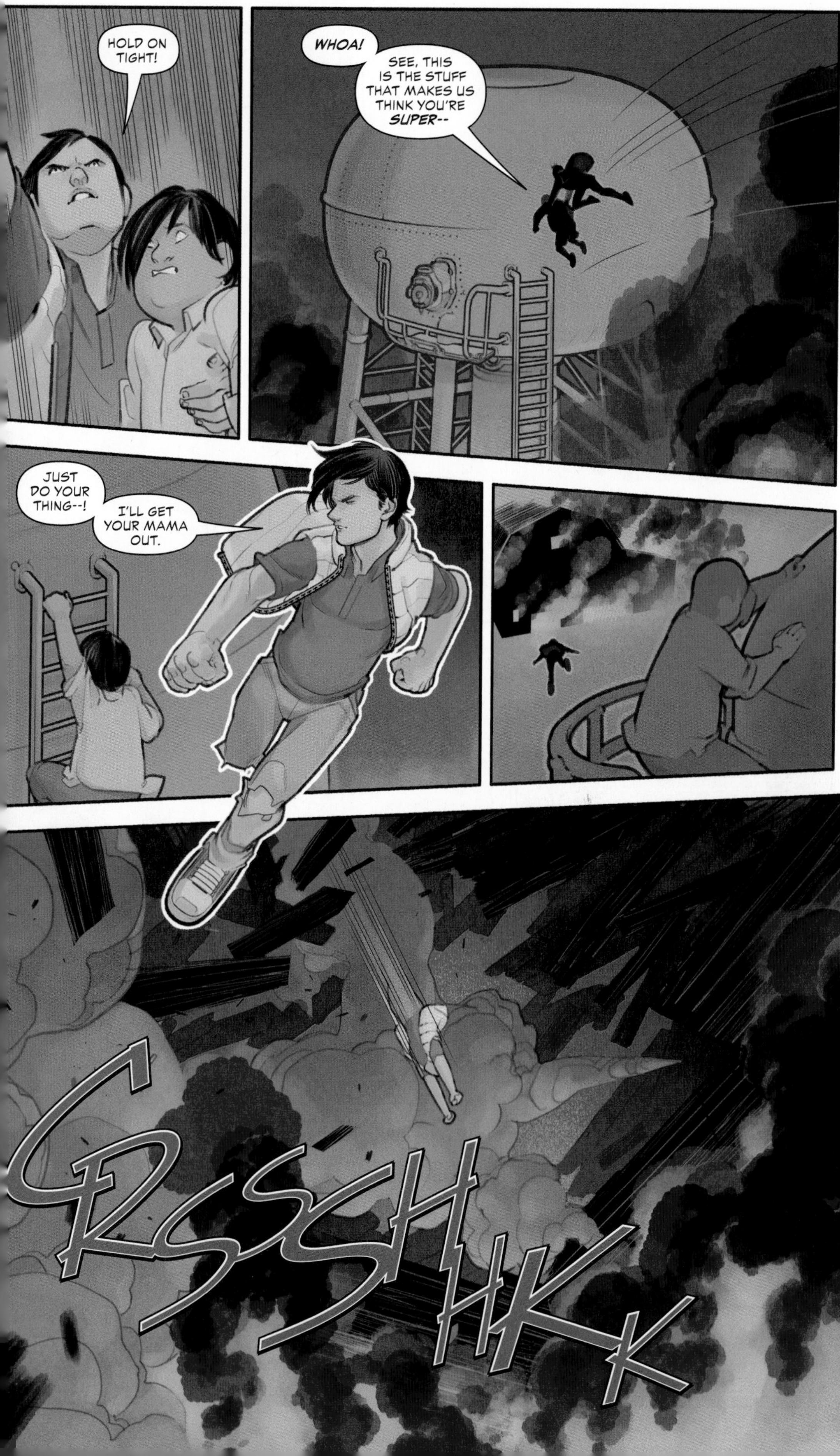
HOLD ON TIGHT!
WHOA!
SEE, THIS IS THE STUFF THAT MAKES US THINK YOU'RE SUPER--
JUST DO YOUR THING--!
I'LL GET YOUR MAMA OUT.
GRSSHKK

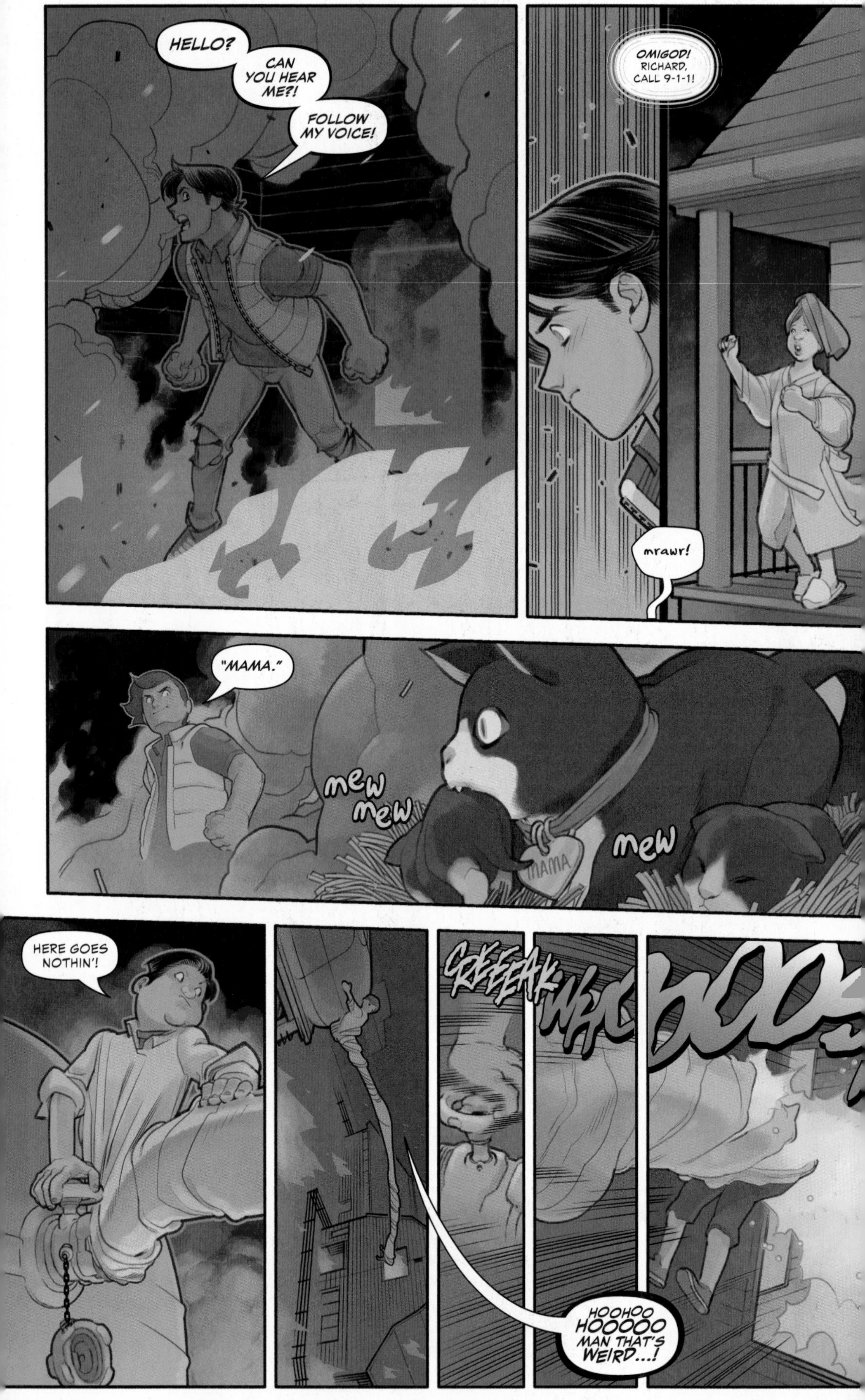
HELLO?
CAN YOU HEAR ME?!
FOLLOW MY VOICE!
OMIGOD! RICHARD, CALL 9-1-1!
mrawr!
"MAMA."
mew mew
mew
MAMA
HERE GOES NOTHIN'!
CREEEAK
HOOHOO HOOOOO MAN THAT'S WEIRD...!

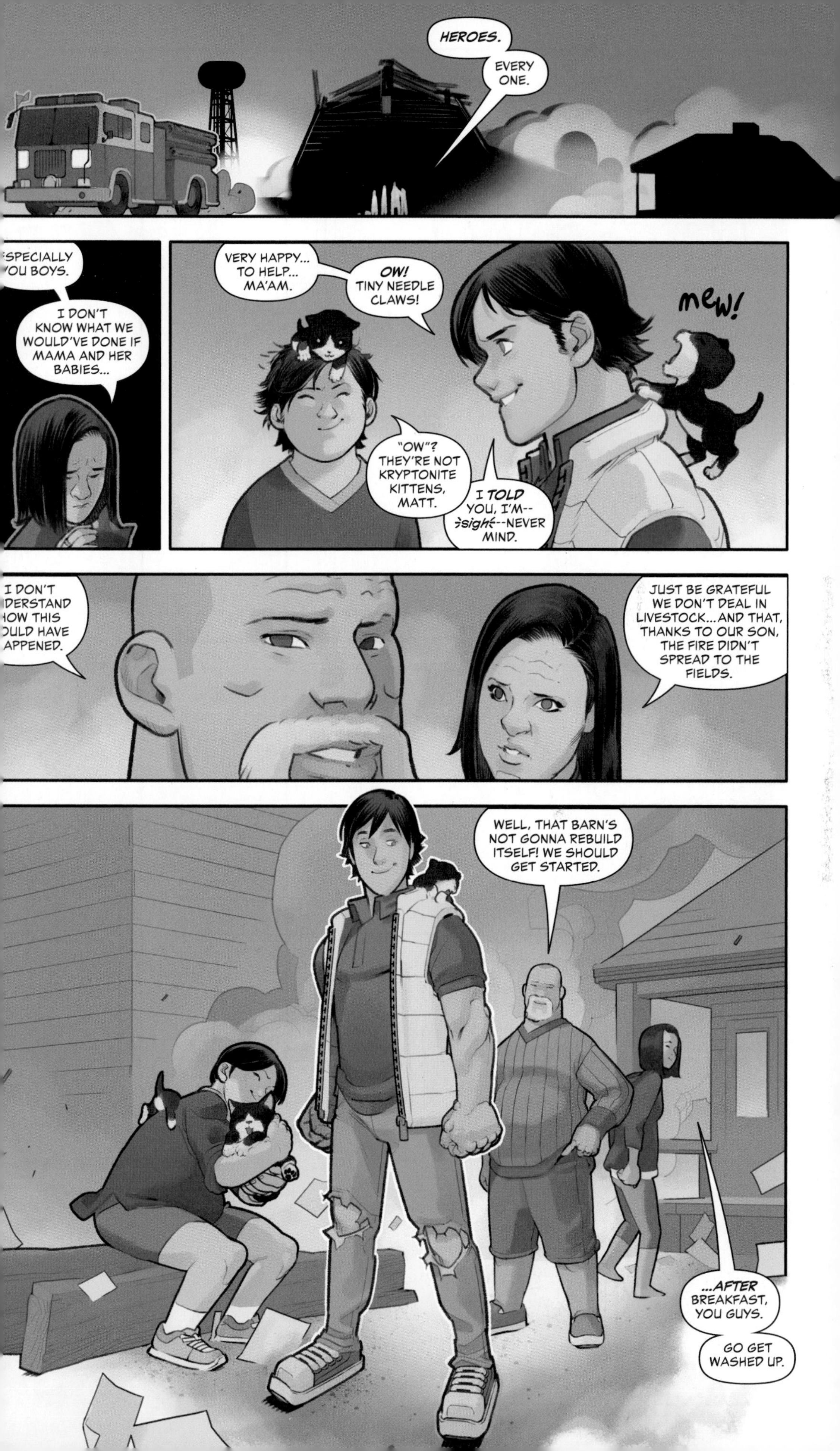
HEROES.
EVERY ONE.
SPECIALLY YOU BOYS.
I DON'T KNOW WHAT WE WOULD'VE DONE IF MAMA AND HER BABIES...
VERY HAPPY... TO HELP... MA'AM.
OW! TINY NEEDLE CLAWS!
mew!
"OW"? THEY'RE NOT KRYPTONITE KITTENS, MATT.
I TOLD YOU, I'M-- sigh --NEVER MIND.
I DON'T DERSTAND HOW THIS OULD HAVE APPENED.
JUST BE GRATEFUL WE DON'T DEAL IN LIVESTOCK...AND THAT, THANKS TO OUR SON, THE FIRE DIDN'T SPREAD TO THE FIELDS.
WELL, THAT BARN'S NOT GONNA REBUILD ITSELF! WE SHOULD GET STARTED.
...AFTER BREAKFAST, YOU GUYS.
GO GET WASHED UP.

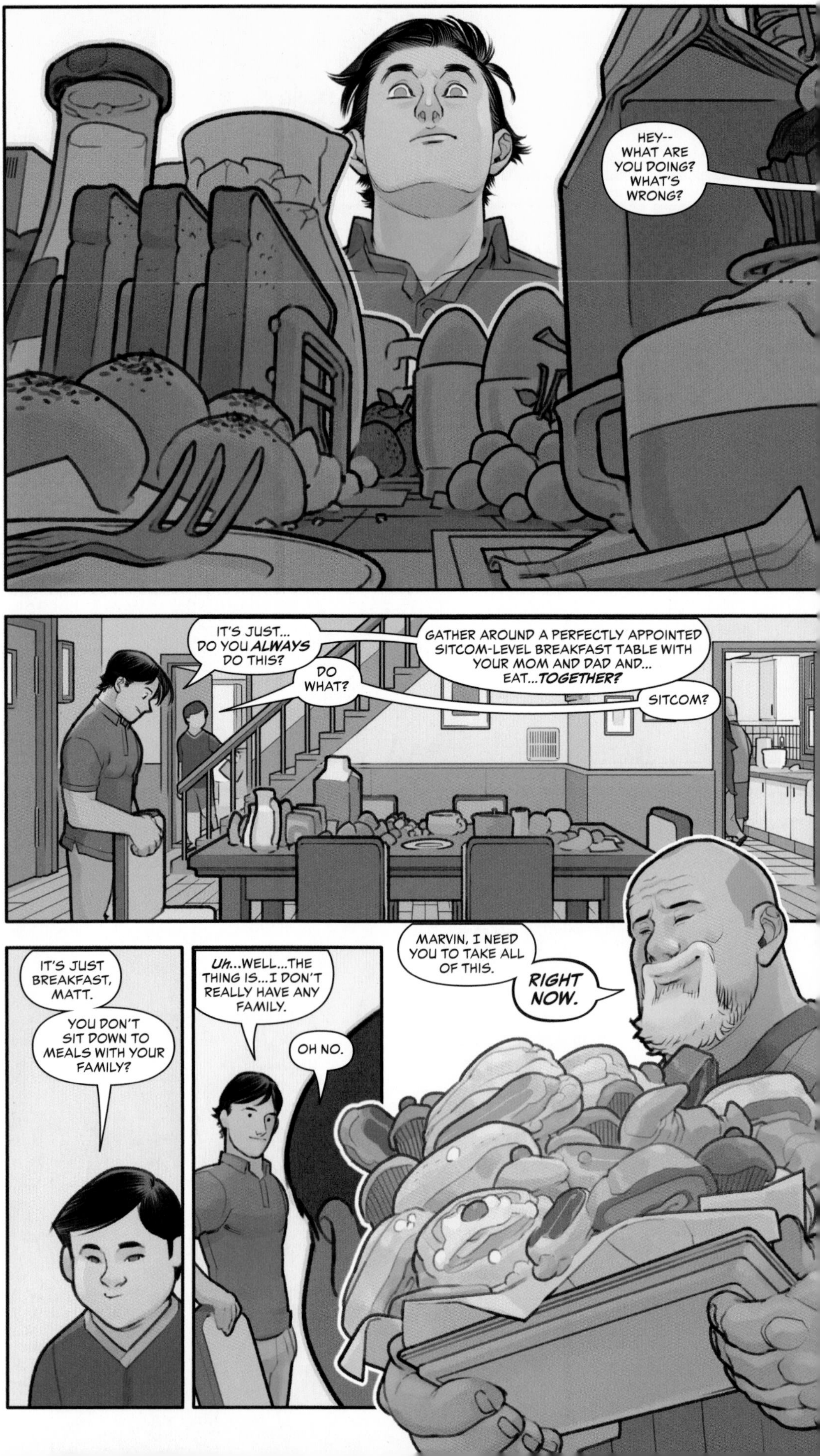
HEY-- WHAT ARE YOU DOING? WHAT'S WRONG?
IT'S JUST... DO YOU *ALWAYS* DO THIS?
GATHER AROUND A PERFECTLY APPOINTED SITCOM-LEVEL BREAKFAST TABLE WITH YOUR MOM AND DAD AND... EAT...*TOGETHER?*
DO WHAT?
SITCOM?
IT'S JUST BREAKFAST, MATT.
YOU DON'T SIT DOWN TO MEALS WITH YOUR FAMILY?
Uh...WELL...THE THING IS...I DON'T REALLY HAVE ANY FAMILY.
OH NO.
MARVIN, I NEED YOU TO TAKE ALL OF THIS.
RIGHT NOW.

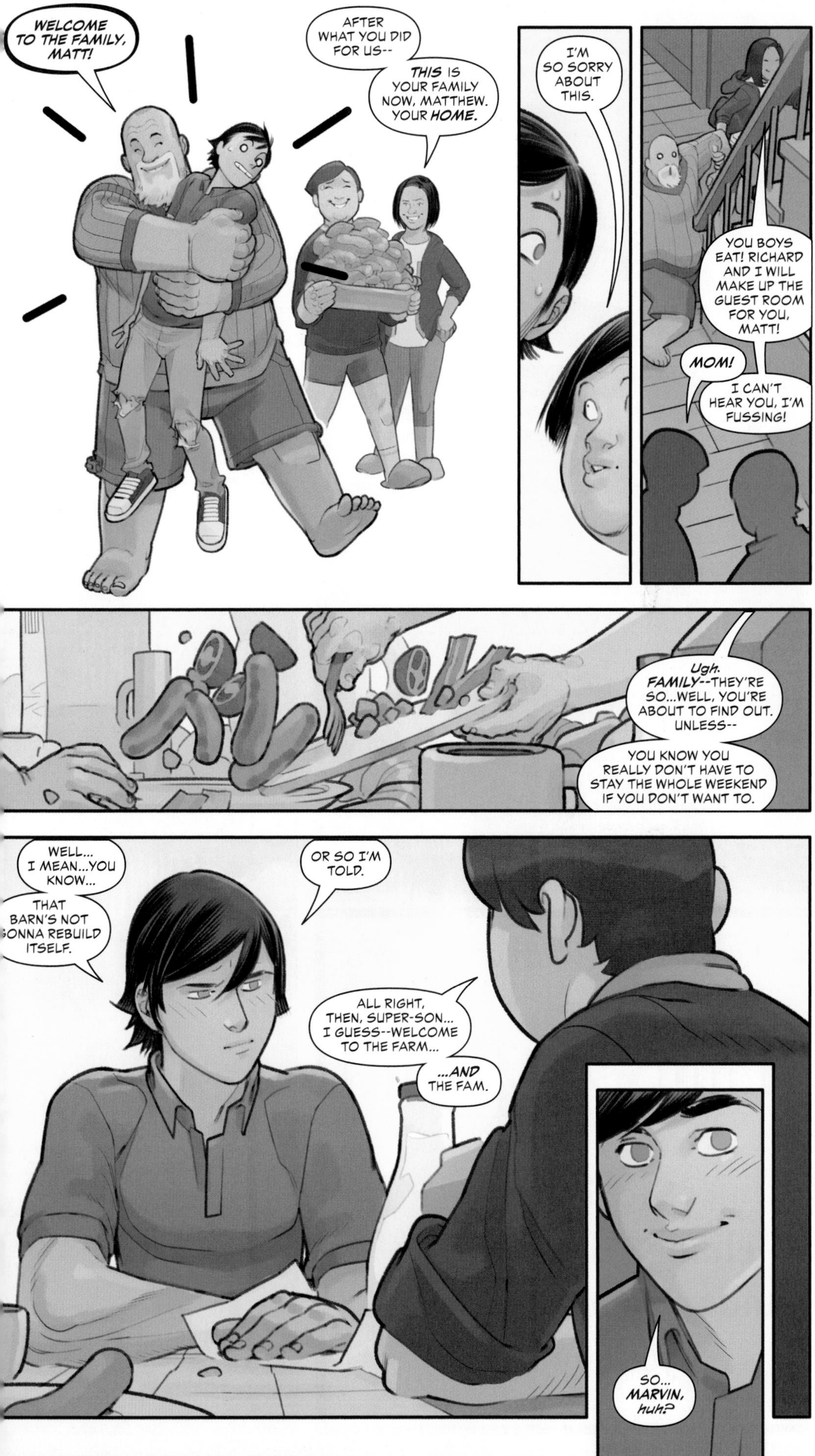
WELCOME TO THE FAMILY, MATT!
AFTER WHAT YOU DID FOR US--
THIS IS YOUR FAMILY NOW, MATTHEW. YOUR HOME.
I'M SO SORRY ABOUT THIS.
YOU BOYS EAT! RICHARD AND I WILL MAKE UP THE GUEST ROOM FOR YOU, MATT!
MOM!
I CAN'T HEAR YOU, I'M FUSSING!
Ugh. FAMILY--THEY'RE SO...WELL, YOU'RE ABOUT TO FIND OUT. UNLESS--
YOU KNOW YOU REALLY DON'T HAVE TO STAY THE WHOLE WEEKEND IF YOU DON'T WANT TO.
WELL... I MEAN...YOU KNOW...
THAT BARN'S NOT GONNA REBUILD ITSELF.
OR SO I'M TOLD.
ALL RIGHT, THEN, SUPER-SON... I GUESS--WELCOME TO THE FARM...
...AND THE FAM.
SO... MARVIN, huh?

SUPERMAN LEVEL SERVICE
AT BIZARRO PRICES!

ALL STAR SQUADRON

MOBILE AP
COMING FALL 202

TERRIFIC TECH

WE'RE MAKING TOMORROW TERRIFIC!

A PROUD SPONSOR OF TITANS ACADEMY

A great metropolitan newspaper

Daily Planet

Stories that change the world by today's most respected journalists!

S.T.A.R

LABORATORIE

SCIENCE

TECHNOLOGY

ADVANCED RESEARC

SPEAK TO MR. CYBORG TODAY ABOUT AN INTERNSHIP!

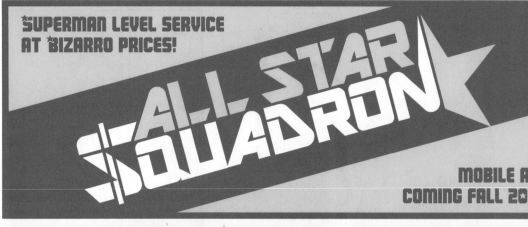

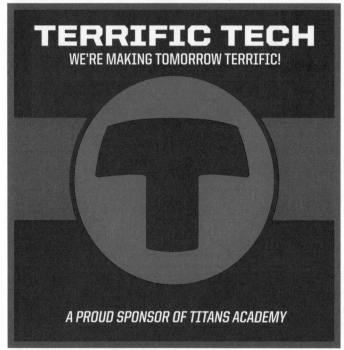

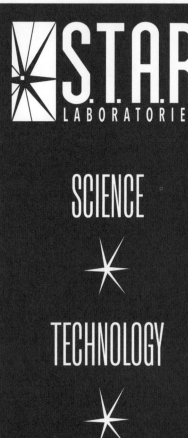

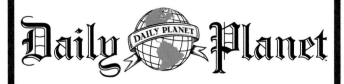

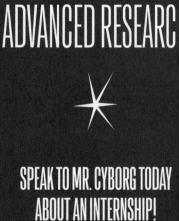

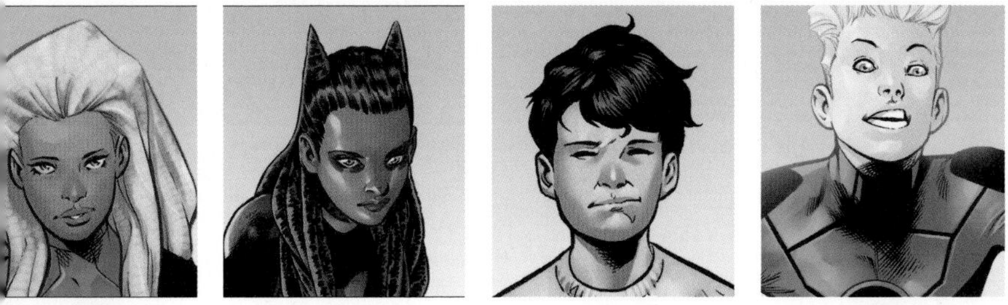

Alinta
Cooper, Merissa
Batson, William
Dane

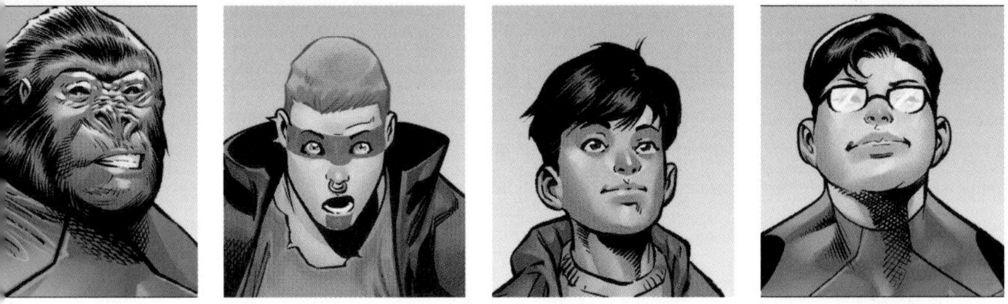

Gregg, Gorilla
LaPorte, Lucas
Montez, Miguel
Murakami, Marvin "Tooby"

Who is your favorite Titan of all time?

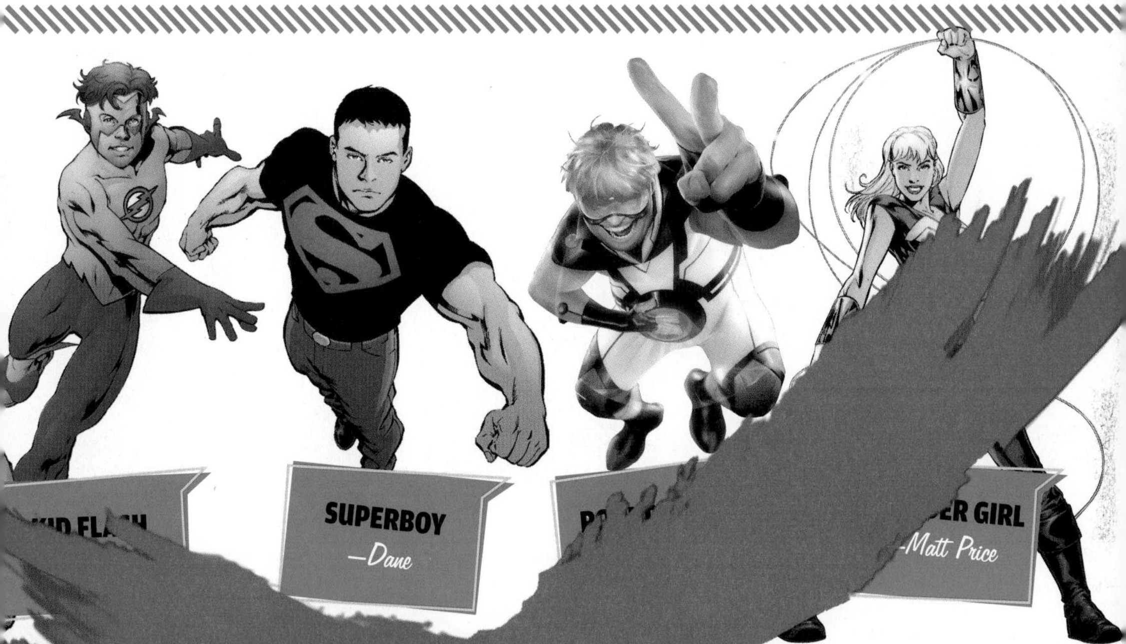
SUPERBOY
—Dane
—Matt Price

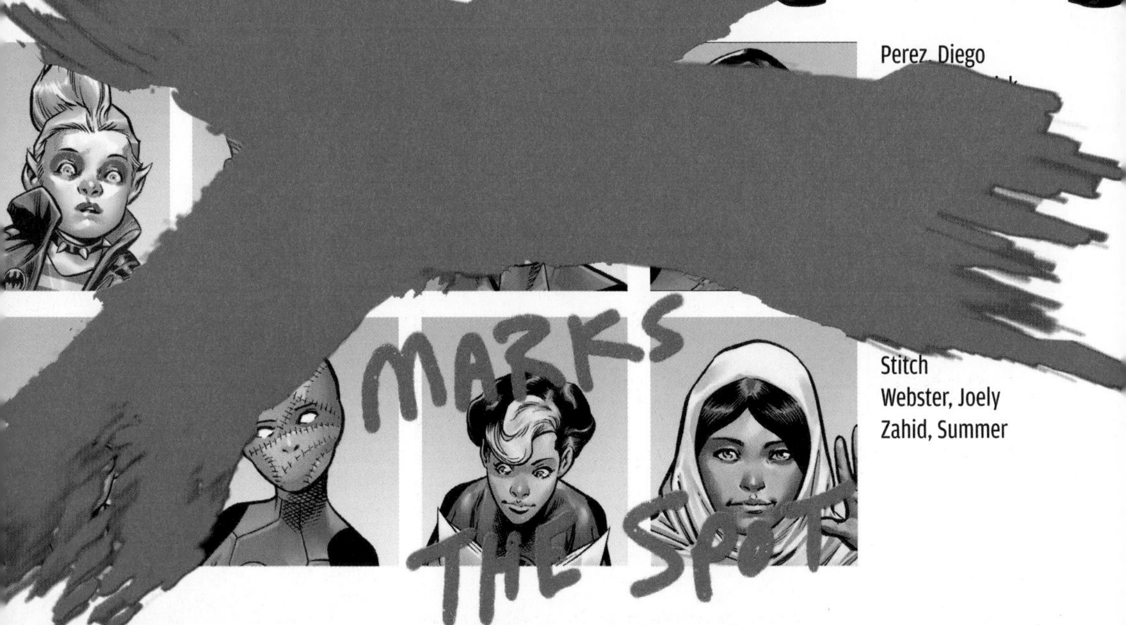
MARKS
THE SPOT

Perez, Diego

Stitch
Webster, Joely
Zahid, Summer

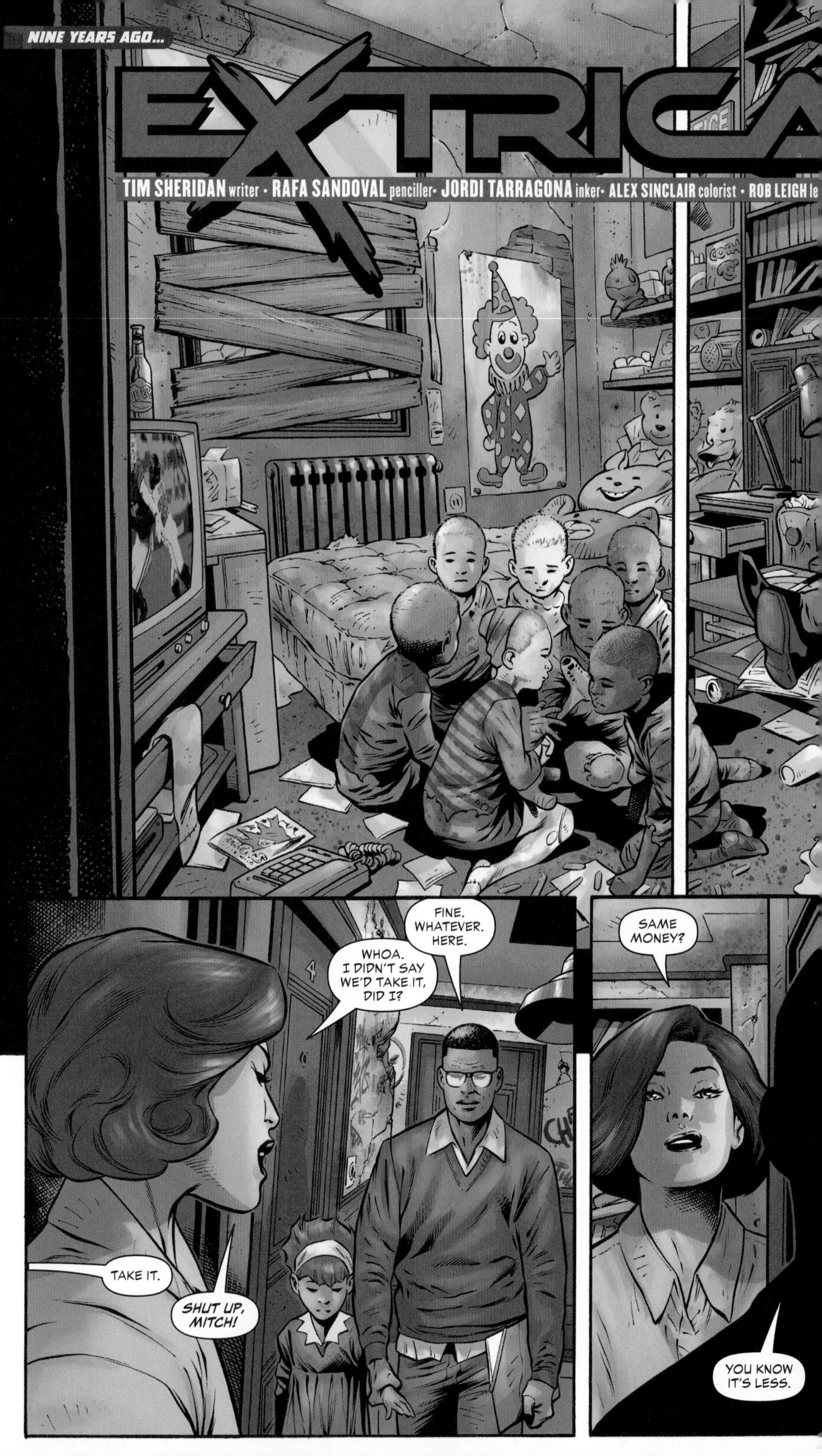
NINE YEARS AGO...
EXTRICA
TIM SHERIDAN writer • RAFA SANDOVAL penciller • JORDI TARRAGONA inker • ALEX SINCLAIR colorist • ROB LEIGH le
WHOA. I DIDN'T SAY WE'D TAKE IT, DID I?
FINE. WHATEVER. HERE.
TAKE IT.
SHUT UP, MITCH!
SAME MONEY?
YOU KNOW IT'S LESS.

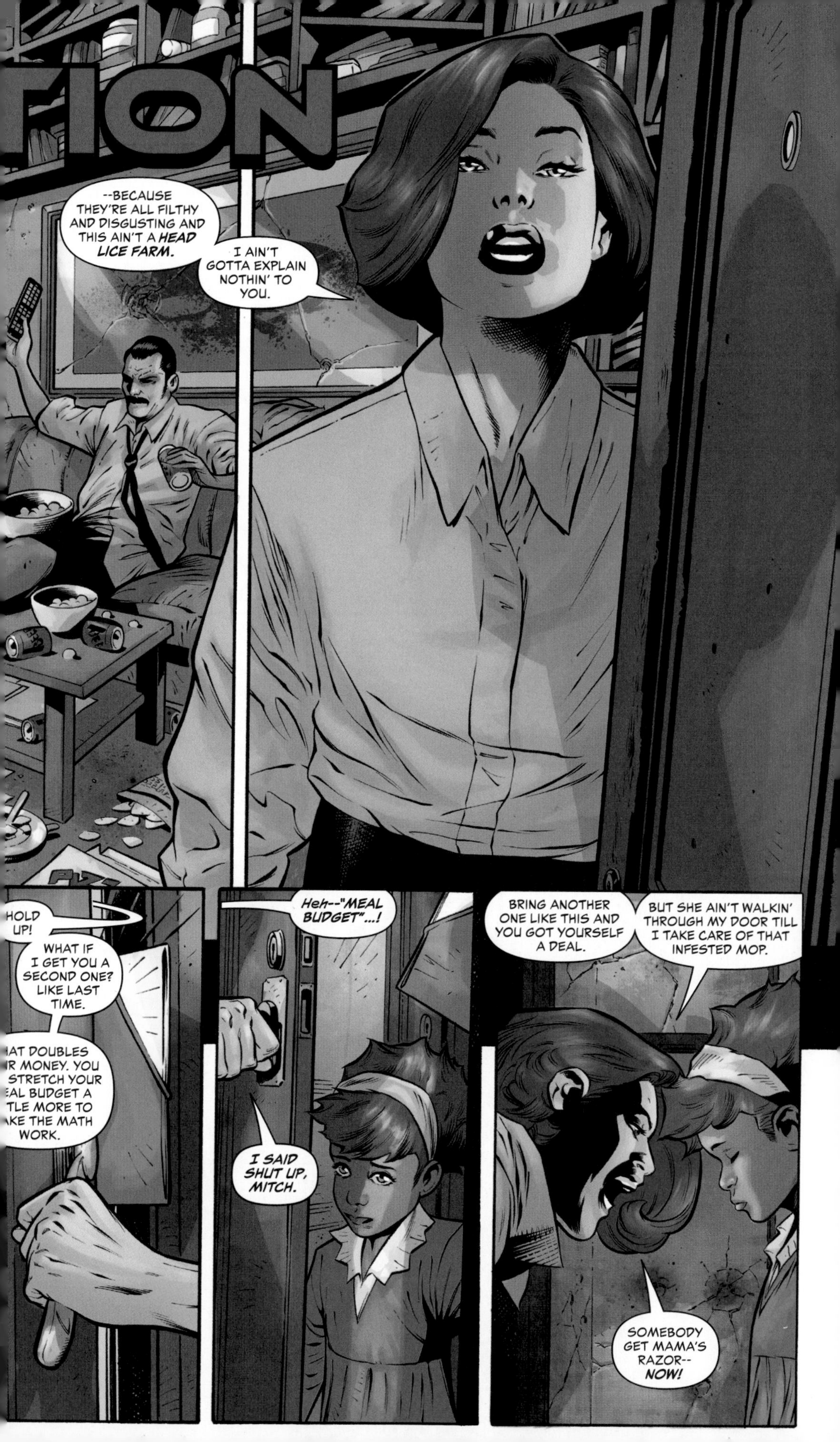
TION
--BECAUSE THEY'RE ALL FILTHY AND DISGUSTING AND THIS AIN'T A *HEAD LICE FARM.*
I AIN'T GOTTA EXPLAIN NOTHIN' TO YOU.
HOLD UP!
WHAT IF I GET YOU A SECOND ONE? LIKE LAST TIME.
AT DOUBLES R MONEY. YOU STRETCH YOUR EAL BUDGET A TLE MORE TO KE THE MATH WORK.
Heh--"MEAL BUDGET"...!
I SAID SHUT UP, MITCH.
BRING ANOTHER ONE LIKE THIS AND YOU GOT YOURSELF A DEAL.
BUT SHE AIN'T WALKIN' THROUGH MY DOOR TILL I TAKE CARE OF THAT INFESTED MOP.
SOMEBODY GET MAMA'S RAZOR-- *NOW!*

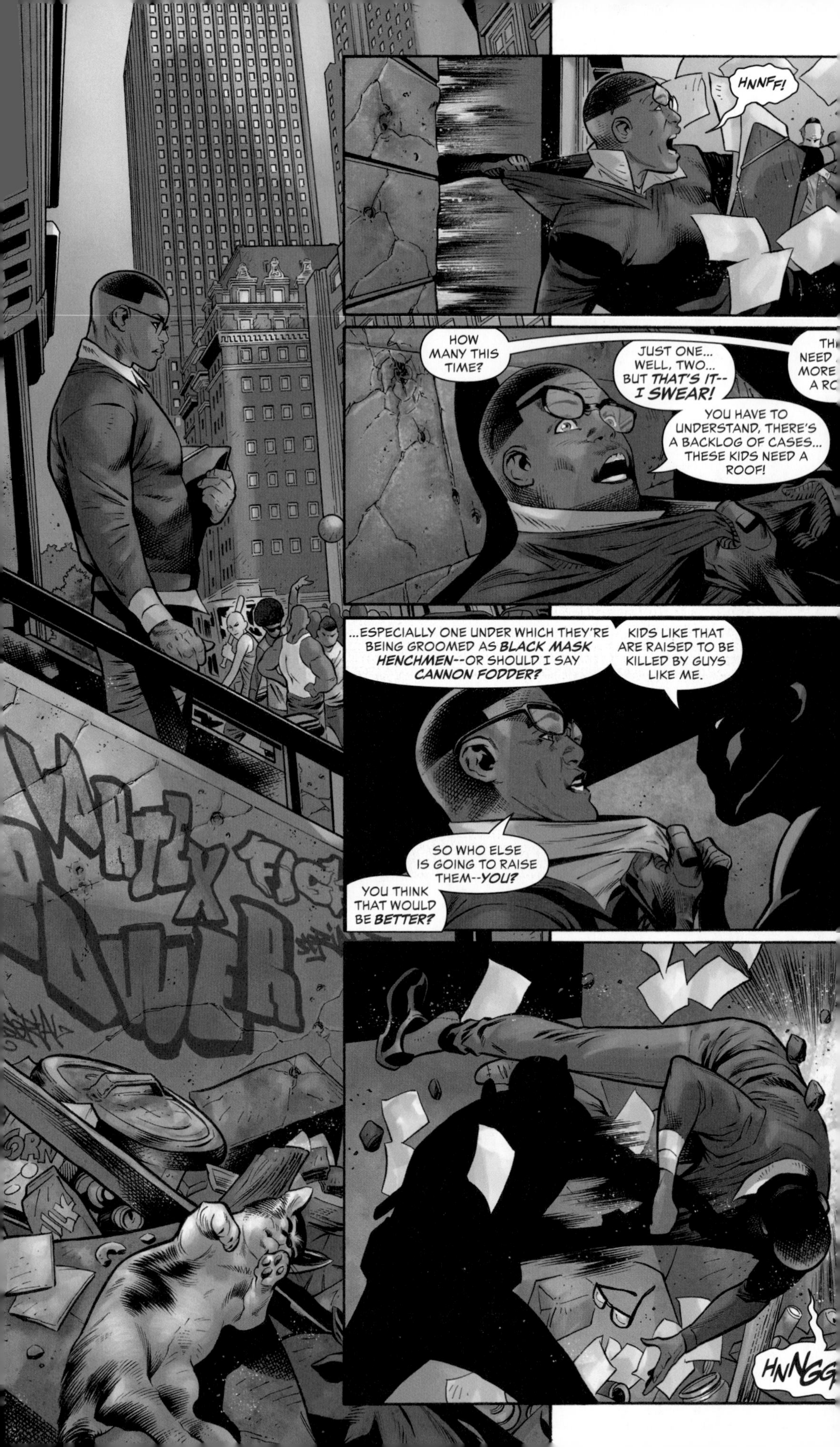
HNNFF!
HOW MANY THIS TIME?
JUST ONE... WELL, TWO... BUT THAT'S IT-- I SWEAR!
YOU HAVE TO UNDERSTAND, THERE'S A BACKLOG OF CASES... THESE KIDS NEED A ROOF!
...ESPECIALLY ONE UNDER WHICH THEY'RE BEING GROOMED AS BLACK MASK HENCHMEN--OR SHOULD I SAY CANNON FODDER?
KIDS LIKE THAT ARE RAISED TO BE KILLED BY GUYS LIKE ME.
SO WHO ELSE IS GOING TO RAISE THEM--YOU?
YOU THINK THAT WOULD BE BETTER?

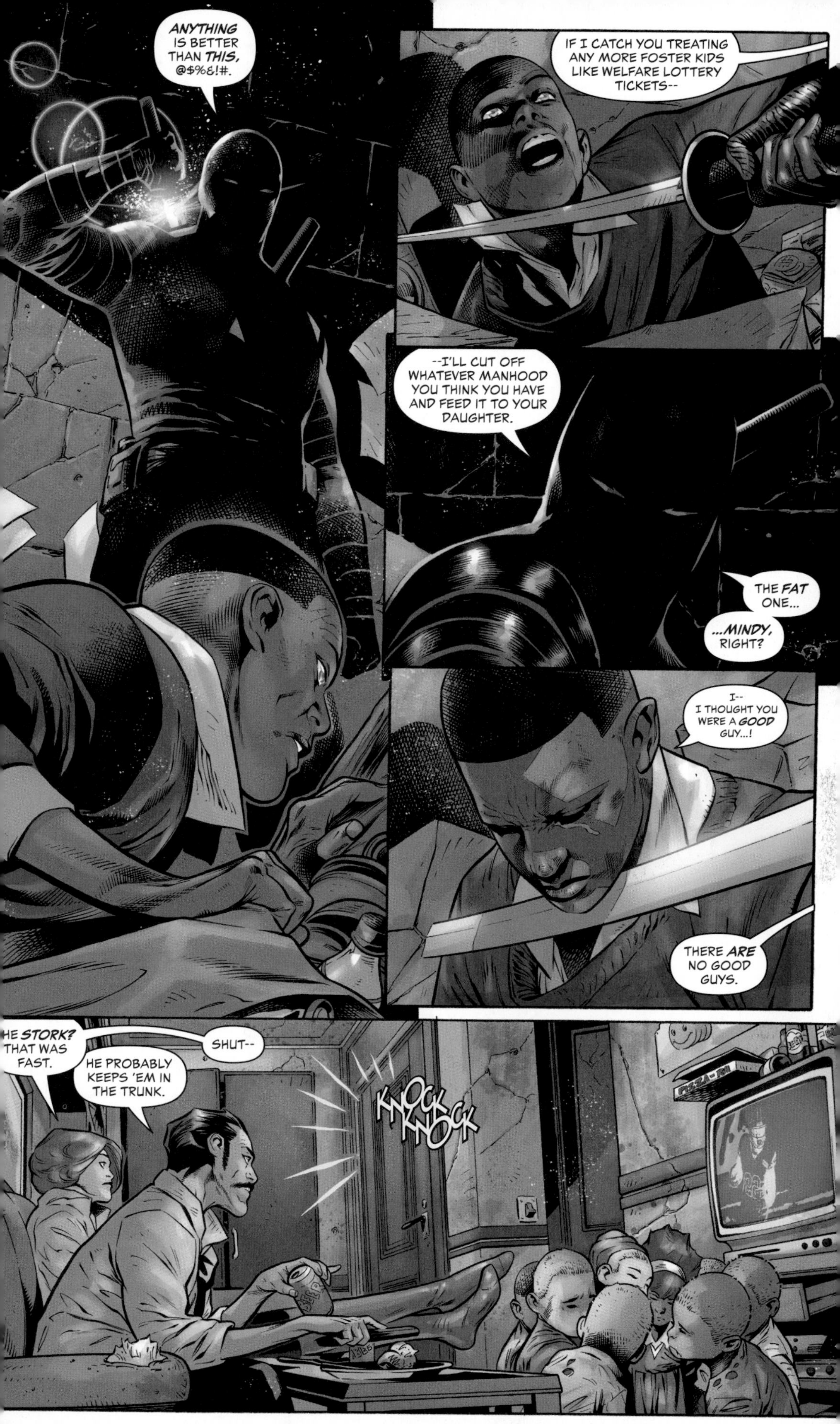
ANYTHING IS BETTER THAN THIS, @$%&!#.
IF I CATCH YOU TREATING ANY MORE FOSTER KIDS LIKE WELFARE LOTTERY TICKETS--
--I'LL CUT OFF WHATEVER MANHOOD YOU THINK YOU HAVE AND FEED IT TO YOUR DAUGHTER.
THE FAT ONE...
...MINDY, RIGHT?
I-- I THOUGHT YOU WERE A GOOD GUY...!
THERE ARE NO GOOD GUYS.
HE STORK? THAT WAS FAST.
HE PROBABLY KEEPS 'EM IN THE TRUNK.
SHUT--
KNOCK KNOCK

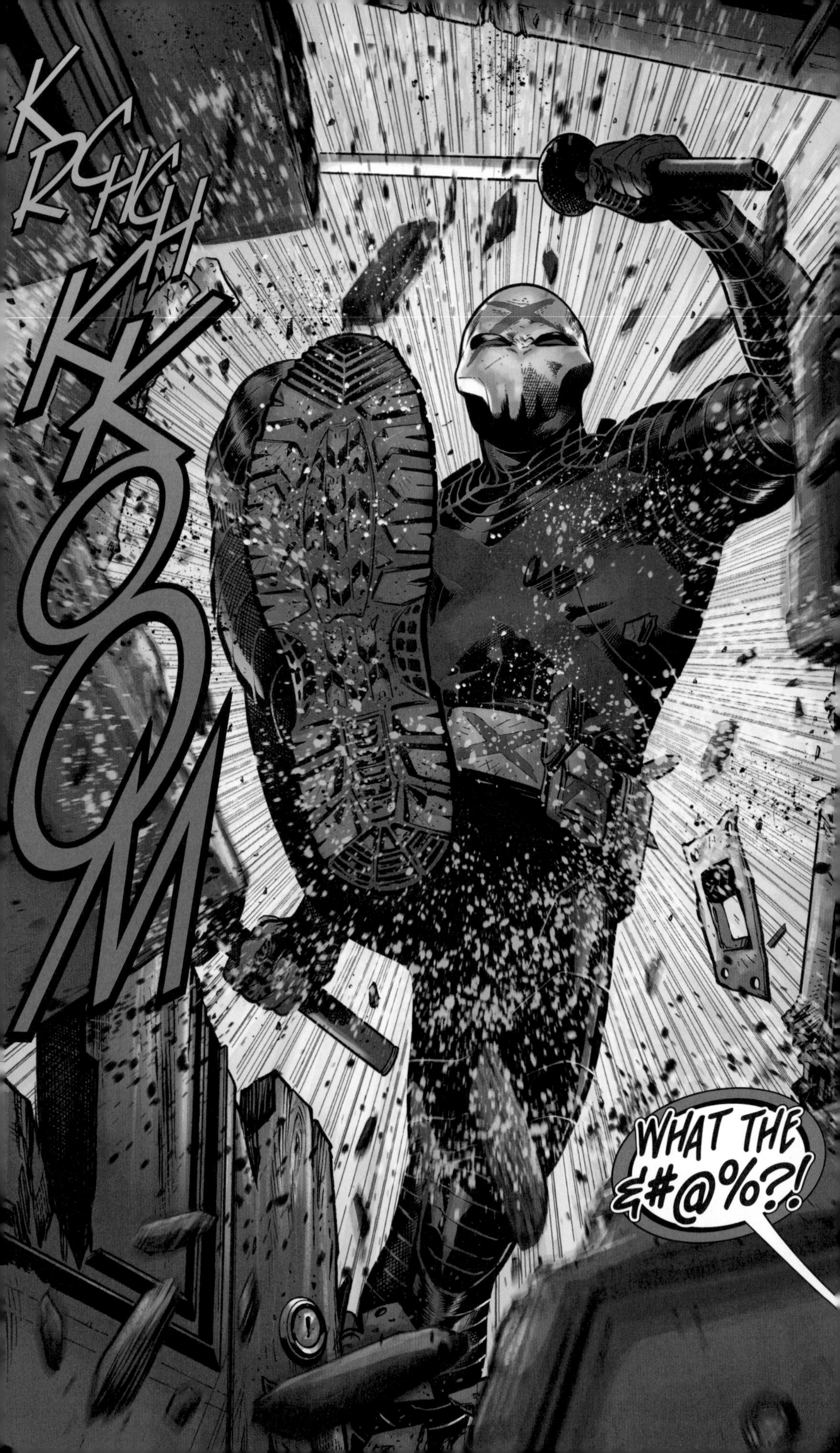
KRCHCH
KHOOM
WHAT THE &#@%?!

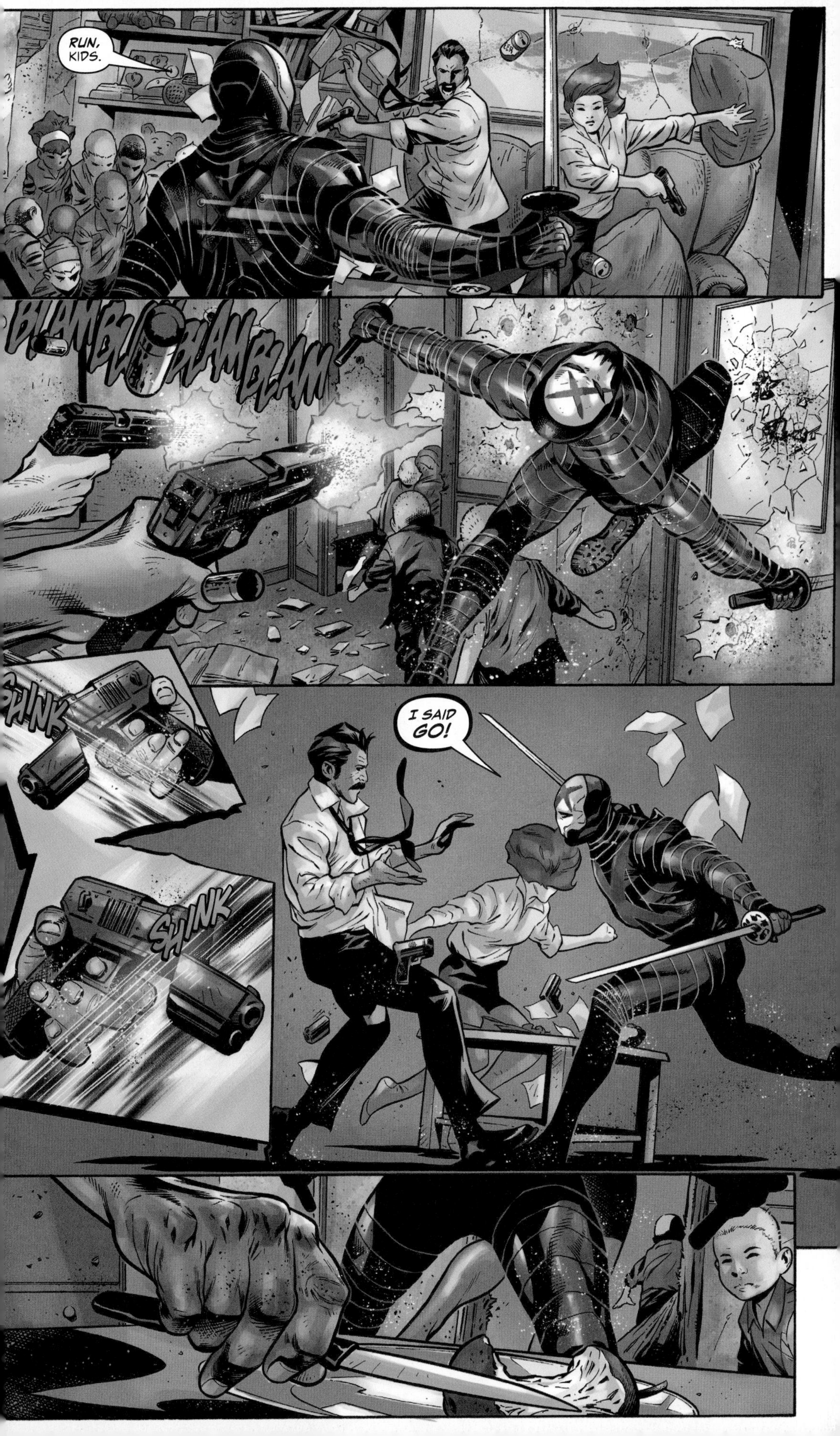

RUN, KIDS.
BLAM BLAM BLAM BLAM
SHINK
SHINK
I SAID GO!

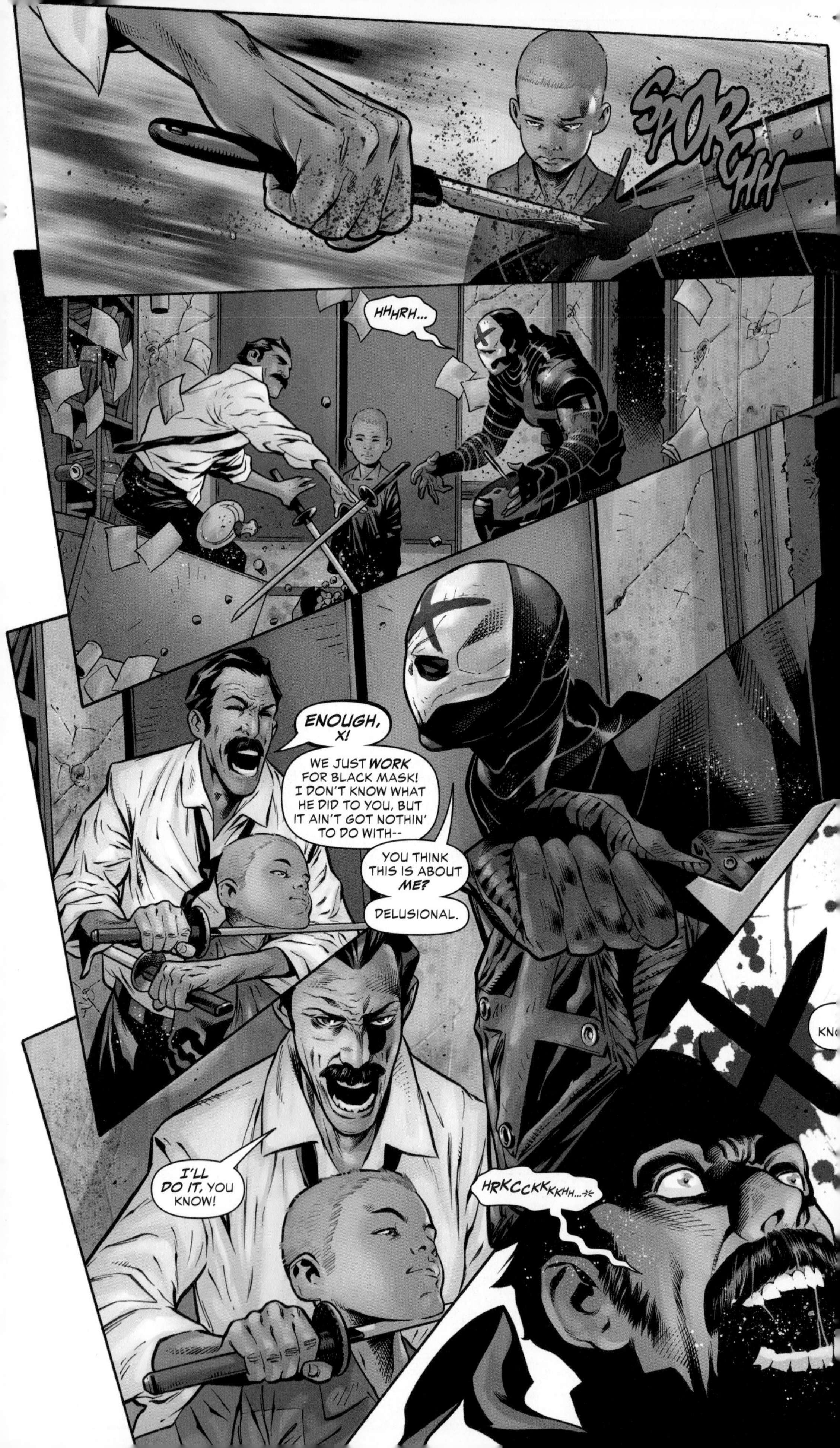
SPORCHH
HHHRH...
ENOUGH, X!
WE JUST WORK FOR BLACK MASK! I DON'T KNOW WHAT HE DID TO YOU, BUT IT AIN'T GOT NOTHIN' TO DO WITH--
YOU THINK THIS IS ABOUT ME?
DELUSIONAL.
I'LL DO IT, YOU KNOW!
HRKCCKKKHH...

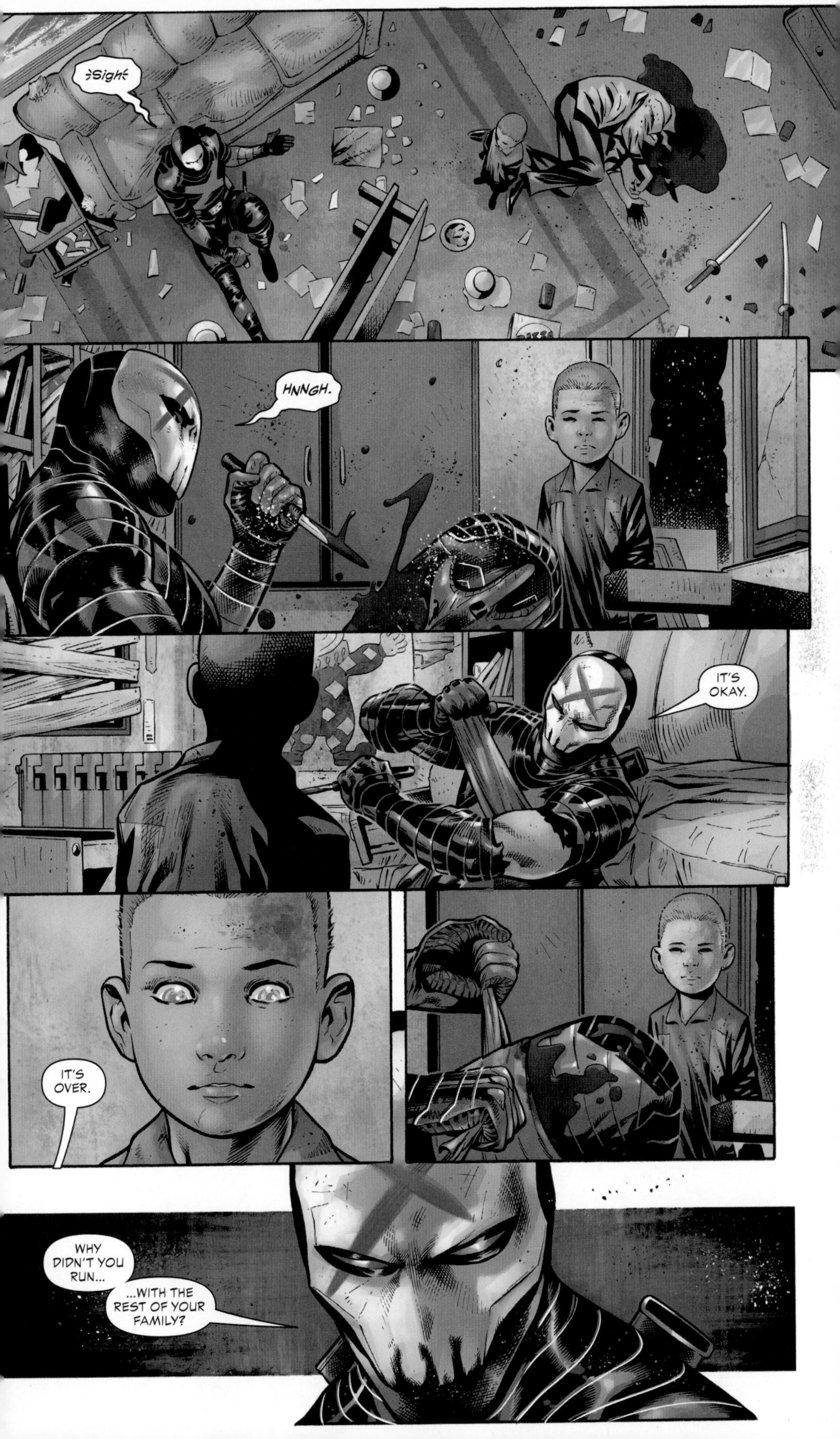

SIGH
HNNGH.
IT'S OKAY.
IT'S OVER.
WHY DIDN'T YOU RUN...
...WITH THE REST OF YOUR FAMILY?

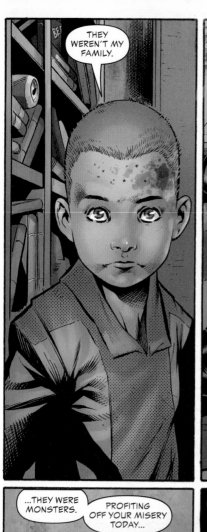

THEY WEREN'T MY FAMILY.

NO.

THOSE PEOPLE...THE ADULTS...

...THEY WERE MONSTERS.

PROFITING OFF YOUR MISERY TODAY...

...AND THEN TOMORROW...

...USING YOU TO FIGHT THEIR WAR FOR THEM.

...TO DIE FOR THEM.

PEOPLE LIKE THAT NEED TO BE STOPPED.

IT'S WHAT WE DO.

YOU KNOW W I AM?

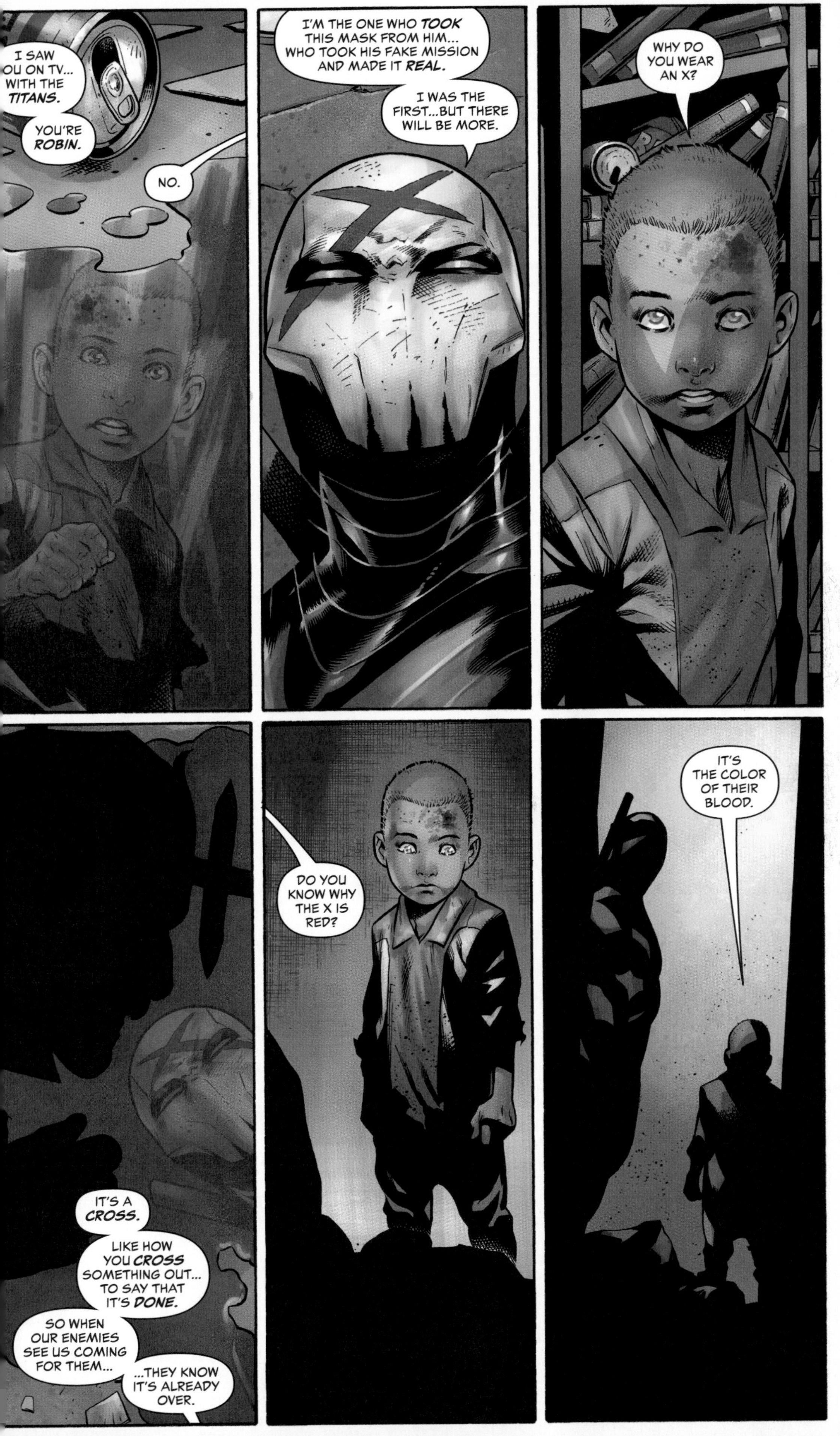
I SAW OU ON TV... WITH THE TITANS.
YOU'RE ROBIN.
NO.
I'M THE ONE WHO TOOK THIS MASK FROM HIM... WHO TOOK HIS FAKE MISSION AND MADE IT REAL.
I WAS THE FIRST...BUT THERE WILL BE MORE.
WHY DO YOU WEAR AN X?
IT'S A CROSS.
LIKE HOW YOU CROSS SOMETHING OUT... TO SAY THAT IT'S DONE.
SO WHEN OUR ENEMIES SEE US COMING FOR THEM...
...THEY KNOW IT'S ALREADY OVER.
DO YOU KNOW WHY THE X IS RED?
IT'S THE COLOR OF THEIR BLOOD.

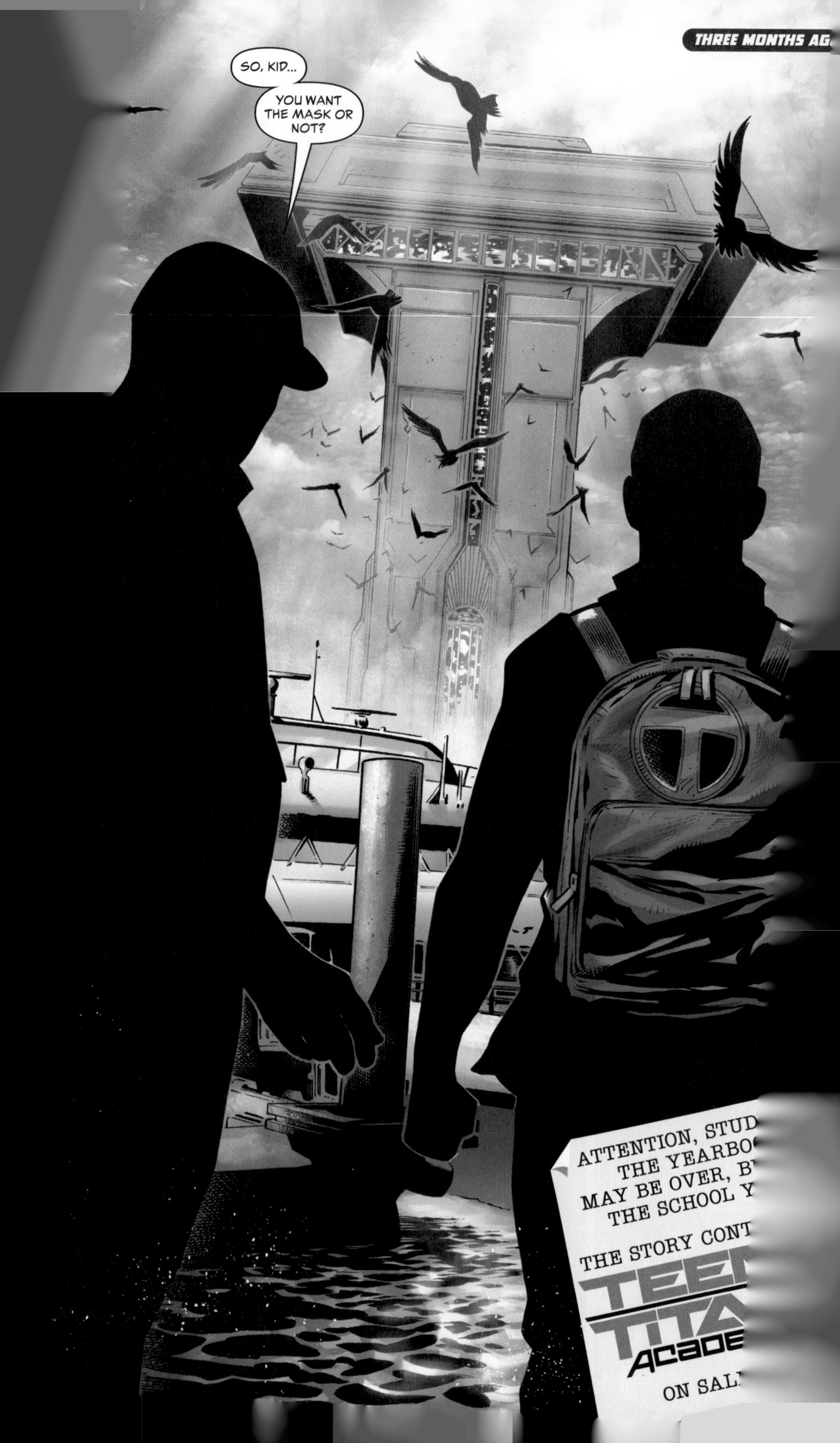
THREE MONTHS AG
SO, KID...
YOU WANT THE MASK OR NOT?
ATTENTION, STUD
THE YEARBO
MAY BE OVER, B
THE SCHOOL Y
THE STORY CONT
TEE
TITA
ACADE
ON SAL

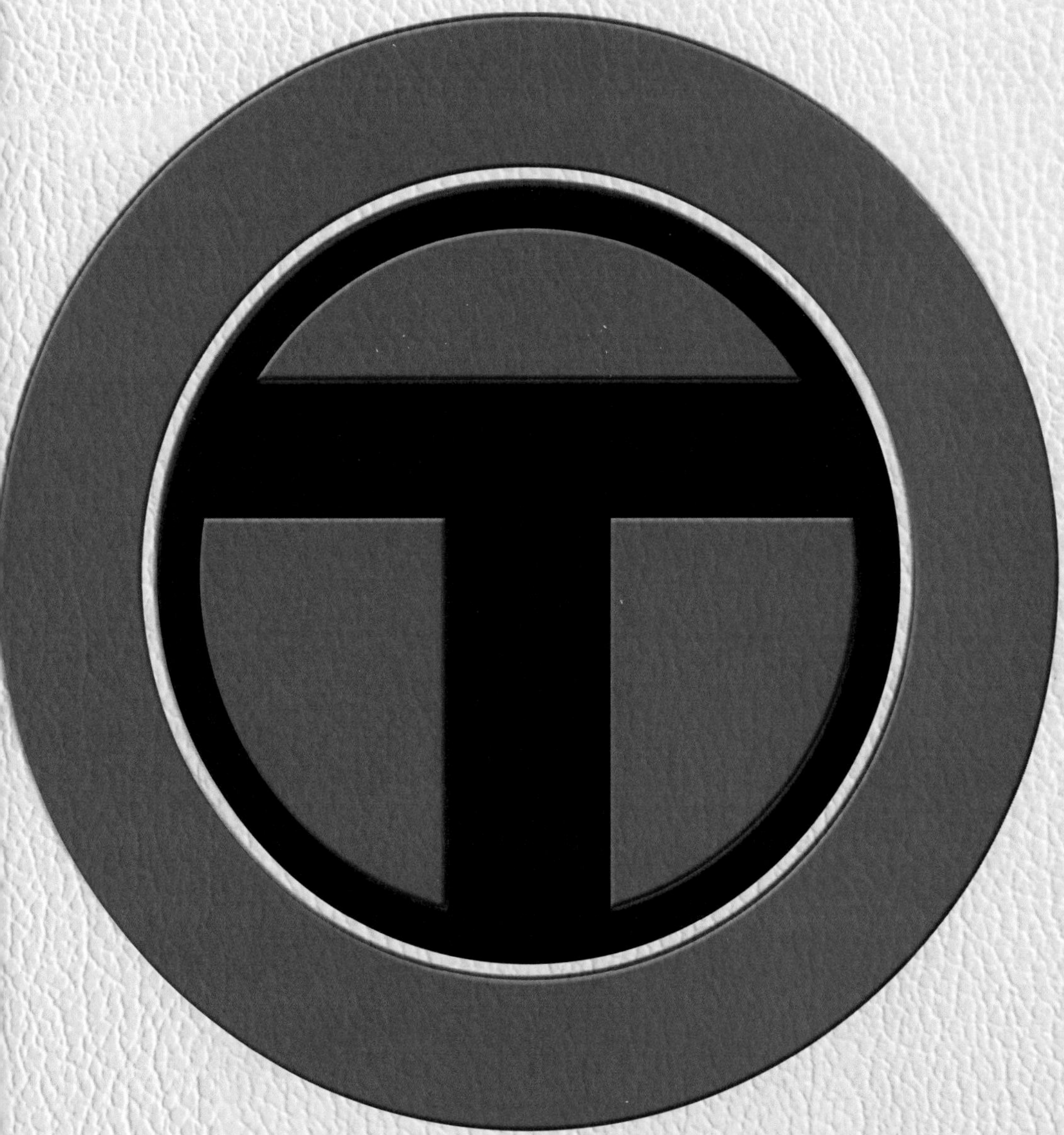

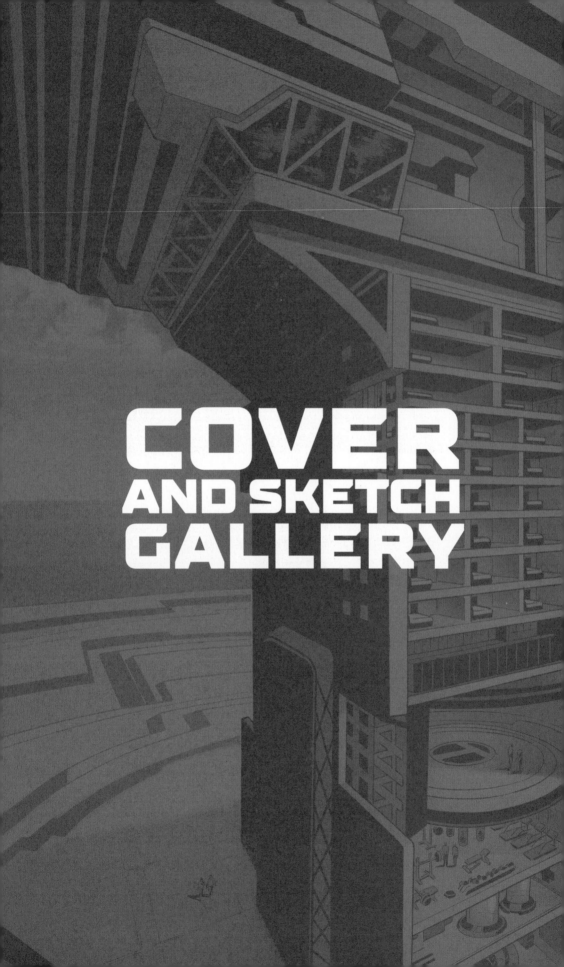

COVER
AND SKETCH
GALLERY

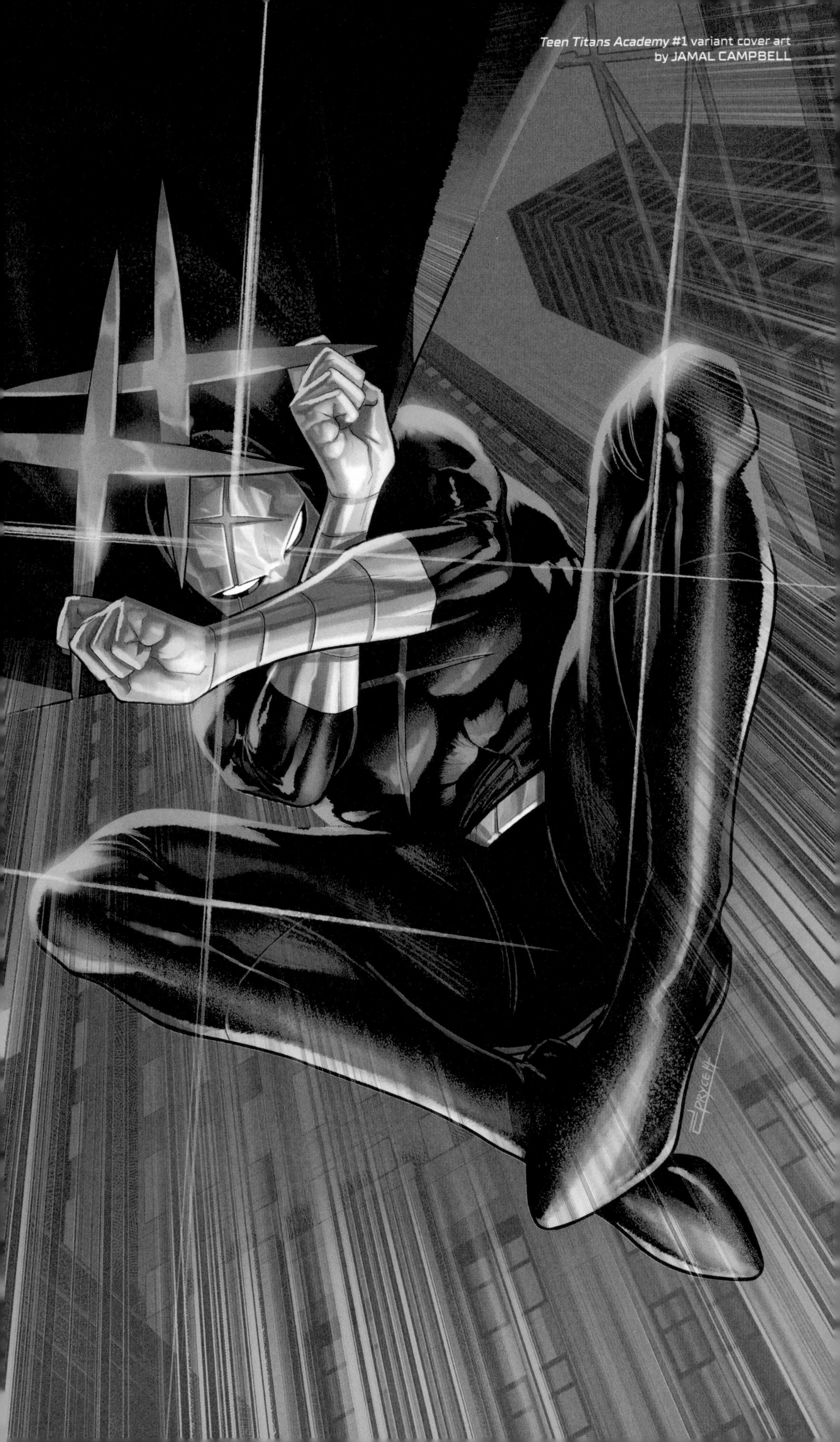

Teen Titans Academy #1 variant cover art
by JAMAL CAMPBELL

Teen Titans Academy #2 variant cover art
by PHILIP TAN and ELMER SANTOS

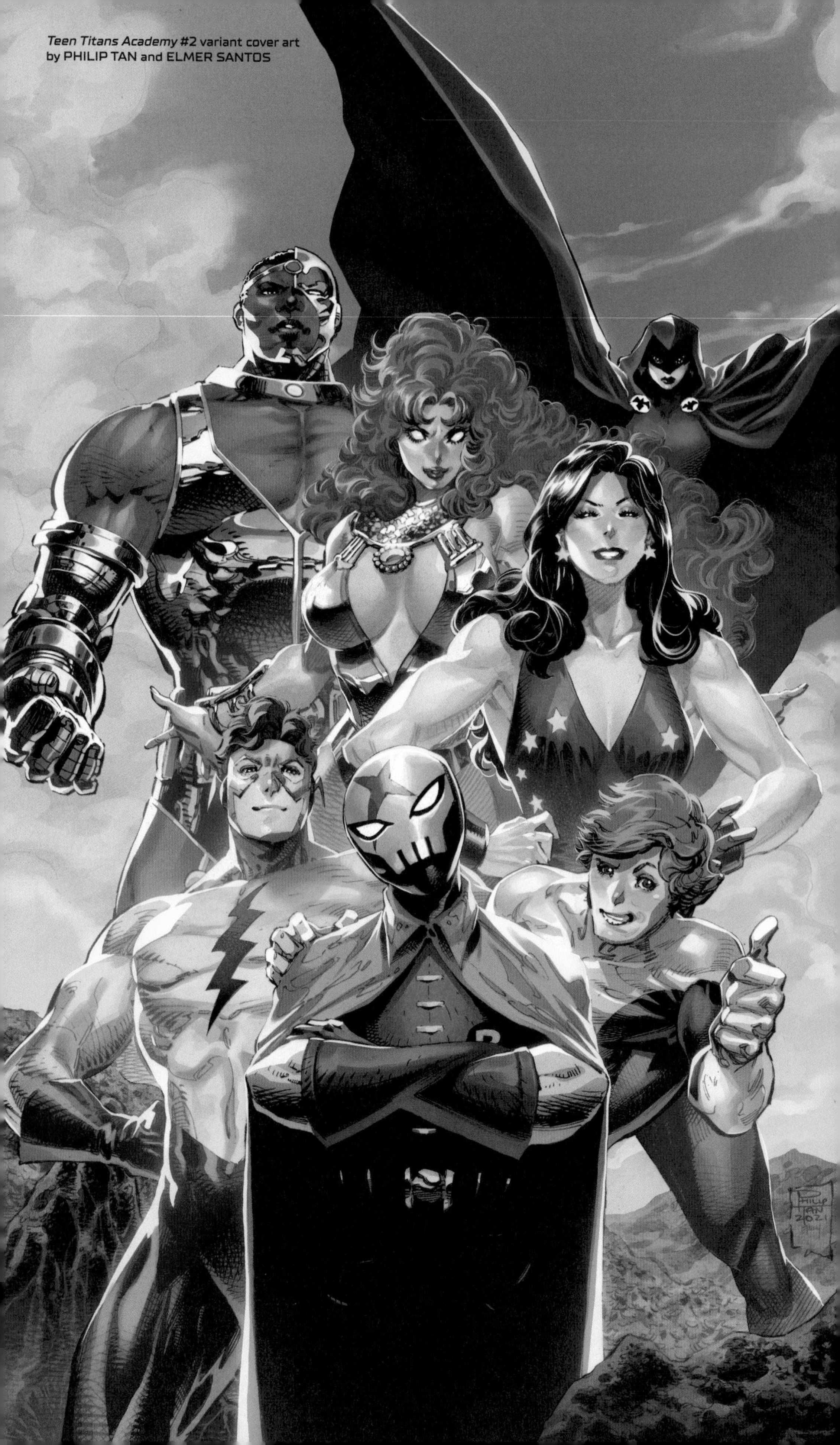

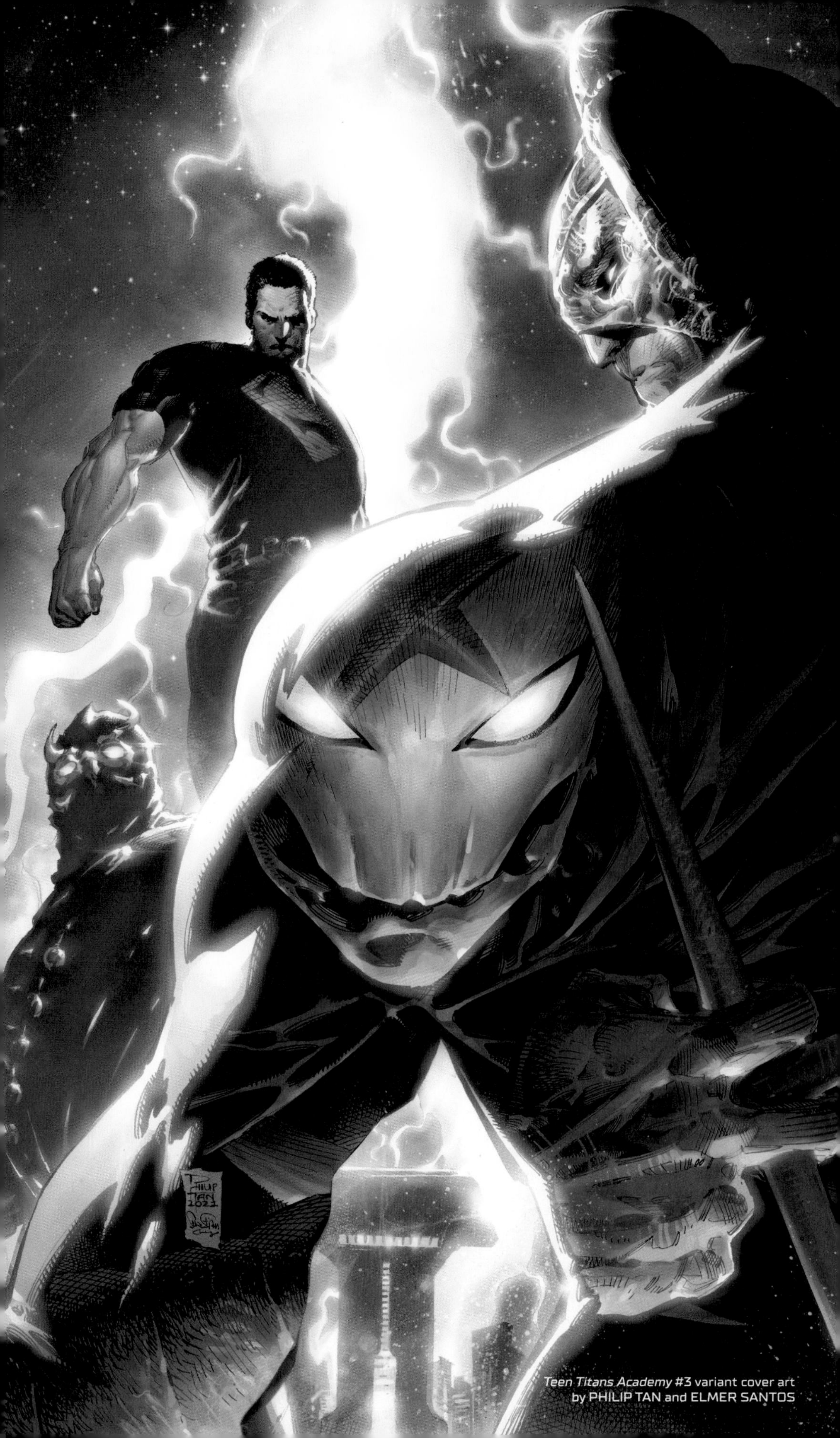
PHILIP TAN 2021

Teen Titans Academy #3 variant cover art
by PHILIP TAN and ELMER SANTOS

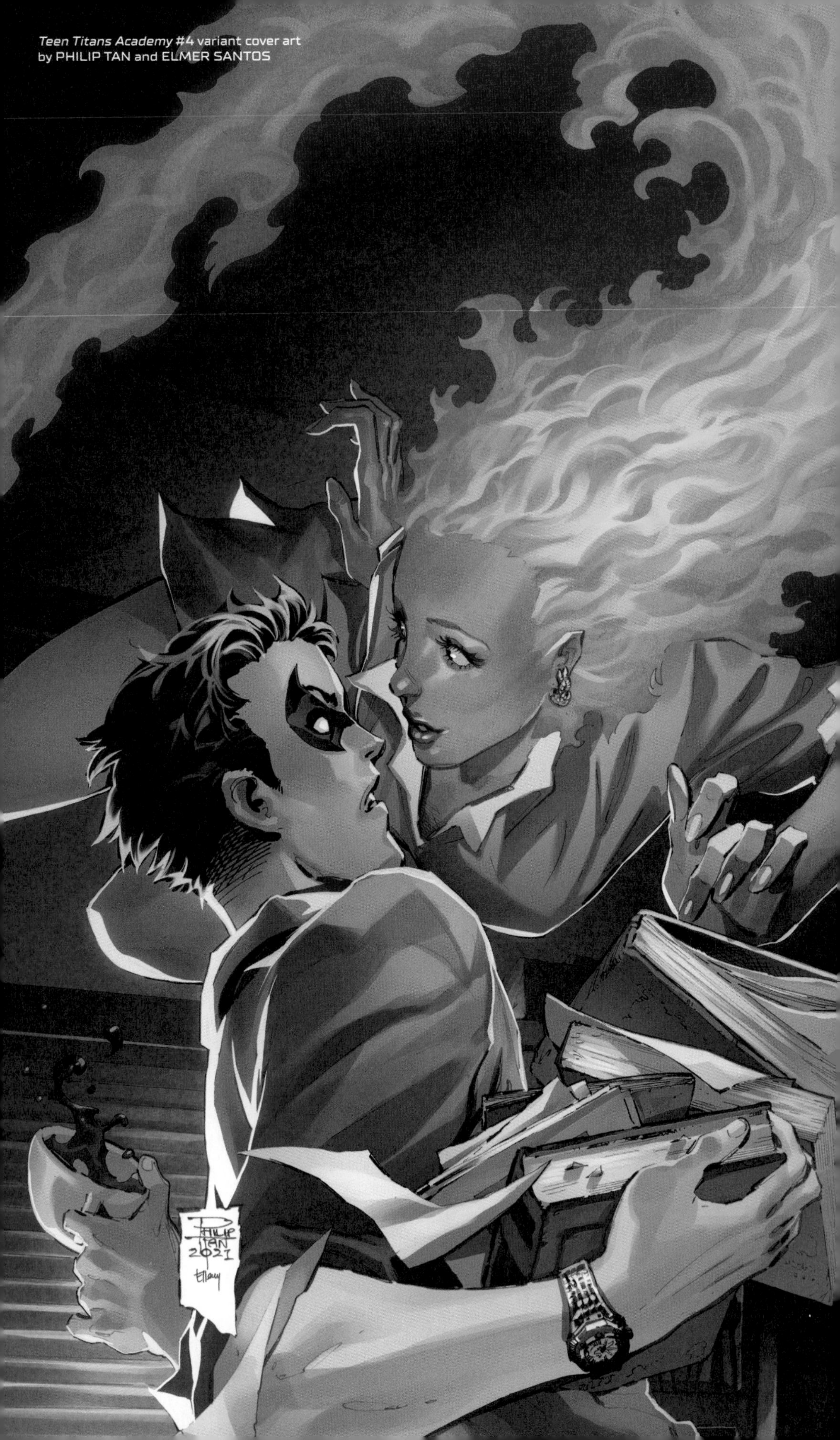

Teen Titans Academy #4 variant cover art
by PHILIP TAN and ELMER SANTOS

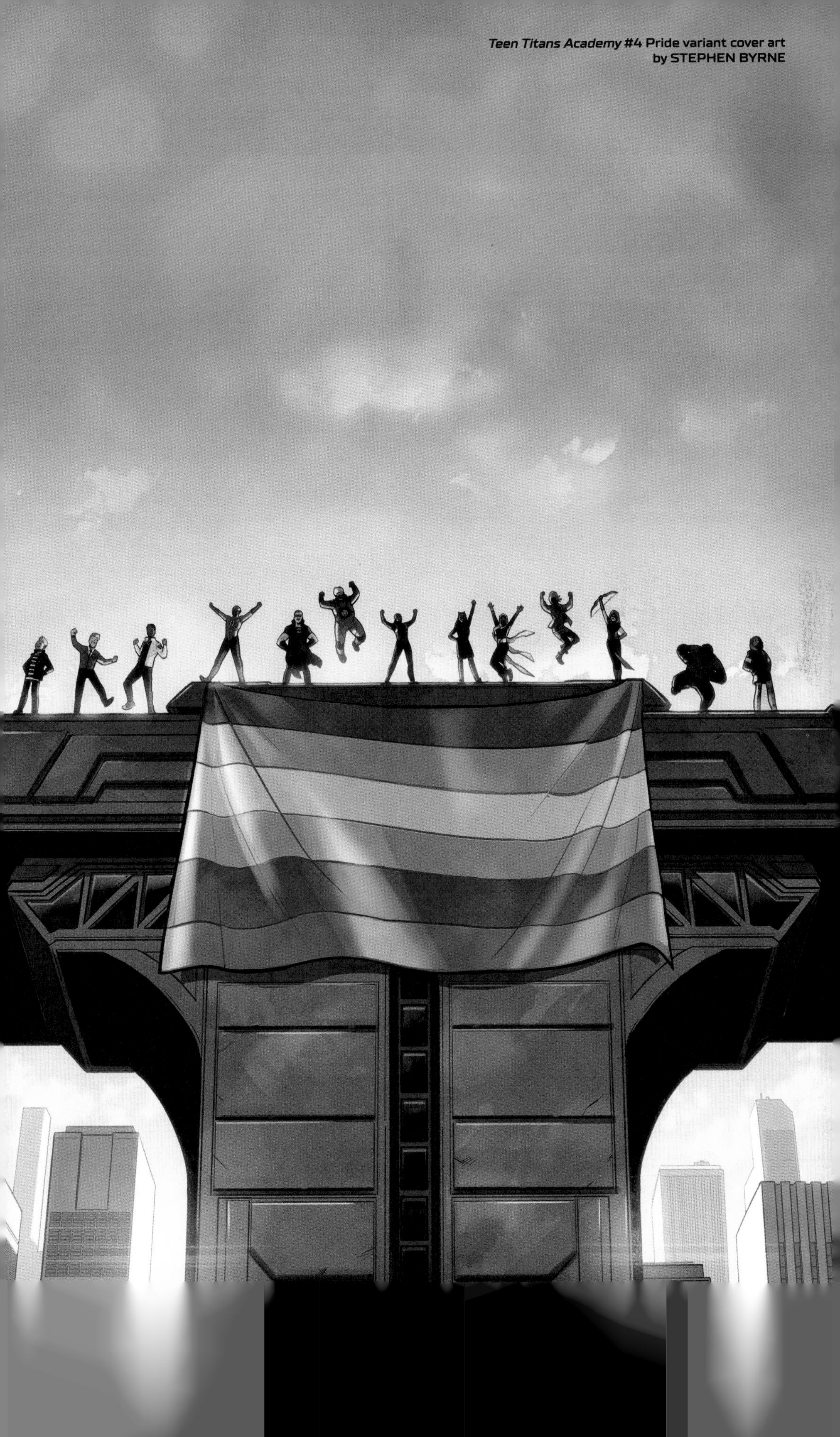

Teen Titans Academy #4 Pride variant cover art
by STEPHEN BYRNE

Teen Titans Academy #5 variant cover art
by PHILIP TAN and ELMER SANTOS

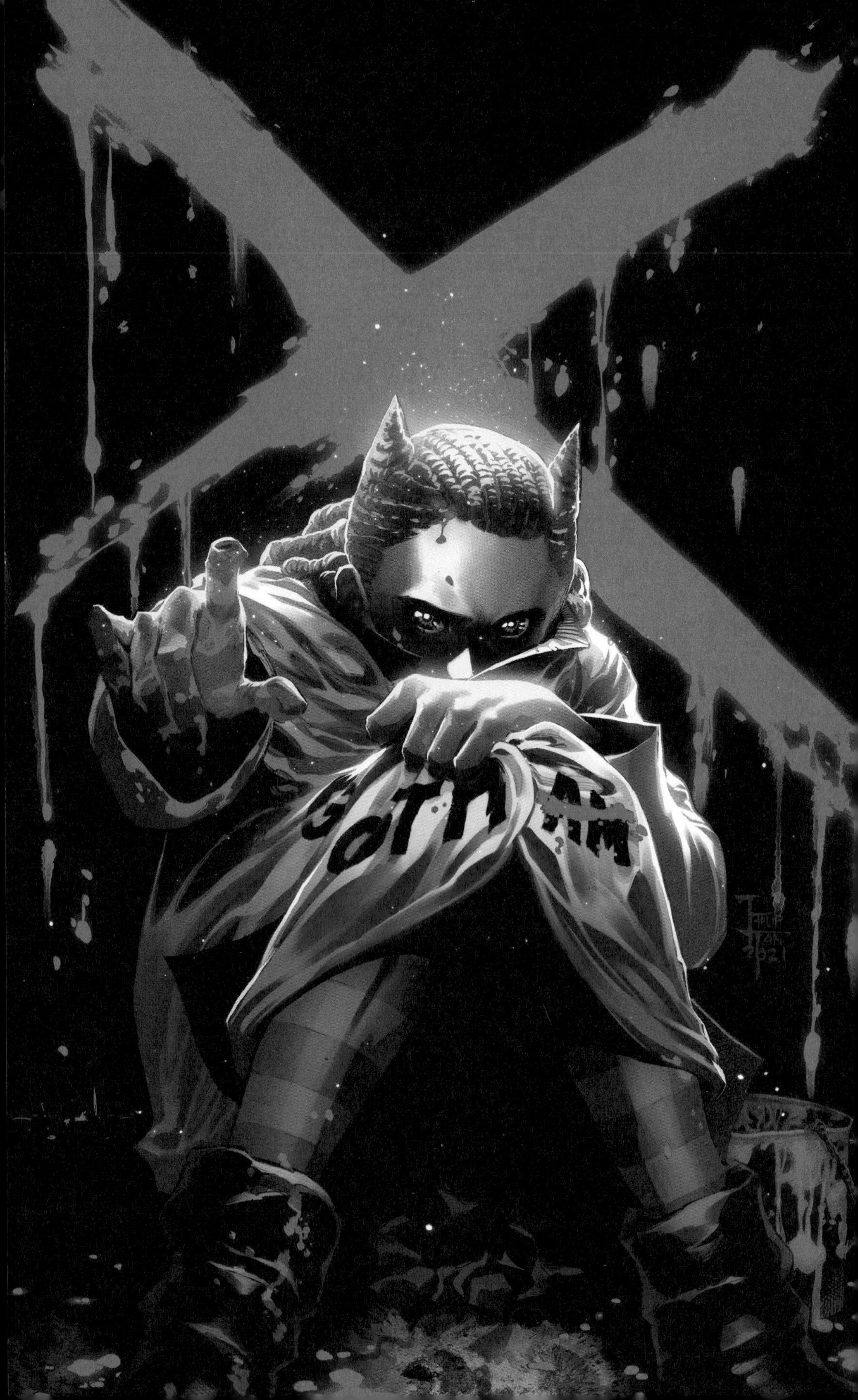
GOTHAM

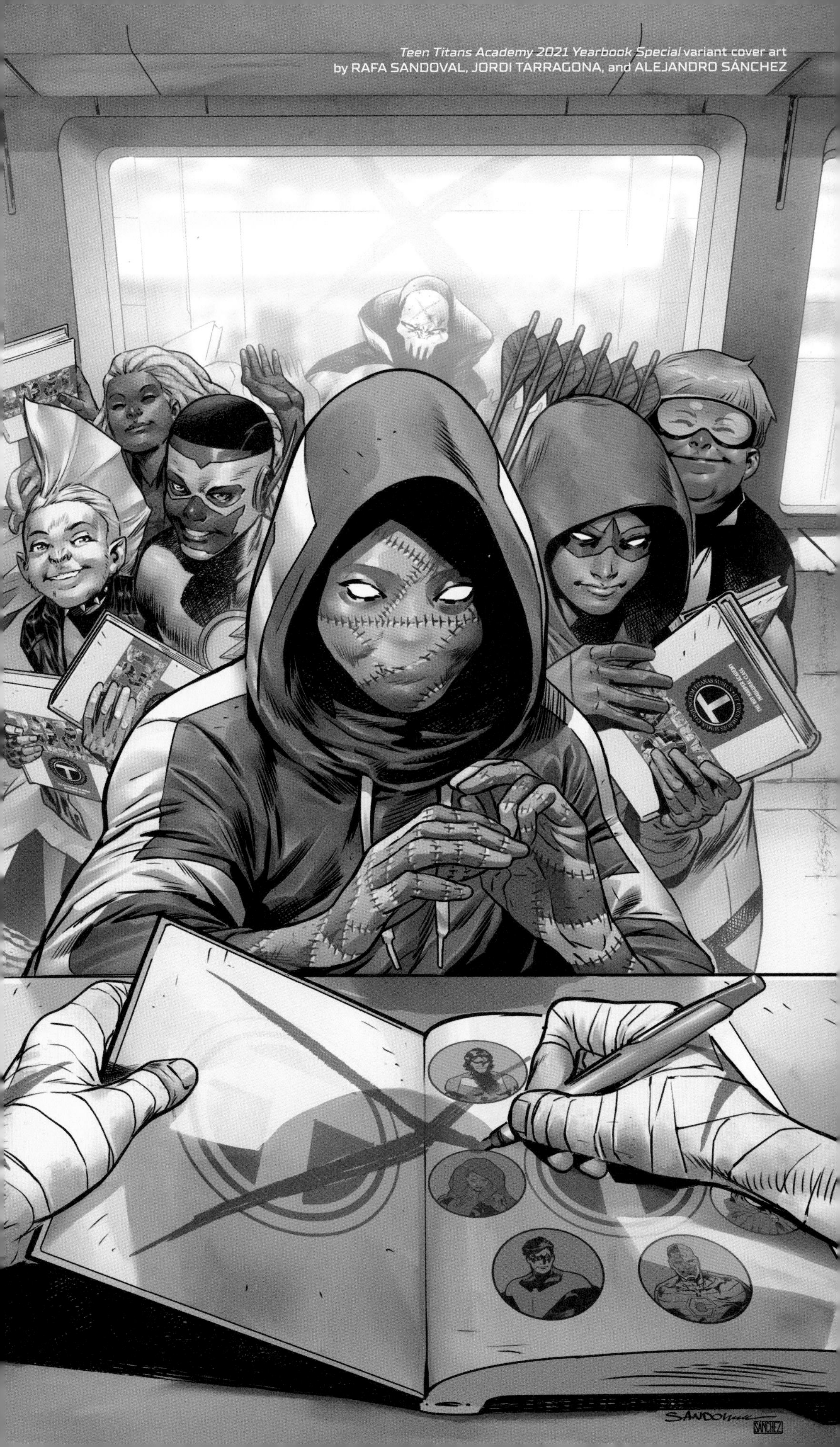

Teen Titans Academy 2021 Yearbook Special variant cover art
by RAFA SANDOVAL, JORDI TARRAGONA, and ALEJANDRO SÁNCHEZ

Cover sketches for *Teen Titans Academy* #1–5 by RAFA SANDOVAL

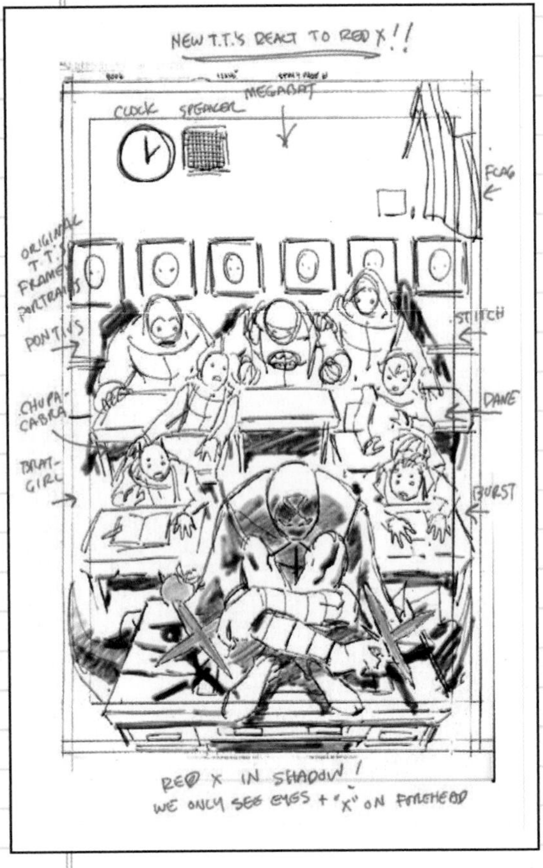
NEW T.T.'S REACT TO RED X!!
CLOCK
SPEAKER
MEGABAT
FLAG
ORIGINAL T.T.'S FRAMED PORTRAITS
STITCH
PONTIUS
CHUPACABRA
DANE
BRAT-GIRL
BURST
RED X IN SHADOW!
WE ONLY SEE EYES + "X" ON FOREHEAD

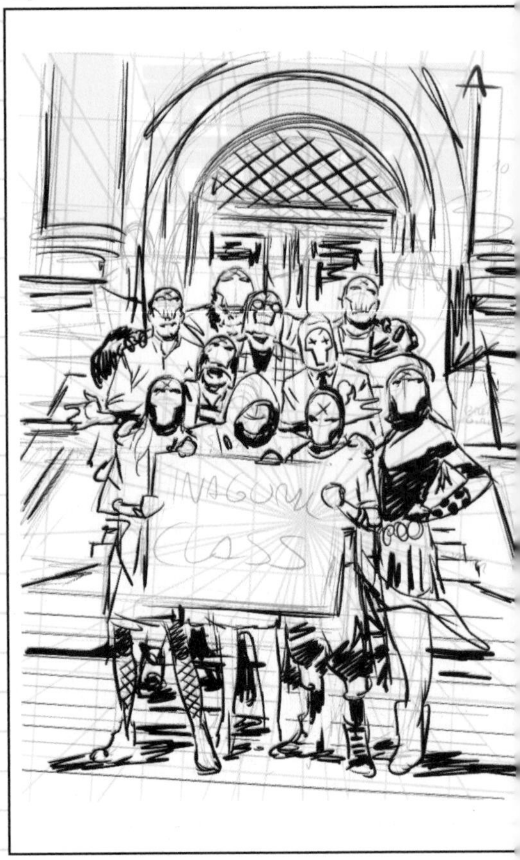
A

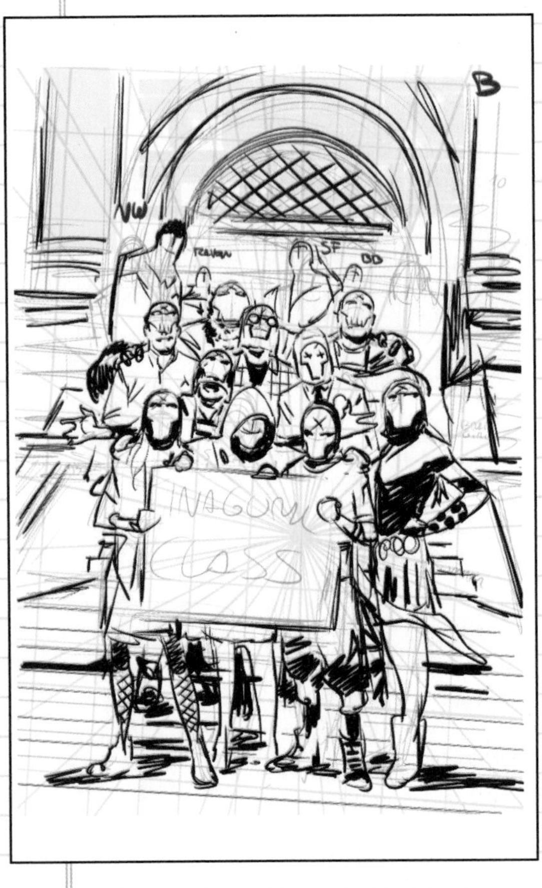
B

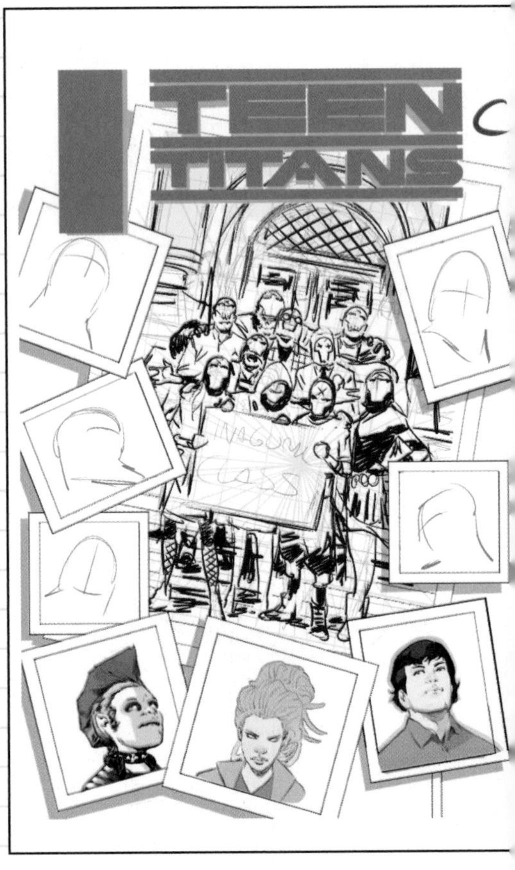
TEEN TITANS
C

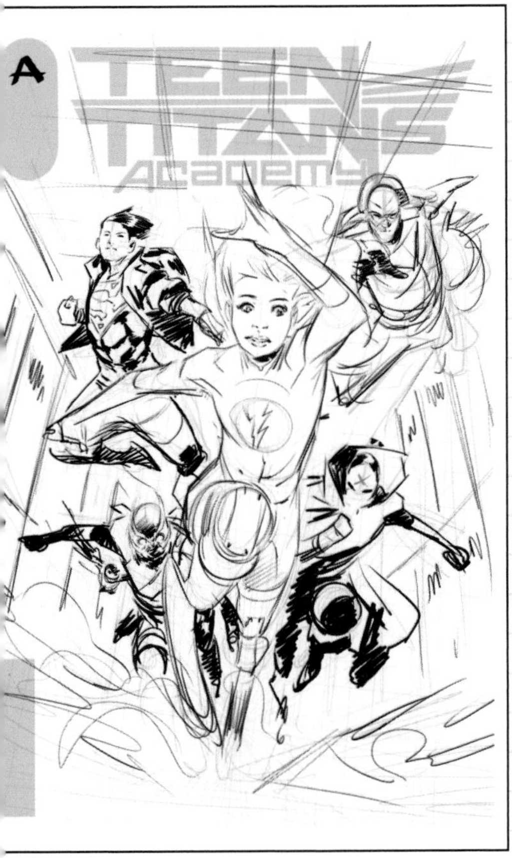
A
TEEN TITANS
ACADEMY

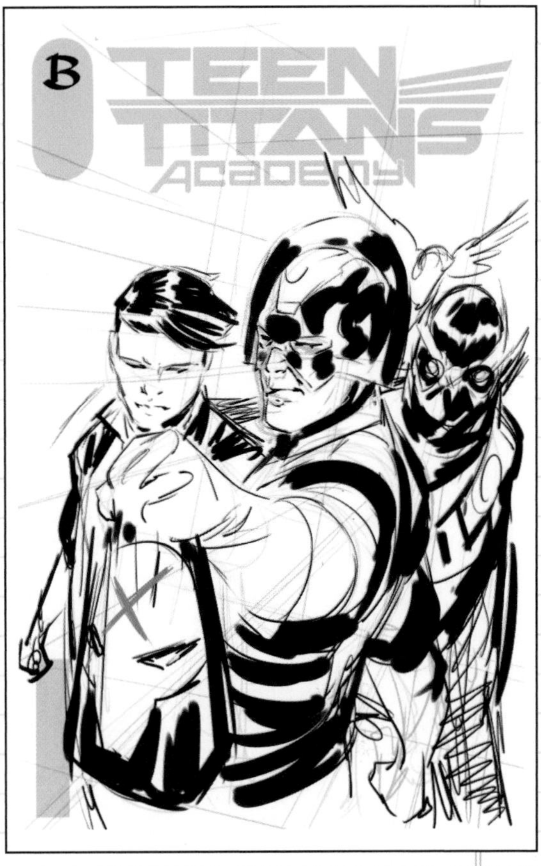
B
TEEN TITANS
ACADEMY

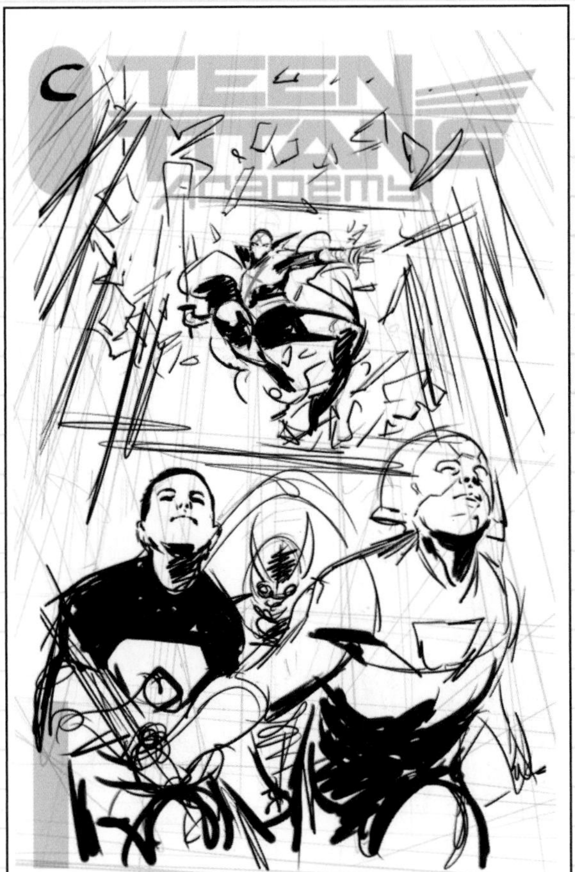
C
TEEN TITANS
ACADEMY

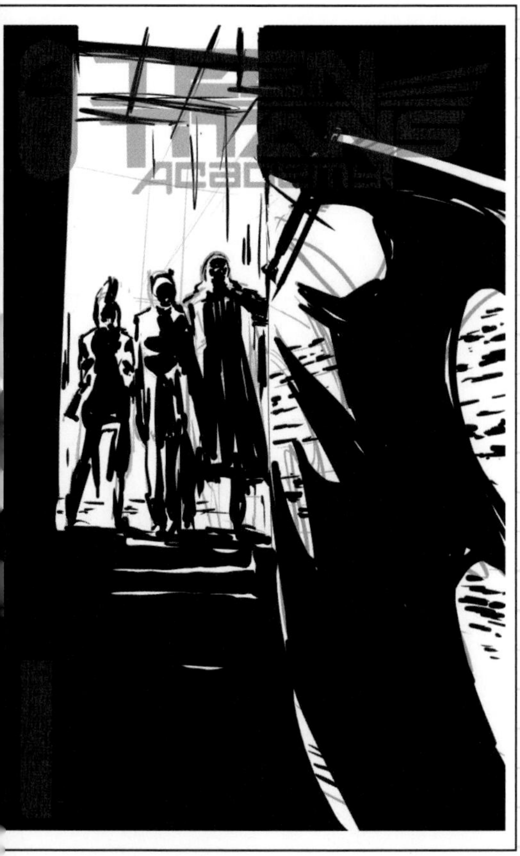

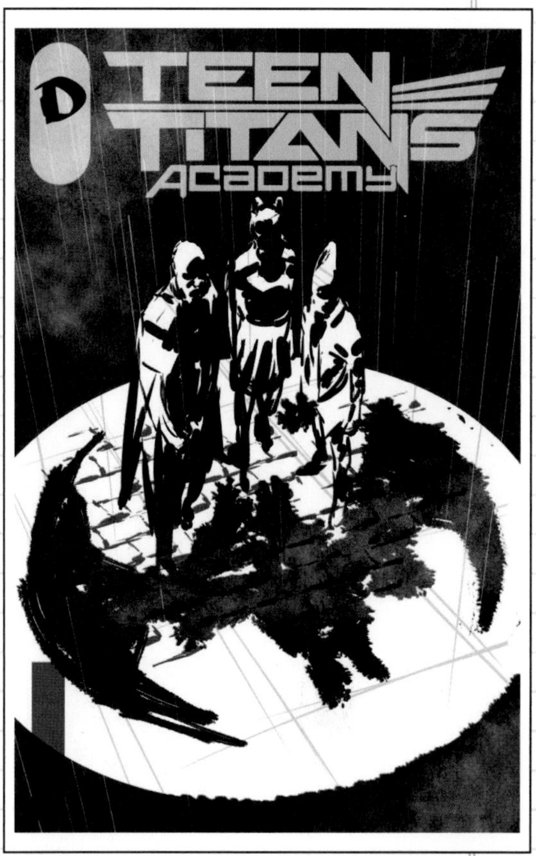
TEEN TITANS ACADEMY

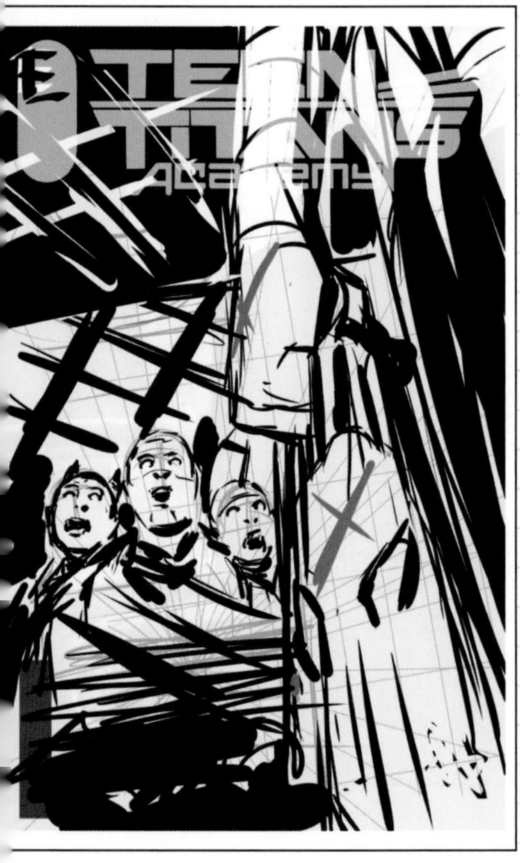

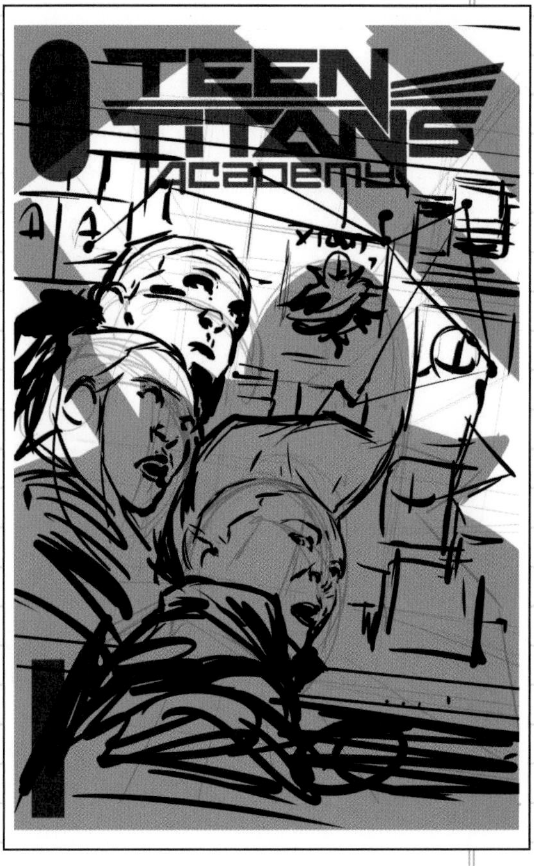
TEEN TITANS ACADEMY

Character studies by RAFA SANDOVAL

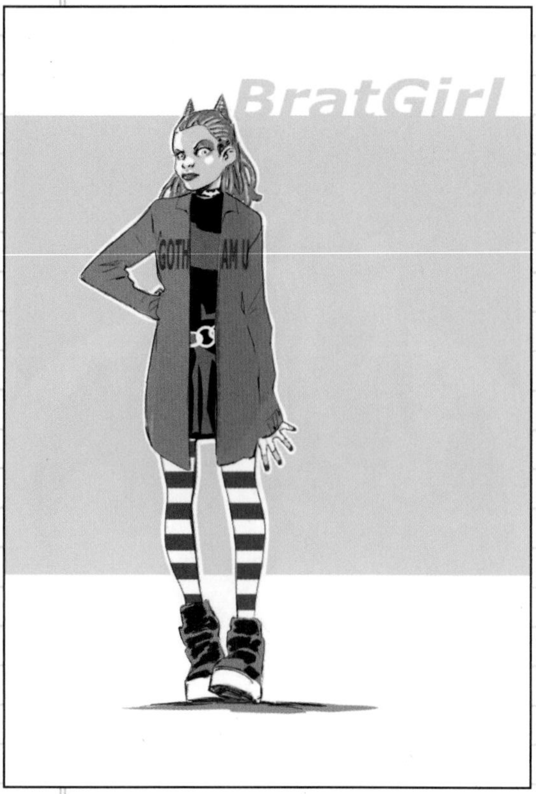
BratGirl
GOTH
AM U

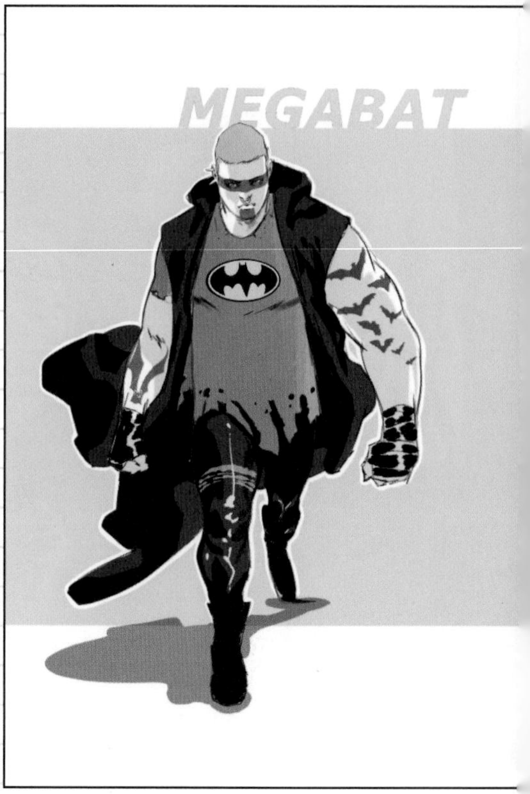
MEGABAT

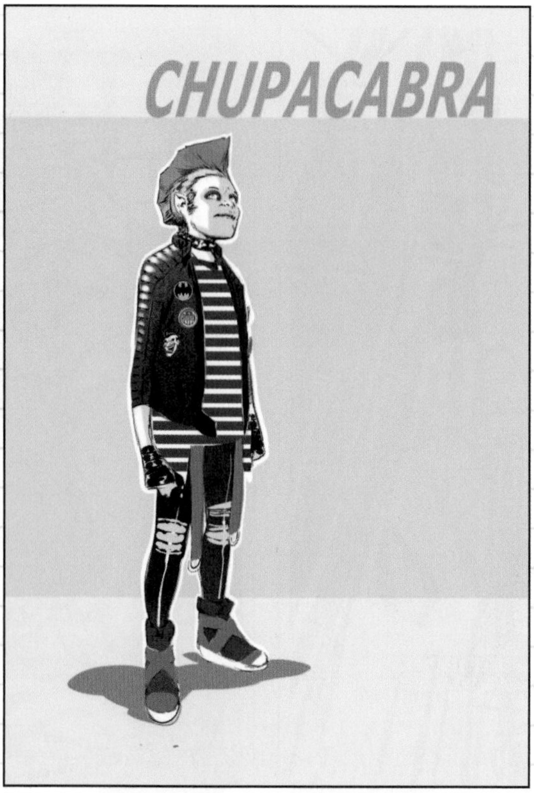
CHUPACABRA

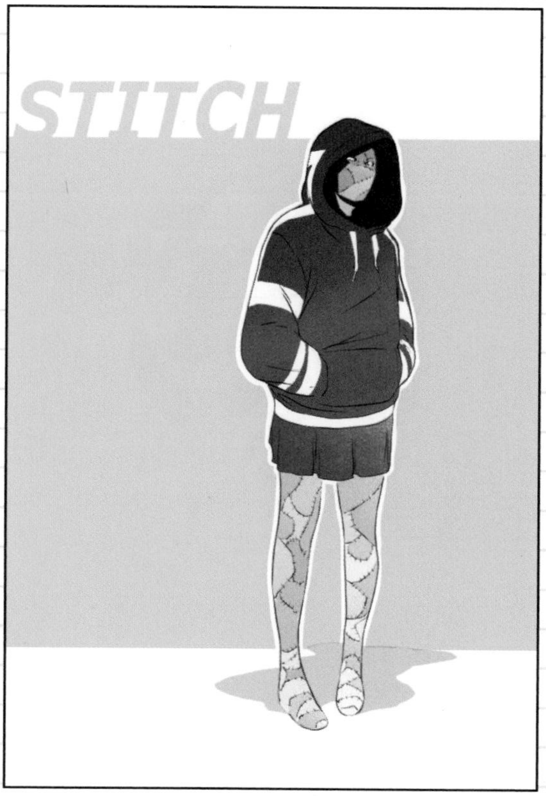
STITCH

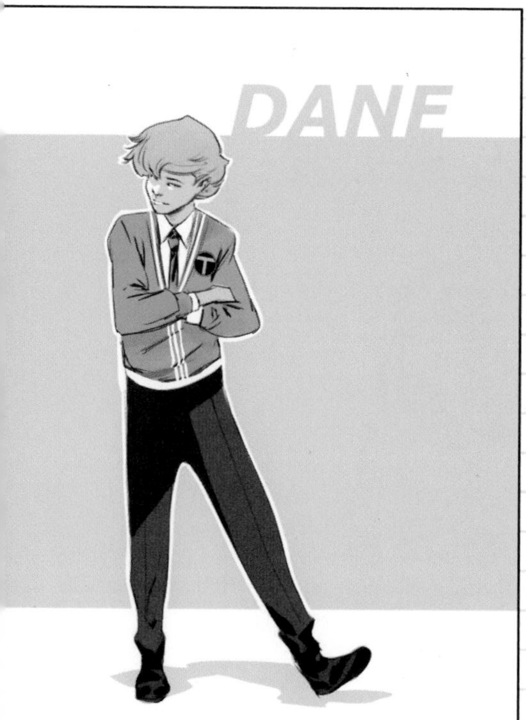
DANE

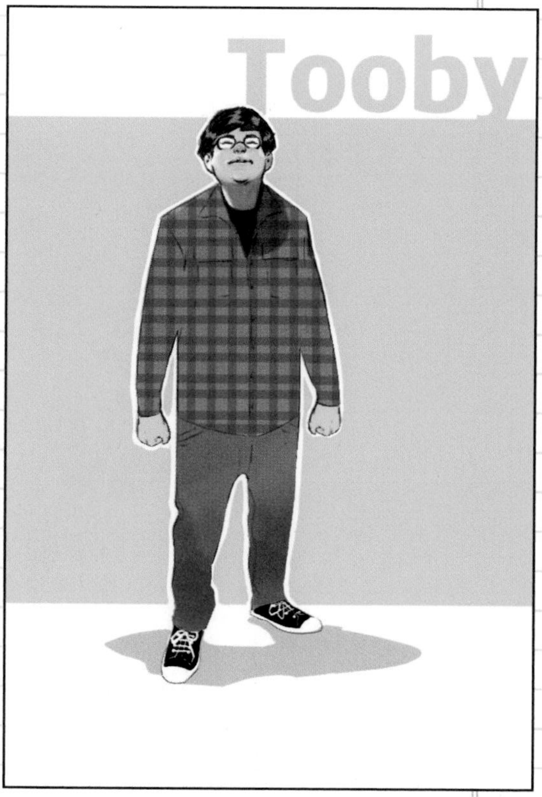
Tooby

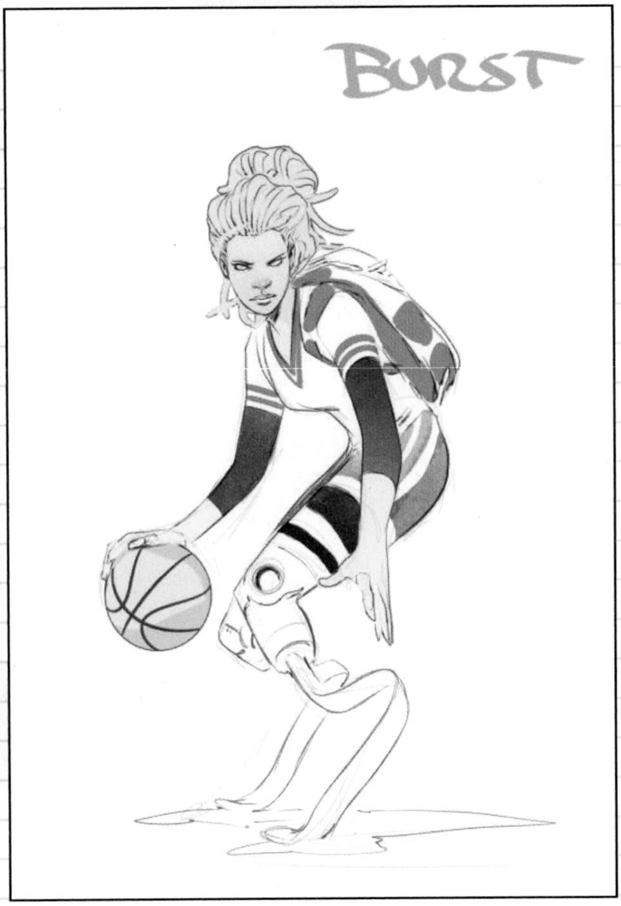
BURST

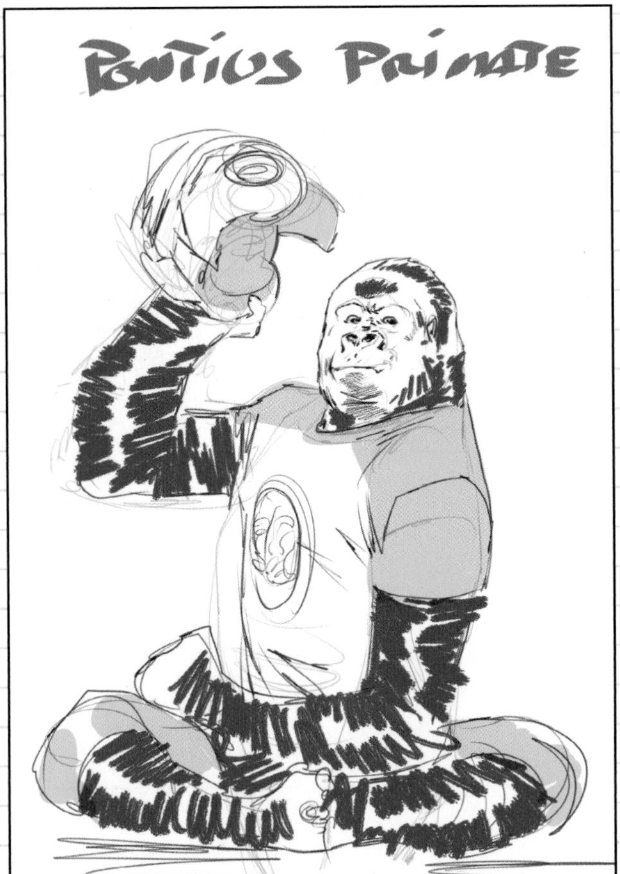
PONTIUS PRIMATE